CU00970048

"Path-breaking in its depth and sophisticati
a key contribution to an evolving field of res
We need new categories of analysis, which N
work with the growing mass of data about our global condition."

—Saskia Sassen, Columbia University, author of *Expulsions: Brutality and Complexity in the Global Economy*

"University presidents have said that globalization was a goal for at least two decades. It is now a reality that is rapidly changing higher education. But with all the attention to student flows, rankings, competition, and fundraising, the primary importance of globalising knowledge can be forgotten. Michael Kennedy's book puts the focus where it needs to be: on how intellectuals and universities work in different global contexts to inform publics and educate students, and on how the global organization of academic work shapes both knowledge itself and the responsibilities of intellectuals. These are issues that academics can't afford to ignore."

—Craig Calhoun, President, London School of Economics and Political Science

"Kennedy argues masterfully that the urgent project of building global knowledge can and should preserve the richness and texture of vernacular ways of knowing. He demonstrates simultaneously his intense commitment to the engaged, context-sensitive social science and keen awareness of the intellectual and ethical dilemmas unavoidable in the production of universally germane knowledge."

—Jan Kubik, Professor and Director, School of Slavonic and East European Studies, University College London

"Michael Kennedy's wise reflections on—and broad experience in working through—some of the key issues at stake in our new global knowledge economy are timely and critical. Kennedy provides readers with important insight into what global knowledge should genuinely mean at a time of pervasive (if also clichéd) globalization. *Globalizing Knowledge* offers fascinating perspectives on issues of monumental significance not just to our societies, polities, and economies but also to our planet."

—Nicholas B. Dirks, Chancellor, University of California, Berkeley

"Information has become the most powerful global asset. With this book, Michael Kennedy makes a plea to all to reach beyond the existing limitations of both academic and political imaginations to seek new sociopolitical transformations. As long as there is a willingness to consciously explore alternatives, humanity will be able to fulfill the promises of progress, resulting in a better world for all. *Globalizing Knowledge* is a major contribution."

—Alfred Gusenbauer, Former Chancellor of Austria

"*Globalizing Knowledge* is a tour de force, grappling with one of the most important challenges of our time—how to develop and mobilize knowledge produced in the university for global problems, and to do so in an equitable way. Michael Kennedy commands an enormous experience in promoting global networks of knowledge, and is well versed in the debates about their possibilities and limitations."

—Michael Burawoy, University of California, Berkeley

"In a changing world, Michael Kennedy introduces an innovative theoretical framework to increase equality in modern countries while also preserving liberty and freedom. Case studies focusing on different countries allow the reader to better understand the context of Kennedy's ideas."

—Ricardo Lagos Escobar, Former President of Chile

"Drawing upon his vast experiences and wide readings, Michael Kennedy has written a cogent and compelling book on the globalization of knowledge(s) and of universities. At once empirically rich and theoretically provocative, it is a necessary book for our challenging and confusing times."

—John Lie, University of California, Berkeley

GLOBALIZING KNOWLEDGE

GLOBALIZING KNOWLEDGE

Intellectuals, Universities, and
Publics in Transformation

Michael D. Kennedy

Stanford University Press
Stanford, California

Stanford University Press
Stanford, California

Printed in the United States of America on acid-free, archival-quality paper

Library of Congress Cataloging-in-Publication Data

Kennedy, Michael D., author.
Globalizing knowledge : intellectuals, universities, and publics in transformation /
Michael D. Kennedy.
pages   cm
Includes bibliographical references and index.
ISBN 978-0-8047-9236-3 (cloth : alk. Paper)
ISBN 978-0-8047-9343-8 (pbk. : alk. paper)
1. Knowledge, Sociology of. 2. Globalization—Social aspects. 3. Intellectuals.
4. Intellectual life—Social aspects. 5. Universities and colleges—Social aspects.
I. Title.
HM651.K454 2014
306.4'2—dc23

                                                                2014015003

ISBN 978-0-8047-9344-5 (electronic)

Contents

Figures and Tables

Figures

Tables

Preface

Globalizing knowledge.

The term is powerful. It is most commonly used when we speak of bringing insights from around the world into a university's research and teaching. But like all concepts useful for mobilizing resources, "globalizing knowledge" conceals much while allowing its connotations to do a lot of work. They do too much work for the critically inclined.

Knowledge depends on information. We are all familiar with the ways in which the information and communication technology revolution has affected the global spread of images, symbols, sounds, ideologies, repertoires, and even ideas. But when we speak of knowledge, we imply a superior sort of understanding. It is more refined, rigorous, and reflexive. Knowledge can't flow so easily as other virtual expressions because it must be sifted, reassembled, and assessed. And that means that its nodes of accumulation and transformation matter even in a world of information flows.

This mattering does not always work in traditionally knowledgeable ways. As reputations globalize, the distinction of knowledge nodes seems to depend more and more on forms of acknowledgment relatively divorced from knowledge as such. Distinction is dissolved into recognition. Recognition morphs into celebrity. Hit lists of the world's most important universities and thinkers then become the most visible arbiters of knowledge quality. This globalizing effect transforms the meaning of knowledge. It flattens the world's learning and commodifies its producers and their products. It also hides the abiding knowledge inequalities that shape our sense of the world.

Many in my discipline of sociology resisted using the word *globalization* for its distraction from the agency and privilege involved in the world's transformation. Words like *imperialism*, or research programs associated with concepts like the world system, highlighted who got what, thus begging us to explain why. Globalization, in contrast, implied a reorganization to which all had to adapt to win, or even to survive. It distracted us from questions not only of who loses but how victory might depend on others' defeats. "Globalizing knowledge" has a similar problem.

When people talk about it, or use other euphemisms, like "internationalizing a university," they conjure a worldly image in which insights flow from across the world to the node they inhabit. However, interests, tastes, prejudices, and power shape that learning flow. They repackage learning's assembly in ways that are hardly neutral, much less scientific or universal. Globalizing knowledge easily masks ethnocentrism's expression, just as it has hidden cosmopolitanism's limits.

Counterposed to provincialism or nationalism, cosmopolitanism is nonetheless shaped by the worldly circuits its proponent values. It's difficult, if not impossible, to imagine a cosmopolitan disposition that is devoid of interests, tastes, prejudice, or power. But to the extent that cosmopolitanism is inhabited by a sufficiently diverse array with a commitment to intellectuality as such, that cosmopolitanism is more respectful of the broader world we inhabit. It is more curious about that world's dimensions we do not yet know. All other things being equal, such a cosmopolitan intellectuality becomes a quality of globalizing knowledge even the critically minded might embrace. Indeed, I would like to think of universities in those terms, at least potentially. A genuinely globalizing knowledge requires cosmopolitan intellectuality. The publicly minded, however, might demand more.

Globalizing knowledge does not necessarily connote anything about people beyond the worlds of learning as such. Many still justify knowledge for its own sake, but many more likely value it for its benefits. They appreciate how it increases the power and privilege of its patrons or augments the public good of the communities in which the knowledgeable and their institutions reside. Just by virtue of that public question, one should imagine the proponents of globalizing knowledge wondering about how public identifications work in their ambitions. And it goes further.

The recognition of knowledge reflects not just its intrinsic value but also the power and privilege organizing the systems in which that recognition functions. Thus, it is difficult for such a lofty notion as globalizing knowledge to be at ease residing only among those already claiming to own it. Imagine, for instance, how much poorer the world would be without the globalization of jazz music, and how racism, class privilege, and art music arrogance conspired in its repression in the last century.

Jazz has traveled the world just as many other products associated with less privileged knowledgeabilities have. This has led some to be concerned for the expropriation embedded in such global flows. Insights produced in communities can be stripped from their producers. The social relations in which that knowledge was embedded can be lost as learning is decontextualized. Globalizing knowledge, neither in its intrinsic qualities nor with its various connotations, has much to say about such exploitations. It should.

Here, I clearly move beyond my immanent concerns for globalizing knowledge and shift into a question that is both pragmatic and associational. After all, intellectuals and their institutions have moved increasingly to consider their public responsibilities. However, the publics to which they refer are typically proximate. Cosmopolitan intellectuals might ask why proximity should rule out distant publics. They should ask us to rethink those obligations on various scales within and beyond the nation. One might even invoke a notion of solidarity so that the choice to bear the burdens of others becomes an intrinsic part of the quest to learn from them. Indeed, I think for globalizing knowledge to become more than a pretentious slogan and comforting complement for cosmopolitan intellectuality, we must understand what a more consequential solidarity could mean in the articulations of globalizing knowledge. This is more than the challenge of difference. This is also a matter of combining diversity's recognition with a question of figuring our ties and the responsibilities that brings with it. Difference and connectivity combine when solidarity animates.

In order to move beyond the slogans and appreciate more adequately these complex relationships between knowledges and global transformations, we need a better set of orienting questions, methodological approaches, and integrating theories than we now enjoy. In this volume, I focus on articulations of globalizing knowledge through which I explore cultural schema organizing the recognition of intellectual responsibility and the valuation of knowledge institutions and networks. I am especially interested to elaborate those

schema that not only conserve and transmit wisdom but also anticipate transformations that could make the world better. I am particularly concerned
with those that engage publics, recognize difference, and acknowledge the
world of flows, especially in terms of energy. This is, then, a cultural political sociology of knowledge *and* change. I not only analyze the dynamics of
knowledge in certain fields but focus on how they might be rearticulated and
designed. In the process, I wish to make global transformations more subject
to inclusive and rational critical discussion in their address and practice.

Those are the intentions, and this is the argument.

The specialization of knowledge has made many doubt the virtue, and even
relevance, of the intellectual as an actor shaping change. However, the term's
necessary reference to questions of responsibility make its sociology essential for
rearticulating the implication of knowledge in change. Not only need we consider how media refashion intellectuals as celebrities and remake possibilities
for their public value; we also need to figure how universities are transformed
in that context. As organizations with their own logics, they do not necessarily express an institutional responsibility derived from their associations with
intellectual responsibility. However, their legitimation depends at least partially
on an affirmation of intellectuality's culture of critical discourse. Questions of
intellectual responsibility thus can have distinctive effect on such institutions
and their social environments. That effect is magnified when associated with
increasingly knowledgeable public engagements. But which publics matter?

The first step in linking theories of knowledge with the practice of knowledgeable *and inclusive* change is to make explicit articulations of intellectual
and institutional responsibility to *various* publics. A second step is to locate
those elaborations not only in their contexts but also in the world of flows.
After all, the increasingly intense movement of, among other things, knowledge, people, wealth, and weapons across borders of all sorts has changed our
sense of the proximities and relevance of various publics. The connectivity
generated by such movements should also, however, reinvigorate our sense of
priorities in the articulation of intellectual and institutional responsibilities.
It invites us to enter the world of design to refashion the kinds of knowledge
networks that can recognize both the challenge of difference and the promise
of connectivity across disparate contexts. In order for that invitation to work,
we need a resonant frame to organize our cumulative effort.

To be cosmopolitan is no longer a philosophical attitude accented with
awareness of the world's diversity and beauty. It is developed in a practice of

learning shaped by thoughts of not only what matters most and why but how the distribution of knowledge across the world shapes our perceptions of what we need to know. When that cosmopolitan disposition articulates the formation and practice of knowledge networks, the possibilities for symbolic expressions of worldly awareness and practices of knowledgeable and consequential solidarity grow. And with that, chances of our world thriving, and even surviving, increase. That, at least, is an article of faith that motivates this volume.

In short, I hope to stimulate an approach and methodology with which intellectuals and their institutions and networks can rearticulate a culture of critical discourse around global public responsibility. Many already claim to be globalizing knowledge. Too few appreciate the range of challenges involved in that articulation. Even fewer offer inspired practice. I hope to augment the significance of those to whom I refer in the last two sentences and shake the presumption of those in the first.

To write such a book that ranges across knowledge cultures and the world appears to reflect incredible hubris, but I offer it with humility. I expect challenges and alterations of all sorts. And that is its ambition: to move a better array of answers and inspire a better set of questions than I typically find within and across knowledge institutions and networks. Too often our culture of critical discourse is caught within the terms of knowledge cultures founded in moments radically unlike the times in which we live, or in emergent spaces without the means to develop ideas and practices with sufficient resource. In both cases, knowledgeable change is hemmed in by organizational cultures animated by power and privilege built to reproduce their own past paths to influence. To judge that constraint as simply wrong is to be sociologically naïve; but to say that is inevitable is to be deadly ignorant.

As I write, concluding composition in January 2014, the world is in immediate crisis. I know, long after this book is published, that the world shall remain in foundational crisis. My hope is that this volume will join with other efforts in moving those with the privilege of disproportionate time to think to act in ways that will help make change more knowledgeable. I count on the power of knowledge networks to make it so, for I have seen already how transformative they can be. At least they have changed me.

I am indebted to many for the transformative learning curve I have enjoyed, limited and rich as it has been.

My formative years (1986–2009) as a professor were at the University of Michigan, where in addition to my duties as a member of the sociology department I had the privilege of directing a number of interdisciplinary and international units, including its International Institute, Weiser Center for Europe and Eurasia, Weiser Center for Emerging Democracies, Center for Russian and East European Studies, Center for European Studies / European Union Center for Excellence, and Program for the Comparative Study of Social Transformations. I also served as the university's first vice provost for international affairs. All my colleagues and students at Michigan were very generous in shaping how I learned about globalizing knowledge.

I have spent much less time at Brown University, but directing its Watson Institute for International Studies has offered exceptional opportunities to learn about the challenges and opportunities of globalizing knowledge, especially for the networks its graduates and donors crafted for its students and faculty. I have been especially moved in this space to think about the connections between international studies, policy making, and public engagements of both actual and virtual sorts. Beyond these networks, students of Brown are the most remarkable, making this liberal arts college in transition to research university a source of abiding energy and transformative vision.

All professors are marked by their institutional homes, but the networks in which they travel are more varied. I have been especially engaged in the networks associated with the regions of my scholarly focus. In addition to sociology circles I have benefited from a variety of conversations in the area studies tradition, most especially in European and Eurasian studies. Those conversations have themselves led to others without obvious regional accent, especially networks shaped by the Social Science Research Council and the Open Society Foundations. Material and collegial support from the Watson Institute for International Studies, the Department of Sociology at Brown University, the Academic Fellowship Program of the Open Society Foundations, and the Social Science Research Council for the project "Engaging Afghanistan" have also helped a great deal. I am especially grateful to all those at Stanford University Press, especially Frances Malcolm, Tim Roberts, Cynthia Lindlof, Jenny Gavacs, and my anonymous reviewers, who have made this book so much better than it could have ever been without them. But in the end, it is the particular individuals with whom we learn over the long haul that count.

The following friends and colleagues, at different points in these last thirty years of my life in globalizing knowledge, have made beyond their scholarly texts the biggest differences in how I have learned about globalizing knowledge: Gerhard Lenski, Tony Jones, Craig Calhoun, Pam DeLargy, Ivan Szelenyi,

Dave Smith, Włodzimierz Wesołowski, Witold Morawski, Renata Siemińska, Ola Jasińska-Kania, Jadwiga Staniszkis, Irek Białecki, Kostek Gebert, Janusz Reykowski, Adam Michnik, Aleksander Kwaśniewski, Zbigniew Bujak, Josef Blass, Marysia Ostafin, Donna Parmelee, Bob Donia, Christine Billick, Mayer Zald,[†*] Genevieve Zubrzycki, John Guidry, Niki Harsanyi, Marty Whyte, Jeff Paige, Peggy Somers, Julia Adams, George Steinmetz, Brian Porter, Al Young, Muge Gocek, Barbara Anderson, John Lie, Doug Northrop, Ted Hopf, Oksana Malanchuk, Alisher Ilkhamov, Marianne Kamp, Rein Voorman, Slavko Hrytsak, Gerard Libaridian, Veena Das, Elizabeth Jelin, Lamin Sanneh, Julie Skurski, Fernando Coronil,[†] Nurcholish Madjid,[†] Glenda Dickerson,[†] Linda Lim, Sioban Harlow, Steven Whiting, Sasha Knysh, Geoff Eley, Ron Suny, Bill Sewell, Sherry Ortner, David William Cohen, Bill Rosenberg, Roman Szporluk, Tom Wolfe, Jane Burbank, Fred Cooper, Gay Seidman, Nancy Cantor, Lee Bollinger, Lester Monts, Gary Krenz, Rosina Bierbaum, Deba Dutta, Earl Lewis, James Steward, Georgi Derluguian, Gayathri Arumugham, Anna Meyendorff, Jan Kubik, Michael Bernhard, Grzegorz Ekiert, David Ost, Marian Kempny,[†] Joanna Regulska, Jozsef Borocz, Gil Merkx, Nick Dirks, Michael Burawoy, Voldemar Tomusk, George Shavarnidze, Tanya Bureychak, Viktor Susak, Linda Gusia, Nita Luci, Shemsi Krasniqi, Mentor Agani, Katherine Verdery, Gail Kligman, Susan Gal, Victor Friedman, Val Bunce, Markku Kivinen, Pami Aalto, David Dusseault, Miko Palonkorpi, Doug Rogers, Lilia Shevtsova, Alena Ledeneva, Keith Brown, Gianpaolo Baiocchi, Cornel Ban, Nukhet Sandal, Naoko Shibusawa, Bob Lee, Jennifer Wood, Tony Bogues, Geri Augusto, Timmons Roberts, Mark Blyth, Ashu Varshney, Peter Evans, Jose Itzighsohn, Rich Snyder, Geoffrey Kirkman, Dietrich and Marilyn Rueschemeyer, Jeff Isaac, Miguel Centeno, Jonathan Van Antwerpen, Joe Karaganis, Tom Asher, Seteney Shami, Steve Damiano, Bill Janeway, John Seely Brown, Woody Powell, Mary McDonnell, Harriet Zuckerman, Ira Katznelson, Michael Watts, Ellen Levy, Mamadou Diouf, Lisa Hajjar, Laz Lima, Ed McDermott, Tomek Zarycki, Lucyna Kirwil, Ramsay Taum, Wu Wen-ching, Ski Krieger, Larson DiFiori, Ania Skrzypek, Alfred Gusenbauer, Ricardo Lagos, Romano Prodi, Charles Taylor, and all my current and former students who form their own quite potent knowledge network (Kennedy 2014b). The students in my 2011 and 2013 classes on knowledge networks and global transformations—Raillan Brooks, Eli Crumrine, Nick Carter, Jen Kao, Allison Kriesberg, Trevor Mundt, Claudia Norton, Vero Testa, Sofia Unanue, Kelly Wess, Mujun Zhou, Lola and Lucy Bates-Campbell, Julia Ellis-Kahana, Julia

* † indicates that the person is now deceased.

Thompson, Juliana Rodriquez, Elizabeth Karin, Katie Cohen, Olivia Pet-rocco, Hania Braun, Hannah Cockrell, Christian Petroske, Sean McAdams, Marcel Bertsch-Gout, Tanya Saxena, and Nik Kalyanpur—were especially helpful to formulating this volume with their inspiration and commentaries. And while I began working on this volume at the turn of the century, between 2007 and 2013 Shiva Balaghi was the most constant and critical companion in my journey across so many articulations of globalizing knowledge. Evidence of her impact is readily seen throughout this volume, and I am grateful for all I have learned from her. My family has mattered more than ever in these last years when I was focused on completing this book. Notably my children, Emma and Lucas; my mom, Ursula; my brother, Ken; my stepmother, Dolo-res; and my cousin Jane have made me far better than I could have been oth-erwise. While I might have global reference, in the end the love and care of family and enduring friends matter most.

And my final thanks are to you who read this, who carry forward my riff on my dissertation adviser's question. When Gerhard Lenski asked in 1966, "Who gets what and why?," he summarized and motivated a great tradition in the sociology of inequality. I invoke his pithiness and commitment to the parsimonious with this question: Who is intellectually responsible, and why? If we ask that in all of our circumstances, we might actually help produce the cosmopolitan intellectuality and consequential solidarity we need to thrive, we need to survive.

1 Knowledge: Articulation and Consequence in Global Transformations

> The trouble with the contemporary condition of our modern civilization is that it stopped questioning itself. Not asking certain questions is pregnant with more dangers than failing to answer questions already on the agenda; while asking the wrong kind of questions all too often helps to avert eyes from the truly important issues. The price of silence is paid in the hard currency of human suffering. Asking the right question marks, after all, the difference between fate and destination, drifting and traveling. Questioning the ostensibly unquestionable premises of our way of life is arguably the most urgent of the services we owe our fellow humans and ourselves.
>
> —*Zygmunt Bauman, "Globalization: The Human Consequences"*

Knowledge transforms social life, institutions on all scales, and the character of the world. But that axiom's limitations, and potentials, are much too poorly understood, especially for how much we believe it to be true.[1]

Knowledge and Change

Not all accounts of transformations attribute terrific significance to knowledge. Environmental shifts, demographic pressures, changes in the mode of production, and alterations in state capacities to wage war or collect resources are among the greater explanations of social transformation. But even in these instances, knowledge plays a typically critical role.

That critical role is most obvious in the commentary beginning this chapter. Zygmunt Bauman offers the characteristic nightmare problem of which not only intellectuals should be afraid. We can dedicate our lives, our institutions, and our worlds to refining our answers to the questions posed by our particular domains of expertise and particular interests or ideologies.

But what if those questions, those domains, those interests and ideologies, are misplaced in their emphasis, direction, or concern? What if we are asking the wrong questions? That's ultimately the most foundational knowledge question, but it cannot be the most consensual. After all, we are far more likely to agree on the importance of a question, or knowledge, when we can see its significance in an already constituted body of knowledge. That, ipso facto, makes any *disciplined* critical question rarely so heretical as Bauman's urgent service. We more typically, especially in this era, focus on technology.

When viewed on the grandest scale, as Gerhard Lenski has offered, this "information about how to use the material resources of the environment to satisfy human needs" (Lenski, Nolan, and Lenski 1995, 42) is the most transformative knowledge of social relations (Kennedy 2004a). From the development of horticulture and then the plow to the revolution in the means by which we communicate with each other electronically, innovations in technology are central to change. And with those transformations, technology becomes central to our ideologies of change.

Those who wish to minimize the energy crisis argue that new modes for extracting fossil fuels will enable us to continue relying on a carbon energy base. Some of those who put their hopes on new greener technologies for saving our planet from global warming put similar stock in the relationship between knowledge and global transformations. And in energy's example, the significance of technology's embeddedness in culture and social relations becomes apparent.

That embeddedness is long recognized. Karl Marx (Marx and Engels [1848] 2012) never argued that the enormous dynamism of capitalist innovation was the single motor of change. It mattered also because it was driven by conflicts within and across classes. Max Weber ([1905] 1930) proposed that what counted was not just matters of accounting; rather, a certain kind of knowledge about God initially moved capitalists to accumulate wealth vigorously. Much more recently, Manuel Castells (2009), Saskia Sassen (2008), and others take the microelectronics revolution seriously, but they explain global transformations by considering the technology's interactions with other social forces. Energy technology optimists don't assume that new and appropriate technologies will emerge by themselves. People who consider the question will argue that one might develop such economically and environmentally consequential technologies only under pressures of market demand or state intervention.

In this sense, the "knowledge" critical here is not just of the technology in question but the accompanying forms of knowledge embedded in the world and about the world that make any technology matter. Are these understandings of the world also knowledge?

Technological innovation typically claims the knowledge mantle with ease given that it reflects an unprecedented combination of information or its application to novel circumstances. But characterizations of markets and demands about adoption of green technology are often debated as if they are ideological rather than knowledgeable interventions into change. The climate warming debate illustrates this problem.

Although most scientists expert in the field debate within parameters assuming unprecedented human contributions to global warming,[2] a few scientists challenge those frameworks. Their interventions in turn lead some beyond the scientific community to charge ideological bias to the scientific majority's discussion. That in turn moves similar charges against these accusers. This debate between minority and majority turns less on scientific terms and more on the ways in which science is shaped by social forces beyond the laboratory, on how knowledge is embedded in, or apart from, the world (Hoffman 2011; Keller 2009).

Categorical thinking about science—is it apart from or embedded in the world?—is all too common and naïve whatever its conclusion. Sociologists are more inclined to ask about degrees of autonomy for science, or forms of influence of the world on science making. But this is not just a sociological question, as the climate science debate illustrates. It is a profoundly important public issue and a place where sophisticated thinking helps. One might ask about the conditions of science's autonomy, building on Robert Merton's (1973) famous account of the ethos of science. One might also consider the ways in which specific scientific problems are tracked through networks and actors both human and nonhuman, as Bruno Latour (2005) and his colleagues would have it. Pithily put, one might argue that one must develop a social science to use science well in public policy (Prewitt, Schwandt, and Straf 2012). These approaches, and this general question about science in the world, are only particulars in a much larger problem.

Globalizing Knowledge

I suspect relatively few of you in reading the preceding passages thought much about what I meant when I referred to the "world." As in many discussions about the relationship between something and "the world," the something is taken more seriously than what we mean when we refer to the world. The world is typically posed as background, everything beyond that something. That vision homogenizes and simplifies all beyond focus. The world is typically cast as if one's own social and biophysical environments are the imagined community of that world, with more distant places and peoples dim reflections, in positive or negative terms, of a more familiar existence.

This kind of ethnocentrism, a familiar sociological condition (Hughes 1961), is becoming less viable with revolutions in information and communication technologies and the relative ease of travel. The physical conditions of the familiar have changed. Some believe that the world is developing a more cosmopolitan disposition as a consequence (Beck 2006), making the globalization of knowledge a matter of everyday life. That cosmopolitanism typically does not engage adequately the challenge of difference (Calhoun 1995), especially when globalization is its vehicle.

Globalization, as concept, had its early academic supporters (Robertson 1992), but especially in my discipline it seemed to have had more detractors (e.g., Arrighi and Silver 1999). It blended too many notions. It was insufficiently distinct from earlier world systems theory. It was too self-congratulatory. Regardless of its intellectual adequacy, the concept took off in the public sphere during the 1990s, aided and abetted by pundits like Tom Friedman (1999). He helped his readers appreciate the distinction of this system that appeared to reduce the importance of state and cultural differences because it focused on flows of both tangible and intangible goods across boundaries.

In this vision, it's especially easy to see knowledge flowing seamlessly across boundaries and differences of all sorts, especially for Friedman's readers. Exemplified by Friedman himself, cross-cultural competence was simple. His readers might trust that most of the world worth knowing already knew the English language. Those places still out of sync would have to put on the "golden straitjacket" (Friedman 1999, 105) Friedman's globalization system demanded in order to be relevant.[3] Universities were very much a part of that system and, in some ways, remain so today.

Higher education is one of globalization's big businesses. The debate around its place in the World Trade Organization's General Agreement on Trade and Services (GATS) illustrated that importance in globalization's heyday (Verger 2009). The globalizing knowledge system was also evident in the alliances universities began striking across the world in the 1990s. The scripts were not too varied. Consider, for example, how the themes offered by the higher education alliance Universitas 21 highlighted their own distinctions in ways that have mirrored so many others:

> providing a forum for university leaders; preparing students for life in a globalised society, inspiring a global perspective through international mobility, stimulating and challenging collaborative thinking, nurturing and developing careers, delivering joint teaching and degrees, promoting innovation in research-inspired teaching, sharing experience and best practices.[4]

I have participated in this world of globalizing knowledge over the last decades. In the beginning I took careful notes, not realizing that I would hear the same leitmotifs over and over again. In one of my first such gatherings at a conference entitled "The University Summit in Kyushu: 2000 International Symposium on Universities' Past and Present," I was especially taken with Sir Graeme Davies, principal and vice chancellor of the University of Glasgow in Scotland. He identified the "global imperative" facing higher education. Among others, he made the following points:

1. "Systematizing internationalization will become more central to the strategic plans and objectives of universities aspiring to the highest status. But international strategies and linkages tend to have second-order priority being pursued only as sources of income intended to augment and sustain the perceived core activities of the universities."

2. More systematic thinking is important, however, because universities "are likely to find themselves in more hostile political circumstances as competition for national and international resources becomes more fierce."

3. "Without careful planning, the most probable outcome in dealing with increasing economic and political pressures will be a set of piecemeal, disjointed, ad hoc responses strongly dominated by local pragmatism."

Even though his manifesto is more than a decade old at the time of this writing, it's remarkable just how little this kind of challenge, and response, changes. However, sometimes one can push the envelope and ask leading questions.

One of my duties during my time as vice provost for international affairs at the University of Michigan (1999–2004) was to think a bit more deeply about what these kinds of international ambitions meant and what we ought to discuss as we proposed to globalize our work. Several Michigan colleagues responded to such questions about the meaning of globalizing knowledge (U-M Faculty 2001). Linda Lim (2001), a professor at one of the schools especially dedicated to globalization within the university, offered the most institutionally critical set of comments:

> In this view, "globalization" of the American university may mean simply offering American programs and teaching American models to foreigners at home or abroad—as in "We have a campus in Singapore" or "We offer programs in London" or "International students are 30 percent of our class," ergo, we are "global." Or it may be taken to mean sending our own students or faculty abroad on "exchanges" for training, internship and research collaboration, many of which involve merely replicating or extending in "their" territory what we already do here, and conducted in our language, not theirs. . . . Importing non-U.S. faculty and students . . . may actually undermine the globalization of the American intellectual universe if it results in institutionalization of the belief that "The rest of the world comes to us, so we don't have to learn about the rest of the world." . . . It is not surprising, then, that so many around the world dismiss "globalization" as a smokescreen for "American domination," and are beginning to resist the spread or at least question the superiority of the "American gospel" of free markets and even of democracy. . . . The hegemonic U.S. university's ethnocentric and parochial misidentification of the intellectual challenge of globalization could actually *diminish* our capacity to understand, interact with, and enrich the "globalized" world in which we live. Only rarely does it acknowledge the importance of globalization in the *intellectual content* of what its members research, study, teach and learn—the language, culture, business or scientific practices of the "other."

Lim's views were not typical in her business school, but after the shock of September 11, 2001, the significance of recognizing difference, and hegemony, became much more apparent.

Understandably, the first and most important thing to do when facing catastrophe is to grieve and then offer compassion and solidarity to those who

have suffered most. I wrote this in my notes during the couple of months succeeding that consequential day:

> The count of 2001's victims numbed our minds; their obituaries, steadily pub-
> lished for months afterward, made us grieve many times over. The variety of
> their life stories made the violence seem even more horrific, for these stories
> showed us that this was not only an attack on America. It was also an assault
> on humanity, leaving families and friends, communities, and nations around
> the world in extraordinary pain. There were no easy words to convey our col-
> lective distress, but there were many acts of individual solidarity that helped
> the victims, the heroes and their kin—the donations of blood, the flow of
> money, the benefit concerts, the memorial observances.[5]

Within the University of Michigan (UM), there were exceptional efforts
undertaken to support grieving students, staff, and faculty. As on many college campuses, on September 12 an extraordinary candlelight vigil assembled
more than fifteen thousand students, staff, faculty, and friends to grieve
together. On September 14, a remarkable concert organized by the UM School
of Music channeled some of that pain. At some point, however, we needed to
consider the ways in which this attack should, or shouldn't, affect our global
mission.

On September 18, I organized a symposium on globalization and terrorism that drew more than one thousand people to listen to President Lee Bollinger, the business school dean Bob Dolan, and experts in religion, security,
violence, and global loss to begin to process this into analytical frameworks.
Dolan's remarks, especially in light of Linda Lim's observations, were most
illuminating:

> A member of my visiting committee . . . said to me, "we were educated about
> global challenges but not educated about real-world perceptions, perceptions that
> we would not like to hear. Our students cannot and should not be sheltered from
> this." And so that, I think, is the change I would take from this—that we have
> to do the research and find ways to really communicate to the future leaders of
> businesses how they can understand the new global realities in order to create a
> situation where we can contribute to society along with our capabilities. (cited in
> Kennedy and Weiner 2003)

Of course, Dolan's observations were most compelling for those embedded in
the globalization system and sympathetic to its promoters like Tom Friedman.

Those who recognized the challenge of difference—whether the difference between the victims of the attacks of 9/11 and those who might celebrate that assault, or between those who saw globalization as a variation on a well-worn practice of exploitation and ignorance by the world's wealthiest classes and those who saw it as a qualitatively new system of opportunity—might just see in Dolan's words a bit too little, too late. And certainly over the last decade, the last century's globalization looks positively anachronistic.

Friedman's thoughts, even when amended by his subsequent publications, show their age. The straitjacket doesn't look so golden, and in fact, Brazil, China, and India, at the least, point to an alternative global order in which what some call "the Global South" leads, and does not adapt to change initiated elsewhere (e.g., Unger 2005, xvi). As a consequence, we have a new kind of knowledge flow, where differences are diminished across a new set of nations in the name of a common struggle against declining forms of knowledge and power. This is a difference increasingly obvious, but hardly the only one that deserves attention when the world is our reference. The problem, however, is how in the world we recognize critical differences.

If we begin with global climate change as our framework, we might focus on the implications of changing water levels for places of different altitudes. Those in island nations likely consider this an existential question even as it appears too remote from the concerns of those setting global priorities. If emerging markets are our focus, as earlier approaches to globalization would emphasize, China and India seem much more important. If security is our concern, one might better begin with the location from which one poses the question of security itself. Policy makers in Washington, Moscow, Jakarta, and Johannesburg have very different proposals for identifying critical differences in the world. And we know that these differences also change over time as the attack on 9/11 and the Arab Uprisings of 2011 make very clear. One might naturalize these differences as expressions of national interest or world epoch, but that misses the opportunity an inquiry into their sociological formation offers for globalizing knowledge.

This range of invocations about knowledge and the world—from the narrative of connectivity inspired by globalization's framework, to the challenge of difference heightened for the powerful by concerns over security or felt everyday by those excluded from worldly privilege—illustrates the challenge. Intellectuals and knowledge institutions and networks can easily overlook that challenge by pursuing a narrow definition of knowledge in the world.

Especially for those intellectuals, institutions, and networks moved by Bauman's worry beginning this chapter, we need to better understand the dynamics of globalizing knowledge.[6] That's especially true if we believe it matters for the world's well-being.

Part of the problem is that the term, like globalization itself, smooths over critical differences in its agents, audiences, objects, networks, and power. This series of cascading differences suggests abandoning the notion of globalizing knowledge altogether. Consider, for example, how sociologists might understand the reference (Kennedy and Centeno 2007). Some of my fellow sociologists can speak of globalizing sociology when they use data from other countries. Others, more familiar with various nations' cultures, might suggest deeper encounters by drawing on those nations' historiographies to refine interpretations of data or produce more context-sensitive questions (e.g., Thornton 2004). Others may even suggest that cultural logics of distant civilizations could alter our sense of space and time in practicing our discipline (e.g., Wallerstein 1999). Those variations also shift as they travel across space. For instance, the Bourdieusian approach we know in France or the United States becomes something else entirely in Poland (Warczok and Zarycki 2014). Globalizing knowledge is, even within sociology, a terrible notion. Yet its reference is inescapable in these times.

I seek therefore to elaborate its broader articulation so globalizing knowledge becomes conceptually clearer. I also work to make that clarification useful in both profound and good ways. Especially then for those inspired by Max Weber's methodological example, let me begin with its ideal type.

Globalizing knowledge refers to the process by which distant regions' knowledgeabilities are implicated in the particular cultures fusing those understandings. The form of globalizing knowledge will vary given the different historical and institutional contexts that shape such learning. Globalizing knowledge is, therefore, relationally composed. The *sociology* of globalizing knowledge concerns the conditions, manners, and implications of that fusion. To develop its sociology, one must be hermeneutic (Kennedy 1987). I would advise we consider that hermeneutic at three moments, drawing on the two familiars involved in proper translation and a third moment of elaboration.

First, the sociology of globalizing knowledge demands that we explain how globalizers recognize learning offered by other times and/or places. Here, the challenge of difference is paramount. Second, sociologists should explain how globalizers fuse horizons, building on those distant recognitions. They should explore how a new common sensibility across planes of difference is cultivated. Finally, as translation occurs across multiple dyads simultaneously, if unequally, synthetic elaborations develop. These articulations are often implicit, but they can become explicit and thus subject to more rational critical discussion. That third moment gives intellectuals and publics, not just the implicated experts, a greater chance to influence how knowledge articulates change. Recognition, translation, and articulation are the three critical moments in the sociology of globalizing knowledge.

My own approach to this sociology of globalizing knowledge is more agent focused than is much work on the sociology of knowledge, translation, and global transformations. This book is about how different kinds of knowledge actors—intellectuals and knowledge institutions and networks—shape, and are shaped by, the mediations of various global flows and contexts through their various professional and public engagements. I have that focus because while I enjoy theory, I am dedicated to its implications for practice, but even in that, theory matters.

I don't have the financial or legislative resources that enable transformational practice as some of the people in my study do. However, my associations with a number of different knowledge institutions and networks have taught me that the cultural schema organizing their work affects how intellectual responsibilities are met and their practices conducted. Thus, while material resources matter,[7] the frameworks through which we recognize them matter maybe even more, especially when knowledge is the coin of the realm.

Understanding, Intellect, and Articulation

The sociology of knowledge has a rich history and an even more exciting present, especially evident with the elaboration of political epistemics. Andreas Glaeser (2011) challenges us to move away from the sociology of knowledge to the sociology of understanding with various modes—discursive, emotive, and kinesthetic—in tow. He emphasizes the importance of figuring how knowledge comes to be validated and how different validation processes can make that knowledge more and less legitimate. That recognition also should make clear to whose networks of authority particular forms of knowledge belong, an inescapable dimension of knowledge politics. Lewis Coser (1965) left no doubt about where he stood and establishes one end of a knowledge politics spectrum.

Coser worked hard to distinguish intellect. In his typically provocative fashion, he writes,

> Not all academic men are intellectuals, nor are all members of the professions; this fact is deplored by some and applauded by others. Intellect, as distinguished from the intelligence required in the arts and sciences, presumes a capacity for detachment from immediate experience, a moving beyond the pragmatic tasks of the moment, a commitment to comprehensive values transcending professional or occupational involvement. . . . Max Weber's famous distinction between men who live off politics and men who live for politics may serve us here. Intellectuals live for rather than off ideas. (1965, viii)

Of course, he bespeaks his time with his gendered references, but he also seems to be from another era with his emphasis on the distinction of intellectuals as such. Not only should understanding be distinguished from knowledge, he might have said, but intellectuals are different from professionals *and* academics. That is quite a distance from the ways in which power/knowledge has come to be discussed around many struggles of resistance and transformation. For example, in a recent collection devoted to struggles in Appalachia, the editors elaborate another end of the spectrum.

> Knowledge is a fundamental component of power: Whose knowledge is considered legitimate? What knowledge is widely circulated? Thus, scaling up involves not only issues of organizational development and linkages, but also the creation of new spaces where people with critical perspectives, experiences, and knowledge can articulate their ideas in forms that are widely accessible at local, regional, national, and international scales. (Fisher and Smith 2012, 13)

Knowledge can be contested across all sorts of gradients of power. Within this Appalachian context, one group of women worked to "conceive new strategies for making our voices heard in bastions of patriarchal power (church, government, academia)" (Dean, Gulley, and McKinney 2012, 112). This was not just between those bastions and women. The Appalachian Women's Alliance grew out of an awareness of how power worked to diminish some within the movement itself. As one person contributing to the volume reflected,

> Class is the hardest issue of all. I have always experienced middle-class white women as being mean. I would try not to engage them in a discussion. If they asked me a question, I would answer briefly, then turn my attention away.

> Again and again I have seen these women watch and wait, looking for a vul-
> nerable area to attack. Only now that I am much older do I have the knowl-
> edge to defend myself and sometimes attack back. (Dean, Gulley, and McKin-
> ney 2012, 112)

The kind of knowledge that comes from learning and sharing among those
without privileged access to education, power, and wealth is not at all the
same as what Coser offers. They stand poles apart. Maybe the Appalachian
example is more akin to the kind of vernacular knowledge those offering two
cheers for anarchism would celebrate (Scott 2012). To say that it is a less validated understanding, as Glaeser's extension might, minimizes the empowerment in the claim that this is an *alternative* knowledge born in struggle and
hope.

One could, as Coser, focus on hierarchies of knowledge. I think it's more
suitable for a sociology of globalizing knowledge to recognize their alternatives and articulations. Instead of thinking about knowledgeability as a hierarchy of more or less philosophically rigorous and empirically grounded
understandings, as an ideology of science might, it is better conceived as many
forms of knowing. To avoid the relativism implied in the adjective, one might
be explicit over the ways in which these alternative knowledges are validated.
One can explore how different practices and institutions variously legitimate
different knowledge cultures and their corresponding social networks.

To study alternative knowledges in such fashion has a long pedigree. Consider the Durkheimian interest in religion's formation, Levi-Strauss's categories of the human mind, or more recent efforts to think through alternative
classification systems and their implications for understanding power (Worsley 1997). Especially with the relative rise of political economic power in the
Global South, and informed by those more and less savvy regarding Edward
Said's (1979) foundational contributions, scholars have worked to consolidate
what knowledgeability based on that global position represents (Chakrabarty
2000; Connell 2007). We are also in new times, however, in which the meaning of place-based knowledge changes. For instance, Jean and John Comaroff
(2011, 48) have argued,

> If indeed rather south-like conditions have become the "grim New Nor-
> mal" in Euro-America, there is clearly a need there too for a return to The-
> ory . . . [by which they mean] the historically contextualized problem-driven
> effort to account for the production of social and cultural "facts" in the world

by recourse to an imaginative methodological counterpoint between the inductive and the deductive, the concrete and the concept, also in a different register, between the epic and the everyday, the meaningful and the material.

Thus, it's not only a matter of figuring the substance of knowledge, or even its grounding. It's the *articulation* that counts (Ortner 2006, 2). The following remains as true today as when Kennedy and Suny (1999, 5) wrote sometime ago, "Articulation is our keyword, a word that is helpful precisely because it provides an important double meaning. A noun that implies expression, something intellectuals are obliged to do to fill their role, it also implies a measure of fit between a cultural product and the social environment that enables its production and makes that product consequential." Articulation, however, has greater theoretical significance than we offered in that volume. It is especially central to the work of Stuart Hall and those he inspired. He appreciated it for the same double meaning that we offered. He also made it more theoretical by emphasizing its opposition to determinisms of various sorts.

> An articulation is thus the form of the connection that *can* make a unity of two different elements, under certain conditions. It is a linkage which is not necessary, determined, absolute and essential for all time. . . . A theory of articulation is both a way of understanding how ideological elements come, under certain conditions, to cohere together within a discourse, and a way of asking how they do or do not become articulated, at specific conjunctures, to certain political subjects. (Hall 1996, 141–42)

It is, one might say, analyzing culture, ideology, and knowledge through the "process of making connections" (Slack 1996, 114).

As in that tradition, I use the word to imply that explicating the relationship among elements of any structure is more important than understanding how any element is foundational in general. In this sense, articulation invites us to move away from the determinism of material forces, the transcendence of ideas and spirit, and even the compulsions of structure, or of freedom, in the elaboration of knowledge consequence. By working with articulation as concept, we are inclined to think about the distinctions of the various elements in vision and how, in any particular moment or practice, they are related to each other to form a particular whole. Especially for engaging globalizing knowledge, we are obliged to consider the conditions under which particular kinds of knowledge become not only visibly important but effective out of sight. And for those interested in practice, it offers a way to figure interventions, respond to their consequences, and cumulate insights and engagements. As I discuss in Chapter 8, it even offers a distinctive mode for engaging a world in crisis where the analyst of transformation explicates connections seen, and unseen, in transformation.

In sum, it's right to pluralize the noun, for knowledge itself has many different qualities, even if we can agree about its association with learning. It varies in substance, from the scholastic achievements of an expert on Plato to the technical and revolutionary insights of the Internet expert challenging our presumptions about wisdom's sources. It varies in its social location, from the acknowledged learnedness of the nuclear physicist or law school professor to the particular insights earned by minority working-class women finding their voice in movements ostensibly dedicated to their empowerment. It varies in its centrality—while it's difficult to overlook the importance of research on DNA for changing our sense of health, we have been formed to overlook No'ono'o and other indigenous forms of knowledge about the interconnectedness of life.[8] But then, this pluralization of knowledge also reflects the place from which I offer my own articulation of knowledge's place in the world within a wide range of sociologies of knowledge.

Sociologies of Knowledge

In the 1968 introduction to Florian Znaniecki's (1986) volume on intellectuals, Lewis Coser (1986, vii) worried that the tradition of engaging the sociology of knowledge could fade. Already by the 1980s, Coser observed the opposite to have happened. In the succeeding decades, the bounty has become truly bountiful. While it could be a joy to tour through the range of alternatives, I only signal some of the most substantial here and address them and others in greater detail as they become relevant later. This initial tour is also useful to help readers anticipate specialists' reactions to my work.

For every sociologist of knowledge, it's hard not to find some Mannheim in the moment. Scholars working in this tradition identify Karl Mannheim as providing the "founding statement" of the traditional approach to the sociology of knowledge with the following form:[9]

(1) Focusing on a particular social thinker (or set of social thinkers), the researcher begins *post festum* with the thinker's ideas already known, fixed in the canonical documents of his or her intellectual tradition or field

(philosophy, economics, sociology etc.); (2) working backward, the researcher then traces the "origins" of those known ideas to external social sources, generally conceptualized in terms of macrolevel economic, political, and ideological conditions, as well as the thinker's class- or group-based interests. (Camic, Gross, and Lamont 2011, 6)

Thinking at such a grand scale, while good for the critical spirit, might not provide much help in institutional engagement. Merton helps.

Robert Merton helped shift American sociology's attention away from this ostensibly European approach to be empirical but dedicated to debunking (Sica 2010). Merton would rather famously focus on the middle range and on science in particular, with its ethos that "encouraged productivity, critical thinking, and the pursuit of continually improved understanding" (Calhoun 2010a, 11). Attending to institutions rather than practices per se, such emphasis marks his era of sociology.[10]

The Mannheimian/Mertonian tension continues to animate differences in the explicit and implicit sociology of knowledge. It took new and especially relevant life for this volume in a debate between Mertonian Piotr Sztompka (2011) and public sociologist Michael Burawoy (2011) on how one globalizes sociology.

With his leadership of the International Sociological Association, Burawoy organized a book around how representatives from different nation-states in the world understood sociologies to vary depending on the place in which one works. This, for Sztompka, violated that Mertonian scientific ethos: Globalizing knowledge means finding common propositions that work regardless of context. To do otherwise risks ideological descent. Burawoy found Sztompka's position to be rooted in a kind of professional sociology that occupies a portion of only one quadrant of the discipline. For overall sociological, intellectual, and social well-being, that knowledgeability should be balanced, Burawoy argued, by other kinds of kinds of sociology (critical, policy, and public). Although I address his framework at greater length in Chapter 4, it's useful to position my work at the start with regard to this debate, for the debate presupposes the best place to stand in globalizing sociology.

Burawoy (1989) once contrasted the sociologies of revolution offered by Leon Trotsky and Theda Skocpol. He noted that the former theorized revolution from within revolutionary practices, and the latter, from outside. One might suggest that Sztompka's sociology stands outside the processes he analyzes, or at least struggles to mark that distance with his Mertonian scientific ethos. However, Burawoy (1990), like Trotsky or even Mannheim, seeks to develop theory in practice. Of course, such a sociology of knowledge need not be Marxist; Dewey's (1938) famous exchange with Trotsky suggests the value of pragmatism's alternative, and complement.[11] Indeed, such sociology need not focus on the present in order to be publicly engaged. Somers's sociology of knowledge illustrates what's possible.

For Somers the struggle over a theory of citizenship and rights is both scholarly and public. In one of her contributions, she argued that the knowledge about the relationship between property and rights is fundamentally wrong, based on a misreading of its historical formation. Instead of rights being the effect of property relations, "the public realm of social relations and membership was the precondition" for property itself; in particular, "participatory and substantive legal rights were the preconditions of independence and freedom" (1995a, 64, 68). Membership, not property, is the key to understanding rights in this epistemology. More than a simple historical misunderstanding, she argues, this misrecognition has seeped into much deeper accounts of the public sphere and our sense of democracy.

Linking social history to a historical sociology of concept formation, she challenges both the philosophical and historical adequacy of separating markets from other social institutions. We do so, she argues, because of the conceptual networks in which we are embedded, not because of the way in which the world works beyond our concepts (Somers 1995b, 1995c). Knowledge cultures, she argues, constitute that analysis through which the world comes to be known. She uses this notion to identify how communities of discourse move to make some types of questions, styles of reasoning, and forms of evidence legitimate, and others not. Concepts, in particular, have "histories, networks, and narratives that can be subjected to historical and empirical investigation" (Somers 1999, 126, 135). This sociology of knowledge, furthermore, can have practical effect, as she and Fred Block illustrate in how another misreading of history legitimates the congressional 1996 Personal Responsibility and Work Opportunities Reconciliation Act (Block and Somers 2003, 2005).

Somers's work illustrates the significance of context in ways few others mark. For example, while many would find arguments about the practical origins of post–World War II human rights work in global fora (Waltz 1999), Somers's example would lead us to look for the deeper historical conceptual roots and regional privileges that move us to recognize how both understandings *and* misunderstandings produce knowledge and practical effect. We need in a sociology of globalizing knowledge to have a much more subtle and open approach to context. Somers's own location is more obvious, however.

Somers is part of a much larger movement in scholarship around elevating the significance of ideas, figuring their sociological conditions, and identifying their grounds in practice (Camic and Gross 2001). Camic, Gross, and Lamont (2011, 3) have recently codified this approach around a nomenclature of social knowledge, by which they mean "descriptive information and analytical statements about the actions, behaviors, subjective states and capacities of human beings and/or about the properties and processes of the aggregate or collective units—the groups, networks, markets, organizations and so on—where these human agents are situated." They invite others to embed analysis of these knowledges in the practices that mediate between the larger social structures and the particular knowledge products issued. And one might do exactly that in the sociology of globalizing knowledge.

For example, one might analyze interdisciplinary associations like the political science–led International Studies Association or subdisciplinary associations like the American Sociological Association's section on global and transnational sociology. Of course, a more traditional sociology of knowledge could look at the work of individual intellectuals who embody that globalizing spirit from Gerhard Lenski to Immanuel Wallerstein to Saskia Sassen. One might split the difference between individuals and institutions to focus on vice provosts for international affairs at large research universities and the demands such positions reflect, and the fields they work to constitute. That is, at least, where I first recognized the importance of a sociology of globalizing knowledge.

Engaged Ethnography, Cultural Politics, and Para-Sites

I hadn't recognized at the time that my work as vice provost for international affairs at the University of Michigan was also ethnographic. At least I hadn't taken it as seriously as I might have. I did, in the course of meetings, joke about it.

As my colleagues would moan about yet another meeting to figure the international mission of the university, I would counter by saying that they complain only because they had chosen the wrong field. If they were like me, a sociologist of globalizing knowledge, this could be yet another ethnographic opportunity. Of course, that *was* a joke, for I had not asked the Institutional

Review Board to approve my methodology and assure that my colleagues, as human subjects, would not be endangered by my observations of their academic practice, or by my humor. In retrospect, I wish I had developed explicitly an engaged ethnography of globalizing knowledge in terms similar to those I had developed during my dissertation research in communist-ruled Poland.

I understand "engaged ethnography" to be "research that seeks through its study and elaboration of vernaculars greater clarity of the ways in which power relations work so as to facilitate greater claims to justice and normative goods among those engaged as well as among those informed by those actions and its study" (Kennedy 2013b, 29).[12] Studying an illegal movement like Poland's Solidarność in the beginning of the 1980s and trying to figure a university's international mission at the turn of the century are radically different. However, in both cases I sought to cultivate a more refined sociological imagination among my interlocutors, and for myself, that might more effectively mobilize knowledge for the public good. It's not obvious which was more challenging.

One reason intellectuals and knowledge were so critical under communist rule was that speaking truth to power was hard only because it was dangerous; it was consequential only because everyone knew the truth but was afraid to say it (Burawoy and Lukacs 1992). Where rules of law are more apparent, lies are more difficult to recognize. Criticisms are easier to offer and much less dangerous because truth is dissolved in procedural loops, so the elaboration of vernaculars, to be critical, should not only clarify how the world is understood. It should also explicate how power relations work to legitimate or problematize the distance of those vernaculars from the claims to justice and normative goods embedded in the rules purporting to organize social life.

For example, the relationship between innocent wishes to internationalize universities and strategic plans to raise funds, especially in times of financial crisis, is not always so obvious. At least it is not typically publicly acknowledged; thus, identifying even best practices among globalizing institutions is not quite adequate to finding their potentials in globalizing knowledge. Sometimes those best practices might commonly hide what is most deserving attention in a culture of really critical discourse. Attending to cultural politics helps therefore.

"Cultural politics" is a much more widely used term than "engaged ethnography" and thus has many more meanings (e.g., Molnar 2005). I use it in

the following sense: "attempts to influence and transform the meanings, identities, values, and representations accompanying the exercise of power and
influence" (Kennedy 2008). Cultural politics draws upon the various structures in which they are embedded and the relationships and contradictions
among them. They are also shaped by events, those conjunctures where relationships among actors and the forces that empower them can shift. Events
can be generated by unexpected flows, or lack of flows, of resources, but they
also can be produced by cultural political interventions themselves. Cultural
political resources can rest in the relationships that exist among symbols and
meanings, and the emotions and identifications attached to them (Sewell
2005). By itself, cultural politics is not enough to understand everything—one
needs to think about how those cultural politics are embedded in history,
networks, institutions, and the distribution of resources. Nevertheless, cultural politics is a very good guide to engaging theory and practice in globalizing knowledge, especially when we are primarily attentive to the schema
that organize them.

Intellectual engagements of social processes are filled with cultural politics. Indeed, intellectuals are often crucial in this field, especially in the articulation of the nation (Suny and Kennedy 1999a). Universities are themselves
embedded in complex cultural politics too, especially around their international missions (Kennedy 2011c). Finding just the right framework, finding
just the right international partners, and finding just the right substantive
missions are not just about globalizing knowledge for its own sake. It's often
about finding the position least likely to offend existing supporters, most
likely to stimulate new sources of funding, or perhaps even make a difference
on terms rarely elaborated beyond vague invocation. Cultural politics is all
about public relations and philanthropic efforts. It can also move to higher
purpose in the constitution of critical interventions.

While I was very pleased to work with colleagues to extending lessons
from the 1989 Polish Round Table negotiations across the world in 1999 Ann
Arbor, that was not an especially difficult cultural political project. Everyone
could be in favor of extending democracy via nonviolent means.[13] In contrast,
to engage the events of 1915 in the Ottoman Empire was exceptionally difficult. Beginning discussion of systematic murders and ethnic cleansing with
the word *genocide* could mean the end, at least at that time, to dialogue among
Turks and Armenians. The book that emerged from that series of engagements (Suny, Gocek, and Naimark 2011) was itself a reflection of cultural

politics. The whole process of scholarly dialogue, not only its final product, is also important to consider if we are to recognize that volume's consequence (Kennedy 2011c).

That Polish and Armenian/Turkish comparison, however, makes the point: When we think about globalizing knowledge, we typically do so from our disciplinary point of view, or our regional engagements, or our institutional mission, or our knowledge network niche. We too rarely compare interventions, investments, institutions, and networks even as we work to understand better our own points of departure. One might even consider those comparisons not only as Skocpol might but as Trotsky exemplified (Burawoy 1989). For that reason, it is important to think about "para-sites."

George Marcus used the term to organize an exceptionally interesting volume in a larger series. He sought new ways to represent the "widespread self-awareness of massive changes in society and culture globally—especially among those who write about the contemporary world—as it is in the facts and lived experiences of these changes themselves" (Marcus 2000, ix). This particular volume Marcus edited was dedicated to developing new kinds of dialogues, new kinds of counterparts, among those in adjacent fields to ethnography. The beauty of the interlocution, he suggests, lies in what it creates: "sites where interpretation occurs, where function is doubled, regardless of how this work arises or where it leads" (5–6). Working with the pun, Marcus suggests that it can extend the "cultural work that subjects do in the construction of a para-site in relation to some level of major institutional function undergoing current transformation" (7).[14]

Transformation, of course, varies substantially. In some cases, we seek to change a curriculum to make its accent more cosmopolitan. Sometimes we work to develop a scholarly dialogue that promises by-products in better international relations, as the Armenian/Turkish dialogue suggested. In other circumstances we develop partnerships with publics both proximate and quite distant. In other cases we articulate the hegemonies of global flows of consequence in order that cultures of critical discourse, rather than concentrations of economic or political power, shape their accounting. With this variety one can immediately appreciate that there is no simple field of practice associated with globalizing knowledge. However, by recognizing the diversity of knowledges, we might develop a better cultural politics and engaged ethnography across the various sites in which we work so that our efforts might cumulate more effectively, more justly.

Over the last thirty-some years, I have been conducting engaged ethnography in para-sites with cultural politics made on the fly. I wonder how much more we might have done had we had a more explicit methodology with which to work.

In what follows, I draw on sites that I know from the inside but treat them as an analytical outsider. I work with that insider information but rely on externally validated documents to pose problems and offer accounts that can illuminate a broader inquiry on how globalizing knowledge works. This is multisited ethnography of sorts but always engaged in a kind of cultural politics in which practice was an immediate object. Its cumulation in this globalizing knowledge project manifests a larger problem that encompasses us all. The cases themselves are not drawn from a careful construction of comparisons chosen to illuminate a puzzle to be resolved by some macroanalytic strategy (Skocpol and Somers 1980). They reflect, rather, an ordered precision of a somewhat chaotic life in international studies ranging across institutions and networks engaging various publics, different contexts, and a couple of global flows with a sense of transformation informed by the duality of structure.

Transformational Sociology

Sewell (2005) builds on Anthony Giddens to elaborate that duality of structure by contrasting the "rules" or "cultural schemas" and resources or actualities that characterize structures in order to have a better sense of how the reproduction and transformation of social relations occur. For Sewell, those schemas range from the deep binary oppositions between the raw and the cooked to the more informal or superficial folkways or conventions that may never be written down but that everyone knows, such as how to respect the queue. Resources are sources of power that might be either human or nonhuman. The strength of a human body, the capacity to command an army, and knowledge itself are "human" resources. Nonhuman resources include, among other things, factories, weapons, and land. Clearly the latter exist independently of the rules with which we organize social life, but no resource can be activated for human purposes without those resources' insertion into the cultural schemas of social life. At the same time, however, these cultural schemas have their power because the resources themselves "embody" the meanings with which they were originally encoded and give those meanings power. Structure is based then on a duality in which schemas give meaning to resources, which in turn can be read by others to find the "truth" of the schema.

The beauty of Sewell's approach does not rest only in its decomposition of discourse or of structure into schemas and resources. Rather, it lies in how neatly this theory of structure can address the big story and the eventful within a historical frame, all with a view toward figuring the consequence of knowledgeability for social and global transformations.

I have synthesized his approach to transformation with five aspects that, for ease of reference, I call the Sewellian list.[15] The first three are especially helpful when considering structural approaches to transformation. The latter two are useful when we emphasize changes in knowledgeability.

1. *The multiplicity of structures*: Any social unit is going to be composed of a variety of structures that are unlikely to be entirely homologous or in synchrony with one another. This variety of structures can lead to conflicting claims and social conflicts.

2. *Unpredictability of resource accumulation*: Enactments of schemas can produce quite unforeseen outcomes, and those outcomes, if sufficiently altering the power relations in a given social unit, lead to a transformation of structure.

3. *The intersection of structures*: Structures with different schemas and different resources overlap and interact in any given setting, making their smooth reproduction always potentially problematic given the contradictions that could emerge from their contact.

4. *The polysemy of resources*: The multiplicity of meaning potentially attached to any set of resources means that these resources can be interpreted in different ways, with various consequences for social transformation. Those with greater authority in interpretation, with greater knowledge, have disproportionate power in this transformation.

5. *The transposability of schemas*: Actors are capable of taking schemas or rules learned in one context and applying them to another. While this capacity is also universally distributed, those with a wider knowledge of different contexts, and different rules across those contexts, should have disproportionate influence in shaping change, ceteris paribus.

Although Sewell is a historian, his theoretical work travels well across time and the world (e.g., Kennedy 1999a; Aalto et al. 2013; Aalto et al. 2012) and is especially suitable for those concerned for the conditions and consequences of knowledgeability in global transformations.

For example, in the introduction to our volume on knowledge politics and global transformations, Cohen and Kennedy (2004, vii) asked, "What are the responsibilities of intellectuals and their institutions before a world in the midst of apparently profound change?" This can be understood as a moral/normative question, which it was in part. But it also had this Sewellian theoretical foundation for practice, as it was transposing questions one typically asked of intellectuals and instead asked of their institutions. It was also unpacking the meanings associated with being a global university so that the contradictory obligations inherent in some of them would be transformed as a consequence of the kind of event 9/11 represented.

Here I don't pretend to resolve the theoretical and methodological issues associated with elevating agency in explaining social life. However, because questions of globalizing knowledge do involve profound normative and moral questions, and because intellectuals too infrequently recognize the conditions of their own consequence, I will be especially attentive to this agentic side of Sewell's approach. At the same time, the conditions of their action—whether in institutions, fields, or networks—are informed by the articulation of the rules and resources at hand in these circumstances. Thus, when we consider how globalizing knowledge works, we need as well to take into account the qualities of knowledge fields, institutions, and networks, not just the commitments of intellectuals, in tracking the formation and consequence of globalizing knowledge.

Sewell's approach informed my knowledge practice and research over these last decades, but it also articulates powerfully with currents developed in recent times around fields (Fligstein and McAdam 2012) and networks (Padgett and Powell 2012). Both field and network studies have their own clusters of experts and consumers whose work doesn't always easily range across universities. Field analysis can alienate those who wish to think of their scholarship as something above, or beyond, questions of power and interest. Network analysis has a different kind of demystifying ethos, one that works relatively well with the intentions of the actors at hand. Network analysts incorporate the rules and protocols associated with network formation in their accounts while at the same time abstract from the meanings actors convey to explain how networks lead to innovation or disappearance. Both field analysis and network analysis are powerful means for explaining outcomes to other experts in their respective specialist fields who are interested in accounts of change. With sufficient translation, the results of their work also can be effective for those interested in the substantive areas under discussion, not only the research question field theorists and network analysts mobilize. I leave it to those experts to figure how their work might refashion my own approach. Sewell's inspiration works well enough.

Rather than approach his historical questions with the quest to explain more general patterns of social life, Sewell seeks to open up explanations of particular instances of historical transformations with analytical tools that have been refined through other empirical explorations. In Jonathan Turner's (2002) sense, this theoretical approach is more an exercise in analytical sensitivity than explanatory generality. I use the five Sewellian transformational propositions in similar ways to explore particular historical cases of knowledge and change. They can clarify the processes in which they are embedded, the conditions structuring them, and comparisons that might illuminate them, which might be most useful for those figuring the theory and practice of globalizing knowledge. But field theory and network analysis can help.

Consider, for example, how public engagements may differ depending on whether one's principal responsibilities lie with institutional leadership or with scholarly development. In Chapter 4, I consider the intellectual consequences of these various commitments to articulate a vision of public sociology from the standpoint of civil society versus a vision of public sociology in the thick of institutional reproduction and transformation. In this, the strategic action fields facing relatively autonomous professors and institutionally obliged administrators are radically different, even while both are apparently within a common field dedicated to mobilizing knowledge for public goods.

One way to move beyond the categorical distinction implied by modifying kinds of responsibility with intellectual and institutional labels, and their accompanying connotations of freedom and constraint, is to think more in network terms. Networks seem to defy the agency/structure problem, being composed and defined by relations themselves, especially when informed by the sense of time suggested previously. However, the very qualities of that relationality mean that networks are subject to greater innovation, and transformation, depending on the location one occupies and the resources one commands.

Manuel Castells (2009, 45–47) makes that point powerfully with his metaphors. Castells calls those with the capacities to constitute networks with particular goals "programmers," for they have a kind of power derived from the network's coordinated action itself. "Switchers" control connections among networks. While he does not propose that we analyze the work of switchers and programmers in terms of intellectual and institutional responsibility, these terms do encourage us to think about how particular locations in networks allow for different measures of consequence, and characterizations of responsibility, in their accompanying practice.

The notion of epistemic community, or the "network of professionals with recognized expertise and competence in a particular domain and authoritative claim to policy relevant knowledge within that domain or issue area" (Eyal and Bucholz 2010, 128), invokes this approach, especially when we might see how that community's particular expertise not only reflects a problem area but, in fact, "performs, shapes and formats" that knowledge object through legislative, interpretive, expert, and mediating practices. Thus, in figuring globalizing knowledge, we should attend to publics, contexts, and flows mediating knowledge practices and products.

Publics, Contexts, and Flows

Eyal and Bucholz (2010), just as Castells (2009), reflect some of the turn toward analyzing communicative practice in the constitution of social relations. No form of social organization reflects that turn better than publics. A public is a secondary association formed by the communicative practices that constitute it, not derived from anything preformed. Of course, resources produced elsewhere and through interaction shape the character of publics, as do competencies generated in other spheres and times. But publics are above all social relations made through communication. Indeed, when sociologists choose to address a public, they help make it so by its naming and recognition. That is one reason why interventions in public sociology are potentially so consequential (Burawoy 2005a).

While markets might also be made by that kind of expert practice in recognition, the other practices constituting markets are focused less on communication as such and more on exchange and accumulation of wealth and goods. Likewise, we might also find in communicative relations the making of states, even nations. However, states and nations are also media of power, made by practices of violence and coercion in addition to communications. Publics are primarily communicative; as one professor of communications has offered, "publics are *emergences* manifested through vernacular rhetoric" (Hauser 1999, 14).

For those familiar with Jürgen Habermas, his influence on this field is obvious, and the previous distinctions I have made reflect his own based on state, economy, and civil society (e.g., Heath 2011). I do find these distinctions analytically useful in general, but for two reasons especially when it comes to globalizing knowledge.

First, although globalization has many different currents, its economic dimension has often led in both popular accounts and knowledgeable engagements, because economic development and trade dominate cross-border ties and expertise can be developed and purchased with the money globalizing wealth can generate. Second, with the resources states have at hand, deploying experts to figure new security regimes and diplomatic ties, alongside all the other matters of state on which foreign policies might focus, is one of the principal avenues for the graduates, and teachers, of international studies. In both cases, knowledge is put to the service of money and power. That medium is quite different in relation to publics.

Although the ideals of Habermas's communicative rationality are often criticized for their distance from the real mechanisms of publicity and conversation, these objections are much more severe when the original point is lost. His discourse ethics were intended to provide a normative reference for analytical critique (Olson 2011). I would take this one step further. If publics are in fact constituted through communication, and knowledge can acquire a greater distinction in that communicative effort, intellectuals and their institutions and networks might play a greater role in shaping at least one dimension of global transformations. Habermas recognizes this: intellectuals, he argues, have greater opportunities to influence other national publics through the development of global public spheres (Habermas 2006; Cronon 2011). Even if that is granted, the spatial dimension of that public engagement deserves more attention.

Those globalizing knowledge occasionally treat as an instrumental problem the ways in which different global contexts become the object of knowledgeable attention. For example, many universities have become especially interested in extending their engagement with China and India, while study abroad offices have become especially enamored of moving their students beyond Europe. Some universities fortunate enough to have donors dedicated to Armenia or Ukraine may find new ways to celebrate a university's investment in Armenian or Ukrainian studies, but the applause rarely reflects an elaborate architecture of globalizing knowledge. Indeed, those overseeing language instruction certainly know that some languages are more difficult for native English speakers to learn, but those different degrees rarely figure into how universities might want to set the bar for, and investment in, different languages of globalizing knowledge (Kennedy 2010a).

One of the aspects of this globalization most taken for granted is language, and the hegemony of English in defining scholarship. Although there are more native speakers of Mandarin Chinese and Spanish, and substantial numbers, in descending order, of Hindi-Urdu, Arabic, Bengali, Portuguese, and Russian native speakers in the world, English is the dominant language of foreign learning, especially of knowledge production in many fields. This tendency is part of globalization's hubris. At the same time, however, much escapes those who remain in English, and more escapes the world when there are few who know a language other than those who grew up with it. And given that a country's wealth is more likely to be recognized not only when its peoples emigrate but when others learn from it in their original tongues, globalizing knowledge can be quite uneven.

When colonial regimes establish particular kinds of hybridities, we are drawn to consider the flows of people who connected them alongside the other goods and services that motivated that tie. While flows of knowledge, people, wealth, and weapons were hardly distinctive to the era of globalization, the intensification of these flows has come to mark it. Arjun Appadurai (2001, 5) even went so far as to propose that "we are functioning in a world fundamentally characterized by objects in motion . . . a world of flows." Some places articulate flows more than others, but some objects flow more than others and draw other objects in their wake.

Images, ideas, and other things that can flow electronically, especially currencies, typically define this world of flows, but I have been especially taken with flows of energy because of the various material qualities it offers, its deep connection to defining the fate of our world, and its immediate connection to defining which places are important for the powerful and which places need not be attended. For those who wish to globalize knowledge, and whose path is blazed by those who seek wealth and power, energy production, distribution channels, and consumption patterns are quite important, even while that observation filters all too slowly beyond the expert domains that claim its study.

These three sets of relations—around publics, contexts, and flows—are central to my own analytical interest in globalizing knowledge. Given the number of injunctions apparent in my writing, these interests are not based on accident alone. They are based on a series of engagements in matters apparently distant from much of globalizing knowledge.

Consequence, Norms, and Reflexivity

"Consequence," "norms," and "reflexitivity" are not terms one typically finds together in discussions of globalizing knowledge. Each has a different anchoring knowledge culture, though their conjunction is critical for this volume's conception.

Consequence is the least elaborate of these notions but the most commonly referenced connotation of globalizing knowledge. With the associations of knowledge with universality, globalizing seems to complete in geographical terms its connotation. As objects flow around the world in ever greater numbers and with ever greater speeds, the idea that knowledge must flow with them, if not also shape them, seems necessary for relevance. Ideologies of knowledge for its own sake continue to anchor many intellectual and institutional practices. However, and especially in times of financial crisis, intrinsic values fade before so many knowledges competing for resources, especially when the consequence of knowledge beyond its advance shapes preferences in allocating funds. Thus, while consequence is critical, especially as institutional and network leaders figure allocations of resources (evident, for example, in the need to specify "impact" in National Science Foundation proposals), theories of consequential knowledge are remarkably underelaborated. We do have recent work on how ideas are consequential in policy work (Block and Somers 2003, 2005) and even in visions of global solidarity (Kennedy 2012b). But this volume is dedicated to figuring how we might better conceive consequence in globalizing knowledge. Figuring norms is much simpler, at least if scholarly reference is one's guide.

On the practical side, those working to universalize human rights have been in the forefront of globalizing knowledge and the roles of norms in both conception and consequence. Scholars working in international law and more constructivist approaches to international relations have relied heavily on normative structures to study globalization's dynamics (Keck and Sikkink 1998; Guidry, Kennedy, and Zald 2000). Some scholars have even theorized this normative dimension as a global resource itself, figuring, for instance, how the European Union uses normative power to advance its own interests (Laidi 2008). The normative not only shapes power and practice but also knowledge itself. We see this in mission statements—the Social Science Research Council, for example, marked its distinction at the turn of the century by emphasizing how it mobilizes knowledge for the public good. That also has foundations in theories of knowledge, especially in "critical theory." As Craig Calhoun (2001a, 110) has put it,

> Indeed, all sociological theory needs (a) to engage in continuous critical examination of the foundations—both intellectual and institutional—on which sociological knowledge rests. At the same time, but distinctly, it needs (b) to approach existing social reality critically, seeing the limits of generalizing from concrete phenomena that are instances of historically conditioned human possibility, not simply universal or unchanging. Finally, it needs (c) to be attentive to the ways in which sociology itself participates in the making of the world, the creation of particular social—and even sometimes material—conditions in social relationships shaped by sociological knowledge and ways of understanding.

This is a matter not only of theory but increasingly of concrete empirical research. In fact, by figuring how the normative is now part of the social, the very distance from public life on which Robert Merton insisted to figure the ethos of science fades before the scholarly engagement of public life (Kalleberg 2010).[16] For Habermas, reason finds its mediation between systems and lifeworld through legal systems and their norms. He thus sees in globalization a profound challenge: How might global governance be realized without global government? Which functions of government might be surrendered to transnational leagues, and which retained for nation-states as such (Cronon 2011)?

However, the critical point for his communicative ethics rests in the fact that reason's potentiality exists only to the extent that movements and civil society remain beyond the administrative reach of institutionalized law. Civil society and its public sphere are the sociological foundations for democracy's immanent critique and thus the motor for democracy's realization through its extension (Haysom 2011).

Michael Burawoy does not acknowledge much of Habermas's work in his earlier scholarship, but the former's turn toward the public university as real utopia suggests Habermas's importance. Burawoy (2012b) seeks to constitute the university as "a community of critical discourse that transcends disciplinary

Plan	Dictatorship	Russia	Past	Particularistic	Bureaucrat	Dependency	Ukraine
Market	Democracy	West	Future	Comparative	Entrepreneur	Opportunity	Estonia

FIGURE 1.1 Knowledge structure of transition culture.

boundaries and sustains the idea of a discursive community critical of the university but also of the society within which it is embedded, and second, a deliberative democracy that roots the university in civil society and engages directly in a conversation with its surrounding publics about the direction of society." But this depends on his earlier argument about public sociology.

Burawoy has promoted a movement for public sociology that depends on distinguishing types of sociology according to the kinds of audiences for which they produce knowledge. Here, publics are critically different from one's fellow academics. However, Burawoy (2005a) also emphasizes another distinction, about the kind of relationship one has to one's work. That is, in part, about norms but also more succinctly about reflexivity, or the degree to which scholars are "concerned with a dialogue about ends," in which the author "interrogates the value premises of society as well as our profession" (Burawoy 2005a, 11). Burawoy (2003) has himself deepened this reflexive proposition with his own methodological innovations.

Reflexivity is all too alien in the worlds of international studies, even if it is an increasingly common term in the social sciences. It guides the theory and practice of globalizing knowledge with consequence, too, at least if the explicit justifications by one of the world's most prominent philanthropists, George Soros (2008), are any indicator. However, for the scholars reading this volume, there are many more obvious intellectuals associated with reflexivity, most notably Pierre Bourdieu. He has offered that sociology ought to "lay bare the social and intellectual unconscious embedded in analytical tools of sociology" and the "unthought categories of thought which delimit the thinkable and predetermine thought" (Bourdieu and Wacquant 1992, 36). This volume is, then, predicated on increasing our reflexivity in globalizing knowledge.

In that spirit and in my previous work, I thought it critical to elaborate the underlying knowledge structure organizing social action. In the case of Eastern Europe's transition culture, I proposed a set of symbols and narratives organized around the movement from plan to market, and from dictatorship to democracy (Figure 1.1; Kennedy 2002a, 108).

Global	Elite	Knowledge	Connected	Global citizenship
~	~	~	~	~
Provincial	Pedestrian	Sense	Isolated	National egoism

FIGURE 1.2 Global knowledge structure based on connectivity.

While certainly that structure was not simply and automatically embraced, its hegemony was extended by arguing about more particular issues within it, such as who was the real source of cultural and knowledge authority in figuring transition's best routes. Globalizing knowledge does not have that same cultural structure or relationship to contest.

As I elaborate in what follows, it is more difficult to establish the general cultural structure underlying globalizing knowledge in part because its structure, not only its emphasis, varies substantially depending on the place of its articulation (e.g., Peacock 2007). Because of the culture of critical discourse underlying knowledge's distinction, discursive authority is also typically contested. That contest over globalizing knowledge challenges its underlying cultural structural stability. For example, one might suggest the underlying structure based on global connectivity shown in Figure 1.2.

For most reading this volume, this is the implicit frame that justifies investments in globalizing knowledge. After all, in order to realize the learning and knowledge one needs to recognize our mutual dependence and common planetary fate, one needs to escape the common sense of one's immediate environs. One needs to embrace the possibilities of sharing knowledge with others around the world. All different kinds of knowledge—in the arts, in the sciences, in the social sciences—can help this mutual recognition. Our identification with one another can be realized through each of these forms of knowledge, making an unqualified and singular expression of globalizing knowledge apt.

This stable structure breaks down first and foremost when connectivity is no longer the implication of a global elite knowledge intellectual chain, and the global reference is not its starting point. One might, for example, think of the case of Edward Snowden, a contractual worker in the US national security establishment who was at the same time deeply embedded in a world defined by connectivity. His theft of documents and release through media might be interpreted through a lens of global connectivity. Those, most evidently in Germany but also across the world, celebrate his whistle-blowing effort on behalf of privacy for all the world's innocents. But when the national interest begins

National	Patriot	Useful knowledge	Security
~	~	~	
Enemy	Traitor	Dangerous knowledge	Threat

FIGURE 1.3 Global knowledge structure based on national security.

the chain, the underlying cultural structure shifts. Consider, for example, this underlying structure associated with a vision of national security (Figure 1.3).

The immediate objection, which is wrong, might be that this is not about globalizing knowledge at all. In fact, this very framework of knowledge serving national security needs has typically animated and resourced area studies, the most substantial investment in learning about other world regions in US universities. However, it does wind up coding knowledge differently. When national interest demarcates, one is immediately drawn to distinctions of knowledge in terms of their utility, and even their danger. If national security is the starting point of globalizing knowledge, some kinds of knowledge or even questions become a threat. One need ask only about the patriotism of Edward Snowden to illustrate the tension (Shaikh and Goodman 2013). Even within the national security frame, one can see that "useful" knowledge is not a very cosmopolitan question, and perhaps a dangerous notion itself.

Scholars and experts can challenge the quality of knowledge per se within the security frame by arguing that dangerous knowledge may not be biased knowledge associated with a nation's critics. Instead, dangerous knowledge may be profound misunderstandings of a nation's "enemies" based on the ideological biases of a nation's ill informed, as suggested in the schematic in Figure 1.4.

Of course, it all depends on how the national interest is defined and who gets to define it. And that, too, is subject to transformation, as is evident in the next knowledge structural moment. Consider what happens to the place of knowledge when public empowerment is the vision of knowledge. In that constitution, one might contrast the plurality of knowledges with the danger of elites, according to their own interest, determining the value of knowledge (Figure 1.5).

Here the question becomes, Which publics, and which elites, define interest? Over the course of 2011–13, the public mobilizations against elites of all sorts have raised profound questions about ideology and knowledge, with the differences between Tea Party critiques of elites and Occupy movements' critiques of elites begging for elaboration and engagement. In each case, the degree to which populist knowledge globalizes is itself likely more limited than when elites with national or global claims to authority judge the value of knowledge as such. Elites globalize knowledge, while publics tend to localize it.

National interest		Expert		Accurate knowledge		Security
Particular interest	~	Ignorant	~	Ideological knowledge	~	Threat

FIGURE 1.4 Global knowledge structure based on expert national security.

Public		Accessibility		Knowledges		Empowerment
Elite	~	Exclusion	~	Ideologies	~	Domination

FIGURE 1.5 Global knowledge structure based on public empowerment.

Really?

It all depends, of course, on which publics we discuss and how publics are themselves constituted. After all, publics vary in many ways, and they can vary just as much in terms of their ethnocentrism as their politics and elite revulsions.

Any of these four underlying structures of knowledge might be adequate for some field or network of globalizing knowledge production. However, because they coexist in a broader contest over articulations of globalizing knowledge, underlying globalizing knowledge structures don't have that same unconscious function that transition culture enjoyed. Instead, we need to pursue a different approach to reflexivity's elaboration.

Although one need not be concerned for these more foundational matters in globalizing knowledge and its theoretical underpinnings, for the scholars working to identify where in the world I situate my work, the foregoing may have been useful. For those concerned more with how I build on these references anchoring knowledge and global transformations, one can simply proceed to the book.

The Book

This sociology could be pursued, as any sociology might, by focusing on the agents seeking to globalize knowledge. One might conduct that work by focusing on particular intellectuals. Indeed, we might simply compare the ideas and biographies of those we have already mentioned—Marx, Weber, Durkheim, Lenski, Sassen, Castells, Merton, Habermas, Bourdieu, Wallerstein, Smelser, Calhoun, Collins, Sztompka, Burawoy, Lim, Glaeser, and others—to conduct that sociology.

Sociologists are especially hesitant to focus only on individual lives, even those of great sociologists, because of our interest in the structures that shape their work. We might then consider universities to be the principal structure shaping those individuals' efforts given that this particular kind of knowledge institution is the principal employer of most sociologists. At the same time, universities are also agents—strategic actors in a world where organizational success is defined, at least in part, by understanding how globalizing knowledge works, or at least effectively contributing to it.

Universities are not the only kind of knowledge institution and, one might argue, are increasingly limited in their role. But they are indispensable for think tanks, research firms, and state information agencies if only because universities are the organizations that train those institutions' future employees. If we were to think about how knowledge institutions are linked, and how individuals within them are tied, we might be inclined to think more about knowledge networks than institutions or individuals.

Networks are a long-standing interest of sociology, but too few think about how networks shape, and reflect, knowledge production and effects. It's especially important to think about networks in a world of globalizing knowledge, especially if one considers them, as Manuel Castells (2009, 20) does, as communicative structures that process flows of information. As these flows of knowledge become digitalized, networks become global if nonetheless selective in their distribution (25). Knowledge becomes more global and virtual simultaneously, moving networks to the center of our sociology of knowledge.

In Chapters 2, 3, and 7, I consider how intellectuals, institutions, and networks define and shape flows of globalizing knowledge. One might identify globalizing knowledge with the most prominent intellectuals whose accounts of the world travel most readily across well-worn networks backed by the most resourced knowledge institutions. However, I am also interested in recognizing how those pathways and *prominenci* come to be identified and what alternatives might be chosen. For that reason, I follow that triplet with another, where publics, contexts, and flows are considered.

Intellectuals, and their knowledge institutions and networks, face a critical challenge. On the one hand, intellectuality can prosper when provided an environment that celebrates the pursuit of knowledge for its own sake. On the other, that quest must be supported by wealthy patrons or by states occasionally requiring public acquiescence if not enthusiasm. To understand how publics and knowledges are related to one another is an increasingly compelling task for many intellectuals, institutions, and networks, the outline of which I consider in Chapter 4. I find it particularly important in these times, not only for the legitimation for knowledge production such engagement might provide. It's also important for the ways in which that engagement could enhance the rational critical qualities of public deliberations and consequently our world trajectories.

Although such ambitions evident in world invocations suggest that I should focus on "global" public spheres, I rather think our efforts are better attended by considering those more attuned to particular interests. National public spheres, for example, even in the European Union, remain dominant for public discussions. For knowledge agents, those more limited spheres defining scholarly excellence are critical. But even these national and scholarly spheres are variable in the degrees to which they acknowledge worlds beyond their borders. Indeed, globalizing knowledge often depends on being able to move beyond ethnocentric starting points to recognize the world from other standpoints. The context of our questions and our concerns shapes the global articulations of our knowledge. To understand the articulations of globalizing knowledge better, we should more critically engage how different contexts shape our approach, either as a foundation for learning or as an object with which to extend learning. To begin to understand those patterns, I explore how English-language scholarship engages the world over time, especially in Poland, Kosova, and Afghanistan.

Globalizing knowledge is not always about how another region's issues enter our own knowledgeable universe. In fact, knowledge often follows other products' entries into our public arenas, into our local, regional, and national contexts. There is no better example of the importance of flows for generating new knowledge than how energy matters. Once something proximately produced, energy is now a global issue, and commodity, and threat. How it shapes knowledge and how knowledge shapes the production, distribution, and consumption of energy have come to be critical issues not only for national security but planetary survival. Flows, not only contexts and publics, are critical to globalizing knowledge. You wouldn't know it if you focused on what most intellectuals, institutions, and networks do.

In the concluding chapters, I consider how to bring together these different agents of knowledge production and the various publics, contexts, and flows that shape them, and are shaped by them. I consider this to reflect not only on sociology's familiar how and why questions but on the "so what" that moves us to philosophy and more foundational intellectual questions. I propose that globalizing knowledge is a critical dynamic for those committed to knowledge for its own sake. I also think it central to the good of the world and thus ought to be more thoughtfully embedded in that world. That, however, will require a sense of cosmopolitanism and solidarity that needs substantially more engagement by the knowledgeable, who are, in turn, an ever growing proportion of our humanity. I hope that such cosmopolitanism and solidarity can form an ever bigger part of ourselves too.

2 Responsibility: Intellectuals in Worldly Theory and Practice

Over the last thirty years, figuring the value of intellectuals seems to have gone out of fashion. Florian Znaniecki (1986) could publish *The Social Role of the Man of Knowledge* in 1940, and Lewis Coser might write in 1965 about *Men of Ideas*, but even their titles suggest the anachronism. Ideas appear still to have cachet (Mandelbaum 2004), but that seems more to do with certain philosophies of history and beliefs that good (and bad!) ideas shape change. There is much less concern with those lives embodying commitments to ideas for their own sake. If we write about intellectuals in general, it is more typically with disdain (Sowell 2009) or perhaps nostalgia (Wald 1987). And while we might write a good deal about knowledge, we typically write out individual distinction by embedding individuals in struggles, fields, and specializations, effectively eliminating the most critical questions of intellectual responsibility from discussion.

In this chapter, I make explicit cultural schemas that allow us to return to such questions of responsibility. I begin by elaborating the distinctions of intellectuality as such, especially in contrast to professionalism, and in articulation with celebrity and public engagements. I also consider those distinctions across different global contexts. Global intellectual references essential to recognizing the world in formation are sometimes difficult to see and, of course, not easily available for grounding one's own worldly theory and practice. There are, however, exemplars of that intellectuality—both networks and individuals—that might inspire intellectuals anew with both a vision of the possible and a greater sociological realism simultaneously.

Recognizing Intellectuality

When we write with critical engagement about how intellectuals shape change, we are much more likely to talk about them in specific ways—policy advisers, IT experts, philosophers, artists, opinion makers, and so on. Even for that field I consider exemplary of intellectuality in today's world—design— the distance from intellectuality's penumbra is apparent. With something so ambitious as Pendleton-Jullian and Brown's (forthcoming) discussion of world building and metatools, their focus on accessibility and communication in design's approach defies intellectuality's association with the precious. It also, by drawing on film production methods and other specialized creativities for definition, masks the profundity of their challenge. Design's implication and revolution return in my own story in Chapter 7. For now, I focus more on the analysts rather than the agents of knowledge and change.

In place of the sociology of intellectuals, most prefer to analyze intellectuals in terms of fields, relationships, and the institutions, networks, and media that shape knowledge work (Eyal and Bucholz 2010). If we do find reference to intellectuals, we are more likely to find them invoked in the nineteenth and early twentieth centuries, at a time when the noun seemed to have fewer qualifiers (Mishra 2012; Kurzman 2008). Some nations, like Germany and France, seem to privilege their intellectuals and their analysis regardless (Boyer 2005; Torpey 1995; Judt 1992, 1998) but, especially in the United States, we don't engage them like we used to. And we lose something critical when we abandon the reference to intellectuals.

We lose the sense of intellectual responsibility. We overlook the distinction of intellectuals from other kinds of knowledge workers. We cease looking for intellectuality's evidence in our leaders. We become unaccustomed to qualities of recognition won with thoughtfulness before wittiness.[1] We miss how learning might make a difference for something more than a career or for the expert resolution of problems others define. Without the sense of intellectual responsibility, it's harder to imagine how knowledge might inspire, not just facilitate, change. That's why, for a volume dedicated to figuring the articulation of knowledge in worldly theory and practice,[2] one might begin by considering the connotations of intellectuality, or at least its exemplars. And we can begin with Marx.

In 2012, Jeff Isaac oversaw the republication of the 1848 *Communist Manifesto* with commentaries explaining its intellectual significance and consequence (Marx and Engels [1848] 2012). The nuanced brilliance and diverse elaborations of that volume's commentaries suggest why the essay was, and remains, so important. It also marks what intellectual means for many: a person whose deep learning and written work bear public consequence over time. This reference also shows that intellectuals can be received in many registers: for some, Marx understood the dynamics of history, while for others his ideas ruined people's histories.[3]

Depending on the circles in which you travel, you might more readily take another nineteenth-century man as the exemplary intellectual. Britain's Cardinal John Newman made the news in 2010 for being the premier celebrity intellectual of the nineteenth century. He was lauded by Pope Benedict XVI for the convert theologian's commitment to conscience and truth (Howse 2010; for background, see Strange 2008). Regardless of affinities, Marx and Newman suggest the power of intellectuality, where the knowledgeable pursuit of truth promises salvation in this world or the next.

The significance of intellectuals is not limited to a distant time, however. Beyond the contemporary United States, intellectuals remain a category of reference, especially in more authoritarian settings or in places where the tradition of the intellectual in the articulation of the nation is strong. They are especially potent when these conditions intersect (Suny and Kennedy 1999a; Bamyeh 2012) as well as in debates about global intellectual responsibilities across democratic and dictatorial conditions (Mishra 2013).

Having worked in Central and Eastern Europe, beginning my studies during the time when communists ruled, I have been especially engaged with intellectuals and the intelligentsia, the class associated with them (see also Falk 2003; King and Szelenyi 2004). In the 1990s, Ron Suny and I could put the study of intellectuals this way without qualification:

> As individuals, and perhaps as a group, intellectuals, "those who create, generate and apply culture" in Seymour Martin Lipset's (1963, 333) phrase, appear to have the greatest effect in their action, and the greatest autonomy in their actions. Intellectuals create different ideologies of national identity within a larger discursive universe of available materials. They do the imaginative ideological labor that brings together disparate cultural elements, selected historical memories, and interpretations of experiences all the while silencing the inconvenient, the unheroic, and the anomalous. (Kennedy and Suny 1999, 2)

The power of intellectuals in studies of postcommunist lands, if not also in those regions' everyday life, remains evident (Bradatan and Oushakine

2010). In the Middle East, their importance is clearly great in both senses of the term. Published in the wake of the Arab Uprisings of 2011, Mohammed Bamyeh (2012, 1), for instance, could find many powerful questions around that region's intellectuals:

> What are the distinctive features of intellectuals in the region? What makes a certain way of formulating ideas more readily propagated, accepted, or debated than otherwise in the public sphere? How do intellectuals influence public life and public debates? How does the work of intellectuals circulate under condition of relative openness or censorship, respectively? What is the audience of intellectuals, and how segmented or stable is it? What are the meaningful ways of measuring the influence of intellectuals in society? What sort of relation exists between intellectuals, "street politics," and civil society? What are the main idioms of public and organic intellectual discourse? What are the institutional venues of public and organic intellectual life, and how effective, stable, or flexible are they? Do public intellectuals provide a common regional discourse that blends together sentiments in more than one country? How are intellectuals connected (in structured or ideational ways) to social movements? Is the level of activity of intellectuals in any given country a good predictor of the quality of political or other kinds of leadership?

Bamyeh's list of questions inspires a series of issues that derive from questions of intellectual responsibility in a particular context. They also travel. He asks, as many of us do, about the power associated with independent thinking and belief in the broad public consequence of learning. The answers to those questions, and the questions themselves, imply a certain capacity to *recognize* intellectual distinction, however.

One is typically drawn in one of two directions when intellectual distinctions are invoked.[4] There are certain kinds of products and practices associated with intellectuality—books, teaching graduate students in university, or explaining to journalists the meaning of a revolution in world historical time, for example. But not all books merit an intellectual association, some teaching seems positively plebeian, and invocations of world history to justify a certain action can sound more ideological than intellectual. And that is where the normative comes in, for invocations of intellectual distinction carry judgments of quality and integrity. Why else would we all so readily recognize, even if we don't speak French, the phrase, *La trahison des clercs*?

Of course, that last sentence was my game with you. If you didn't recognize the reference to Julien Benda's (1927) volume, then you were already doubting your intellectual credentials. If you did recognize it, you could have wondered at my pretension. Regardless of your interpretation, this little exercise illustrates that intellectual distinction depends on both the qualifications of the intellectual and the cultural capital of the audience assigning that identification. And here again, another intellectual reference is made, for cultural capital today conjures specific association.

Pierre Bourdieu has done more than others in recent memory to make cultural and other forms of capital central to sociology and the human sciences. He uses capital to refer to the relative ability to acquire power and privilege in fields specified by particular rules of contest. *Cultural* capital is acquired through others' recognition of taste, cultivation, and education in that person. To identify someone as intellectual is not just to recognize a status, however. It establishes that person's relationship to others in a field of practice defined by the stakes and rules of intellectuality. Bourdieu (1988) used this famously to analyze Parisian intellectuals in 1968, but his orientation is more widely deployed to study other relationships between culture and politics and the place of intellectuals in that conjunction (e.g., Swartz 1997; Büyükokutan 2011).

One implies two things when identifying a person as an intellectual: that intellectuals' practice has a certain consequence derived from distinctive knowledge, and such consequence is independent from other kinds of power. If an intellectual's worth is simply defined by his promotion by a state, we might call him an ideologue rather than intellectual, especially if we don't appreciate that state or individual. If we admire the findings of a biomedical researcher but learn later that her grant came from a pharmaceutical company profiting from her research results, we will discount her learnedness. If the scholar's account depends on divine inspiration, or authority, we might also hesitate. Although the scholarly products of the Dalai Lama and Pope John Paul II certainly inspire intellectual respect, their association with authority beyond knowledge as such leads many to put them in a different category altogether.[5] While divine inspiration is certainly allowed, autonomy from all powers, be they sacred or profane, is typically critical for recognizing intellectual distinction.

Edward Said's (1996, 120–21) work is often invoked by those who wish to make this point: "The morality and principles of an intellectual should not constitute a sort of sealed gearbox that drives thought and action in one direction and is powered by an engine with only one fuel source. The intellectual has to walk around, has to have the space in which to stand and talk back to authority, since unquestioning subservience to authority in today's world is one of the greatest threats to an active, and moral, intellectual life."

Although the ethos of science may not apply to all intellectuals, its emphasis on autonomy surely does. That is one reason why Robert Merton's concerns bear weight here. If "true knowledge" is our ambition, then assuring an institutional setting for intellectuals to pursue their scholarship without "extra-scientific influence" is critical for "advancement of knowledge" (Panofsky 2010). Because the institutional autonomy of science is itself a historical accomplishment, preserving that autonomy matters, and recognizing its importance for delivering intellectual distinction, critical. Consequence also matters, however.

We can find consequence among intellectuals in a wide array of fashions. A certain reinterpretation of a classic text might start a new trend in research. A statistician might help us identify a new way to figure interaction effects among variables. Academics may even act like social movements to establish new fields of influence within scholarly worlds (Frickel and Gross 2005), but not all intellectuals like to think of their consequence being limited to academic affairs. That complicates our concerns about autonomy in marking intellectual distinction.

For those concerned with social transformations, especially their global extensions, intellectual relevance cannot depend on distance from power. Intellectuality's consequence depends on alignments with power, whether in defense of certain virtues or in pursuit of certain kinds of justice, whether by advising ministries of foreign affairs or by participating in social movements. One might, as Edward Shils (1972, 7), offer a kind of equivalence between intellectuals who elaborate the potentials in a given system of already existing values and intellectuals who reject them. Those following Antonio Gramsci (1971) might rather evaluate those alignments within a larger philosophy of history, distinguishing the work of "traditional" intellectuals, who justify existing arrangements within a certain cultural hegemony, and organic intellectuals, who articulate the interests of classes who seek their transformation. Some might be more inclined to embrace a "sociological interventionism," as Alain Touraine does, looking to "increase the capacity for action of individuals in the intervention groups looking for the movement through the group"

(Dubet and Wieviorka 1996, 59). Still others with a more Nietzchean and Heideggerian bent might rather follow Petr Sloterdijk (2012, 5), who identifies more than ten tendencies seeking to embed reason in the real world, thus hauling back intellectuals "from the beautiful deathlike site of disinterestedness to the arena of cognitive real politik."

It is exceptionally difficult, if not impossible, to establish neutral, or even rational critical, alignments of knowledge and power. Whenever we invoke any normative goods, like justice or security, we inevitably, even if only implicitly, establish alignments. In our address of these goods, we mark for whom and through which agents these goods might be realized. However, terms matter. If instead of justice and security we focused on exploitation and dispossession, gestures of openness toward ruling and ruled classes, toward authorities, citizens, and stateless, are differently constrained. Intellectuals, if they are to have social consequence, cannot remain apart from power. With such acknowledgment, one can also open up the nightmare question.

When might intellectuals form a *class for themselves* rather than elevate truth or buttress the power of others? Might all that intellectual talk be ultimately self-interested? Many have worried about that possibility, especially those who have seen socialism's appeal for intellectuals (Kennedy 1992a). Some even have proposed that society ruled by communists, especially as the system matured, was just such a system (Konrad and Szelenyi 1979). However, increasingly few intellectuals across the world, especially after the failure of communism's revision in 1968, embraced such a view (Kennedy 1991). If one values intellectuality and its requisite autonomy, to view such a society that represses intellectuals as the expression of their distinction is, at the very least, a contradiction. Worse, and more likely, it is a means to denigrate the qualities of intellectuality as such.[6]

Rather than try to identify a historical system that extends intellectual power, one might consider what binds intellectuals together. What might, in the words of an earlier sociological generation, make intellectuals a class *in statu nascendi*? Alvin Gouldner (1979, 83–85) offered a productive way to think about intellectuals as a universal class, if flawed, only because their class "subverts all establishments, social limits, and privileges including its own . . . (and) bears a culture of critical and careful discourse which is an historically emancipatory rationality." I find this identification of intellectuals' culture of critical discourse to be a very productive way to think about the collective accomplishment, and distinction, of intellectuals. For it to be more than an idealization of what we would like to think of ourselves, we need to figure a way to identify its variable expression.

Craig Calhoun introduced the questions that follow to distinguish among public spheres. We begin to see in them how we can recognize degrees of intellectuality in social interaction.

> We need to know not only how active communication is and how inclusive and open participation is, but what the qualities of the communication are. We need to attend to the processes by which culture is produced and reproduced in public, and not only treat it as an inheritance, or private product of individuals or small groups. We need to ask how responsive public opinion is to reasoned argument, how well any potential public sphere benefits from the potential for self correction and collective education implicit in the possibilities for rational-critical discourse. And we need to know how committed participants are to the processes of public discourse and through that to each other. Finally, and not least of all, we need to ask how effectively the public opinion formed can influence social institutions and wielders of economic, political, or indeed cultural power. (Calhoun 2003b, 248)

To the extent that societies are organized around those rational and critical deliberations in public spheres, and those publics are themselves inclusive and discriminatory only on the basis of qualities of argument rather than around any characteristics associated with power, then these societies might be more intellectual in their constitution. And here, then, we begin to approach the real cultural sociological problem.

Recognizing intellectuality works at many levels. We might try to decide who is, and who is not, an intellectual based on the quality and autonomy of his work. We might also figure the relationship between the intellectual and her judges, to see whether their assessment reflects an audience sufficiently intellectual to judge. We might also wonder to what extent the company an intellectual keeps is sufficiently informed by the culture of critical discourse so as to allow claims to flawed universality rather than charges of collective self-interest. And we need to consider how intellectuality is recognized variously across systems and cultures. But why bother?

To struggle over the meaning of intellectuality allows us to focus on questions of responsibility in ways that other discourses prohibit. *The Political Responsibility of Intellectuals* (Maclean, Montefiore, and Winch 1990) is especially helpful and previously inspired substantial reflection and cursory summary (Kennedy and Suny 1999, 12):

> As Plato would have it, or as Benda argued, the treason of intellectuals is to abandon the commitment to a superior and ever more cultivated universalistic reason (Lock 1990). Others argued that an intellectual's primary responsibility is to the craft, a textual responsibility, and one abandons intellectual responsibility when one violates that code of textual responsibility (LeCercle 1990). Indeed, intellectual responsibility is most apparent when moral action is conducted through modes of intellectual practice, rather than in explicitly political engagement. But even with that intellectual craft, intellectuals cannot be relieved of political or moral responsibility since it can, and must, be practiced within their field (Tamas 1990). For these authors, then, intellectuals have a different kind of political responsibility, perhaps even an elevated one, but one that is to be kept separate from popular politics. Ernest Gellner (1990) however, offers caution by arguing that it is frankly difficult to recognize intellectual treason when any conclusion is reached by intellectual means; perhaps the greatest treason is to easily identify others who are guilty.
>
> On the other hand, several of the authors emphasized that one cannot separate very easily intellectual responsibility from a more general political responsibility. For instance, the defense of truth seeking cannot be limited to intellectual affairs, since the real world impinges on those intellectual affairs, and truth seeking is not only the province of intellectuals, but of all actors (Montefiore 1990). Indeed, intellectuals have more responsibility than ever before, given that technological prowess now threatens not only human communities but the biophysical world itself. (Levy 1990)

When intellectuals from liberal capitalist societies noted the difficulty of distinguishing intellectual from political responsibility, the limits of their generalization quickly became apparent. East Central European intellectuals, informed by their responsibilities to speak truth to power under communist rule, had reason to be reticent. After all, the communist insistence that all parts of life be subject to surveillance and political obligation changed the terms of intellectual practice. To be professional and give onto Caesar what is Caesar's by avoiding explicit politics was, for many, the only way to be both intellectually responsible and not in prison or exile. Intellectual responsibility in liberal capitalist societies is a lot simpler, if one measures it only by expression. It's a lot more difficult if one tries to appreciate its consequence because that intellectual responsibility stands in uneasy relationship to professional distinction.

Professional Distinction

The sociology of professionals, as of intellectuals, is less fashionable today than it was in mid-twentieth-century global sociology. However, we can learn much from that era. For example, the distinction of professionals articulated then resembles many qualities of intellectuals and scientists. Both emphasize autonomy through self-regulation and integrity through codes of conduct. However, professionals were also viewed differently from intellectuals. Professions were conceived to be more functional than critical in a world where society's biggest challenges could be addressed best by ever more specialized expertise embedded in legitimate associations and institutions.

As that sociology of professions developed, one could wonder how self-interest and public goods articulated with one another, especially as professionals controlled their own credentialing and consequentially the market for their services (e.g., Larson 1977). Both functional and critical takes on professionals can also be extended to academics. With the terrific growth of higher education's faculty and students, some argue that university-based intellectuals have come to look more like professionals than collectivities of intellectuals (Rhoades 2007).[7] Such a claim is, however, typically more than an analytical observation.

Some like to distinguish professionals from intellectuals within the academy and, inevitably, identify themselves as intellectual. With that professional term, intellectuals mark others who stay within relatively narrow specializations both for inspiration and audience. Some view Michael Burawoy's 2X2 classification of knowledge types in sociologies, and in universities, as just such a dismissive gesture:

> I use the term "professional" to refer to the academic who pursues knowledge within and accountable to a community of scholars. I think of them as having an instrumental orientation to knowledge because they are, for the most part, as Thomas Kuhn wrote, puzzle solvers, working within paradigms, whose foundations—methodological, theoretical, philosophical, value—we take for granted. Or in Imre Lakatos's framework we work within research programs, defined by a negative heuristic, that is a set of assumptions that we never relinquish. Of course, many a professional academic objects to being labeled as

having an "instrumental" approach knowledge, they have a far more grandi-
ose vision of themselves as pursuing knowledge for knowledge's sake. . . . In
the eyes of the "professional" it is often far more easy to see instrumental
knowledge as defining the policy scientist who advises clients (corporations,
governments, NGOs) concerning problems that they define. But one should
recognize, as we will, there is considerable variation here in the degree of
autonomy vouchsafed to the scientist, the degree to which they become the
servants of power or on the other hand, bring their own agenda to the policy
table. Still, I consider this instrumental knowledge in as much as the client's
problems ultimately prevail, and the policy scientist exists to define the most
effective means to solve those problems (or to legitimate a solution already
arrived at), and the likely consequences of pursuing the particular means.
This dimension is becoming ever more important as the university's relations
to private corporations expand and intensify. (Burawoy 2012b)

This distinction between intellectuals and professionals also animates the
more public sphere. Pankaj Mishra does not mince words:

I think the very fact that we have to ask this question about intellectual
responsibility shows how serious the problem has become in our time, and
how much of a dodo the unaffiliated intellectual has become. Even writers
and intellectuals with a great deal of integrity and courage have become too
professionalized, too career-oriented, and too concerned not to upset their
peers, not to mention those they regard as their more famous and successful
superiors. Many people we think of as intellectuals are basically global professionals, very adept movers in the networks of Oxbridge, the Ivy League, the
London School of Economics, think tanks, Davos, and Aspen. They regurgi-
tate, with some embellishments, the wisdom they have picked up there. The
result is a stultifying sameness in the intellectual public sphere: loud echo-
chambers in which you have a whole class of writers and journalists saying
the same things over and over again, people who may not seek proximity to
power but who are careful not to provoke its wrath lest they be cast out of
the charmed circles they feel they depend on. This professional docility and
its codes of omerta are what allow people like Ferguson to flourish. And of
course the state's institutions are always looking for intellectual respectability
from historians, sociologists, and journalists. (W. Ali 2013)

We need not view the distinction between intellectual and professional as
a put-down. As Foucault notes, the expert has displaced the writer as the

"universal" intellectual. Referencing J. Robert Oppenheimer, the atomic scientist who headed the Manhattan Project, Foucault (1980, 128–29) writes,

> For the first time, the intellectual was hounded by political powers, no longer on account of the general discourse which he conducted, but because of the knowledge at his disposal. . . . (The specific intellectual) is no longer he who bears the values of all, opposes the unjust sovereign or his ministers and makes his cry resound even beyond the grave. It is rather he who, along with a handful of others, has at his disposal, whether in the service of the state or against it, powers which can either benefit or irrevocably destroy life. He is no longer the rhapsodist of the eternal, but the strategist of life and death.

Oppenheimer is of course distinctive, even while his life and mind should inspire additional reflection on intellectuality (Thorpe 2006). Further, not every discipline or profession has that kind of life/death moment, even if each enjoys/suffers the specialization Foucault describes. The qualities of specialization vary across fields of scholarship, however, with variable implication in knowledge institutions and networks. Consider, for example, the social sciences in US universities.

Specialization is easier when context is taken for granted. When a scholar works within a particular time, place, and field that most other scholars recognize, the possibilities for narrowness grow as the search for distinction in a crowded field becomes ever more intense (Collins 1986). Within the US academy, specialization in American electoral practices is much greater than specializations around the loya jirga, for example.

As the number of specialists in a field grows, their relative influence is greater within those institutions that hire them. For example, those specialists on electoral studies are likely more influential within most US universities than are those who are expert not only on the loya jirga but on Afghanistan. They may be even more influential than those expert on the whole of Asia.

One might even wonder whether experts in election studies have more influence within US academic institutions than experts in all of international affairs. After all, those with the electoral studies expertise do control important parts of political science, and disciplinary departments control the labor markets and credentialing systems in which degrees are awarded and careers made (Abbott 2001). One might therefore argue that the specialists who have captured significant parts of disciplines, as opposed to internationalists who have no disciplinary distinction, are more likely to influence priorities within universities. That hypothesis deserves much more careful research, and, if true, further research to consider its implication for globalizing knowledge. The answer is not self-evident, nor is the relationship among intellectuality, professional recognition, and global reference.

Miguel Centeno and I have analyzed the dynamics of globalizing knowledge within sociology (Kennedy and Centeno 2007). One part of that study was to ask US-based sociologists explicitly associated with "international sociology" at several departments, which are known for their position in the field or international commitments,[8] to identify which five books or articles, published in the last fifty years by those working in American sociology, were the most important contributions to scholarship in their field.[9] If consequence matters in recognizing intellectual distinction, the authors our colleagues identify might deserve the association. Patterns were evident in responses.

Three figures were mentioned most often: Barrington Moore, Immanuel Wallerstein, and Charles Tilly. Moore's 1966 volume was typically celebrated, but our respondents more readily identified Tilly and Wallerstein with their oeuvre and the schools of scholarship and students they produced. Few in our discipline and even beyond would contest these three being identified as intellectuals, given the quality of their work and the breadth of their impact.

Other scholars were mentioned, if not so often. Moore's student Theda Skocpol was the only woman on the list and was typically celebrated for her 1979 work on revolution. Scholars mentioned more than once whose careers were mostly outside the United States—Bourdieu, Foucault, Perry Anderson, and Gosta Esping-Anderson—were invariably identified with Europe or the Mediterranean. Those who worked on China were likely to mention Andrew Walder. Sociologists who worked in more demographic traditions found Blau and Duncan's 1967 work an inspiration or Douglas Massey's corpus most inspiring. Those who focused on development would mention Peter Evans, and those on transition, Ivan Szelenyi. Nobody would doubt everyone mentioned in this paragraph to be intellectuals for the same reasons Moore, Wallerstein, and Tilly would be identified. But they all reflect a certain specialization, a niche, a network that shapes recognition.

First and most obviously, scholarly pedigree matters. For example, demographers, networked through their professionally distinctive conferences, associations, journals, and training, are likely to identify those who contribute to figuring how population patterns shape societies and global transformations. Political sociologists, less tightly networked but with some affinities made through overlapping associations, are more likely to celebrate those who address states and social movements. Those who identified Wallerstein, for example, were unlikely to mention Massey.

Regional reference also shapes these networks. Political sociologists are more likely to focus on Europe and North America than the rest of the world, despite the absence of place-based knowledge in their claims to expertise. Those who study China are more tightly integrated with their journals, training, and especially distinctive language and cultural sensibilities. They will likely identify experts on that nation as their exemplars and will refer to their place-based expertise in their biographies. China experts can *appear* more narrow than the comparative and historical Europeanists and Americanists, therefore.

Europeanists might enjoy increasing coordination through studies of the European Union. Given European global powers, Europeanists, like Americanists, can cover the world in ways that China specialists, much less those who specialize in Afghanistan, do not. At least have not yet. While this is true in sociology, it is especially true in political science. International relations scholars grounded in dominant world powers are much freer to write about a wide range of places in the world than are those with contextual expertise in places that don't have such geopolitical reach.

We shall attend much more carefully in Chapter 5 to these questions of substantive and regional specialization in articulations of globalizing knowledge. However, it is important in recognizing intellectuality to think about how networks grounded in substance and regional reference work in more general claims to knowledge. Some specializations are more general than others. At least they appear to be so.

Network theorists offer important variables for this conceptualization. One might consider network distribution and multiplexity in these various academic specialties. Especially if one combined these structural features with more cultural dimensions associated with roles and positions, one might be able to understand better how different kinds of specialist work become more central in knowledge production. And with that centrality, its occupants are more likely to be able to claim the consequential side of intellectuality. At the same time, because claims to intellectuality are not simply a matter of network position but cultural association, the assignment is far from automatic (Moody 2004).

This association between network position and cultural claims is important to consider over time. Consider, for example, demography's changing position. During that time when Otis Dudley Duncan's POET (population, organization, environment, technology) (Duncan 1960; Duncan and Schnore 1961) was a prominent heuristic device for understanding social change, demographers could be central to sociology's engagement of the world. As modernization theory faded from view, and power relations across the world became more prominent in defining the course of change (Gilman 2003), demographers and political sociologists became more distinct as methodologies and intellectual worldviews diverged. While there are scholars who can still cross these domains rather well, it's striking, especially in studies of "development," just how distant experts on population and politics can be from one another. With that, disciplinary coherence declines, and the capacity to recognize intellectuality beyond subprofessional competencies fades.

Rather than pursue these specifics further, we can reach a general conclusion: There is no simple pyramid of disciplinary distinction in sociology because scholars have come to value different qualities in knowledge production in ever more specialized fashion. Networks shape intellectual recognition within sociology, and those networks can be increasingly isolated from each other. If we understood how those networks functioned, we might understand better how professional distinction is won and how intellectual recognition might be awarded as expert domains were crossed. We might also look beyond peer groups to recognize distinctions of knowledge.

Public and Celebrity Intellectuals

Just a couple of decades ago, many wondered where the "public intellectual" went and, with that, the broader significance of intellectuality in US culture. The signal contribution in this debate was Russell Jacoby's (1987) text. Tania Lewis (2001, 221) argues that his and others' angst reflected the "story of the increasingly professionalized and politicized nature of intellectual culture in the United States, a process that for most cultural commentators is characterized as one of intellectual *decline*." That discussion presumes, however, that we know what a public intellectual is. Bamyeh (2012, 2–3) recently consolidated discussion of public intellectuals with this characterization:

> Public intellectuals may be understood as articulate thinkers whose role consists in either: (1) popularizing existing, complex intellectual systems for the benefit of a public rather than academic audience; (2) founding original systems of thought in a language that captures broad public audiences; or (3)

expressing existing public sentiments, feelings, and attitudes in intellectual and systematic but accessible formats (be it in the form of philosophical theses, literary works, expository exegesis of "tradition," systematic analysis of current affairs, or popular artistic experiments). There are many venues for the dissemination of the works of these respective intellectuals: popular treatises and commentaries; memoirs; literary works; old and new media; and so on. But persons identified as public intellectuals tend to be those that add intellectual substance to the public sphere; crystallize what is otherwise called "street politics" into intelligible and referenced arguments; provide ideational support for the further evolution of civil society as well as social movements; and establish or defend criteria for the quality of social leadership.

Once again, context matters much. While debating the qualities and distinctions of public intellectuality is easily compelling in the Middle East and Eastern Europe, the angst over the very existence of public intellectuality in the United States could lead us down a familiar road to ask about what makes the United States peculiar. Before we leap for explanations, we should refine our sense of that which we want to explain. We may not appreciate sufficiently the cultural and historical articulations of responsibility and public intellectuality in the United States. Robert Merton helps.

One of sociology's most important figures, Merton thought the discipline's distinction depended on keeping its distance from public engagement; to get too close to the public fray meant taking normative stands that could not have scientific foundations. This did not mean complete disengagement. For instance, Merton introduced the notion of "self-fulfilling prophecy" in the broadly read *Antioch Review* so that the lay public might have crisper concepts with which to exercise its deliberative reason (Kalleberg 2010, 190). In those days when the autonomy of (social) science was critical, at a time when normative questions appeared secondary to the expert questions about how to manage modernity, this seemed, to some at least, a viable relationship between publics and knowledge, but the times changed. During those 1968 days of rage at Merton's Columbia University, the pose of liberal neutrality proved increasingly difficult to couple with discourses of intellectual responsibility. Merton's own cultural capital declined as issues of intellectual, and public, responsibility melded into a new engaged vision of scholarship (Calhoun 2010a).

We should, thus, consider the conditions under which articulations of intellectual responsibility become necessarily public in reference and how those publics vary. For example, under conditions like what Bamyeh describes, to avoid the normative is impossible. In his collection, authors identify public intellectuals in the Middle East over at least the last century as vanguards, tradition transformers, and migrants mobilizing around gender, religious, and transnational identifications. One can see in these very foci the challenge of remaining apolitically professional.[10] These themes are not, however, what contemporary US discussions have in mind when public intellectuals are invoked. Because publics vary, so do the articulations of intellectuals and intellectuality.

Although not everyone draws on Gramsci in this stream of discussion, his emphasis on organic intellectuals is important for their role in articulating what is not already recognized and understood in "public" discussions. In particular, with his emphasis on the multiplicity of power and the value of standpoints in their recognition, Gramsci's (1971, 9) notion that all people are intellectuals even if they are not always recognized for that function grows in importance.

Bamyeh and his colleagues take that in important directions for extending our sense of intellectuality's consequence and variety. And in their worlds, as in the worlds dominated by communists, if not to the same degree, ideas become more consequential when domination is less remunerative than coercive and symbolic/ideological.[11] Where domination is relatively invisible through surveillance, manipulation, and discipline, intellectuals can say what they want without consequence because their words have relatively little public value.[12]

Under conditions where truths are easily articulated but have little consequence given the cacophony of truth tellers without claims to intellectual distinction, the intellectual seems to have little weight. Indeed, when reflecting on the significance of Konrad and Szelenyi's (1979) volume twenty-five years after its publication, I offered that the power of truthful articulations before power seemed to count less than the witticisms of truthiness:

> The conditions of public discourse in commercialized media and fragmented internet culture require critique of consequence to be connected to outrageousness. . . . Bluster is better, demanding only notice, not a sophistication that recognizes an intellectual's disrespect. Perhaps we should welcome those who wish to constrain academic expression—indeed, those who would monitor professors for their expressions of intellectual diversity might, ironically, raise the value of ideas as they seek to limit them with harassments of various

sorts. But this, it seems, is guerrilla intellectual war on the sidelines, distrac-
tions from the real contests over the exercise of power, designed to focus the
contest on pseudo-academic values while making the real debates ever more
distant from intellectual engagement. . . . With all due apologies, I might even
speculate that Michael Moore is the Ivan Szelenyi of our times, and *Dude,
Where's My Country* [Warner, New York, 2003] is the real sequel to *The Intellectuals on the Road to Class Power.* (Kennedy 2005)

After I offered this comment at the special forum at the 2003 American Association for the Advancement of Slavic Studies dedicated to discussing the impact
of Konrad and Szelenyi (1979), Michael Bernhard, the forum's organizer, rightly
suggested that I should look to Comedy Central's *Daily Show* host Jon Stewart.
And now, ten years later, most would recommend that purveyor of truthiness,
Stephen Colbert, as the public intellectual par excellence. As you groan, maybe
we should change the term. He is at least a celebrity intellectual. And for many,
that particular combination calls oxymoron to mind.

Although in 1973 Lewis Coser marked the type's emergence and anticipated its survival, he has little appreciation for it. That's not surprising, for he
distinguishes intellectuals simply as those who "live for rather than off ideas"
(Coser 1965, viii). Coser (1973, 50) notes that celebrity intellectuals tend to be
judged on the "basis of the exchange value on the market of intellectual commodities," assuming a kind of "fetishistic character" valued for their public
rating. Bypassing more cultured status judges (i.e., those who can address the
substance of ideas), the celebrity intellectual depends on passing through the
gatekeeping function of journalists and talk-show hosts (48). Coser finishes
his essay by looking at the limits of Erich Segal's, Charles Reich's, and Mar-
shall McLuhan's celebrity intellectuality.[13]

If he were alive today, Coser might very well have addressed Niall Ferguson as the exemplary celebrity intellectual in this framework.[14] This would
especially be likely following charges that Professor Ferguson abandoned
intellectual rigor in public expressions of partisan fury.[15] When intellectuals
appear to be motivated more by interest than integrity and ideas, they lose
their credibility as intellectuals. But then intellectuals in general crave recognition, and the value of truthfulness in that recognition varies.

Recognition is critical currency among intellectuals. To be cited, to
be sought for one's opinion on the affairs of the world, to be inducted into
various honorary societies, to be given a fellowship in recognition of one's

genius,[16] to be invited to lavish gatherings of the world's elite whether in Yalta or in Aspen, are all indicators of recognition's value for intellectual distinction. After all, one cannot acquire the status without someone else conferring it. But for the traditional *and* critical intellectual like Coser, recognition by one's peers is radically different from recognition by an undifferentiated public mediated by markets, or even an elite public reproducing its influence. Even if celebrity and intellectual are like categories in the search for recognition, the audiences make the difference. But so do the times.

While subsequent interpreters recognize what Coser argues, where, in the words of Tania Lewis (2001, 222) the celebrity intellectual "privileges entertainment over information, affect over meaning," she also argues that we should get over apologies for the conjunction; we should recognize that "the material reality of contemporary intellectual practice is inseparable from the sphere of mediatized celebrity." While Paul Krugman might have more intellectual gravitas than Niall Ferguson, both have acquired celebrity status. Two other political economy intellectuals illustrate the point even more clearly than Krugman and Ferguson, for in this next comparison, qualities of intellectuality are not at issue.

During 2012–13, two volumes appeared that challenge conventional accounts of how capitalist economies function. William Janeway (2012), a PhD in economics but also a venture capitalist of considerable accomplishment, received much public attention and acclaim for his critique of dominant conceptions of the innovation economy. Mark Blyth (2013), a purer academic, appeared later in the academic year with his volume on the history of austerity as a dangerous idea. Blyth didn't have the same professional networks Janeway enjoyed, but he did have another pathway to celebrity: a video that went viral, popularizing his critique of austerity two and a half years earlier.[17] On June 3, 2013, Janeway's volume ranked number 253,774 on Amazon, while Blyth's book hit 8,238. Janeway and Blyth are both celebrity intellectuals of sorts, but they are clearly of different types with different media and networks enabling their recognition.

Celebrity intellectuals are not only to be found among economists and political scientists, of course. Feminists have in particular made this conjunction central to their knowledge culture, finding the development of feminism to work as well within the "celebrity zone," not just the worlds of intellectuals and politics (Wicke 1994). Pussy Riot's embrace by celebrities from Madonna to Bjork and the efforts extended to associate their punk prayer protest in Moscow's Cathedral of Christ the Savior with more intellectual traditions of dissent all point to the power of this combination (Rutland 2012).

Within the United States, African American intellectuals have been especially likely to find the conjunction. Sometimes their intellectuality leads, as is the case with Cornel West. In other circumstances, mass media move professors into the culture, as Melissa Harris-Perry has found with her talk show on MSNBC. But this is not limited to US culture by any means or to academic discussions. One Australian paper even constructed a list of the top-twenty celebrity intellectuals in their country who "affect the public sensibility" ("Brain Power" 2005).

Constructing such lists in the public sphere is part of making intellectual celebrity. This is always a little embarrassing for intellectuals, however, especially if they are responsible for filling out the names on the list. If list makers self-identify as "serious" intellectuals, they will likely recognize the irony in composing such a list. To protect themselves from serious intellectual critique, they will try to make the list making more intellectual, or at least apparently empirical. Consider, for example, the joint effort of *Foreign Policy* magazine and *Prospect* to identify the most influential public intellectuals, which ultimately included thinkers such as Noam Chomsky (1), Naomi Klein (11), Slavoj Žižek (23), and Clifford Geertz (55).[18]

Assuming that you have skimmed the list, I can tell you that I have played another game with you, which began earlier when I identified distinguished sociologists, which itself began for me when scholars replied to my inquiry about those influentials. Some among my respondents expressed their discomfort with the question and declined to answer; more expressed their discomfort and answered anyway. Even when people did not object, in deference to our friendship or collegiality, no doubt they harbored the same concern I had: Intellectual distinction is not made with lists. However, public recognition can be extended with them. Coser might say that if peers award distinction, then that may not bear the burden of commodified celebrity. Still, rankings rankle intellectuals whatever the jury.

Lists like the top one hundred public intellectuals are, however, intriguing for how they help constitute global publics by naming those intellectuals the publicly engaged should know beyond their own more immediate environs. Translations do that, in part, and that is how I came to know and appreciate Václav Havel long before meeting him, long before such lists were made. But lists like the one mentioned could move others interested in globalizing knowledge production with publics in mind to consider more quickly a wider range of intellectuals than they otherwise might. Lists like this enable

us to move beyond our familiar bounds, beyond our own international reference group made with our discipline, our politics, our tastes. Lists like this
undoubtedly globalize knowledge, or at least its facsimile. I appreciate that
function, but the larger geography it represents needs to be articulated more
explicitly.

Foreign Policy (*FP*) has continued to make lists like these. The international relations community, those who read *FP*, do consider themselves global
and need such references more than others for professional purposes. Especially if one shifts away from publics to policies, it becomes much more plau-
sible to imagine ideas of consequence and their makers. That is certainly what
FP does with its annual "portrait of the global marketplace of ideas and the
thinkers who made them."

Such lists offer something to those of us who are interested in globalizing knowledge. *FP* helps constitute recognition for individuals by their naming and, by their distribution across fields and nations, helps identify which
nations produce what kinds of important ideas. By mapping the globalization of knowledge, *FP* produces implicitly a kind of geography of intellectual
distinction.

The 2011 list (Pavgi 2011) certainly reinforces the power of American ideas,
since the United States was the source of about half of the big thinkers in the
world. The American academy is especially dominant; nearly 90 percent of academics who offered big ideas in 2011 worked in the United States. Big finance
thinkers and politicians of vision were relatively evenly distributed between the
United States and the European Union, with a smattering of political visionar-
ies in other parts of Europe, Asia, Australia, and South America. The Internet
became an especially important field for new ideas in 2011. Here again, most of
the ideas seem to come from the United States. The only place where big ideas
were relatively evenly distributed across the world comes from activists. In the
wake of 2011's Arab Uprisings, it could hardly be otherwise.

The Arab Uprisings, especially the struggles emanating from Tahrir
Square, were different from the celebrity intellectuality *FP* seems to promote.
After all, both in dominant global public narratives and in Egyptian scholarship itself, the intellectuality of the uprisings was distributed more evenly
across civil society than unevenly between intellectuals and their people.
That, however, is a matter for more scholarly attention by those more expert
than I to unpack. Nevertheless, we can see quite readily one of those effects in
an alternative network of intellectual recognition.

Forms of Global Intellectual Articulation

As we witness these remarkable social transformations, we can also see the development of exceptional new intellectual networks inspired by, and extending, their impact. Although it is hardly limited by an identification with the Arab Uprisings, the ezine *Jadaliyya* represents a new kind of collective, a networked public intellectuality that is not defined by celebrity but by connection, critique, and translation.[19] Written not only by experts for experts, its scholarly profile has a distinctive public face. As the creators describe it,

> *Jadaliyya* provides a unique source of insight and critical analysis that combines local knowledge, scholarship, and advocacy with an eye to audiences in the United States, the Arab world, and beyond. The site currently publishes posts both in Arabic and in English. *Jadaliyya* is run and produced on a voluntary basis by an editorial team and expanding pool of contributors committed to discussing the Arab world on its own terms. Where others see only a security threat, conflict, or data on a graph, we see a region inhabited by living communities and dynamic societies.[20]

Jadaliyya's public impact, within and beyond the United States, has been substantial. According to its editor, as of January 2012 it had reached 1.5 million readers (this does not count articles that were forwarded, and other methods by which *Jadaliyya* is read). The website has seventy thousand visitors per week and is read in 210 countries, especially in the United States, United Kingdom, and Egypt (Bassam Haddad, pers. comm., February 2, 2012). Beyond the spread of its readership, the site's very concept is worth noting, developing a form of public engagement with scholarly integrity through this medium. Bassam Haddad, a political scientist who was *Jadaliyya*'s initiator and has been a central member of its editorial team, recalls the impetus for creating the ezine:

> By 2010, my colleagues and I had gotten really irritated by the fact that, although the news cycle had narrowed and narrowed, there was no medium to capture the middle ground between daily blogs and peer-reviewed scholarly journals. At one end, there were daily blogs: often very creative, scholarly, and energetic. But they were also one-person efforts. On the other end were peer reviewed articles in journals that can take six months at best to get out information and analysis. There was a huge unoccupied vacuum between the

two. We created *Jadaliyya* to fill that vacuum. The website we created was not just another website. It is perhaps the closest thing to a peer-reviewed alternative to traditional scholarly journals that is produced and available online on a daily basis. (Haddad 2012)

I find two dimensions of *Jadaliyya*'s work especially important for reflecting on global public intellectuality.[21] Although the journal has no manifesto and presents pieces that are quite diverse in orientation, the spirit of the journal is decidedly critical and especially attentive to "power relations locally and globally" (Haddad 2012). The project shows that a contextually grounded approach that engages public issues, illuminating the power relations that shape them and their interpretation and public accounting, can be both analytically powerful and popular. Indeed, three of the five "top hits" through 2011 on *Jadaliyya*'s website address gender and sexual power, racism and Orientalism, and corruption and dictatorship directly (Mikdashi 2011; Balaghi 2011a; Abul-Magd 2011).[22]

By making its publications freely available worldwide and enabling translation immediately and without cost, this publicly engaged scholarship can enter a different set of power relations made by the horizontal ties facilitated by the digital revolution. Tracing those translation networks will, no doubt, be part of a future historical sociology of knowledge production. For now we can recognize the knowledge revolution in practice. Publicly engaged scholarship can go beyond the constraints of time and control characterizing conventional academic, and press, publishing. *Jadaliyya*, if it would be willing to accept the notion as a compliment, offers a vision of "Publicly Engaged Intellectuality 2.0."

Though these scholars writing for *Jadaliyya* may not be on *FP*'s top one hundred list, they are typically more publicly embedded than the stars whose ideas express the policy relationship *FP* celebrates. Their penchant for critique from a more public standpoint, and from beyond the metropole, also resonates with a range of globally articulated scholars who are perhaps better known.

Partha Chatterjee, Gyan Pandey, Homi Bhabha, Gayatri Spivak, Dipesh Chakrabarty, and other scholars originally from South Asia have transformed the US and global academies in profound ways. Not only have they brought their contextual expertise on South Asia into globalizing human sciences but they have clearly challenged Western conventions with their work. Generally speaking, they argue that the theoretical paradigms and methodologies born

in metropolitan and colonial conditions can actually divert one from understanding properly the conditions facing not only colonized and postcolonial
societies but also the colonial powers themselves. Drawing on my own enduring engagement with nationalism, I have found Partha Chatterjee's (1986, 1993)
challenge considerable. He explains how even nationalism, that which is supposed to be the property of a nation, is conceived within a global framework
that can undermine the indigenousness of community expression. For this
reason, I especially appreciate efforts to ground social thought in its global
places (e.g., Connell 2007).

Although South Asians have had a growing influence on the academy with
their elaborations of subaltern studies, postcolonial studies, and other interventions (e.g., Prakash 1990), other world regions have also made their mark
in relatively prominent ways. The world region in which I have worked lon-
gest, Central and Eastern Europe, has also had its range of scholarly influence,
magnified by appreciation for the conditions of knowledge production under
communist rule that made them. Wolfe and Pickles (2013, 109) are quite per-
ceptive about those times and after 1989 in the "return to Europe":

> After 1989, when political power no longer promoted and justified itself
> through a culture-wide project of ideological identification and official ver-
> sions of Marxism had largely lost whatever purchase they once had, these
> ideas developed in resistance found new avenues of expression. For many
> intellectuals, the return was marked by a newfound legitimacy for the lib-
> eral theories of individual rights or critical (Western) Marxism they had
> encountered through underground channels, as well as appreciation for the
> benefits of neo-liberal capitalism. Hayek's account of centralized state power
> leading to the road to serfdom, for example, which was received "like fresh
> water" (personal communication) in clandestine seminars under state social-
> ism, informed the decisions of many liberal and neo-liberal reformers in CEE
> after 1989. . . . Most of the reforms were designed by politicians, bureaucrats
> and intellectuals, decisively influenced by this rediscovered and reinvigorated
> sphere of liberal thought.

And with these changes have come many opportunities for scholars with
commercially valued skills to serve institutional interests in media, government, and business realms; those with more basic, or academic, forms of
cultural capital struggle to find their place. Professionalism can trump traditional and critical intellectualities.

Nevertheless, as Wolfe and Pickles indicate, the peculiar contradictions of communist and postcommunist pasts have produced scholars of great accomplishment, including Slavoj Žižek, Julia Kristeva, Tzvetan Todorov, Jan Patočka, Mircea Eliade, Emil Cioran, and Leszek Kołakowski. Unlike those of postcolonial scholars, their regional origins are far less marked, by themselves or others, and thus the significance of their formative contexts disappears from view. Their global reference becomes, one might say, grounded far more in the arguments they make than with reference to the contexts from which they come. And with that blending into general intellectual status, they create many fewer opportunities for those from similar origins to generate recognition or to build networks with that regional accent in mind.

Of course, some write about this. I especially appreciate how Leszek Nowak framed the issue. Referring to the great Polish writer Witold Gombrowicz and his reflections on the issue, Nowak (2012, 53) writes,

> Either he will be true to the Polish problematic but will remain a second-class writer, or he will try to become a world-class writer but carrying with him the baggage of provincial culture he will remain a second-class writer. However hard he tries whether in the direction of the national or the universal, straw will be stuck to his shoes. This is because he, as a Pole, really has straw stuck to his shoes. (2012, 53)

Writing in a "provincial" university against the dominant trends of Polish, much less European, writers, Nowak treated provincialism more as a disposition intellectuals themselves embraced, not a failure of their recognition by others more highly placed. Of course, one might not treat these in "either-or" terms but consider how they vary by more discriminating knowledge cultures.

Consider, for example, the terrific recognition afforded Tadeusz Kantor—a giant in theater (Kantor 1993) and critical to thinking about the articulation of the national and the global (Kubik 2006). However, only those grounded in Poland and/or theater may be inclined to recognize his distinction. How might one generate the attraction to move into Polish culture?

A relatively new artistic/intellectual formation, Slavs and Tatars, illustrates just the opposite. Self-described as "a faction of polemics and intimacies devoted to an area east of the former Berlin Wall and west of the Great Wall of China known as Eurasia, the collective's work spans several media, disciplines, and a broad spectrum of cultural registers (high and low), focusing on an oft-forgotten sphere of influence between Slavs, Caucasians and

Central Asians."[23] The anonymous collective invites engagement in this region but diminishes the importance of their own biographies in exploration. Their growing recognition in the art world could inspire similar effect as subaltern studies, albeit in very different professional networks, as their influence travels more across museums and exhibitions than universities and editorial pages.

Venues do matter for this kind of recognition, of course. Although I have already discussed celebrity intellectuals, of which some are comedians, the world of jokes can itself be a window onto intellectual recognition. Consider these examples of "intellectual" humor reported on *Slate*:

> **From user guitartard:** "Is it solipsistic in here, or is it just me?"
> Why it's funny: Because if it's solipsistic in here, it really is just you. Or rather, just me.
> **From user phattmatt:** "Jean-Paul Sartre is sitting at a French cafe, revising his draft of Being and Nothingness. He says to the waitress, "I'd like a cup of coffee, please, with no cream." The waitress replies, "I'm sorry, Monsieur, but we're out of cream. How about with no milk?"
> Why it's funny: Because Sartre believes that an absence of something is still something. Plus, coffee with no milk tastes a lot worse than coffee with no cream. (Waldman and Oremus 2013)

And the list of good jokes goes on in the original. The significance of recognizing intellectuality in this works even better in its full complement, but I think you might get humor's articulation even with these first two. First, that it could appear in a blog already indicates the value of intellectual as a category of humor. Second, that it's an "idiot's guide"—a type of publication for all sorts of things, from karate to Marxism—is itself a joke, implying that the typical reader might not get the esoteric humor behind it. Third, it's also likely necessary for most. Few enjoy intellectual foundations that range so well, from philosophy to psychiatry and linguistics as the full list carries. Nevertheless, notice the intellectuality privileged in the choices: there is no Arab literature, engineering humor, or veterinary jokes in the lot. Even in the world of humor, intellectual recognition is stratified.

Recognition, of course, is not everything. Those working in global networks are often dedicated to minimizing their own distinction in an effort to create broader effect. Those who study global knowledge networks in the policy world, for instance, find it much more productive to envision their intellectuality through the various roles that they play: as storytellers, net-workers, engineers, and fixers (Maxwell and Stone 2005). Those roles are not likely to make an individual achieve the recognition associated with intellectuals.

On the other end of the spectrum, however, intellectuals can become prominent as political figures and known for their political more than their intellectual role. Sometimes they can hold on to their intellectuality; Coser (1965, 135) opined that "Masaryk, Wilson, Leon Blum, Nehru, Disraeli and Gladstone" managed to wield "power without losing their intellectual quali-ties."[24] Suny and I worked to elaborate a theory of national intellectual practice in which we made relatively little categorical distinction between those who remained identified as scholars and those who identified more as politicians. What mattered for us was the *quality* of their practice as national figures.

One definition of the intellectual refers to actors by virtue of their prod-ucts, which are in some way construed as the formulation or manipulation of symbols of national meaning. This understanding, however, slips easily into making intellectuals and other political elites relatively interchangeable, since political elites use symbols in their own legitimation. In these terms, one could argue that Kosciuszko was an intellectual-activist, moving beyond the legislation associated with modern intellectuals toward mobilization of these ideas in the popular imagination and social action. He in many ways devel-oped a better intellectual politics as he elaborated a more powerful politics of emancipation that included the normatively superior position of extend-ing the whole of Polishness to any estate and any ethnicity. Let us consider intellectual practice as our mediating account, understood as a combination of intellectual resources (cultural capital, sophistication of intellectuality, autonomy of activity, prestige, and articulation with other kinds of power), forms of intellectual activity (organization of more exclusively intellectual associations, implication in state power, mobilization of popular movements, cultivation of new readerships, etc.), and kinds of intellectual products (social movements, state action, exemplary performances or exhibitions, litera-ture, etc.). We might then consider how these shape the nation's formation and alternatives and even decline in association with other conditions. We can also seek to understand the formation of intellectual practice through the structures of the nation, economy, state, and everyday life, among other things. (Suny and Kennedy 1999b, 401–2)

One of the best ways to consider these alternative potentials is to consider intellectuals biographically. I find learning about and from those who have exemplified intellectuality in the articulation of the nation and global futures particularly useful for extending the sense of worldly theory and practice.[25]

Intellectuals and the Articulation of the Nation: Havel, Lagos, Ghani

One must be careful in making assignments of intellectuality to those in political authority. It is well known that Joseph Stalin wished to command the same kind of intellectual authority as Lenin and Trotsky (Leites 1953). Far more recently, Muammar Qaddafi worked with globally recognized intellectuals to validate his own authority with claims of being a real "thinker" (Calhoun 2012a, 23–23). The public relations firm headed by Harvard professors even defined their mission this way: "to emphasize the emergence of a new Libya . . . [and] introduce Muammar Qadhafi as a thinker and intellectual" (Monitor Group 2007). We do need to develop an approach to this matter that allows us to do more than think in ad hoc or post hoc fashion, much less as consultants assigning intellectuality for hire. There is, however, a good person with whom to begin whose intellectual credentials are generally not doubted.

Václav Havel is one of the exemplary public intellectuals of the twentieth century for many reasons, not least of which is his commitment to living in truth.[26] His dramatic productions and essays and his courage as dissident and prisoner all inspired many who sought exemplars of intellectual responsibility.[27] Havel was active earlier, but his leadership in the formation of Charter 77—a citizens' initiative whose first act was to document the discrepancy between law and reality in communist-ruled Czechoslovakia—led him to write one of the most important political essays of the twentieth century.

"The Power of the Powerless" (the Czech words *Moc bezmocn ch* capture the oxymoron even better) develops a relational theory of power that encourages resistance to authorities with pretensions, and ambitions, of totalitarian rule. It highlights the significance of individual choice and individual responsibility. To reflect on the deeper questions of human existence, and to live in truth, is not a game for the ivory tower. For Havel, this was the foundation for freedom. To act *as if* the rule of law were in effect, even when it is not, was one strategy for cultivating individual responsibility under communist rule and for limiting the power of those who would deny human dignity. Those keywords of today's political theory—*resistance* and *civil society*—can certainly find powerful inspiration and innovation in that essay. The challenge of his presidency was even greater, for intellectual responsibility to one's own ethical terrain might be easier than for those whose obligations also include institutional responsibility.

In his critical biography, John Keane (2000, 441) named Havel's effort a "crowned republic," drawing on the eighteenth-century political philosophy of Friedrich von Hardenberg (a.k.a. Novalis). In this postmodern version, Havel used his office to inspire the cultural innovation that moves a citizenry to become the reflective and responsible agents on which freedom and the good society depend. In his view of transition, President Havel argued that one needs to build into the making of markets the fundamentals of that virtuous civil society he admired while in the opposition. During his 1992 "New Year's Address to the Nation," Havel maintained that effective markets rest on the foundation of trust, honesty, humility, reliability, and other virtues that can be cultivated only through a strong civil society (446–47). His presidential leadership also offered lessons in globalizing knowledge, even in such a field as foreign policy.

His famous 1989 apology on behalf of Czechoslovak citizens for the expulsion of ethnic Germans in the wake of World War II gained him relatively little applause at home. It did, however, mark a different kind of international politics. Its humility and willingness to recognize responsibility in the most difficult of times signaled an approach to international relations that put ethical dilemmas ahead of political calculations at home. He wrote, "Just as our 'dissidence' was anchored in this moral ground, so the spirit of foreign policy should grow and, more important, continue to grow from it" (Havel 1993, 99).

This orientation toward foreign policy might elevate human rights over national interests. It also might reduce national sovereignty in favor of European integration. But it also creates a new global space. It helps create an international culture that encourages civil society's extension beyond national boundaries. Just as an open and vital civil society is important for making effective markets in postcommunist circumstances, its global approximation would be critical for cultivating an ethically desirable globalization that is otherwise shaped by markets and the compression of time and space afforded by the revolution in information technology. That, at least, is how I took President, and not just Playwright, Havel.

Václav Havel led us beyond what either the most powerful president or the most accomplished intellectual might realize by putting fundamental moral questions of our age on the first page of our global political agenda. Shouldn't the protection of human rights override questions of national sovereignty? Doesn't our ambition to control the world lead us to overlook those questions that depend on the cultivation of individual responsibility for our spiritual and environmental well-being? Whatever our answers, these questions reflect the qualities of an intellectual, and a political leader, with a sense of global responsibility. In that spirit, President Havel tried to change the meaning of presidential power but also challenge what it means to be an intellectual. His example invites us to consider the relationship between intellectual and institutional responsibility, something that is typically not discovered in the elevation of intellectual distinction. Ricardo Lagos offers another critical example, even if his own story is not so well known.[28]

Ricardo Lagos was president of Chile in 2000–2006 and then president of the Club of Madrid. He then became one of Ban Ki-moon's special envoys on climate change. His work has been among the most important for developing a more cosmopolitan sense of progressive politics, as will be evident in Chapter 8, and was absolutely central to the emancipation of Chile from dictatorship in ways that are remarkably similar to Havel's opposition in communist-ruled Czechoslovakia. He even belongs to Havel's generation, if on a different side of the world.

Lagos was born in Chile and earned his PhD in economics in 1966 at Duke University in North Carolina. By 1969, he was the University of Chile's chancellor; he attributes this early ascent to university administration to student politics at the time.[29] He was also traveling in the circles of Salvador Allende, a candidate for president first in 1964, but then, as the leader of a popular coalition, a winner of the presidency in 1970. During Allende's presidency, Lagos had various appointments—director of the Economic Institute and of the Latin American Faculty of Social Sciences, and as part of Chile's delegation to the United Nations. Although a socialist, he criticized Allende's policies for the ways in which they stoked the economy so that inflation soared (Lagos 2012b, 26).The United States nonetheless helped ruin this socialist project—in fact, President Nixon charged Secretary of State Henry Kissinger with undermining the Chilean economic experiment, empowering its military, and enabling democracy's death in Chile (32).

When Pinochet called the coup on September 11, 1973, the military disappeared many with whom Lagos served. Lagos himself was not taken, but he left in February 1974, knowing that this Chile could not be for him. He went first to Buenos Aires, then to the University of North Carolina at Chapel Hill, where he was a visiting Kenan Professor in 1974–75. An April 1975 conference, resulting in an important conference volume (Gil, Lagos, and Landsberger 1979), represented his strategic and analytical thinking in exile at the time. He was able to go back in 1978 as a representative of a branch of the International Labor Organization, with some diplomatic protection as a consequence.

Lagos's academic style still led during this period, but with subtle public effect. In a 1982 interview for the popular magazine *Cosas*, he explained that there would be an economic meltdown, a consequence of those Chilean economic policies inspired by the Chicago School of neoliberal economics. This assessment was not only informed by Lagos's individual economics expertise; it was also based on his having formed a think tank, Vector, to redefine the country's socialist thought (Lagos 2012b, 47–48). Ultimately, however, Lagos's challenge to Pinochet was not limited to publishing and analysis.

For the next several years, Lagos became more involved in clandestine politics, playing the bridge builder in the socialist camp while simultaneously arguing against a violent response to Pinochet. He was also a major force for the broader opposition to Pinochet that formed in 1983: the Democratic Alliance. In December, the socialists appointed him their spokesperson, launching his political career (Lagos 2012b, 58–59).

Much intervened during those five years of more active political opposition to the dictatorship, including the good fortune that he survived imprisonment and murder conspiracies by the Pinochet government. His greatest moment may have been on TV on April 25, 1988. In anticipation of a plebiscite designed to reappoint Pinochet, Lagos said the following in response to a question about voting "no" to that renewal. He pointed his finger at the general, who was watching from his home:

> When the cameras started rolling, I began like a sprinter, jumping up from the starting line to get straight to the point. "It is the beginning of the end of the dictatorship," I told Correa [the journalist onstage] whose practiced television smile gradually vanished as I spoke. I kept going. "General Pinochet has not been honest with this country. First he said, . . . first *you* said, General Pinochet, (that) you had goals but no deadlines. Then, General Pinochet, you had a timeline and imposed the constitution of 1980. I will remind you, General Pinochet, that you said on the day of the 1980s plebiscite, "President Pinochet will not be a candidate in 1989." . . . And now you will have the country

pass through another eight years, . . . with torture, assassinations, with the violation of human rights. . . . To me, it is inadmissible that a Chilean would have such ambitions to power, to be so bold as to stay for 25 years in power!! Others have never been (so ambitious) sir, and you will have to answer . . . and you will have to answer between yes and no, and you will be summoned (to answer) for what you did. (Lagos 2012b, 10)

The opposition won the plebiscite on October 5, and a coup was averted by the democratic opposition's coordination with parts of the military. Lagos and his allies, according to a newspaper, "with a pen and paper" defeated the dictatorship (Lagos 2012b, 104). Intellectual responsibility led, but with terrific public consequence. Living in truth, and speaking truthfully, was not just something dissidents managed under communist rule. It was also something socialists managed under a United States-backed right-wing military dictatorship.

Lagos's tenure as president is generally considered one of the most dynamic in Latin America.[30] His concern for inequality reflected his socialist roots, and the policies he initiated around the spread of education (Lagos 2012b, 125–33), housing, and health (186–98) show that enduring commitment. One can point to a number of innovative policies and practices that reflect Lagos's own intellectual agility, depth, and networks—his counter-cyclical economic policy saving surpluses from good times (176–78) is one that most will celebrate, but it is not only in applause that we can recognize his intellectual distinction. Indeed, we might see in his introduction of free-trade policies an example of intellectual leadership, an example made especially clear by his being a socialist (179–86). As he explained, being a socialist in some places might mean protectionism, but for a country like Chile, free-trade agreements (FTAs) were the most effective way to modernize. Each negotiation would produce its own winners and losers within Chile, but overall, there would be winners: manufacturers in the FTA with New Zealand, and farmers in the FTA with South Korea, for example. More important, by getting into the global economy, he could explain how this would lead to the country's modernization: to sell apples on the world market, one had to have paved roads so that the apples would not arrive bruised! He enjoyed a sincerity, an accessibility, that made him publicly attractive even while his intellectual engagement enabled him to escape public constraint when need be.

The limits of intellectuality and political power in the southern hemisphere are also apparent in his story. Lagos recalls the times when US president George W. Bush made his case for war against Iraq. Lagos worked hard to prevent the attack. Chile was at the time a member of the United Nations (UN) Security Council and one of the votes Bush sought to legitimate invasion. Lagos probably didn't need his intellectual foundations to recognize the inadequacy of the Powell case for war before the UN, but he did need that agility to figure a way to halt the invasion. He tried working with Tony Blair on different UN resolutions around Iraq, different from the one-sided versions Bush was pushing. But most fundamentally, he was trying to reinforce, in this moment of crisis, an international regime of law that could not be manipulated at superpower will. Small nations need an international system to be equitable, he writes (Lagos 2012b, 212). But that time, he could not manage.

I recognize Lagos to be in the same spirit as Havel, one that recognizes the world as it is, but understanding it so well as to try to change it pragmatically with powers at hand. Havel may have the spirit of the dramatist and Lagos the spirit of an economist, but both have worked with the range of the intellectual assuming responsibility for not only their words but worldly affairs.

While Ricardo Lagos is less prominent than Havel, it may be that Ashraf Ghani is even less broadly recognized among political intellectuals in the articulation of their nations,[31] in part because Ghani has never been Afghanistan's president—his candidacy in 2009 was not successful. He was, however, Afghanistan's minister of finance in 2002–4 and has been considered for appointment as UN general secretary and World Bank president. As I write, he is one of two leading candidates to succeed Hamid Karzai as Afghanistan's president. Regardless of that election's outcome, Ghani is certainly one of the most intellectual of political leaders in the world today. His work has been among the most important for putting Afghanistan to the heart of discussions of sovereignty, democracy, and global flows of development, as will be evident in Chapter 5. In some ways, his intellectuality is even more directly foundational for his political engagement than the philosopher/playwright Havel and economist Lagos.

With Soviet influence growing in Afghanistan in 1978, and with the invasion in 1979, Ashraf Ghani's planned return to Afghanistan was derailed. He stayed in the United States to earn his PhD in anthropology at Columbia University. He began a normal academic career relatively devoid of political engagement until 1991, when he left Johns Hopkins to work at the World Bank. This departure from tenure-stream positions for this policy-making world is not typical, especially for anthropologists. However, during my interview with him in 2000, he indicated his concern for how development projects were dominated by the logics, first of engineers and then later of economists. He sought to bring to development projects a more institutional and organizational approach to change by bringing different disciplinary backgrounds into transnational organizational politics.

Despite his general engagement in the world of development, Ghani remained extensively involved in Afghan affairs, illustrated by his regular broadcast through BBC and Voice of America in both Pashto and Persian before the end to Taliban rule in 2001.[32] He would subsequently learn that Afghan publics knew his voice very well as a consequence of this radio work. Ghani entered the political world, therefore, through multilateral institutions after an academic career.

Ghani began in 1998 to advise Lakhdar Brahimi, the special representative of the UN's secretary general (Rashid 2008, 54). Ghani ultimately became a central figure in designing the Bonn Agreement, made between November 27 and December 5, 2001, which established the interim authority ruling Afghanistan after the Taliban's ouster. The June 2002 emergency loya jirga appointed Ghani finance minister. Here is a typical assessment of his role:

> Ghani was one of the most brilliant Afghans of his generation and the most capable minister in the cabinet. He worked twenty hours a day in order to reorganize the Finance Ministry, introduce a new currency, and establish a new tax system. He encouraged educated Afghans to return home to help him, and persuaded wealthy Afghans abroad to provide investment. . . . He built up the Finance Ministry from nothing. There had been no power or phone lines, no Internet, and no experienced staff. He hired the Chicago law firm Baker and McKenzie as consultants to help him run the AACA and asked Transparency International for help in creating mechanisms to prevent corruption. He hired the British firm Crown Agents to procure goods for the government so that donors would be satisfied that there was no corruption, and BearingPoint to provide a financial management system. Within a few months, Ghani had fifty foreign advisers trying to reestablish the various departments of finance and trade while reorganizing other economics related ministries and the central bank. (Rashid 2008, 179–80)

Ghani knew how the international aid complex—that assembly of advisory, donor and recipient organizations and their suppliers—functioned, as he had previously worked in the World Bank. He hired many consultants, but he also sought to base the relationship between the Afghan government and aid organizations on partnership, not on clientelism. His 2009 presidential campaign also suggested that intellectuality.

His English-language presentation illustrates just how much his expertise informs his sense of Afghanistan's future:

> On March 31–April 2004, he presented a seven-year program of public investment, Securing Afghanistan's Future, to an international conference in Berlin attended by 65 finance and foreign ministers. Described as the most comprehensive program ever prepared and presented by a poor country to the international community, Securing Afghanistan's Future was prepared by a team of one-hundred experts working under the supervision of a committee chaired by Dr Ghani. The concept of a double-compact, between the donors and the government of Afghanistan on the one hand and between the government and people of Afghanistan on the other, underpinned the program of investment in Securing Afghanistan's Future. The donors pledged $8.2 billion at the conference for the first three years of the program—the exact amount asked by the government—and agreed that the government's request for a total seven-year package of assistance of $27.5 billion was justified.
>
> Throughout his career, Dr Ghani has focused relentlessly on poverty eradication through the creation of wealth and the establishment of the rights of citizenship. In Afghanistan, he is attributed with designing the National Solidarity Program, a program of bloc grants to villages in which elected village councils determine both the priorities and the mechanisms of implementation. The program has been rolled out across the country and has become so successful that other countries around the world are seeking to emulate it. Dr Ghani also partnered with the Ministry of Communication to ensure that telecom licenses were granted on a fully-transparent basis. As a result, the number of mobile phones in the country jumped from 100 in July 2002 to over a million at the end of 2005. Private investment in the sector exceeded $200 million and the telecom sector emerged as one of the major sectors of revenue generation for government.[33]

Ghani refused to join the presidential cabinet formed after Karzai's election in October 2004. He has said that he refused to compromise his position, arguing that neither Afghan authorities nor their international supporters would undertake the reforms that would continue the trajectories of change the initial years of Afghan democracy produced. For the succeeding four years, Ghani stayed out of Afghan politics. He became chancellor of Kabul University for a short time, but it was a cabinet-appointed position, so Karzai removed him even from this. Ghani recalled ministers saying that he was training more students to be like himself through this position, and one Ashraf Ghani is more than enough (Ghani 2011).

Ghani did, however, manage to create something of public consequence rooted in substantial intellectual innovation. His National Solidarity Program, "arguably the only success story in post-Taliban Afghanistan" (Chopan and Daud 2009, 98), is exemplary. This program is celebrated by the president of the World Bank Group (Zoellick 2008) and is also highlighted by American think tanks dedicated to US security in ways that show how democracy and development go together (Nagl, Exum, and Humayun 2009):

> In contrast to Western-led initiatives, the NSP is distinguished by the degree to which Afghans are personally invested in its projects. The high degree of Afghan participation stems from the way the program is structured: Afghan citizens are involved in every aspect of the decision-making process, from project selection to implementation, and the expenditure of funds is publicly tracked and monitored by villagers. Project results are tangible and of immediate use.
>
> Moreover, the NSP also generates institutions at the local level that are crucial to any vision of a future, self-sustaining Afghan state. The elected Community Development Councils remain intact after project completion, and in some cases these structures have resolved protracted conflicts. The CDCs have also started to federate spontaneously, with dozens of villages pooling resources and completing larger scale projects that no one village could afford or manage alone. Building on this natural demand, the program has now facilitated the formation of District Development Assemblies, where the dozen or so CDCs in a district send representatives to a district level body to discuss, plan and organize larger projects. In this way, the NSP is helping villagers establish relationships as Afghan citizens that bridge traditional divides.

It is striking to see just how prominently the National Solidarity Program has been featured in Western discussions. One might attribute its promotion, as well as its association with Ashraf Ghani, to be part of Ghani's own presidential campaign in 2009, mobilizing support in the international and internationalist Afghan communities. Additionally, one might see it as part of the World Bank's own self-recognition, not only for Dr. Ghani's past employment there but also for the organization's commitment to community-driven development.[34] Regardless of the reason for its recognition, Ghani and this particular initiative deserve broader engagement by those interested in worldly theory and practice in global transformations.

Ghani remains quite prominent in Afghan affairs and in global networks around development. Being more than a decade younger than Lagos and Havel, and working in a nation only little more than a decade into democratic transition and still wracked by war, the times are not so propitious for figuring the public consequence of his intellectuality. We can, however, consider its scholarly consequence more.

Havel, Lagos, and Ghani each embody a distinctive set of abilities, with substantial intellectuality among them. They also are exceptionally energetic, profoundly dedicated, and remarkably aware of circumstances, and they embody what it means to be a critical intellectual engaging, not only opposing, power. They do so in different ways, reflecting different periods and places. But where in the world would they be connected?

Articulations of Intellectuality

To conclude this chapter with Havel, Lagos, and Ghani is meant to challenge. It could easily appear to invoke discussions of leadership, to produce new notions of celebrity, or to reproduce those conventions associated with Coser's men of ideas beginning this chapter. But if one juxtaposes these *prominenci* with our previous discussions of globally networked public intellectuality around *Jadaliyya* and the diverse set of intellectuals marked by names like Szelenyi, Chatterjee, and Balaghi, their example should inspire different points. I offer five with which to anticipate the book's elaboration.

First, ideas are a particularly limited way of thinking about how intellectuals develop worldly theory and practice, much less consequence. Even if shorthand, the notion of ideas misleads. Intellectuals contribute not only through concepts but by embodiment of new relationships. They can offer novel rhetorics and develop new symbols. They craft new policies and practices. They do this in books but also in states, social movements, and design studios. They sometimes do this in obvious ways, but sometimes the ways are hidden. In short, we should view intellectuals as far more than embodiments of ideas. A sociology of knowledge that focuses on ideas misses the production, distribution, consumption, and diversity of knowledge itself.

Second, as we move away from ideas, we also can move away from the categorical thinking that is too often associated with studies of intellectuals. Some probably still doubt whether Havel, Lagos, and Ghani merit membership in the intellectual class, especially once they assumed reigns of political authority. After all, they are hardly autonomous from institutional powers, one of the greatest qualities of intellectual distinction. Here, however, we can appreciate the value of shifting terms, away from a matter of intellectual distinctions toward the distinctions of intellectuality.

Marshaling truthfulness, evidence, reason, and vision beyond political conventions and calculus, while challenging power on different scales in their name, all seem to me evidence of *intellectuality* in practice. We can readily recognize these qualities when these men challenged power from their academic, and oppositional, perches. We may have even celebrated their ties with publics, civil society, and subordinate classes. But in power too, each of these men has transposed schemas from one circumstance to another in the pursuit of intellectually grounded claims to realizing better worlds. It's in the qualities of particular practices, rather than in the attributes associated with curricula vitae and awards won or even positions occupied, that we may find the best measures of consequential intellectuality.

Third, even if we consider intellectuals as individuals associated with ideas of consequence, those distinctions are made through networks of learning and support. Lagos survived and helped end the Pinochet dictatorship thanks to his association with Latin American and European socialists and intellectuals. Ghani's intellectuality could be mobilized with greater consequence because of his connections to the global development community and his associations with multinational and national political communities in addition to his Afghan ties. Havel's distinction was recognized, in part, through the global human rights network mobilizations following the Helsinki Accords. He could challenge conventional foreign policy as president more effectively with those anchors in mind. As we consider how intellectuals matter, we should focus as much on the networks of which they are a part as on the lives they have led.

Fourth, networks enable individuals to survive and sometimes thrive, but that's not all. Intellectual consequence is realized in overlapping networks of recognition that have different qualities of authority and historical and spatial resonance. Havel's distinction was won in European and US circles because the power of the powerless could enhance the normative foundations of the West's position in the Cold War. That legacy could carry through the first decade of the twenty-first century. In contrast, explicitly political networks challenging US power define Lagos's importance. Even as president, with arguably more accomplishment as both oppositionist and president, Lagos does not have the recognition that Havel enjoyed, a lack that can be ascribed to past US geopolitical inclinations. Lagos certainly enjoys more recognition than Ghani, however, for to struggle in Afghanistan against corruption within and enemies without, all with allies that undermine sovereignty even as they try to shed responsibility, hardly wins applause in any significant audience no matter the quality of ideas. Yet qualities of intellectuality can build alternative networks for the production and validation of alternatives. Recognizing Ghani's place is a start.

Finally, intellectuality is distinguished in reception, not in production. Although some distinctions might be realized better below the radar, it's difficult for their replication, elaboration, and transformation to be found without their identification and amplification. Havel was celebrated widely, and even when his positions were controversial—as in his support for NATO's war against Serbia in what he called the first war launched in the name of human rights—they could not be simply dismissed. Lagos, too, has increasingly broad global recognition, but the most obvious networks on which the extension of his ideas might travel, those around social democracy, are themselves in transformation. They are developing energy but are not yet at takeoff. And Ghani is especially caught, not only for the place of Afghanistan in the world but for the lack of broader networks of recognition establishing his place, which is the reason we need to do more than question the qualities of ideas. We need to ask about institutions and networks that support not only critical intellectuals outside power but those engaged with it.

Are knowledge institutions and networks designed in ways that enable articulations of globalizing knowledge to find their best public paths? Their most critical engagements? The best combinations of worldly theory and practice? Or are we, in our media-frenzied search for celebrity and recognition by those who already have money and power, falling prey to that which Coser (1973, 48–49) pointed out forty years ago?

The path has been opened up for a type of intellectual who can free himself from the control of standards embedded in distinct cultural circles and personified by distinctive status judges. He can bypass them, so to speak, and address himself directly to an undifferentiated public of superficially educated consumers. These large masses of men and women are not equipped to judge the accuracy, the mastery or depth of a contribution, but they are sufficiently well-educated to judge a work in terms of surface characteristics of style and presentation. They are likely to ask not whether what is asserted is true or significant, but whether it is startling. What counts among them is not whether a work contributes understanding or knowledge, but whether it provides the shock and *frisson* of brilliant novelty.

I very much appreciate Coser's concern for quality, but I am also concerned for the challenge of recognizing quality when biases based on power and privilege are already so deeply embedded in our knowledge institutions and networks and not just our corporate media and states. We face a challenge in articulations of globalizing knowledge that go well beyond any particular intellectual's ability and any single network's mobilization. We may not be so limited as we think, however, especially if knowledge institutions might become all that they could be and more globally reflexive than they have historically realized. Respect for intellectuality is foundational, but these institutions will realize their potentials only when concerns over intellectual *and* institutional responsibility guide us.

3   Legitimations: Knowledge Institutions and Universities of the World

Knowledge institutions take many different forms. We see them most readily as universities and then colleges. We are likely, if pressed, to put think tanks and various research arms of other kinds of organizations—of states, corporations, and associations in civil society—in the category. In fact, the category seemed to expand its ranks in the 1990s, exemplified by the World Bank's self-characterization as the "Knowledge Bank." Its ambitions to provide a "Development Gateway" not only promised a comprehensive development project through knowledge sharing but inspired a wide range of other actors to adopt the World Bank's methods around knowledge management (King 2005, 73). In the end, however, universities anchor all these knowledge institutions. Taken as an institutional system, the university is an appropriate organizational foundation for considering the articulations of globalizing knowledge.

That consideration is usually undertaken in discussions of internationalizing the university, which typically insufficiently address the organization's distinction and its recurrent contests. Normally, it only implicitly recognizes variations in knowledge organizational forms and capacities. Those variations are themselves deeply implicated in an increasingly globalized market and prestige hierarchy in higher education, a subject considered further in Chapter 7. In what follows, I make explicit those cultural schemas that hide challenges around globalizing knowledge within universities. With my faith in the culture of critical discourse, I believe that by making those contests explicit, we might develop a more intellectually and institutionally responsible approach to globalizing knowledge.

Recognizing Universities

Lewis Coser (1965, 280) called the university the "most favorable institutional setting for American intellectuals for several reasons":

1. It provides a milieu in which men sharing a common concern with the untrammeled pursuit of knowledge can communicate with one another and thus sharpen their minds in continuous interchange.
2. It affords its professors regular remuneration, which, although far below that prevalent in a number of nonacademic professions, allows them a middle-class lifestyle.
3. It provides security of tenure for senior academicians. This point and the last one together account for the fact that the academician is institutionally protected from the vagaries of the market place so that he can devote himself to his work without being distracted by economic pressures.
4. It has institutionalized the time allocation of academicians in such a way that they can devote a major part of their working time to independent thought and autonomous research.
5. Finally, and most important, it grants academic freedom to its members.

From that same generation, Edward Shils (Shils et al. 1972) led a committee at the University of Chicago to figure university excellence. Their report began this way:

> In intellectual matters, at least, the whole amounts to more than the sum of the parts in isolation. A university faculty is not merely an assemblage of individual scientists and scholars; it must possess a corporate life and an atmosphere created by the research, teaching, and conversation of individual scientists and scholars which stimulates and sustains the work of colleagues and students at the highest possible level.[1]

Such ideals motivate the excellence of universities and legitimate their place in society. Universities do not obtain their power and privilege by being hospitable to intellectuals, however.

Universities typically gain their distinction in systems of power and privilege for their contributions to society or to particular interests in that society. We can readily read universities through the lenses of national and public needs and the desires of their sponsoring powers. This tension between function and interests is also readily apparent in how we have analyzed universities.

Studying universities as such has long been an important object for scholars of higher education.[2] These efforts are typically housed in universities' schools of education. A few sociologists have taken it up (e.g., Gumpert 2007; Rhoten and Calhoun 2011). Retired university administrators frequently offer their wisdom about the challenges, while a few others write about what makes some of their number exceptional (Padilla 2005). However, as crises in higher education develop in ever wider arrays of expressions, manifest most dramatically and contentiously at the University of Virginia (Rice 2012), a growing number of boards think that the best way to address the problem is to dismiss the university's chief. That is, after all, the way that it's taken care of in the innovation economy where so many university board members work and from which they draw lessons for their university oversight.

In the wake of these transformations, engaging universities has changed. A growing number of consultants promise to plumb the future and figure how to adapt to the new technologies promising radical transformations in learning (Christensen and Eyring 2011). Universities also have become the object of an increasingly vigorous "critical university studies" (J. Williams 2012). Scholars in this domain seem to channel the spirit of Thorstein Veblen ([1904] 2005) as they offer a wide array of causal stories for the death of the real university. In particular, worries about the corporatization of the university, and the decline of faculty authority, lead many of these critical agendas (Ginsberg 2011), with massive online courses the new object of debate and attention (Newfield 2013). Very often, the analysts' disciplinary, if not political, accent is apparent in these debates, much as it is visible in articulations of a university's globalizing knowledge.

Those global articulations might appear, as in medicine and engineering, to work through the creation of global expert standards. They may, as in environmental studies, public health, and architecture, struggle over the relationship between local conditions and global trajectories. Too often, as in public policy and international studies, missions articulate an international commitment even while national preferences dominate the frame. These important tensions about globalizing knowledge, however, are typically sub-ordinated to disciplinary debates.

The arts are especially useful for moving us beyond those familiar zones in considering the dilemmas of these various global articulations. They help us recognize efforts to transcend worldly problems both by appreciating the beauty of human creations and by working with the arts to move insights more deeply into the human condition and its conflicts. The arts can, unlike other disciplines committed to ever more specialized discourses, bring schol-ars together because *intellectual* culture, not just professional culture, requires cultivation in these modes of expression.

However, to the extent the arts and intellectuality are lost in the universi-ties' drive to solve problems defined by actors beyond the culture of critical discourse and to realize prestige within ranking systems defined by science and technology, universities increase the risk of failing institutional respon-sibility's test. Thus, the university's challenges, and the world's needs, must become more prominent in our culture of critical discourse so that intellec-tual and institutional responsibility can be addressed simultaneously. While many critical intellectuals were trained to distrust functional social explana-tion, it's important to reconsider in the address of universities.

Universities do, after all, meet functional need. Universities train work-forces appropriate to the nation's era: teachers, engineers, doctors, and then computer scientists, neuroscientists, biomedical engineers, and nuclear physi-cists. Those functions also go beyond the manifest. During one of my visits to University of Prishtina, I was reviewing this list of functions with one of my hosts. Pellumb Kelmendi, rather puzzled, looked at me and told me that I was missing the most obvious function: These universities keep youth engaged. If these young people are not engaged in university life, regardless of where it leads in a career, they become a destabilizing force. Universities keep them occupied, at least until students no longer believe that university learning leads to lucrative livelihoods.

In these days of rising student debt and crisis economies, those assump-tions could animate disenchantment if not outright rebellion. The cultural schemas that universities not only train workforces and create opportuni-ties but are also essential to the successful economy and society *are* critical. Indeed, for one school of thought, that kind of institutional script is redefin-ing the world with universities as their agents. For them, a *belief* in higher education's function is driving global change.

To be modern and respected, nations need reputable universities. Nationalism did not only demand that each nation have its own literary language and national poet. It also required intellectual concentration in that knowledge institution that defined modernity. An apt academic expression of that common sense can be found in one of my discipline's leading schools of global sociology.

Higher education depends on global "environmental meanings, definitions, rules, and models" (Meyer et al. 2007, 188). In this line of thought, professionals associated with knowledge institutions set agendas for global transformations, emulating those already successful within those terms. Although we do see terrific variations in degrees of institutional autonomy and differentiation, we can see globally isomorphic tendencies in university emphases on research, enrollment patterns, and curricula (194–95). And with this isomorphism in university form, we have increasing resemblance in societies across the world.[3] Universities come to map reality and in turn help constitute it by increasingly privileging a certain constitution with a global over local edge (Frank and Gabler 2006). This world society school on higher education makes a good case for seeing universities as the key institutions producing global transformations: "Much contemporary social change—on issues such as the environment, human rights, indigenous people's movements, economic policy, and the like—can be traced in some significant part to a global web of "knowledge society participants" (Meyer et al. 2007, 205). Those in this school can document increasing homogeneity over time, toward a model of university and society that is increasingly rationalized and secularized with growing emphasis on individual agency and public knowledge. However, their accounts of change rest mainly on correlation and emulation and less on struggles and alternative possibilities lost.

Intellectuals working to channel knowledge toward productive and transformative engagements of publics across the world clearly need to identify the similarities and differences among universities across the world. They also need to figure how priorities in their development come to be established within the terms world society scholars establish. European scholars may be more likely to carry out this kind of research in their own critical engagements with the European Union's Bologna Process (e.g., Tomusk 2007a). We might even generalize their critical approach with this kind of nightmare sequence of questions: To what extent are these transformations in university structure, culture, and practice generated through cultures of critical

discourse that Gouldner, and others, use to define the distinctions of intellectuals? Even worse, to what extent are they snuffing out intellectuality as
such? Tomusk (2007b) worries, for he sees in the globalizing rationalization of
university systems the intellectual's replacement with the knowledge worker.

Need that be the outcome, or is that disenchantment a peculiar penchant
of the European process? Universities are increasingly coordinated across
institutions, both within nations and across the world. Newsletters like *University World News* or publications like the *Chronicle of Higher Education* illustrate the communicative efforts to consolidate university powers and sense of
network and belonging to wider global transformations.

In this chapter, I focus on the conditions of and some of the contests animating change within universities. In particular, I find the account of the
"great American university" by a sociologist and Columbia University's former provost, Jonathan R. Cole (2009), to be an especially useful place to start
in a review of the university's distinction. That is true because of the percep-
tiveness of his account and because changes in universities like his can create
ripple effects in other universities across the world.

Recognizing University Function

Instead of beginning with what the university has lost, as most critical university studies do, Cole begins by establishing the university's place in the world.
It's worth considering his method, for it reflects both the Mertonian sociology
of science he learned from Merton directly and a viewpoint on university value
that characterizes leadership of many of the most highly ranked universities.

Cole (2009, 202, 205) identifies the university as central to contemporary
society:

> We depend increasingly on knowledge as the source of social and economic
> advance, (and) we require an increasing proportion of our young people to
> be trained, even beyond their undergraduate education. . . . Our economy is
> knowledge driven and the leading industries are microelectronics, biotech-
> nology, new materials science industries, telecommunications, computer
> technology (hardware and software), civilian aircraft, and robotics.

But why can't these be provided in commercially tied research sites? Cole
argues that the university has benefits beyond instrumentalities, even if they
all derive from its distinction.

Cole frames it this way: "Universities are singular places where knowledge and discovery have intrinsic value, where they are often pursued without 'products' in mind" (246). He also identifies, building on his mentor Robert Merton, a list of twelve ideals that define the culture of the research university: universalism, organized skepticism, creation of new knowledge, free and open communication of ideas, disinterestedness, free inquiry and academic freedom, international communities, the peer-review system, working for the common good, governance by authority, intellectual progeny, and the vitality of community (61–70).

Cole is also clear about what makes for an excellent research university within this value system, this time with thirteen elements: faculty research productivity, quality and impact of research, grant and contract support, honorific awards, access to highly qualified students, excellence in teaching, physical facilities and advanced information technologies, large endowments and plentiful resources, large academic departments, free inquiry and academic freedom, location, contributions to the public good, and excellent leadership (110–15).

His three-chapter account documenting the indispensability of the knowledge produced by America's great universities is one of the most important parts of the book. In the biological and biomedical sciences, he highlights how university work on DNA has fundamentally changed our ability to deal with health. Nothing quite compares in the physical sciences to the place of genetics in the life sciences, but innovations in the machines that understand the physical world, from telescopes to supercolliders, provide important stories. However, none of them is quite so remarkable for everyday life as the development of computer technology.

In regard to the social sciences and humanities, he is most likely to introduce concepts that have become part of our everyday life, noting in particular those Mertonian insights associated with the self-fulfilling prophecy and the notion of unintended consequences. Cole aspires to make this an interactive history, more than a list, where other university agents publicize how universities make a difference.[4]

Cole composes these discoveries to highlight the indispensability of the research university. He also marks the variable relationship different discoveries have to their producers. Discoveries in the humanities can, more or less, rely exclusively on what universities themselves can mobilize on their own. Social sciences are more likely than humanities to rely on external foundations for larger-scale research, exemplified, for instance, by the dependence of the University of Michigan's Institute for Social Research on that funding. But the biggest discoveries typically require even more substantial partnerships. For example, the computer was developed through a complex web of relationships involving research universities, the military, major government funding agencies, and industrial laboratories (Cole 2009, 275). Here again, the relationship of the university to external actors is itself variable by field and over time. The meaning of institutional autonomy, therefore, varies not only across but within universities.

Worries about the loss of academic independence have a long pedigree. However, the debates at the start of the twentieth century do not resemble those at the start of the twenty-first. The research university has, of necessity, given up the imagination of independence that captured the elite private university at last century's start (Lowen 1997).[5]

Stanford, led by Harvard, Chicago, Columbia, and Yale, received significant private foundation support in the 1920s for the development of academic science. But with financial ruin in the 1930s, it had to transform one of its key ideological self-understandings—its independence from government. Initially, Harvard, Yale, and more than 130 other private institutions refused government support, arguing that to be private, a university had to be independent of all political influence, to remain "remote from the pressures of democratic society" (Lowen 1997, 33). But economic crisis overwhelmed this argument and led to new sensibilities about what it meant to be a great private university. It also led to new mechanisms, like contract overhead, that allowed previously more acceptable industrial patronage to be linked to federal support without changing the university's sense of private self.

With more and more of the university's budget depending on external sources rather than university endowment, new questions could emerge about academic freedom, departmental autonomy, military patronage, and, ultimately, who might define excellence. Indeed, questions about political interference became both simpler, and more complex, in this context. Sometimes it's easy to see political interference. Cole (2009) in fact recounts the ways in which the Red Scare following World War I and the McCarthy era following World War II mobilized the movement for academic freedom and helped set the terms for its meaning and defense. He also recounts how the interventions of the second Bush administration and other civic groups reminded many universities' leaders and publics about the importance of defending that freedom so hard won in earlier eras. I'm not sure, however, that we are developing the sense of academic freedom that we need.

Most of the scholarship around academic freedom focuses on state-funded universities, in part because the challenges are most obvious there. Some, like the University of Michigan, are guaranteed by charter their independence from political interference, but interference easily finds its way. For example, at the start of the century's second decade, the state prohibited the University of Michigan from offering benefits of marital or civil union to same-sex couples. The state argued that university employees should be subject to the same rules as state employees, who also have been denied benefits for same-sex unions (Landen 2011). Private universities set their own terms here, although the dispute between Catholic universities and the state around support for contraception (Grady 2012) illustrates another limit on university autonomy.

One might approach university autonomy in another fashion, however. Instead of considering departures from the ideal in the exceptional case, one might consider those larger social forces structuring university dispositions in the first place. Michael Burawoy (2012b) has been especially prominent in these debates in recent years. He has moved from his focus on public sociology as a perspective in scholarship written from the standpoint of civil society toward the engagement of the public university as "the battleground of competing real utopias." He is concerned about social forces that would make the university a "profit center living on its own self-generated budget through the commodification of the production and transmission of knowledge." He is right to anticipate this, for just such a vision has become real in the promise of many, most eloquently from the former chancellor of the University of North Carolina at Chapel Hill, Holden Thorpe (Rohde 2012).

Thorpe and Buck Goldstein (2010), his entrepreneurial colleague, argue that the distinction of the research university rests in its capacity to address global problems like hunger, water shortages, climate change, and inequality. Indeed, the difference between private and public university is nearly lost—it's mainly about big science and more external funding for research, where private and public universities are presented on equal footing. In Thorpe's vision, this is no loss of public engagement but rather the increase of capacity to address critical issues. And because faculty address these critical global issues, this is no loss of academic freedom, just an increase in knowledge consequence.

Not all universities have the capacity to become such a world-class entrepreneurial university as the University of North Carolina at Chapel Hill.

Here, the hubris of the most elite becomes apparent, or at least the losses faced by most public universities most acutely evident. In order to emulate the most successful, universities with fewer capacities need to invest in ways that their own external funding does not allow. This leads them to pass on the costs of higher education more and more to their students, while decreasing investments in "normal" university functions. Burawoy (2012b, 7) captures the tragedy: "All this contributes to the degradation of higher education at the same time that students are paying ever more money, taking out greater loans, and worst of all facing slimmer job prospects."

Public universities experience this in most dramatic fashion, for private universities in the United States have always cost their students more. However, these private universities have made the challenge of public universities even greater. The wealthy private universities have increased their own accessibility to those with lesser financial means and to those who have been historically excluded from higher education, based on their racial, ethnic, or religious backgrounds. Indeed, it becomes something to celebrate, as Lee Bollinger (2012), Columbia University's president, offered:

> Especially in this era of economic insecurity, the argument is made that diversity in post-secondary schools should be focused on family income rather than racial diversity. Of course, we want both. When universities are granted the freedom to assemble student bodies featuring multiple types of diversity and possess the resources to support "need blind" admissions with full financial aid, the result is a highly sought-after learning environment that attracts the best students.
>
> Consider Columbia, where our undergraduate student body has the highest percentage of low- and moderate-income students and the largest number of military veterans of our peer institutions, as well as the highest percentage of African American students among the nation's top 30 universities.

This move toward need-blind admissions has indeed made Columbia, and other schools with substantial endowments, much more "public." Arguably, as public universities become more costly, well-endowed private universities become more financially accessible for the most accomplished applicants from all classes. They might appear, in terms of diversity, even more utopian than public universities. That achievement helps mask the point Burawoy makes, however.

Private universities, even more than public universities, are obliged to continue to demonstrate their value to those who would extend their endowments. Private university leaderships depend far less on meeting the expectations of faculty and far more on meeting the expectations of governing boards and donors, at least in comparison with those who would lead public universities. To the extent donor expectations are in sync with the values of academic freedom and university autonomy, there is no manifest problem. But there is no method to assess how the culture of critical discourse works to guide university governance, and an external logic of market viability may be taking over.

Ernst and Young, the accounting firm, sounded the challenge to Australian universities in no uncertain terms in the fall of 2012 (Bokor 2012). They argued that most universities operate with business models that will make them nonviable in the next ten to fifteen years. They will have to merge their work with other for-profit sectors, especially around digital technologies, and find new ways to develop "applied" research. Based on a six-month study interviewing more than forty actors, they found one respondent's reply particularly prescient: "Our number one competitor in 10 years' time will be Google—if we are still in business" (Maslin 2012). This kind of talk is, however, unreasonably worrisome.

One of the leading scholars of complexity, Scott E. Page (2012), makes a strong case for why universities are not at risk, even while they must adapt to survive in the environment the accounting firm describes. It's true that Google is doing some of the same work that universities do, but because it is a private institution, it cannot produce the same public goods that universities produce. It also cannot provide that safe haven that universities offer young people whose lives are most at risk between the ages of eighteen and twenty-two, whether due to violence or risky behavior. And it can't have the same range of research that modern universities offer. Page does believe that universities need to be reorganized so that expertise is cultivated deeply and in broader and more flexible combinations. Universities are resilient, in the end, and they will survive. It's not clear, however, from Page's commentary what kinds of universities will adapt in this new environment. Consider the transformations under way threatening university self-governance.

Governing bodies of knowledge institutions normally are loath to interfere publicly in what are properly academic discussions, like the qualifications for tenure. But they can shape discourses of success around university leadership by invoking different authorities for how to measure it. Quality is one marker, but anticipating future markets is another. This is one reason offered for the remarkably abrupt attempt to fire Terry Sullivan from the presidency of the University of Virginia (Stripling 2012). One doesn't know how general those conflicts are, but it would not be surprising if other boards are using reflections like those of Ernst and Young as opportunities to redefine what universities ought to be. Globalizing knowledge within universities can't be understood without these organizational contests in mind. At the same time, we should not forget that globalizing universities has a long pedigree.

Global Universities

At the beginning of the twentieth century, the president of the University of Michigan, James B. Angell, who also happened to be a former US ambassador to China, remarked on the number of students coming from abroad, from Japan, China, Egypt, Turkey, South Africa, and Europe. This global diversity, according to President Angell, would help "cure students 'of narrow provincialism and to comprehend in some measure the complex life into which (they are) soon to be ushered'" (Morgan 1999, 3). One can hear the same thing from most university presidents today when they speak of the need to globalize. Of course, their theoretical references change (Rhoads and Szelenyi 2011), but the underlying rationales—the need for the highly educated to be cosmopolitan—has not.[6] The conditions of crossing borders have changed profoundly however.

This change has taken place around many dimensions. The most telling and profound may be in the conception of the university itself and its relationship to those beyond its conventional public. The University of Michigan's then president, Lee Bollinger, made the point succinctly in a lecture during the convocation awarding Václav Havel an honorary degree in September 2000:

> We need to consider the extent to which we are going to take on an identification with people outside of our own borders. . . . We do not have the same sense of collective responsibility, of shared responsibility, of shared identification with those individuals as we do with people in our own society. Over the past century, this university and many like it have added to our sense of responsibility to our state a sense of national responsibility as well. We supplemented the identification with citizens of the state with that of citizens of the nation. The question now is the extent to which over the next century we will entertain the idea of a broader identification. (quoted in Kennedy 2001b)

Bollinger's invitation was the right kind of leading question. It also reflected the times in which he offered it.

Globalization, in that moment, led in defining the qualities of higher education's engagement with the world by linking the information and communication technology revolution to the importance of crossing national and regional boundaries in scholarship and learning. It assumed an international cosmopolitanism at the core of higher education, and its business. As Gil Merkx (2003) put it, this era was characterized by the development of a university-wide mission in the internationalization of knowledge. In that moment, a wide array of professions came to use globalization as their marker of achievement and the narrative with which to change their systems of credentialing and recognition. Internationalization's extension also led university presidents and chancellors to identify the distribution of internationalism's benefits across the whole of the university as a priority.[7] Those who would lead this transformation also had to contend with other older sensibilities of the university's worldly place and with those rooted in them (Tarrow and Hall 1998).

Many universities had, for example, long-standing historical ties to China, deriving from early twentieth-century missionary efforts. This led those universities to develop substantial historical, cultural, and language-based efforts in extending learning about the civilization. These earlier investments in Orientalism blended with subsequent investments in area studies to produce often well-funded and quite coherent groups of faculty and students, if relatively few in number.[8]

My intention in writing about area studies expertise as a continuous rather than categorical variable during those times was designed to smooth over contests around China's engagement at the University of Michigan between those associated with area studies and those associated with globalization (Kennedy 2000a, 2000b, 2001a). Instead of seeing these as contesting forces over the resources to be acquired in China's address, I proposed that they be seen as mutually reinforcing, even in contest.

Indeed, one of the finest discussions I have heard occurred around a question prompted by a psychologist's presentation of differences in perception across the world. He argued that East Asians perceive the world differently than do those raised in the West, with the latter focusing more on object, the former more on the object's context. For the area studies experts in the room, this kind of difference was disturbing, especially as they worked so hard in their area studies traditions to move beyond the essentializing difference that so marked their origins in Orientalism.[9] But using that history, the area studies scholars moved into an engagement of these psychological methods and data sources for identifying the origins and reproduction of difference in cognitive processes.

The fruits of this debate might be found in refinements around the data and their interpretation. More substantial effects developed in the character of relations among parts of the university and the appointments that solidified them. In particular, recruiting Shinobu Kitayama and Twila Tardif to Michigan's psychology department and Japanese and Chinese area studies centers, respectively, reinforced the fusions of expertise and new qualities of discussion developed in these encounters. They helped Michigan move beyond abiding differences rooted in knowledge culture wars, but those differences paled in comparison to the emphasis on difference following September 11, 2001.

Very shortly after Bollinger's speech recommending new forms of identification with others beyond our borders, universities had to develop a new sense of the world in light of those attacks. I referenced this shift briefly in the Introduction, but it needs to be viewed again in its articulation with area studies.

Area Studies

Area studies within universities have had an abiding and strong tie to a vision of the world defined through the lens of security. Russian and East European studies, in particular, developed with concern about the Soviet Union in mind.[10] David Engerman (2010) has detailed how the particularities of the Russian studies field both reflected and shaped the meaning of the Cold War.

It's striking to note that the security mission of area studies sometimes led, during the formation of research centers, to the exclusion of researchers who knew Russia best on their campuses. They instead drew on scholars who claimed to understand the character of the world and its dynamics. For example, Harvard's Russian studies was especially influenced by sociologists, some of whom, like Talcott Parsons, could never claim area studies expertise. Others, like Alex Inkeles, might have had area studies expertise, though he did not think of himself in those terms (Engerman 2010, 55). Those at Harvard who knew Russia better—Merle Fainsod, Michael Karpovich, and Pitirim

Sorokin—were not part of the Russian Research Center's (RRC) founding story (46). In fact, Parsons appointed Clyde Kluckhohn, an anthropologist specializing in Navajo studies, as the first RRC director (45–46).

Security in those days was defined quite broadly. It required having a better sense of Russian economy, culture, society, history, and politics on their own terms. Scholars played a large role in defining how those terms should be understood. Area studies could even moderate ideological extremes with its complicated stories woven with sophisticated theories that compensated for limited data. And different disciplines engaged the problematic all from within their own knowledge culture, while area studies as such valued their contributions differently.

The disciplines potentially closest to area studies ideology—linguistics and literary studies—did not fare well in the intellectual development of Soviet studies, even if a number of faculty were hired to extend language learning. Roman Jakobson was clearly an intellectual giant, though he was underappreciated in the elaboration of Soviet studies as a field. And while the semiotic approaches he pioneered anticipated much contemporary discourse analysis, cultural analysis in Soviet studies was more concerned with understanding "the Russian mind" and Soviet values than it was with theorizing about the virtual structures of action.

Economics was initially considered crucial, because Soviet economic capacities—of great geopolitical and military importance—were so little understood. Yet at the same time, because economics' disciplinary debates were so preoccupied with methodology and the esoterics of available econometric data, the field of Soviet economic studies was exceptionally small and easy to erase even before the Soviet Union disappeared. Russian history, however, remained at the core of Russian studies throughout the Cold War and after because archives and collaborations became more broadly accessible and the area's turn toward social history converged with developments in the disciplinary mainstream. Too, history has occupied a central place in area studies more generally.

Political science also has been at the core of area studies' interdisciplinary array, but sociology is surprisingly central to the founding story of Soviet studies: the Soviet Union was the "other" modernizing society whose convergence with America had to be theorized and measured.[11] That academic interest was, however, less sustainable because it did not fuse with the security establishment itself.

In contrast, political science, with its interest in and association with the making of American foreign policy, provided much better translators, and travelers, between the worlds of scholarship and security. The flow between government and particular institutes, like George Washington University's Institute for Sino-Soviet Studies, enabled a relatively autonomous field of political science/Soviet studies to be established, one that did not have to attend to qualities of the discipline as much as to a certain kind of policy-relevant knowledge (Engerman 2010, 257–58). One might look to the US ambassador to Russia between 2012 and 2014, Michael McFaul, as one of the most exemplary successes of this kind of fusion.

When political science leads university global efforts, the tensions between area studies and global studies can be kept in the family, so to speak. International relations scholars and comparative politics experts can figure ways to transpose the debates within their discipline to broader university contexts. But area studies, once it moved beyond the security establishment to become part of the university fabric, was not defined by political science or even social science alone.

Through the first decade of the twenty-first century, the leading area studies centers of the United States were generally identified with winning grants from the US Department of Education to become National Resource Centers in particular regions. Looking at the principal faculty contacts in January 2009 for grants through 2010,[12] one can appreciate where leadership in area studies lay, at least for that time period, a distribution that I detail elsewhere (Kennedy 2010a).

Faculty working in language and literature and other cultural studies departments like religion dominate leadership in area studies. More than 25 percent of all National Resource Center directors worked in such units. This is a deceptively broad category, as these scholars more often than others have their own area studies associations or indigenous cultural producers as their principal intellectual reference groups. Unless they attend the Modern Language Association meetings and treat comparative literature and other such global fields as their main reference, they are not so coherent a group as other academic associations, but one should not underestimate the significance of this group in defining any particular area studies unit. In each, the modal category of faculty associates is typically from the relevant language, literature, or philology units.

Despite the numerical significance of literary and cultural studies for area studies as a whole, other fields are represented in its leadership positions. In

2009–10, historians led among the directors, followed by political scientists and anthropologists. There were also a few sociologists, geographers, economists, architecture scholars, and art historians directing centers, in addition to one musicologist and one scholar of information science. Although there are important variations across regions, historians enjoy the strongest grounding in area studies' elaboration and defense, given their location within the university between humanities and social sciences, their substantive if not geographical range, and their more exclusive identification with the core competence of area studies in contextual expertise. To the extent historians remained within their area studies formation, however, they were unlikely to weather the challenge of globalizing the university.

Area studies faced a dilemma in its relationship to the global university. It could benefit with resources or status from the extended attention university administrators and those in distant disciplines could offer, but it could no longer so simply define its projects in area studies terms. Area studies leaders had to engage other fields on the others' terms. Very often, those fields, especially if offered by the wealthier professional schools, would treat the area studies projects as sources of data and travel advice. In some universities, however, new umbrella positions and organizations were created to advance that global mission, which could, in turn, enhance area studies work.

My position as vice provost for international affairs at the University of Michigan was created with that coordination in mind. Its authority was augmented by directorship of an International Institute that combined all area studies programs with other international ones. That combination provided an opportunity to enhance both area and global studies simultaneously, which involved administrative work as well as intellectual articulation to move beyond the conventional understanding of area studies.

Area studies was more a folk concept during the Cold War, understood but underdeveloped in theory, although in the decades since the Cold War's end, much has been done. Tansman (2004, 184) illustrates the commonsense understanding with which we began as "an enterprise seeking to know, analyze, and interpret foreign cultures through a multi-disciplinary lens." Walder (2004) took it much further in knowledge theoretical terms by emphasizing that translational capacity as variable. Not every area studies expert is fluent across languages, knows relevant histories, understands contemporary and historical institutional arrays in the region, and, especially when there is national variety in that region, knows its full diversity.

One might also, following Dirks (2004), move beyond questions of translation to historicity. One could inquire into the degrees by which a knowledge culture comes to be aware of its historical formation and resists the ignorance of former (and ongoing) biases. Dirks (2004, 363) promotes a postfoundationalist history, "in which attempts to grapple with the fundamental historicity of modernity in South Asia would necessarily be combined with critical attention to the historical formation of basic categories for the representation of South Asia." It's not only a matter of translation, one could say, but also reflexivity, so we were especially concerned to elevate its theoretical elaboration within the International Institute with an emphasis on contextual expertise (Kennedy 2000a):

> The International Institute comprises one of the nation's broadest assemblies of interdisciplinary centers and programs organized around area studies. By advancing contextual expertise—expertise in the languages, cultures, histories, and institutions of particular nations and world regions—these centers and programs enhance the capacity of the faculty, students, and staff to engage the world's diverse vernaculars and institutions and the movement of peoples and practices across the world. At the same time, the Institute refines the epistemological foundations and research competencies associated with contextual expertise and its relationship to other kinds of scholarship.

This clearly moves area studies well beyond security and becomes part of globalizing the university itself. Indeed, this kind of articulation offers an opportunity to extend contextual expertise: to become a *truly* global or international university, one that is comprehensive, requires area studies programs in all world regions. But that, of course, is only the interest of a few. It's critical to figure the relationship, or articulation, of area studies with other parts of the global university.

The Professions Engaged

Although I have identified significant currents of global articulation in most US universities—through globalization's pulse, security's frame, and area studies' contextual expertise—the impetus to move beyond the nation for scholarly reference and public consequence travels well beyond these knowledge cultures. For this reason, it's important to recognize just how globalized professional schools came to be over the 1990s, albeit in very different ways.[13]

Professions organize different bodies of knowledge and occupy very different statuses in power and privilege; consequently, they deploy different strategies to advance their interests. Given this variety, there are critically important differences in the ways in which different professions, and different groups within professions, view the world.[14] Still, as professions, they share some qualities.

They are reproduced through higher education; one can therefore reshape professions by engaging higher education. They also have relatively clear hierarchies; by shaping leading professional schools, one also increases the chance of reshaping an entire profession by encouraging the transformation of the most influential. There are critical debates particular to each of the professions, but it is also possible to read some debates across professions. Given the politics of globalization itself, all the globalizing professions had to ask, at some level, for whom they globalize.

These questions dominated much of the professional school discourse of global universities at the turn of the last century, even as their discussions were mostly conducted in-house. They were typically not introduced into other parts of the university or in articulation with a field identified with globalizing knowledge more generally.

In order to develop this articulation for a conference so dedicated, Lainie Weiner and I analyzed the articulations of the world in five leading schools in nine fields.[15] Because of the importance of going beyond the website "front region" (Goffman 1959) to get off- and backstage in understanding the dynamics of intellectual transformation, I also relied on the case I knew best—the University of Michigan—when it was not otherwise part of the assembly. Drawing on website representations about missions, special features, curricular programs, and other activities, we painted brief portraits of this professional variety in international engagement, especially in their relationship to contextual expertise.

Professional schools differed substantially in how they treated this global articulation. Perhaps more than any other field, schools of architecture and urban planning identified with the contextual expertise of area studies. This should not be surprising given that this combination of fields is itself organized around space and place, if in typically two very different ways. Although originating as an offshoot of architecture, after World War II and especially in the 1960s, urban and regional planning developed a stronger focus on social and economic space, with social science and policy affinities predominating.

The humanities and the creative sparks of the arts are more important in shaping the design concerns of architecture. This disciplinary range characteristic of architecture and urban planning also characterizes area studies. Deans of these schools and directors of area studies thus could share common concerns and strategies for cultivating interdisciplinarity across humanities and social sciences. The more obvious commonality is the common premium placed on identification with places and peoples from abroad.

Although there has been substantial overlap with the contextual expertise of area studies, architecture and urban planning deans have often ridden the second wave of internationalism, expressing their concerns in the language of globalization. Consider MIT's mission from that period:

> Our outlook is global. Students and faculty come to the School of Architecture and Planning from all over the world, and our alumni are to be found everywhere. We are vitally concerned with understanding and responding to today's complex interactions of local communities and cultures with systems of global interconnection, and with preparing students to work in a world where time and difference are electronically compressed.[16]

By combining the language of globalization with the traditional focus on particular places abroad, one might find in architecture and urban planning that very synthesis one seeks in the articulation of a broader scholarly mission. However, the value of looking to this profession rests not only in its fusions but also in the dissonances its global ambitions produce. Whose globalization is it anyway? Scholars in this field have debated it substantially (e.g., Rubbo 2001; UIA/UNESCO 2003; Wampler 2001).

Schools of environmental studies typically organize the world in different ways from those of other parts of the university because they attend to the biophysical rather than (or in addition to) the political or cultural environments. This environmental approach is a different kind of contextual expertise, one that incorporates the human factor as one element among many in the assessment of the ecosystem, within a framework that also thinks about the world as context. In many ways, it is easier in such knowledge cultures to shift beyond the American viewpoint because it is easier to speak of global needs in biophysical rather than political terms. Global warming exemplifies.

At the end of the 1990s, this global emphasis was especially evident in the website welcome by then dean James Gustav Speth of the Yale School of Forestry and Environmental Studies:

"The increased awareness that environmental concerns are moving into the international arena will require that US environmental policy be more in concert with other nations, thus giving birth to a new field of environmental diplomacy."[17]

They explicitly stated their wish to build a "truly global school of the environment." Duke University's school said much the same thing, if in an even more compelling fashion:

"In this dawn of a new millennium, we now know that many environmental problems are global in nature. The health of one forest, the integrity of a single barrier beach, and the quality of the air we breathe, are not just isolated problems. These environments have shaped the evolution of our world and define its future."[18]

Area and environmental studies found common ground when environmental work required extensive fieldwork among those whose distance from US cultural presumptions was greatest. For those who must learn local languages and rely on indigenous peoples for environmental expertise, the synergy with area studies became even more powerful. Berkeley's approach to environmental design was explicitly focused here. It emphasized

how the physical environment, in the so called "third world" nations of the world, is shaped by larger global, cultural, historic, social, economic and environmental factors. . . . Unlike similar areas of study in other schools, the Berkeley program is premised on two interlinked concepts: first, that the study of other cultures, societies, and peoples is a fundamental exercise for the creation of a better physical environment, and second, that the first world can learn from the experiences of the third world as much as it can contribute to it.[19]

Like the environment, schools of public health also have global reach, if typically with more particular regional articulations. Although Johns Hopkins University explicitly linked some of its international public health work to global environmental change,[20] most schools of public health had two traditional foci in their international programs: the epidemiology of infectious diseases and population planning. Indeed, it was more than curricular. Both emphases were designed from the beginning for students from abroad and for US health professionals to work in international agencies and collaborative projects abroad. And both have had a traditional focus on the developing world. Given that long-standing mission, schools of public health could proceed relatively autonomously from larger university missions. In this sense, one hardly needed the university at large to extend internationalism in public health. Synergies were, however, occasionally transformative.

When Michigan's International Institute made public health a primary focus (Harlow 2001), the value of moving across disciplines was nowhere more apparent than in the results of various projects and publications devoted to analyzing the relationship between science-based risk assessment and international trade law (Harlow 2004). Efforts like these combined the contextual expertise of area studies faculty with the expertise of health science professionals with consequence.

Global health has become more central to visions of the whole of universities, and not only the province of the particular public health school. This means, however, that public policy schools had to move over.

Struggles for Professional Authority

Of all the professional schools in US universities, public policy potentially had the greatest claims to leadership in globalizing the university, given its origins in association with American government. But it had that authority only if a policy school had a credible international capacity, which has varied substantially across universities. In fact, in many universities, public policy typically addressed local and national concerns, while foreign policy and international studies were melded in the liberal arts colleges (Vitalis 2002, 2010). Because internationalism had become so important in globalization's definition of public policy, all schools have come to mention their global reach, but only some could claim leadership in this area.

Most schools of public affairs emphasized that they trained people from around the world in public leadership and public governance. These articulations were especially prominent in dealing with matters associated with the social science end of area studies, whether in studies of democratization and governance, economic reform and development studies, ethnic conflict and nationalism, or security studies. They also developed centers devoted to particular issues in international affairs—Princeton University's Woodrow Wilson School, for instance, had centers devoted to migration and development, international organization, and programs devoted to leadership in international affairs, international political economy, US-Japan relations, international security, and other areas. Harvard's Kennedy School had centers devoted to science and international affairs, human rights policy, Asian economic development, and China public policy. But the relationship between these schools and the broader university is always complex. This was especially true in the social science end of area studies.

With Harvard's particular structure, area studies and professional school initiatives had little incentive to collaborate; rather, they had more reason to multiply initiatives and replicate competencies. Thus, most of the area studies centers at Harvard were relatively distant from professional school concerns, even to those professional initiatives so obviously tied to their own world regions. At Columbia the relationship was slightly different and reflects the relative triumph of the liberal arts over the School of International and Public Affairs (SIPA) when area studies were moved from SIPA's authority, so that the SIPA dean then reported to the vice president of arts and sciences (who also happened to be dean of the faculty of arts and sciences). This is typical: there is far more international studies *and* social science expertise outside public policy schools than in them. The space left for public policy thus depends on the quality of its ties with other units and the openness of those units to engaging matters of public policy. The Watson Institute for International Studies at Brown University illustrates this opportunity and challenge well.

Moved by Thomas Watson Jr.'s experience as ambassador to the Soviet Union under Jimmy Carter, the former CEO of IBM wanted his alma mater to become more prominent in discussing the relationship between American foreign policy and international affairs. Though there were a few scholars with that interest on the campus, during the 1980s and 1990s Watson found it more productive to bring people with diplomatic experience into the initiative's leadership, regardless of what faculty in corresponding units claiming academic authority would wish. By endowing the institute, Watson might have thought he would assure the institutional foundation for this shift to the world of policy and publics in ways its liberal arts might not otherwise. Over time, however, the relative autonomy of the institute declined as joint appointments with conventional disciplinary units increasingly determined institute priorities. Disciplines came to shape the mission of what the institute's international studies should be. For example, one of Watson's original and motivating interests, diplomacy, was not a priority for those disciplines. At the same time, research missions evolve, and Watson's original concern to address global problems abides in a form suitable to the university's own cultural politics.

Each of these stories has more complex underlying narratives, but the underlying metanarrative was that foreign policy experts lost control over globalizing knowledge as other fields became more important. However, law schools maintained a privileged position. Legal expertise provided much of the intellectual foundation for internationalism historically. Legal scholars helped develop the constitution of transnational organizations like the United Nations and elaborate transnational documents like the Charter of Human Rights and the transnational organizations in its support. They helped create constitutions for emerging democracies, international trade law, and arguments for or against the appropriateness of preemptive military strikes. Thus, legal scholars could also provide leadership in globalizing knowledge within universities and in transnational fora. But as universities continued to globalize, their own sense of their scholarly organization and relationship to other units changed.

Of course, law schools' internationalism can function in much the same way as any other school's internationalism, based especially on the arrival of students from abroad. LLM or JSM degrees are often designed to help link an American legal degree with concerns based in an international fellow's home country. Stanford "was most explicit about transcending the traditional divisions of public international law, private international law, and comparative law, however, because 'these categorizations are no longer particularly useful because of the overlap between international regimes, the activities of nonstate actors, and the various practices through which law and lawyers engage in the international system.'"[21]

Within and across the university, law school faculty are almost always central in the development of centers for human rights and the activism that attends them. Yale's Orville H. Schell, Jr. Center for International Human Rights was established in 1989 to "increase understanding of human rights issues, equip lawyers and other professionals with the skills needed to advance the cause of international human rights and assist human rights organizations."[22] New York University's Global Public Service Law Project, created in 1998, was developed to "increase awareness and understanding of the variety of public interest lawyering done in different contexts across the world."[23]

Typically, these contexts are "various," without any particular places in mind, but a few law schools identified particular and enduring commitments in those days. Michigan noted its investment in South Africa with an externship program,[24] and to Cambodia with internships available for work in human rights organizations there.[25] It also offered joint degrees with several area studies centers. Yale was also particularly committed to a few places: It offered support for its students to work with law students in Chile, Argentina, and Brazil to extend democracy's potentials. It also developed a China Law Center to increase understanding of China's legal system and assist in China's legal reform process.[26]

This suggests one other important dimension of international law: It can collaborate with activists who work with those at the bottom of society and with those defining the rules from the top. For example, Yale's global annual constitutionalism seminar brought together supreme court and constitutional court judges from around the world to discuss matters of common concern.[27] Michigan's work in refugee and asylum law focused on developing theories of and strategies for defending the rights and their legal protections of those beyond their nations.[28]

New York University's law school became quite famous for its own internationalism, using that strategy as a means to catapult its status from a respectable school into one of the top five schools in the nation by the end of the 1990s. Globalization is, as the school itself wrote, "not a catchword limited to adding courses to cover 'hot' international topics or to respond to passing demands for relevance. It's a fundamental organizing principle."[29] Its project on transnational justice was explicitly linked to transitional societies in the search for retroactive justice. Typically, however, courses like these on transnational justice were not made available to other parts of the university. And while law school deans often ascended to university presidencies—Lee Bollinger, John Sexton, and Jeffery Lehman were just a few from this period— their globalizing sense often meant abiding autonomy for law schools and informal influence in the university's globalization.

Business schools offered a different kind of influence. Like schools of public policy, business schools often overlapped with conventional scholarly disciplines and could rouse academic contest. Unlike public policy schools, business schools had a considerable autonomous financial base that enabled their insulation, if not appropriation, of faculty expertise across campuses. They also claimed a privileged position during globalization's wave of internationalism.

Some business schools were long accustomed to developing an international approach, but they became especially prominent in debates about globalization's potentials as they figured how to develop a "global" company. Business leaders therefore had much to learn in business schools about globalization's limits and potentials and how to balance within their firm global efficiencies and local context.

Pennsylvania's Wharton School may have been the most international of all the business schools during that decade, at least in its representation. It offered joint degrees and certificates in international studies not only bridging the campus but also linking to other US institutes (to the Hopkins School for Advanced International Studies), to INSEAD in France, and to Singapore. Its Lauder Institute of Management and International Studies exemplified the linkage by combining "an outstanding management education with intensive exposure to a foreign country's culture, politics, economy and language."[30]

Perhaps the exemplary business school initiative was one in which deeper awareness of global opportunities shook professional sensibilities about business as usual. Anticipating his famous bottom-of-the-pyramid argument, C. K. Prahalad along with China expert colleague Kenneth Lieberthal argued that corporations needed to struggle against the presumptions they bring from their richer markets when working to build markets in developing countries (Prahalad and Lieberthal 2003). That struggle against presumption is not always apparent in many professional contexts.

Globalizing Professional Standards and Connections

Even when the school is global in its mission and its courses and has many students from abroad, as the leading engineering and business schools tend to have, parochialism can predominate. This dilemma of defining internationalism is evident when internationalism assumes that extending American sensibilities and databases is the same as globalizing the mind and capturing the intellects of other areas. It is, therefore, critical to consider how internationalization not only extends American academic reach but challenges the presumptions on which that reach is extended.

Physicians are the exemplary profession, and their schools are typically the most autonomous and powerful within the university system. Medical schools also started "going global" in the 1990s for reasons associated with globalization rather than development, with a new global economy, information networks, standards, and interest in US academic medicine.[31]

Most of the top medical schools had international exchange programs, international health programs, and established partner institutions and made international research a priority, although each also had a distinctive element. The most highly ranked school, Harvard, has developed an explicitly international component since 1994, with a commitment to provide quality health care to "citizens of the world" within their own communities.[32] Learning abroad was a common theme for most of the leading medical schools. Pennsylvania's Office of International Medical Programs was the only medical school to explicitly mention its link to those beyond the health sciences, with particular emphases on four places: Africa, India, the Middle East, and St. Petersburg.[33]

Sometimes medicine's global ambitions were based on capturing new markets for services, drawing wealthy foreigners to America for care, but there was much more to this professional globalization. There *were* global standards that contributed significantly to the well-being of broad sectors of the population abroad. The value of global vaccination programs was well understood, for example, but physicians agonized over how insulin treatment of diabetes might be extended more widely. Those who discussed such global standards assumed that about 40 to 60 percent of what allopathic physicians do should be based on a global standard, but they also knew that much remained to be learned about critical cultural differences. With experience, physicians learned that one could not build health capacity effectively in different world regions without significant contextual expertise going into the assessments of need. Michigan's OBGYN program, for example, had been tied to Ghana for some time, facilitating other research projects in the region and developing especially powerful collaborative relations and consequential learning.[34]

Sociologists often identify engineering as a "failed" professional project but only because their profession is less self-regulated and more closely articulated with corporations (Larson 1977). Globalization, therefore, became prominent in the definition of this profession's schooling when it became important to the corporations with which this profession is closely tied. Because of these ties to the corporate world, however, the field tends to be highly differentiated, and therefore it is useful to consider more specific elements of the profession.[35] Nevertheless, just as in medicine, the global economy, information networks, standards, and interest in US academic practice lead the motivation to go global (A. Nowak 2002).

At the time, one of the most dynamic aspects of the field rested in the linkage between the globalization of engineering expertise and the challenge of cultural and political differences. Science, technology, and society programs typically articulated this interest, but very often from the points of view of historians and sociologists of science and technology rather than the more applied or experiential interests of engineers themselves. It was unusual when such programs took hold within schools of engineering. More typically, engineers were driven by the technological questions of their field and the questions of corporate clients.

Corporate clients were, however, increasingly interested in the challenge of political difference. They encouraged universities to focus on developing global standards for manufacturing. Their academic colleagues were additionally interested in ways to explore cultural differences. Then Michigan engineering professor Debasish Dutta became increasingly interested in how globalization, technology, and culture were related, in part stimulated by his teaching a global design course taught simultaneously at Michigan, Seoul National University, and Delft University (Dutta 2001).

In their first year, Dutta's students focused on how to design a coffee pot that would successfully manage different tastes. For example, Korea had to have a pot that would make instant coffee, while European and American tastes were stimulated with a slower roast. One Norwegian student from Delft took the point to a different level. She asked whether the aim shouldn't be to design a pot that helped express and refine local tastes rather than introduce modules that could merely accommodate them. Whether in the design of a washing machine or the placement of a coffee cup holder, understanding cultural tastes became increasingly critical to developing appropriate products for global audiences. The question became one about how technology might not just enable broader reach but open up better questions and establish more responsive ties. Schools of information, moving from being the homes of library sciences to the architects of global information infrastructures, began to lead the way.

In stark contrast to most professional schools, only two of the top five schools of information—Berkeley, Syracuse, Pittsburgh, Illinois, and Michigan—explicitly referenced the international at the turn of the century. Pittsburgh's mission statement said,

> The SIS faculty, staff, students, and programs—uniquely interdisciplinary, multicultural and international by design—are dedicated to the building of a global society and an informed citizenship based upon the foundation of knowledge made possible only through access to reliable and useful information.[36]

Michigan's mission statement and representation of initiatives was far more explicitly worldly than others:

Unprecedented change in the use of information is reshaping our personal
activities, our community and organizational practices, and our national and
global institutions. In managing these transformations, *our society* [emphasis
added] too often focuses narrowly either on extending technology or revis-
ing social policies. We need an integrated understanding of human needs and
their relationships to information systems and social structures. We need uni-
fying principles that illuminate the role of information in both computation
and cognition, in both communication and community.[37]

The emphasis on place was nearly invisible, however. Consider the ways in which
"our society" structured the imagination. Which society was "our society"? Is it
the global society mentioned by Pittsburgh? Or is it a vision of the United States,
understood as global because globalization is US (Kennedy 2002b)?

Internet internationalism was clearly different from all the other professional approaches to globalizing knowledge because of the ways in which the
"death of distance" structured the field's imagination. Vosco (2000, 38) typified that era's position: "The convergence of computer and communication
technologies permits people to meet anywhere at any time, thereby making
possible the ubiquitous exchange of information from the simplest two-per-
son exchange to the operation of the multinational conglomerate, with its vast
requirements for moving information and ideas, rapidly, efficiently, and with
close to complete security."

Of all the professional fields I surveyed, work in schools of information
sciences has changed the most in the time following the century's turn. The
technologies have changed, but the reflexivity involved in anticipating the
consequences of that transformation for learning, communication, and even
conceptions of the self have been dramatic (e.g., Thomas and Brown 2011). One
of the more practical applications of this can be seen in the work of Derek
Cogburn and his colleagues as they seek to advance the "socio-technical infrastructure required to support geographically distributed collaboration and
knowledge work, particularly between developed and developing countries."[38]

The fusion of information science dispositions with other disciplinary traditions has been especially productive, apparent in the ways in which architecture and information science have combined to lead us to rethink higher
education itself. For instance, Ann Pendleton-Jullian (2009) has proposed that
we rethink entirely university design, moving from a model dependent on the
transmission of knowledge to students with disciplined information based on

facts to one that depends on students moving across disciplinary boundaries, relying on an entrepreneurial spirit to learn what they need when they need it.

Globalizing knowledge through new capacities in information sharing might be the most revolutionary, and their fusion with questions of design, most transformative. The artistic imagination also underlies that visionary practice in ways that might enable transformative outcomes, but the arts can also distract from principles quietly imploding as the transcendent is celebrated.

The Arts Transcendent

Many would argue that the arts can transcend all differences. That assumption was certainly an important part of the Cold War: The number of tours taking American musicians across the world could astound. From the University of Michigan's Symphony Band in 1961 (whose tour across the USSR inspired its conductor to say, "Music is the greatest instrument in the world for peace" [Glenn 2012]) to Dave Brubeck and other jazz diplomats (Davenport 2009), through efforts to transform contentions in the Middle East after the Cold War, music promises harmony. Consider how Turkish philanthropist A. Nihat Gökyigit developed his "Three Seas Orchestra," bringing at least one performer from each nation bordering on the eastern Mediterranean, Black Sea, and Caspian Sea into a single symphonic orchestra to play both Western classical music and music of these peoples, suitably adapted for Western symphonic form (Kennedy 2003). This is quite an inspiration. One might wish to consider in these terms the historic accomplishments of Russia itself.

Russia, like Turkey and the Ottoman Empire, has been the great power on the Western borderlands, but unlike the Turks, managed to insinuate much of its high culture into the core of the Western artistic canon. From at least the nineteenth century onward, Russian art music helped define the Western form—from the most famous in Prokofiev, Stravinsky, Tchaikovsky, and Shostakovich to the lesser known in Balakirev, Lyadov, and Lyapunov. Russian music and dance stirred the Western European and North American cosmopolitan soul. I mention this familiar accomplishment of Russian statecraft in the arts to enable me to set the foundation for the worldwide celebration of St. Petersburg's three hundredth anniversary in 2003, which in turn allows me to focus on a slightly more manageable subject for the transcendent arts. The University of Michigan invested substantial resources in "Celebrating St. Petersburg" to put itself at the academic heart of a worldwide celebration of St. Petersburg's "cultural brilliance."

More than any other in that decade at the university, this project illustrated the capacity of the university to focus its resources on a single theme
in the articulation of international affairs. It relied on the transcendent arts
to mobilize its efforts. With performances by, courses with, and commentaries on some of Russia's greatest artists; a conference organized around the
redesign of St. Petersburg's cityscape; a theme semester and study abroad
opportunity focused on Russian culture and history; and an exhibit at the
University of Michigan's Museum of Art (UMMA), one suggests, but does not
exhaust, the breadth of the celebration. With regular mention by the university's president, considerable investment by its news and information service,
and substantial efforts by the university's Center for Russian and East European Studies, especially its key administrator, Marysia Ostafin, "Celebrating
St. Petersburg" won center stage at the University of Michigan. The UMMA
exhibition, however, offers one of the best lenses onto the main thrust of the
celebration in part because of its own relative "stability" evident in the single
collection on loan and the catalog that accompanied it (Steward 2003).

The Collections of the Romanovs focused on how the Romanovs—from
Peter the Great to Nicholas II—collected fine and decorative arts in order to
build their Russian state as part of a Western cultural world. Using works
on loan from the State Hermitage Museum in St. Petersburg, this exhibition
simultaneously demonstrated the embrace of transcendent arts even as it
offered its own clarification of the relationship between power and aesthetics.

First, the curators emphasized that artistic objects were deeply interwoven with
forms of power. Peter I, for example, brought European craftsmen and artists to
his new capital city in order to help make it a great European capital. Even Anna
Ioannova, ruling for the decade after Peter's death, acquired artistic objects to
demonstrate her power. Elizabeth I, ruling after Anna's death in 1740, commis-
sioned silver service dessert sets from English silversmiths, and later developed a
porcelain factory to rival the English. Catherine the Great, however, completed
this trajectory, building up the European arts in the Russian state imaginary the
most. Although Peter I, Catherine I, and other tsars manufactured Asian appreciation with ornamentation associated with Chinese, Japanese, and Persian
elites, this was all cast within a European identification, one that found these
Oriental tastes part of the cosmopolitan tastes of the time. (Steward 2003, 16)

Of course, this identification with the West was cast with empire, if of a different type, in mind. Russia's empire was contiguous, defined by religious

authority and rooted in a chronology of refined empire, as art historian Alexey Leporc (2003, 32) emphasizes in his description of the second floor of the Hermitage, in the Gallery of the History of Ancient Painting:

> Here the chronology would stretch from the first icons from Constantinople to Kiev, by the Russian Princess Olga in the tenth century to the foundation of the Academy of Arts in 1757, thus stressing the overall development of art from antiquity to Byzantium before moving on to art created on Russian soil. The accentuation of this continuity made the gallery a projection of one of the most important concepts in Russian statehood: Moscow (or St. Petersburg, depending on the period of history) as the third Rome.

One of the principal pieces of the collection, the Berlin Dessert Service, captures this sense of empire powerfully. Presented to Catherine the Great by Frederick the Great of Prussia in 1772, this multifigure table decoration, with the Russian empress at its center, is surrounded by invocations of ancient gods and their strengths, below which were "kneeling figures of representatives of different peoples and classes in Russia." The whole ensemble was complemented by twelve figures in national military costumes and finally, the conquest of peoples, including Turks and other non-Christian figures in light of the recent success in the Russo-Turkish War (Kostiuk et al. 2003, 181).

There was much more to celebrate in Ann Arbor about St. Petersburg than those pieces on loan from the Hermitage. With the recognition accorded Russian culture by aficionados of ballet, theater, and art music from Boris Godunov to Shostakovich, Russian cultural brilliance not only radiated. It also helped Americans understand better their own heritage. After all, Russian culture helped constitute American multiculturalism in the arts, evident in Balanchine's contributions to the making of American dance.

This celebration was not entirely transcendent, and cultural contests abounded. This was especially apparent during the architectural symposium, where the profound debate over how the city's redesign was to be recognized: Was this city to be treated as a museum or as a place that was, and continued to be, on the cutting edge of the arts (Senkevitch 2003)? These cultural contests were, however, entirely manageable within the university context because they replicated conventional positions within the university.

Art historians could stand at a distance and explain the functions of artistic display in the quest for power and privilege among not quite-Western tsars and tsarinas. Architects could disparage the St. Petersburg public's poor taste, or that of its (post-)Soviet bureaucratic creators. The international arts community could refine their taste and access the emotional energy derived from proximity to the most creative. Indeed, the presence of Mariinsky Theatre maestro Valery Gergiev in Ann Arbor helped constitute the cultural power of the university when he not only performed but participated in a course for the university's students.

One additional element enabled this celebration to be so successful: its nearly complete oversight of Russia's particular kind of empire and, in particular, its definition as a Christian empire that helped destroy both the Persian and Ottoman Empires. This could be overlooked because Russia itself, while proud of its role in partitioning Iran with the British and in defeating Ottomans from the Crimean Wars onward, developed around a tension between its Russian soul and its westward gaze. That westward gaze demanded empire, and Russia's bore especially complex ties to Islam, from its Christian associations through its Soviet successor.[39] But just as imperialism could be overlooked in the definition of Western democracy, so too could this religious difference be overlooked in the definition of Russian art. Celebrating St. Petersburg helped a university of the world avert Russia's historic tensions with the Muslim world, and America could enjoy that relief in light of the ways in which Islam overwhelmed most global imaginations after September 11, 2001.

The Arts Engaged

One cannot approach the corpus of Glenda Dickerson's art and say that it seeks to produce transcendent art that winks at power. Quite to the contrary, her work engaged power as it illuminated African American experience, especially African American women's experience. And with that, she sought to redefine the way in which we viewed the world. Instead of taking a break from the pain of 9/11, her work obliged us to view it differently.[40] With her leadership of the University of Michigan's Center for World Performance Studies, she invited her audiences' focus in a new and powerful way.

Glenda conceived and directed three performances of *Kitchen Prayers* in Ann Arbor in December, March, and May 2002 and then, between July 10 and July 19, 2002, she and her troupe—Walonda Lewis, Denise Lock, Kim Staunton Ramsey, and Lisa Richards, with the assistance of Kenneth Daughterty—performed in Istanbul. She performed the play a few times more, in a few other places, but I saw only those 2002 performances and thus focus my remarks on them.

Kitchen Prayers began as an American reflection on September 11, 2001, and a consideration of the kinds of losses others throughout the world have experienced through violence. It brought together classical tragedy, ethnography, and contemporary headlines. This was an especially woman-centered reflection; it focused on how war, disease, and violence affected mothers and their children across the world. In America it began with the particular experiences of five women onstage as they recalled the losses and fears they experienced on September 11. Glenda in particular worried about her daughter; Anitra was at the time of the attacks traveling on the A train beneath the Towers. Anitra survived, but of course many did not, including Yvette Adams, a black service worker who was in the World Trade Center that day.

These performances privileged African American perspective, experience, and loss. For example, in the final performance in Istanbul, the troupe returned to an earlier presentation, drawing the headlines from the obituaries of the black fathers, sons, brothers, and husbands who also were firefighters lost on September 11. While applauded in Istanbul, this privilege was not obviously so comforting in an American context. I recall one reaction from the first performance—"Why does Glenda conceive this in solely African American terms? Wasn't this a loss felt by everyone? Shouldn't we be together in this?"

This was a critical performance in many ways. In contrast to the Russian arts heralded in the St. Petersburg celebration, this performance put to the center of its artistic performance the problems and inequalities the St. Petersburg arts sought to transcend, to skirt, or to critique with allegory. Of course, there were important exceptions to the St. Petersburg assembly; one might look at that year's performance of *Boris Godunov* as a none-too-subtle critique of Russian state power in the performance's present. But this performance was not offensive to its American audience, in dramatic contrast to what Glenda's play offered in Istanbul.

After the final performance in Turkey, one young Turkish woman asked whether one could really say that those people lost in the World Trade Center were "victims." She said she abhorred violence and nationalism and was herself an advocate of human rights across borders, but then she stated in a matter-of-fact manner that these people were casualties of war. The cast was shocked. Denise told her that but for a last-minute change in plans on

September 10, she would have been just such a casualty. Our Turkish inquirer responded that this was unconvincing; accidental locations happen. After all, those killed by American weapons at the wedding in Afghanistan just a couple of weeks earlier were also innocent, and the commentator suggested, maybe even more innocent because they were not associated with the superpower setting the terms for war.

It is inconceivable to most, if not all, Americans that those who died on September 11 in any way deserved their fate, regardless of their association with the superpower. While there are also many Americans who will not accept the notion that innocent deaths like those at the Afghan wedding are ever justified, there are equally many if not more Americans who will accept "collateral damage" as the unintended consequences of war. Perhaps this young Turkish woman found that this acceptance of American power's insufficiently discriminant violence justified the victims of 9/11. My Turkish friends assured me that this is an extreme position and that Turkey is America's best friend in the Muslim world. But they also said that many Turks found the American presumption to redefine the world in the wake of 9/11 to be the underlying problem that makes racial differences among Americans appear to be rather slight in the overall scheme of things.

This extreme disjuncture of sensibilities born of a particular conjuncture built on more enduring cultural politics. For Glenda and her cast, nothing their audience could say could be torn from the experiences of black people in the West, in their origins as slaves, in their struggle to be free. But in the performance's failure to critique the West, and in the appropriation of Turkish materials without sufficient expertise, many Turks found a familiar Orientalist disposition. To appropriate the Turkish story in this way plays the Orientalist card, one observer told me, regardless of blacks' position in America. The safest strategy would have been for the troupe to stay within their experience, to represent only themselves or the category they are perceived to embody, and to share those representations across the world.

That's possible, and common, and ideally designed for creating epistemic communities with more or less common understandings of the world with varying languages at home. Maybe it is best to represent only oneself, for it provides the surer ground of cultural ownership and enables safe affinities to be recognized rather than to be proposed. But that method also suppresses some of the more difficult conversations that ought to be engaged. *Kitchen Prayers* in Istanbul certainly prompted new conversations about the politics of race and gender, within the United States and across the world, while refashioning presumptions embedded in the cultural politics of globalization itself.

Glenda Dickerson was a distinctive artist, but the importance of working with art to highlight the challenge of difference, not only recognize the transcendence of beauty, is critical to much of area studies too. This was especially apparent in the responses to my survey among area studies scholars about their place in globalizing knowledge (Kennedy 2010a).

Consider, for example, a musicologist working in a tradition beyond Europe and America. In order to get a job in a school of music in the West, he reported to a survey that he had to know the art music of the Western tradition in addition to his own focus. And that suggests the theoretical and methodological innovation possible in area studies and the arts by thinking about grounding and translation anew. As that musicologist said,

> Without the language skills, no one can understand (this tradition of) music. The same goes for any music culture with a rich and documented history. Thus, only American schools with Title VI centers that can provide language classes/support, regular lectures and workshops can sustain faculty and students learning cultures and musics outside Europe and North America. . . . Ethnomusicology students at (his university), for example, are so limited by school and program rules which prioritize studying of European art music that they depend on the centers to learn the facts and issues about the cultures/regions that they study. A musicology student studying French music in the school will get a good education about French music within the school, but the same cannot be said about an ethnomusicology student studying (another nation's) music. They need that (area studies center) to supplement their quest for knowledge. (Kennedy 2010a, 211)

In short, this example in musicology, building on Dickerson's dramaturgy, suggests that the relationship between knowledge production across locales cannot be read simply through the lenses supplied by the contexts in which one grows up or is educated. The arts can offer an incredibly powerful lens through which the basic insights of area studies—about the challenge of translation, the significance of grounding, and the importance of learning deeply about other places—can come through. And these commitments can resonate powerfully with other university priorities, especially around diversity.

Many from Hawaii can especially appreciate that resonance, as the University of Michigan's Amy Stillman (2003) expressed so powerfully in her own argument about what a university of the world could look like:

> My ancestors were voyagers who used the stars, winds and waves to navigate across thousands of miles of open ocean. Surrounded by water, they were never limited by it. Land locked people without maritime traditions experience the ocean as a barrier. They move across land with great ease but stop at the water's edge. Islanders, in contrast, see the water as a highway and move across it with ease. Pacific traditions of navigation involve reading of all the signs, the directions of winds, waves and currents, the colors of the water and clouds, the variety of birds and marine life. From the deck of a canoe a horizon is never finite and moving through the world is as fluid as the winds and the waves.
>
> To be a university of the world, I suggest, is to fully engage with the infinite horizons of our diverse humanity on a scale that is truly and inclusively global.

This is not, however, just a matter of perspective. Power is laced with that diversity. In a not so subtle challenge to the celebration of internationalism, Stillman said,

> Area studies courses examine overseas populations. Should we not also be studying those communities now resident in the United States whose ancestry traces to those lands both distant and foreign? . . . If we can recognize how the horizons of knowledge might be limited by not fully engaging with otherness in all of its facets then we can also see the important opportunity of this moment to affirm our commitment to understanding diversity globally by beginning right here at home.

Indeed, the challenging articulation of multiculturalism and its tensions with power are hard to miss. As we consider globalizing knowledge across the university, this question of representation and respect for difference and authority in the world's study is powerful, especially when international studies overlaps with particular ethnic/racial dynamics within a nation.

A theoretically informed area studies and most ethnic/racial studies projects should find common ground in the kinds of cultural politics of knowledge they address, even if their conclusions may not be the same. But then they typically don't define the main currents of globalizing knowledge in universities because that challenge of difference they emphasize is difficult. Recognizing diversity's many dimensions also typically does not align with how more powerful actors articulate the terms of the world.

Articulations of the Global University

The ironies should be obvious by now. For the most part, I have discussed the global university with reference almost exclusively to universities within the United States. In that fashion, I reproduce the very problem Michael Burawoy and others cite: presuming that what happens in the United States, especially among its elite knowledge institutions, defines the course of university work on a global scale. To some extent, as the world society theorists argue, this is empirically true, although much work remains to be done on why that is the case with the data they consider. More comparative studies of curricula, structure, and personnel could be developed, especially with regard to what it means to be a global university.

Rhoads and Szelenyi (2011) help. They compare four universities' conceptions of global citizenship: University of California at Los Angeles (UCLA, their own); Central European University (CEU) in Budapest, Hungary; Guangdong University of Foreign Studies (GDUFS) in Guangzhou, China; and the University of Buenos Aires (UBA) in Argentina. How, they ask, do these universities shape the sense of rights and responsibilities in a world where obligations and expectations beyond nation-states anticipate a new kind of citizenship? In particular, the authors are concerned to elaborate how economic, political, and cultural sensibilities of these rights and obligations work in knowledge institutions increasingly challenged by neoliberalism.

By itself, the diversity of these institutions marks the challenge of talking about the articulation of *the* global university. While each has some powerful expression of global mission and identifications, only CEU is manifestly global and without particular definition by its Hungarian surroundings. Its language of instruction is English, its faculty and student body are only minimally Hungarian, and its mission is increasingly global in its wish to bring knowledge to bear on the challenges facing the philosophy and practice of open societies in the world, not only in the postcommunist region. At the same time, CEU's location within Hungary and the European Union means that it must face the particular rules and regulations of institutions in that environment, much as UCLA, GDUFS, and UBA face in their own respective environments.

The authors conclude that the different environments facing each of these universities lead them to emphasize different debates in the address of global citizenship, even while they more or less agree on the increasingly global nature of key policy and practice issues. Rhoads and Szelenyi (2011, 275) wonder whether universities should "promote certain types of citizenship among students and faculty, or should they avoid making value judgments regarding the nature of citizenship?" They conclude that universities *ought* to supplement a familiar focus on individual success in local contexts, especially with a more emancipatory and collective focus on global well-being.

My spirit is with them, but I think their injunction is not much different from the ones on the lips of university administrators at the beginning of the twentieth century. Particularly charismatic leadership in combination with collaborative college faculties could rally around that kind of vision of global citizenship, but generalized idealism is most likely effective in smaller universities and colleges defined by their liberal arts curricula. In the larger universities on which I have focused in this chapter, where the research priorities in different knowledge cultures tend to define the trajectories of learning, ethical injunctions are likely to fall if not on deaf ears, then on ears attuned to more particular musics.

Most university transformations in these places occur within vernaculars that are not only nationally accented but defined within relatively particular knowledge cultures organized around disciplines and schools of thought. For that reason, any discourse of global knowledge institutional responsibility must resonate with actually existing contests and collaborations. I have, therefore, spent much of the preceding chapter outlining the qualities of academic engagement involved in defining the global university in both general terms and with specific examples. I highlighted possibilities emerging from within and across disciplinary and professional knowledge cultures.

In general, some within universities seek to globalize their standards for excellence without concern for hegemonic expression; others seek to extend their hegemonies by understanding global differences more adequately. Still others see these global differences as ways to challenge reigning assumptions about how the world works and how it ought to work. It's too simple to talk about the contrast between globalizing knowledge from above and from below, but to ask that question at least raises the question about knowledge for whom, and whose language, metaphors, histories, and institutions should shape the parameters of the conversation.

The answer to that question depends on the field of scholarship. Scholars in engineering and medicine will discuss globalizing knowledge differently than those in area studies. And the latter are different still from those who focus on global trade and national security. Still, we would be mistaken to presume that dialogues across these more specific knowledge cultures cannot move university cultures. We would be wrong to assume that these particular disciplined and professional knowledge cultures can't do more for the global public good. I believe that public good to be more likely in view when priorities are developed through cultures of critical discourse that cross disciplinary and professional boundaries. Indeed, those formally trained in network theory would likely argue that innovations tend to take place in the structural holes of networks, not in the actually existing clusters of knowledge production.

I have discussed a number of such innovations, but these particular examples don't necessarily cumulate. They mostly tend to reinforce particular programs within or across more substantial departments and schools. They might, however, become something more, especially if they are brought to bear on the larger questions animating university-wide debate.

Financial pressures on universities have stimulated a great deal of discussion around the most compelling functions of universities, which in turn shapes how universities address their fund-raising strategies and their top priorities for investment. It's easy to see universities trying to replicate those great transformations in knowledge production that have happened over the last decades, with developments in studies of DNA and of microelectronics leading. It's not surprising, then, when universities decide to invest in those parts of the university associated with science and technology. It's much more difficult to identify those consequential transformations when patents are not pending and start-ups are not ignited. It's especially difficult to identify which investments in globalizing knowledge matter most and why.

While most university agents, from presidents to professors and students, all celebrate the importance of becoming more global in awareness and citizenship, there are few examples of how university policies and practices have moved beyond early twentieth-century notions celebrating a more cosmopolitan disposition. The rationales have remained the same, even as the rationales' techniques have grown in power and participants grown in diversity. And therein lies the distinction of the global university, and its challenge.

As universities become increasingly global, they also become increasingly professional, which means that knowledge becomes increasingly specialized, and with it, the capacities to judge true distinction rely increasingly on narrower bands of expertise. Within that dynamic, units defend their professional prerogative in strategies typically not befitting a culture of critical discourse but rather a bureaucratic field of contest. Of course, the bureaucratic rules are different, with appeals to research distinction animating the discourse of allocation and assignment. Nevertheless, it is often difficult to go beyond those bands of expertise arguing for excellence within a field. That happens when patents are won and start-ups emerge. But that is not the only way to recognize public goods, which explains why Burawoy's (2012b, 10) invitation to reframe the public university is so powerful:

> Critical discourse, however, cannot be confined to the internal organization and mission of the university, it must also embrace the place of the university in the wider society, especially if it is to contest the regulatory and commercial models. Furthermore as it thinks of itself in society, it also engages in a critique of that society and its support for the formal rationalization of governance and commodification of research and teaching. In this vision the university is not a passive player submitting to the force of external forces but an active and self-conscious ingredient in the very constitution of society. It is, to use Alvin Gouldner's (1979) term, a community defined by a culture of critical discourse.

Burawoy writes as a sociologist, and one might find many in my discipline eager to contribute to such a culture. At the same time, Burawoy's invitation to that culture also has a disciplinary and political ring that could discourage the broader university from the initial conversation. It's possible that some engineers and physicians could join in a critique of commodification and that some political scientists and lawyers will also worry about the formal rationalization of governance. It's more likely, however, that we could find common ground first without the critique of constraints, and rather in the embrace of intellectual and institutional responsibility before the world. That demands that we figure what in the world we mean by those twin responsibilities.

I would propose that we begin with the question of publics, for in that subject the student's place is most evident.

4 Engagements: Knowledgeable Publics

Publics have become increasing critical in the world because of both global and intellectual transformations. At the global level, the revolution in information and communication technology has made publics much more significant. As one expert reflects,

> Global publics, once informed, increasingly have the power to confer legitimacy upon, or withdraw it from, policies of governments and firms. By increasing the ability of global publics to acquire and evaluate information for themselves and by limiting the ability of governments and firms to conduct diplomacy in secret, ICTS have heightened the need for governments, firms, and civil society organizations to communicate effectively to global publics. (Pigman 2007, 53)

While much more might be done to analyze this process, it can't be done well without recognizing how the notion of public has itself changed.

The concept of "public" is not new, but the way it is used has become distinctive in the last couple of decades. As discussed in the Introduction, the "public" has changed. Many have previously conceived it as a relatively local or proximate object of reference invoked by others to justify action. It has come to be understood more properly as a form of social interaction that depends above all on communication among participants of different proximities alongside their increasing self-awareness of that condition and its consequence.

This scholarly turn opened the way for more fruitful encounters between humanities and social sciences, given the importance of discourse and communication to the constitution of this sociological object. This interaction is not only a matter of ties among network positions but also expressions of connectivity through different poetics where the personal and impersonal blend to create identifications and recognitions, and even transformations in understandings if not also practice (Warner 2005). While publics are thus a social fact in the Durkheimian sense, they depend on a certain kind of performativity and reflexivity demanding attention to the group's constitution in time and place. Unlike many sociological referents, this social fact is not determined remotely by a sociological function, historical role, or structural location. Unlike earlier conceptions of class, social groups, or revolutionary subjects, publics are communicatively constituted and not structurally determined.

In this chapter, I develop this notion of public, especially around the role of knowledge in its constitution. By focusing on the social responsibility elevated in public sociology and the ways in which the Occupy movement articulates knowledge, I consider how higher education might not only refigure its public engagement but also consider its global ties in these terms.

Among sociologists, two scholars have been especially critical in elevating publics. Craig Calhoun's approach is most useful for those who work to articulate knowledge institutions and publics, while Michael Burawoy's approach is especially helpful for redefining how sociologists, as disciplined intellectuals, engage publics from the standpoint of civil society and its relation to social movements.[1]

The Social Responsibility of Public Sociology

In his 2004 presidential address to the American Sociological Association (ASA), Michael Burawoy (2005b) delivered an argument "for public sociology."[2] He offered eleven theses in elaboration and has written many other essays anticipating, and subsequently developing, this argument, available in this volume's Bibliography. Several special issues of journals and edited volumes have also complemented and challenged his arguments, to which he has generously offered responses and rejoinders. This initiative has been among the most productive and prolific efforts of ASA presidents accompanying their presidential addresses, and it promises to transform the internal structure of

American sociology.[3] And in his guise as the president of the International Sociological Association, we have seen a dramatic shift in the scale of this action. It is fair to say that this has become one of the most powerful social movements within a scholarly discipline to transform the relationship of a discipline to publics.[4]

Although his eleven theses are the best way to begin thinking through his account of public sociology, I think Zussman and Mira (2007, 5–6) are correct to emphasize understanding public sociology in relation to the other kinds of sociology he identifies—professional, critical, and policy:

> Professional sociology, Burawoy acknowledges, is the sine qua non of other sociologies, supplying "true and tested methods, accumulated bodies of knowledge, orienting questions, and conceptual frameworks." In contrast, critical sociology is the "conscience of professional sociology," constantly questioning the foundations, both normative and descriptive, of professional research programs. Critical sociology insists that sociology "confront the pressing cultural and institutional problems of the time" rather than lapsing into obsessive attention to issues of "technique and specialization." Yet critical sociology, as Burawoy understands it, is also marked by its unrepentant academic character, a preoccupation with abstract research programs rather than the common sense and actual experiences of those for whom it purports to speak. Policy sociology, unlike either professional sociology or critical sociology, does speak to audiences beyond the university. But it does so, Burawoy argues, "in the service of a goal defined by a client," and provides "solutions to problems" formulated elsewhere, or particularly in its pathological forms, "legitimates solutions that have already been reached." . . . Public sociology is bound to civil society—that vast array of associations and movements that stand apart from both the state and economy.

One of the most important distinctions Burawoy makes is between instrumental and reflexive knowledge. Instrumental knowledge is relatively more familiar in the elaboration of sociology, but reflexive knowledge also has an important pedigree. In that tradition, Burawoy (2007a, 34) understands it to be "concerned with a dialogue about ends" and that it "interrogates the value premises of society as well as our profession." In short, sociology for what and sociology for whom are the guiding questions, which also evoke another ASA president (Lee 1986), indicating reflexivity's abiding presence in the discipline.

Beyond these types of sociology, it is also quite useful to think about varieties of publics to whom public sociology might be addressed. Burawoy distinguishes two kinds in his second thesis about the multiplicity of public sociologies. He associates a traditional public sociology with publics that are "generally invisible in that they cannot be seen, thin in that they do not generate much internal interaction, and passive in that they do not constitute a movement or organization, and they are usually mainstream." He contrasts that with an organic public sociology "in which the sociologist works in close connection with a visible, thick, active, local, and often counterpublic . . . labor movement, neighborhood associations, communities of faith, immigrant rights groups, human rights organizations" (Burawoy 2007a, 43). Burawoy's choice of adjective is quite deliberate, for his sense of public sociology here is very much in line with Gramsci's notion of organic intellectual. Both accounts, of course, preceded the movement that changed our sense of public engagement and should change our idea of knowledge.

The Occupy Movement as Transformative Public

In one of the more literary efforts early on to explain Occupy Wall Street (OWS), the novelist and *Times Literary Supplement* columnist Michael Greenberg (2011) explained that *Adbusters* out of Vancouver hatched the idea for OWS in 2011's midsummer.[5] The movement took off "when combined with anarchism, the hactivism of the WikiLeaks phenomenon, and the arcane theories of Guy Debord and the so-called Situationists on the May 1968 student demonstrations in Paris." Later that summer, he writes, Anonymous joined the movement, the hackers whose association with "V for Vendetta" iconography is most apparent in the Guy Fawkes masks they wear.

It is difficult to estimate the real range of the Occupy movement across the United States and the world, but at one level, the digital imagery of this movement may be just as important as more familiar sociological data, as shown in this map from October 30, 2011, of how the Occupy movement spread (Figure 4.1).[6]

Although some of those dots indicate very few protesters, others indicate substantial numbers. Spain, with its 15 M movement, clearly led the world in protest on October 15, 2011 (Baiocchi and Ganuza 2012), with the Italians, Portuguese, Chileans, Germans, and Greeks not far behind. Given the size of their nations, the Croats and especially Slovenes were out in force. London had one of the longest-enduring encampments. We see Occupy's extensions

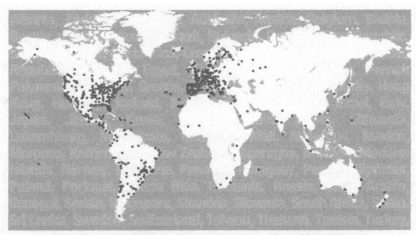

THE WORLD HAS SPOKEN
1,039 Occupation Events in 87 Countries

FIGURE 4.1 Global distribution of Occupy protests, 2011.

across Turkey and Brazil, transforming the meaning of occupy itself (Baiocchi and Kennedy 2013). Ukraine's Euromaidan protest is a variation on this kind of protest, one to which I attend in Chapter 8.

Occupy Wall Street protesters enabled the global movement's focus, or at least its verbal referent. I turn later to the global dimensions of the protest, but for now, New York City, because it has been the hub at some level, deserves extensive attention. Todd Gitlin's (2012) is one of the first substantial accounts and a remarkable step forward in transformational sociology.

Gitlin, active in the 1960s movements himself and a longtime sociologist focused on media and movements, has been extensively engaged with Occupy. He interviewed some of the pioneers and learned their stories and the inspirations that moved those relative few in mid-September to occupy Zuccotti Park in Wall Street. Another intellectual, however, is a critical part of the story.

Joe Stiglitz—Columbia University professor, Nobel Prize winner, former chief economist for the World Bank—published in May 2011 an essay in *Vanity Fair*, whose title might suggest the connection to Occupy Wall Street: "Of the 1%, by the 1%, for the 1%." Gitlin provides some of the evidence for its direct inspiration. More important is the powerful message Occupy Wall Street enacted, articulated, embodied. Gitlin (2012, 19) captures the power of the 1 percent/99 percent formulation: "Couching the issue this way was a stroke of messaging genius, since it turned the tables on right-wingers who insisted that any campaign for economic justice and progressive taxation amounted to class warfare. If the 1 percent were responsible for rampant inequality, then the status quo was not warfare at all, but a rout." Although there were, at times, thousands living in the park, their support extended much further. The activists themselves were especially savvy at figuring ways to gauge it.

Gitlin (2012, 28) reports that, in the fall of 2011, some three million Americans identified with Occupy. But beyond the challenge of estimates, what exactly identification and antagonism mean is difficult: a growing number, over time, began to disagree with the Occupy movement's tactics, even as the message about inequality began to become more broadly accepted and critical to public debate (43–44). That distinction between tactics and message complements an important distinction between what Gitlin calls the inner core of the movement and its outer movement of potential supporters like the lobby MoveOn, trade unions, and progressives in electoral politics.

The inner movement of Occupy Wall Street and its extensions elsewhere developed their own community, with their own local culture and rituals (Gitlin 2012, 73–79). They developed a remarkably functional division of labor, with media, health, sanitation, and other areas engaged (80–89). While their self-organization was impressive, their rules also complicated their practice. The movement's insistence on direct democracy, consensus, and inclusion limited organizational efficiencies; like much of the broader society, the movement was unable to address matters of class and racial difference as effectively as one might imagine a movement dedicated to empowerment of the 99 percent (92–99). However, the point of intellectual engagement with a mobilized public is not just to point to limitations but also to recognize achievements and, by extension, potentials. Gitlin does that.

Occupy developed a new sense of what it means to be effective, resisting articulation with the world as it exists, refusing to play by the rules that have led to the rout of the 99 percent by the 1 percent. Gitlin (2012, 142) gets it:

Occupy does not want to be mainstream. It is, at its core, an outsider movement, deeply committed to a radical departure from political norms. That is its identity, an identity only reinforced by its early flush of success. And such success imposes burdens. Success? Is it reasonable to speak of success when the plutocracy prevails, when big money still dominates official politics, when the investment banks and their executives thrive with impunity under minimal regulation, when corporate power still rules markets and melts icecaps? Despite a world of change it has not achieved, the movement can still take a certain success to heart—can *feel* success—even if, at some level, it still disbelieves what it has wrought. It burst out of nowhere. Its interior bonds, many of them, are intense. Enough of its inner life satisfies enough of its inner core. Arrests, and the insults and injuries meted out by the police and their ideological cheering squads, consolidate bonds. If the working groups and decision-making structures are only intermittently functional, they have created a sort of way of life. However outlandish that way of life may look to traditionalist outsiders, outlandishness is—to the core—proof that they are authentically resistant.

This inner core is not just a simple expression of a way of being. It represents its own intellectuality, struggling to find authentic resistance in a world whose rules and resources can be overwhelming. It's not just resistance that is distinctive.

The movement's core radicals were remarkably diverse, and even eclectic, but Gitlin (2012, 130–39) found their commitment to nonviolence foundational. I think he is right to argue that this nonviolence may have well been the movement's most effective posture, realized through peer pressure. It was not just rooted in strategy but in a genuine spirit that was always, potentially, at risk (113–21).

The knowledgeable foundations for this nonviolence deserve further study even with Gitlin's important contributions. Too often the nonviolence of social movements is treated as simply rational, or an expression of some popular will, rather than a reasoned and reflexive recognition of a movement's relation to power (Kennedy 2002a, 288–95). We are more likely to appreciate that recognition if we recognize the individuals who are part of the movement, whose intellectuality mattered.

Gitlin (2012, 66) found most of the activists quite earnest, and one might also say, both quite inspiring and inspired. He referenced Amin Husain:

A soft-spoken but burningly intense and eloquent Midwesterner from a poor Palestinian-American family, he spent years living in Ramallah, on the West Bank, where he became involved in the First Intifada and saw the inside of Israeli jails. He studied at Cambridge and Columbia Law School. Soon enough, he had graduated from dumpster-diving (during law school) to earning $185,000 a year, plus bonus, handling financial transactions and private equity (doing midsize deals, he told me, rattling off the figures "250 million to 1 billion") for the major corporate law firm Cravath, Swaine & Moore. This wasn't the life he wanted. He quit. The next thing he knew, he was living in

Budapest, listening to acid jazz, writing on napkins. Refashioning himself as a video and performance artist back in New York, during the Arab spring, he and Brooklyn artist friends put out "communiqués," leaflets drawn from Middle East newspapers with the headlines translated into English. He joined Occupy from day one. (150–51)

Husain reappears in Gitlin's volume, where he demonstrates the profound intellectuality with which he approaches the movement. He reflects on the movement's involvement in opposing foreclosures and evictions of people victimized by the predatory lending causing the housing bubble, and its tensions with broader revolutionary goals:

> "Everyone has to be less ambitious, less certain they're right. We are going to be what we want to see. That was the spirit that was powerful in Liberty Square during the first weeks." (Gitlin asks) Is this utopian? "This is not about utopia, but about empowering. It's like Tahrir Square saying: 'We will govern ourselves.' Imagination is what wins. You have to release people's potential." (183)

Husain expresses one of the most profound challenges for the movement: how the inner core and the outer ring of struggle against inequality's extension relate to one another. Gitlin's account of the relationship between the lobbying organization MoveOn and the Occupy movement illuminates.

While on the one hand, the organization supported, or used, the movement's radical critique, the movement distrusted the lobby "the way social democrats once fretted about the many-tentacled Communist Party" (Gitlin 2012, 148). Further,

> From a certain point of view, MoveOn's aid threatened the integrity of the horizontally organized community. That kind of success was corrosive. Recognition was a certificate of legitimacy from authorities who did not deserve their authority. The movement thrived on a sense of beautiful marginality, but rapture was attached to a sense of vulnerability, for it was good to be supported but bad to be trendy. It was good to be sought after, bad to be captive. It was good to be a community banded together in warm solidarity, bad to be smothered by hypocrites. (148)

Occupy's inner core was not wrong. Gitlin articulates this when he writes,

> If the last decades have demonstrated anything—indeed, if the history of American capitalism demonstrates anything—it is that the social

arrangement known by the God-term *the market* is perfectly content with vast inequalities. As for the political class, its reliance on big money inhibits, if it does not outright extinguish, whatever reform impulses well up from time to time. Given the power of money in politics, the political class is too inter-locked with lobbyists, Wall Street, and the rest of the corporate galaxy to care enough to take the political risks. Democratic vitality is both the prerequisite and the outcome of a continuing mobilization to make the conditions of life more decent and fair. (169–70)

Occupy recognized this dilemma of co-optation in its theory and practice. It struggled to develop ever more innovative practices to inspire new recruits and remind those beyond, symbolically, of the character of the struggle. They also worked to find direct ways, beyond changes in policies, to affect lives. This was most notable in the movement around lost housing; through a "movement of repossession, deforeclosure, and housing occupation," Occupy sought to find new ways to show their consequence (176). Movements must learn not just to grow but to survive.

Studies of social movements have become quite rigorous over the last three decades or so, and we are likely to see a bounty of works dedicated to the dynamics of the inner movement and its relationship to organizations of affinity. We should also attend to the ways in which this mobilized public transformed our sense of intellectuality and how its knowledgeable engage-ment might change our sense of the future. Well beyond Husain, Gitlin, and Stiglitz, Occupy has been an exceptionally knowledgeable movement, innova-tive in practice, in concept, and perhaps in consequence.

The Knowledgeability of the Occupy Movement

Although conventional intellectuals like Stiglitz may have inspired generally, and for the movement's core intellectuals, David Graeber may have been the most immediate scholar-in-sync, conventional intellectuals did not make the Occupy movement. The movement instead transformed them, based on an intellectuality around alternative media that empowered and extended the movement itself. Gitlin (2012, 24–25) explains:

> Occupy was not hanging on the mainstream imprimatur. The movement had its own media. A media team called Global Revolution provided a live stream video feed. One key member, Vlad Teichberg, a thirty-nine-year-old Russian immigrant

who had walked out of a lucrative job creating and trading derivatives on, yes, Wall Street, moved to what he described as "a hard-core anarchist punk house" in Brooklyn, thrown himself into antiwar video operations, gone to Madrid in the spring to do media with the *Indignados* encampment, and was rigging laptops so they could function as the movement's own video cameras. "The live stream is, in a way, the central nervous system of the entire operation," organizer Max Berger told *New York*'s John Heilemann. "Because in moments where the police have tried to fuck with us, it's our first line of defense. And it's been a big part of how we disseminate our information, raise the money, everything."

Teichberg was not alone. The man who estimated the three million supporters based on Facebook likes, Shen Tong, also left a job on Wall Street to add to the movement (28). This is a different kind of intellectuality, less dependent on external referees and validation, on credentials and distinction. It is an organic intellectuality, but without Gramscian pretense. It can be diminished by adjectives like *savvy*, but it is, perhaps, a more consequential intellectuality. Before we embrace the digital organic intellectual, however, we should consider how this mobilized public transformed knowledgeability.

Many individual faculty and students became an important part of Occupy knowledge production and dissemination by extending what they did in support of and articulation with the Occupy movement. They elaborated poetry and sculpture through its place; they gave lectures on the place of human rights across the world; they elaborated a more transformational understanding of capitalism.

Established academics also took the movement seriously. Some made it the focus of courses, while others used its mobilizations and rhetorics to develop alternative visions of the future. The Social Science Research Council, the network of networks seeking to mobilize knowledge for the public good, made the imagined alternative futures inspired by Occupy central to its work.[7] In short, the Occupy movement made some professional, policy, and critical sociologists, and social scientists, all more public.

Intellectuals were not the only actors transformed. Universities as such also provided support for Occupy. For example, New York University archived the deliberations of the Occupy movement think tank (B. McDonald 2012). While we saw individuals and some universities lending their scholarship to this public mobilization, the Occupy movement itself elevated the value of the university as such by allying explicitly with movements focused on universities and support for enrolled students.

FIGURE 4.2 Occupy LSX, January 12, 2012. Photograph by Michael D. Kennedy.

A number of "Occupy Universities" were also developing in major urban centers,[8] even if their reading lists were not so broad as what typically develops in conventionally credentialed universities. London developed this especially well. With its "Tent City University,"[9] the movement on the steps of St. Paul's Cathedral was especially dedicated to the value of higher learning (Walker 2012; Figure 4.2).

Beyond lectures and discussions, the Occupy movement supported libraries of interesting range. Although we might await the ethnographies of the movement to understand better how in practice these libraries functioned, their symbolic location in the Occupy movement's reconstruction of place showed that this was a movement not only dedicated to identifying problems. It was also ostensibly devoted to understanding better how the organization of knowledge produced the inequalities and injustices the movement highlights.

As the photographs indicate, the centrality of knowledge for these public mobilizations is not limited to the United Kingdom but is a central theme of

FIGURE 4.3 Occupy Wall Street, November 12, 2011. Photograph by Michael D. Kennedy.

the US mobilizations as well. Occupy Wall Street's library was symbolically important not only for its size and location but especially in the eviction of Zuccotti Square (Figure 4.3).

As one blogger recalled the tweets of the OWS librarians, "NYPD destroying American cultural history, they're destroying the documents, the books, the artwork of an event in our nation's history. . . . Right now, the NYPD are throwing over 5,000 books from our library into a dumpster. Will they burn them?" (Boog 2011).

At the same time, many in the Occupy movement protested the ways in which the costs of higher education has indebted so many, with poor labor markets making the indebted unable to find the work that would enable them to pay off their loans. The initial inner core of the OWS movement in fact included many recent college graduates outraged by the student loan debt they had and the job prospects they didn't (Gitlin 2012, 21; Figure 4.4).

Higher education figured prominently in the Occupy movement, and the Occupy movement figured increasingly prominently in the work of scholars.

FIGURE 4.4 Occupy Wall Street, November 12, 2011. Photograph by Michael D. Kennedy.

We would miss a critical public/university nexus if we considered only how the Occupy movement invoked higher education. Occupy also took place *through* higher education.

Mobilizing Publics through Higher Education

The defense of public universities through the Occupy movement articulates clearly concerns over the "neoliberal" university. In one essay on the Occupy Berkeley movement, a graduate student explained: "What's at the heart of the privatization is a bringing in of the market logic, and the kind of exploitations and the inequalities associated with the market . . . into parts of life and relationships that we used to see as parts of our responsibility as co-citizens" (Eidelson 2011). And the critiques spread around the opposition of neoliberalism and the public university.

Publics have become especially prominent in the rearticulation of higher education mainly because public support for universities has declined precipitously in the United States and much of Europe. My colleagues, especially from California, have written at length about what has happened in their home state, where the neoliberal challenge to the public university is most apparent not only in fiscal retrenchment but in active contest. Struggles to defend that public university, through its redefinition "as the place where maximum access is synthesized with the highest quality" (Newfield 2008, 272), are increasingly critical.[10]

Chris Newfield's simple expression of the public university is a terrific starting point, along with his observation that this is not a new contest. The assault on public higher education began in the 1970s just as "the American middle class was starting to become multiracial, and as public universities were moving with increasing speed toward meaningful racial integration" (Newfield 2008, 3). When Wendy Brown (2009) says that the privatization of higher education is about "narrowed access, expanded inequalities, destroyed shared purposes, devalued knowledge and research that is not entrepreneurial or applicable, research that is contoured toward corporate and away from public ends, constricted academic freedom, eroded shared governance, and education that is rich, deep, broad and critical radically eschewed," we are tempted to frame the relationship between publics and universities as one of common victimization before neoliberal assault and fiscal retrenchment.

This viewpoint extends across the world and is especially well developed in the United Kingdom, notably around a movement called the "Campaign for the Public University." In short, the Campaign's White Paper argues against "the application of a market model to higher education and emphasizing the social benefits and public value of universities over the private benefits to individuals and the economy" (Dawes 2011). At the same time, together with their sympathetic critics, they seek to move beyond the notion that the public university is just the antithesis of the "neoliberal university." From their argument, you might say that the public university is one dedicated to deepening and extending a more sustainable democracy, whereas the privatizing impetus turns the university into an extension of market logic. Figure 4.5 illustrates a possible contrast.

Embedded in this contrast is something Michael Burawoy (2012b) identifies as a "real utopia." Here, the culture of critical discourse (CCD), instead of privatizing logics or aspirations defined by external regulation, establishes priorities and decision making around them. Comparing publicly committed and privately animated universities is not, however, the only distinction offered in this moment of neoliberal/public contest. One might also consider how this core academic public has joined with other publics in the contest around neoliberal transformation.

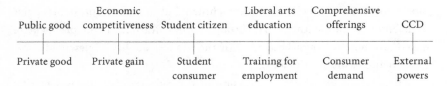

FIGURE 4.5 The cultural system distinguishing public from private university.

In the United Kingdom, but also more broadly (D. Greenberg 2012), the defense of the public university may have been sparked by increases in tuition and declining state funding, but it has morphed into something more. Publics are demanding greater transparency in politically accountable financial decisions (Dawes 2011). Student protests over increasing tuitions are joining with trade unions mobilizing over cuts to public expenditures, and the Occupy movement's more general critique of how inequality distorts democracy. And just as Occupy continues to innovate, so do the movements around public education, especially when the authorities of that public education abuse their control over the means of violence.

Although the use of illegitimate force by University of California, Davis security on November 18, 2011, is exceptional, the widely circulated image of the incident is now iconic. The image, itself part of the movement's transformation, shows a police officer shooting pepper spray at students resisting, nonviolently, orders to move. That officer, and the entire hierarchy to which he is responsible, came to be held accountable for misusing force in the assurance of security. Michael McQuarry (2011) describes how the exercise of arbitrary violence shifts the meaning of Occupy university movements away from questions of inequality toward another focus on the limits of accountability within universities themselves. It might also be a question of publics.

Police are, of course, critical to security, but the important question raised by the UC, Davis action, and others, is not only who is responsible but with whom campus police identify and why. The UC, Davis incident stimulated a nationwide discussion and turned attention toward another public mobilization that in fact preceded the Occupy Wall Street movement.

One of those discussions took place on November 22, 2011, when Ed Schultz, host of MSNBC's *The Ed Show*, declared that "everyone can learn something from the Madison police department and its handling of protests."[11] He went on to interview Madison, Wisconsin, police detective Brian Austin, a representative of the Madison Professional Police Officers Association.

FIGURE 4.6 Wisconsin firefighters mobilized in solidarity, February 16, 2011.
Photograph by Lucas W. Kennedy.

Austin spoke with pride about a mobilization in February and March 2011 of hundreds of thousands of people to defend collective bargaining rights for state employees (Figure 4.6). He indicated that there was no violence between police and protesters because there existed an open dialogue between them from the top of the hierarchy through the rank and file. Their harmony was facilitated in this instance because the 99 percent clearly included off-duty police officers, firefighters, teachers, and nurses, all of whose collective rights and unions were being threatened by newly elected Governor Scott Walker. When Governor Walker sought to evict those who occupied the State Capitol, off-duty police officers assured both safety and resistance because on-duty officers saw their comrades among the protesters.

Sagrans (2011) offers a terrific collection of essays and reflections on the movement to resist this bill. Wisconsin's lessons are better told by its activists and analysts, but the movement's explicit alliance with unions, notably of the public service sector and its police and firefighters, signaled not only a strong working-class base but also a challenge to authority that did not fall prey to discourses of disorder and dangers to public health or well-being.

Explicit, and abiding, support by neighboring (but not all) businesses also helped make clear that mobilization was not wrecking merchant liveli-hoods. In many ways, the rhetoric of solidarity so important to Occupy was quite real in Wisconsin and is something to be considered by the rest of Occupy movement and those who wish to elevate the publicness of universi-ties. And they might learn even more from the sociologists at the University of Wisconsin.

The Teaching Assistant Association of the University of Wisconsin, Madi-son was part of this mobilization from the start. Taylan Acar and colleagues (2011) provide an exceptionally interesting account of its first seventeen days and how the micropolitics of occupying the Capitol proceeded. It is fortunate that so many social scientists were involved in the mobilization, perhaps less for their contributions to its politics and more for how we might consider this movement's lessons for the future trajectories of the Occupy movement. For in those founding moments, the common class identification of teaching assistants with other state employees was the basis for an extraordinary mobi-lization. Higher education was not distinctive, as such, but the employees of higher education brought considerable resources to this labor movement with much broader aims.

In this example, one might find the real distinction of public universities in the Occupy movement: to the extent they share status or class identifica-tions with other state employees, the basis for a broader public mobilization against the politics of austerity becomes apparent. Wisconsin, some have argued, is the exemplar for the movement to defend public universities from the neoliberal assault. At the same time, we also need to recognize its general-izing limits.

Public universities are not the only sites of the Occupy movement. In fact, private universities have become quite important in them as well. Undergrad-uate Julie Pittman was one of the leading activists at Brown University. Apart from a few brief protests, she and other facilitators kept the university move-ment focused on Occupy Providence, even as the movement worked to figure "a stronger relationship between Brown and Providence" (Carr 2011). Staying off campus was a deliberate effort across some private university publics. In an interview for Duke University's *Chronicle*, Pittman reported, "Although it would have been easier to stage a protest on campus, discussing issues of eco-nomic justice and participatory democracy within the student body is not as powerful as engaging with community members about the issues. . . . There is a real difference between a very privileged university having a mini-occupation and us raising awareness, starting dialogue and encouraging people to be more involved with Occupy Providence" (Oshima 2011).

Duke University reporters interviewed Pittman to provide contrast, because Duke's Occupy movement was campus focused, even enjoying university administration support (Oshima 2011). Harvard's Occupy movement has also been campus focused, as one of its activists recalled: "We have pitched our tents precisely to make a case for a more open university, devoted not to its own profit and the reproduction of a social and technocratic elite, but to the benefit of the now-famous 99 percent" (Djagalov 2012).

When Occupy movements are limited to private university campuses, the contradictions of the private university and the public mission become apparent. Harvard, for instance, prohibited the public from entering its Yard, and the movement never quite managed to figure its relationship to staff on campus, especially janitors seeking better working conditions. That dilemma is unlikely on public university campuses, especially if students are themselves previously organized into a union, as teaching assistants were at the University of Wisconsin, Madison. And that begins to differentiate the story.

When we think about publics constituting higher education, we need to begin by thinking about how various segments of proximate publics relate to each other. On one end of the spectrum, we have public universities where faculty and students are unionized, sharing status with other laborers in a system. In that very constitution, they wind up making a public that is based less on university values and more on wage relations and the status so derived.

When we think about universities without faculty and student unions, those relationships across class demarcations within the core public are based less on status and more on certain communicative capacities. In some circumstances, students will support various kinds of staff in their efforts to improve their working conditions. In other circumstances, as at Harvard, these matters will become "too divisive" (Djagalov 2012). In this example, these mobilizations become more like publics than like classes because they are constituted as much by communication as by status. And when that happens, it's quite useful to think about publics alongside classes rather than collapsing them into a common problem of neoliberalism's assault on public goods.

Regardless of the distinctions made, there is one major substantive point to take away. These transformations of public knowledge are constituted by new and powerful partnerships in formation, developing through the mobilization of new publics in support of knowledge. These deserve more attention, but we should not assume that these mobilizations are always seeking to elevate the knowledge institutions themselves. We need a public sociology that not only identifies with civil society but can bring public values into the institutions. Public sociology is both critical to resistance and movements and vital for responsible institutional leadership.

Public Sociology with Institutional Responsibility

Burawoy is of course not the only proponent of public sociology.[12] In many ways, Craig Calhoun occupies a very similar intellectual space, both having worked from within prominent positions in American sociology to make both the critical and public sociological vectors more viable. They are also quite different from each other. This is evident in Calhoun's (2005, 360) concern with Burawoy demarcating public from professional, critical, and policy sociology, and by implication, making sociologists choose whether they stand with civil society, policy makers, a narrow band of professionals, or an even narrower band of those who believe themselves essential to the flicker of hope:

> Sociology will, I think, be very different if the ideal of the university as a public institution is not sustained. This is not only a matter of state vs. private funding, of course, but also of academic norms, of state regulation as distinct from funding, or the institutional forms private philanthropy takes on. We need to ask a whole complex of questions about what it means to serve the public good, how vital public communication is to this, and how different kinds of institutional supports shape both public communication within the community of scientists and communication between scientists and broader publics. The need for a stronger sociology of publics which Burawoy mentions (and which I endorse and even hope I help along) is vital not only for the project of understanding the other arenas into which sociology may be introduced, but the contexts of our own work. Good "professional" sociology is sustained not simply by formalized peer review at journals or funding agencies, but by a vital public communication among sociologists in which theories, methods, findings, and arguments can be debated. Indeed, peer review often limits debate, not least when it focuses more on the avoidance of errors than on the interest of arguments, but also when it encourages substituting

an apparently neutral abstract scale of "quality" for a more multifaceted and open engagement with different ideas.

Craig Calhoun has promoted a form of sociology in which the constitution of publics around issues has become central. Their critical evaluation becomes possible due to his embrace of a Habermasian normative problematic that allows for the articulation of institutional responsibility in more nuanced fashion. Calhoun (2001b, 162) conceives publics as

> self-organizing fields of discourse in which participation is not based primarily on personal connections and is always in principle open to strangers. A public sphere comprises an indefinite number of more or less overlapping publics, some ephemeral, some enduring, and some shaped by struggle against the dominant organization of others. Engagement in public life establishes social solidarity partly through enhancing the significance of particular categorical identities and partly through facilitating the creation of direct social relations. Beyond this, however, the engagement of people with each other in public is itself a form of social solidarity. This engagement includes, but is not limited to, rational-critical discourse about affairs of common concern. Communication in public also informs the sharing of social imaginaries, ways of understanding social life that are themselves constitutive of it. Both culture and identity are created partly in public action and interaction. An element of reasoned reflection, however, is crucial to the idea of choice as a dimension of this form of solidarity—to the distinction of public culture from the simple expression of preexisting identity.

Like the other contributors to his 1993 edited volume, Calhoun can only celebrate the multiplication of publics that flow from the criticism of Habermas's then relatively integrated sensibility. Calhoun's (1995) commitment to the challenge of difference, and his desire to confront the possibility of incommensurability among publics, identifies a major and still unreconciled problem in Habermas's work, one to which Calhoun points.

This irresolution rests on Calhoun's distance from postmodern pessimisms and his enduring commitment to the search for that self-correcting sensibility animating the enduring enlightenment project, a commitment he shares with Habermas. His general and abiding interest in the ways in which solidarities and differences are reconciled in better and worse ways through publics animates his work.

This kind of approach is recognizably Habermasian, but it also owes a great deal to Hannah Arendt. Calhoun wants to emphasize that publics are not only about communication but also about performance; not only about decision making but also about identity formation. With Arendt, he wants to think about public spaces as places for free action and critical judgment, whose relationship is not close to being adequately understood (Calhoun and McGowan 1997, 14). We should also be able to understand better the conditions under which publics might make better decisions and facilitate resistance to evil (20).

We can clearly see Calhoun's scholarly agenda. He asks that we (1) consider the conditions under which solidarities of various kinds of groups are formed; (2) assess the ways in which these groups, internally, replicate the conditions of open and free public discussion elevated by Habermas, but whose performative and formative dimensions are noted by Arendt; and (3) consider the ways in which these groups might, on the basis of their own reflexive dispositions and communicative competencies, move more independently from systemic needs; in order (4) to consider how well these various publics might, in articulation with various powers, recognize and address needs near and far. And with this, he opens up the question of institutional responsibility.

Through his own institutional leadership, Calhoun has elaborated that quest in a number of ways. As president of the Social Science Research Council, Calhoun moved the organization to consider the relationship between intellectual and institutional responsibility and security head-on, in both conventional (e.g., Calhoun, Price, and Timmer 2002) and electronic publications.[13]

Calhoun also has engaged in substantial fashion as an individual scholar and an institutional leader in the response to the "Minerva Research Initiative" undertaken by the US Department of Defense. That, in turn, spurred a substantial amount of discussion in a variety of academic settings. The American Anthropological Association has been especially prominent in the discussion, and the Social Science Research Council, under Calhoun's leadership, sought to facilitate a more multidisciplinary discussion.[14] Calhoun's own account reflects the deep faith he has in the power of critical reason and the responsibilities of intellectuals to engage their institutions. His commitment to normative questions is apparent in his questions about the proposed new relationship between the academy and the military. He writes that a new normative framework is needed to guide relationships between civilian academics and the military. The implicit normative framework in place fifty years ago was violated by Project Camelot and similar operations and is discredited as well as outmoded. The arguments underway will not be very fruitful so long as they are simply for or against cooperation with the military or taking funding from the military. It is important, rather, to work out a good and open understanding of how such cooperation might work, what risks are entailed, what are the warning signs of problems, and what to do about them. Conversely, there should be an understanding of the opportunities and the conditions on which those opportunities are extended. Suspicions won't vanish overnight. They will be alleviated by the experience of successful collaborative work based on mutual respect, including better understanding of differences of perspective. Normative issues arise not only in direct relationships between military funders and civilian researchers, but also in relationships among academics. For example, what are the appropriate obligations between advisors and graduate students? How should military funding be considered in tenure reviews? When a large-scale project is organized as a consortium, how should differences among its participants be addressed? What are the implications of Pentagon funding for efforts to build relationships with researchers in other countries? (Calhoun 2010b, 1102)

While many intellectuals can avoid these questions, given their lack of or resistance to the assumption of institutional responsibility, their institutions become implicated much more easily, if not necessarily.[15] Intellectuals who lead knowledge institutions must develop a much more critical disposition on such matters.

Calhoun himself moved to assume the leadership of the London School of Economics and Politics after an instance of failed institutional responsibility. Money from the Qaddafi family called into question the institutional integrity of the school, dragging down several notable intellectuals' statuses with it. Typical of his style, Calhoun poses the question as something not just a matter of moral responsibility but one of public sociological sense and core intellectual mission:

Clarity about core intellectual mission is vital. This does not mean that universities should be insular, or even that their work should be useful only in long-term and indirect ways. Universities can provide immediately practical knowledge; this is the most important way for them to have a short-term impact. And as intellectual communities that pursue, share, and respect knowledge, universities can also play other roles. A museum exhibition can attract audiences and promote tourism. An architecture school can help solve urban design problems. But the most important contributions do not come in short-term, instrumental projects; they come as the result of longer-term academic work. This is true for the eventual impact of fundamental research, but it is also true in a number of other ways. Ties formed among intellectuals can solidify relations between nations; knowledge shared can improve the efficiency of bureaucracies or markets; social science can inform the quality of public debates and public policy. But for serious intellectual work to thrive, it cannot be entirely governed by instrumental outcomes. This is a distinction of universities from for-profit businesses and governments. Unfortunately, many funding agencies—even public funding agencies—forget this as they seek to impose short-term, instrumental impact assessments on universities. (Calhoun 2012a, 28–29)

The story here is about compromise occasioned by elites with crashing legitimacy following revolutions and civil war. However, the matter is not entirely different from other occasions when extra-scholarly interests compromise intellectual integrity or the integrity of institutions associated with intellectual legitimacy. The importance of keeping focus on this core mission is, therefore, all the more important in regard to public engagement. But universities must be clear about what they mean concerning publics.

The Publics of the University

Drawing on my knowledge of one of the leading US "public universities," the University of Michigan, I have proposed that all universities consider the kinds of publics they constitute with their own communicative action.[16] The most obvious is the core academic public, evident in the first cell in Table 4.1, which is also the most familiar to the discussion of the public university. The entire argument about excellence and accessibility refers most readily to this core public of students and the alumni who were once in that company. Their association is voluntary, thus implying that "public" quality in ways that faculty and staff association is not, given their status as employees. That point introduces an important question of stratification within publics.

Faculty are certainly constitutive of that core academic public given their contributions to its communicative sensibilities. Here, through faculty

TABLE 4.1 Proximate university publics and their articulations

Academic values	Public as context	Public as partner
1. Core publics among campus faculty, students, staff, and alumni	2. University as employer, investor, culture provider, and contractor	3. Service learning and scholarship in civic engagement

assemblies of various sorts, they form a real, active, and potentially mobilizing public. Students are similarly capable, even though they don't always have the cultural capital in claims making. When they become alumni, they can have more capital, if not always cultural, in augmenting their influence.

University administrations typically invoke these publics to promote or justify certain directions. They often treat these publics as rather "thin," as constituencies to be addressed and referenced and only ritually engaged. Crisis can prompt new public engagements and new formulations of the public good for the university. They are not always enduring, and sometimes fleeting. Brown University faced just such a crisis in the fall of 2013, though we do not know yet the consequence of that contest.

The Taubman Center for Public Policy invited former police commissioner of New York City Raymond Kelly to give the endowed Noah Krieger Memorial Lecture on October 29. He intended to speak, in his words, on "proactive policing."[17] A substantial number of students protested that event, claiming that such tactics depended on racist profiling. They, according to some, shut down the lecture. That action, in turn, prompted a storm of discussion on whether Brown University supported free speech or not (Jaschik 2013). It also, however, prompted important discussion on how race and class shape the terms in which freedom of speech is itself considered (e.g., Khalek et al. 2013).

This debate engaged the proximate public, including its alumni. For instance, Elizabeth Castelli (class of 1979) wrote to the university's president that this was not a matter of free speech but of endorsing a practice those in New York recognize to be racist.[18] And the matter went global. In the *Guardian*, Doreen St. Felix (2013), one of the protesters, elaborated the movement's trajectory, not only the shutdown of speech. She also challenged the claim that Brown was functioning only as a neutral space allowing for the free exchange of ideas. Instead, she said, the university is "deeply enmeshed within that structure of systemic injustice. Discourse facilitated, legitimized, and moneyed by the few in power is not true 'discourse' at all."

In this contest, we come to appreciate the importance of open public discussion within universities and the challenge of assuming an even playing field for that discussion. Were it not for the donations establishing the lecture and the informal networks that facilitated Ray Kelly's invitation to Brown, the matter would never have been broached. Were Brown's protesting students and Providence allies not connected with publics considered victimized by stop-and-frisk in New York City, they would not have experienced such a visceral reaction to Ray Kelly's invitation. Understanding free speech is critical, but so too is the way in which inequalities are built into that very constitution of debate.

However, we should also consider how this debate reflects the stratification of Brown University's core proximate public itself. In this contest, we see only those communicatively privileged—faculty, students, academic administrators, and alumni. Staff are often, depending on rank, among the least privileged in public discussions, although there are circumstances, events, in which they become publicly prominent.[19]

To a considerable degree, the discourse about privatizing the public university has been about transforming the qualities of publicness *within* the university, even if that has rarely extended to treatment of nonfaculty staff. If the defense of the public university involves changes in labor contracts, and those contracts involve both staff and academic classes, then the quality of publics becomes more egalitarian and less academically hierarchical. And we can see that happening across the world today.

This is not a simple class conflict, however, given that the knowledge dimensions of the contest are not only expressed in terms of class consciousness and its associated hegemonies and counter-hegemonies. They are also expressed with respect for a deeper concern for what we know, how we know it, what purposes that knowledge serves, and what publics that knowledge engages. The core academic public, then, has different contours depending on the character of the academic institution, but it is on the front lines of defining the terms of the public. Other publics also have a critical stake in that definition.

"Public as context" in Table 4.1 is also a familiar part of the privatizing public university articulation. Here, contributions of the university to its immediate environs' well-being are made, and the boundaries of publics identified. The most immediate and obvious public is that which is legislated: the preferential status of a public university's citizens within the state in

TABLE 4.2 Proximate public articulations of university value

	Individual goods	Public goods
Economic values	1. Value of degree for career	2. Contributions to local economy
Justice values	3. Accessibility to disadvantaged	4. Contributions to local public good
Symbolic values	5. Status by association	6. Public goods made through partnership

admission and tuition, with the presumption that one is training citizens for the state's future good.[20]

That core proximate public can be demanding. And in some circumstances, it is in terrific need. To build on the tabular sensibilities I have already introduced, one might introduce distinctions within this "public as context" (Table 4.2). These distinctions are not hard and fast, of course, but they do signal some important differences. First, we see the most common notion of university value: how it contributes to an individual's career. What is a degree "worth"? Second, we move toward a more collective articulation of that point by asking how the institution as such contributes to the economic well-being of its local context.

Third and fourth, we move beyond economic questions to broader notions of public goods. We also can consider the degrees to which individuals of limited means, having faced difficult circumstances, are able to gain access to and succeed in that university. One of the best indicators of this in US universities is the percentage of students receiving Pell Grants, and here, Rutgers shines as a public university fulfilling its mission (D. Greenberg 2012). On a more collective level, one can also consider how a university's presence in a community contributes to the qualities of life for those beyond it—in health, cultural opportunities, and other public goods.[21]

Fifth and sixth, we consider more active engagements. I have in mind the value of sports teams for the fifth cell: while they have economic benefits to a locale, and they might offer some public goods, their significance for the public goes beyond consumption into a powerful public (sports fan) identification with the university. My own time at the University of Michigan leads me to wonder not only how able university administrators are prey to the commercial pressures of college sports but also how they can turn the loyalties made in places like the Big House (Michigan's football stadium) into pride for the ways in which the university can lead in the halls of the Supreme

Court. Of course, the obverse can also be true.[22] We need not consider only the moneymaking sports, however.

One of the most exceptional initiatives for sports extending the proximate public good takes place through wrestling. Although it is a national movement, I have watched, and learned from my students' research, how "Beat the Streets Providence" builds grit among the less privileged middle school students it brings into the sport.[23] That Brown University and other Rhode Island higher education wrestling teams actively support the initiative indicates just how much can be done, with relatively few resources, in that articulation of knowledge, sports, and public engagement.[24]

That last example and the sixth cell of the table invite consideration of another identification that can also take place through partnership in the making of public goods. Most universities have this kind of outreach; Brown University's Swearer Center for Public Service exemplifies that sense of partnership.[25] This kind of partnership need not be the focus of a particular university center, however. It can also become part of a university's core commitment, where a public becomes something more than context for university work, so in Table 4.2 I refigured "public" to distinguish public as context and public as partner. This is a vital distinction, especially when you consider how different private universities engage their proximate publics.

Brown University won national attention in 2012 for the criticisms various public leaders of Providence offered the university and its measure of support for the city (Kiley 2012). It also became a center point of the local public sphere. On February 2, 2012, reflecting on Providence's proximity to bankruptcy, the local paper reported on its front page that, among other things, the city's mayor "is seeking higher payments from the city's tax-exempt institutions, especially Brown University" (Mooney and Pina 2012). It was not just a matter of elite negotiations. Passions flamed. The chief of the firefighters union, Paul Doughty, said, "I think Brown's actions are particularly disgusting" (Soens 2012). The local paper went on to elaborate why, with Brown's $2.5 billion endowment, there is such fury: "Brown, whose voluntary and property tax payments are currently less than $4 million, owns property worth more than $1 billion. If fully taxed, city officials say the Ivy League school would have to pay more than $38 million annually. Doughty said Brown should realize if Providence fails, so does Brown because 'who wants to go to a college in the middle of Detroit?'" (Mooney and Pina 2012). That last question not only fails to endear the man to people like me who have spent a good deal of time in southeast Michigan but also connotes other troubling comparisons. Nevertheless, it anticipated mobilization.

During the university's next corporation (board of governors) meeting, firefighters picketed the university to protest its failure to support the city (Soens 2012). Brown University students added their voice to the protest, with one student saying, "I am ashamed that my university is making residents in Providence feel like their very real economic realities are not our problem. And, I'm deeply troubled by our failure to recognize that the members of the Brown community are also, and more importantly, members of the Providence community" ("Students Press Brown" 2012). Building on that student's dismay, even a neighborhood paper, the *East Side Monthly*, got into the mix, challenging the university's president, Ruth Simmons: "Simmons, as a former board member of Goldman Sachs, Pfizer and the like, comes with almost overpowering big vision credentials. The corporation board that runs the school certainly boasts world class credentials in terms of fundraising and networking, though likely it doesn't know very much about the 'real' Providence, nor perhaps really cares" ("Looking Ahead at Brown" 2012).

As the negotiations between the city and the university continued, the sense that Brown is a "city on a hill" risked implying something more than its lofty intellectual status. Indeed, Brown's relatively poor relationship to Providence was made even more starkly problematic by the contributions Harvard (M. McDonald 2012) and other Ivy League institutions made. Brown and the Providence mayor finally figured a mutually satisfactory agreement before Ruth Simmons's successor came on board (Pina 2012).[26]

During those days, Brown worked hard to communicate how it contributes to its local public good. On February 15, 2012, the principal splash of its website's home page was dedicated to how Brown's building construction is partnering with a broader effort to create job opportunities for disadvantaged residents of the state. Featuring "Marc Nixon, a construction laborer working on Brown's new aquatics and fitness center," his "career success story" becomes an example of how "Brown is one of Rhode Island's biggest participants in Building Futures, an initiative that helps workers like Nixon move into careers in the construction trade" (Baum 2012). Its alumni and supporters also have been moved to the public realm. Also featured on its home page, Charlie Kroll (2012), chief executive of a software firm and Brown graduate, wrote to the local news,

As the chief executive of Andera, a venture-capital-funded technology company based in Providence, I am particularly concerned that the terms of any agreement not impede Brown's ability to be a strong and vibrant partner in the Knowledge District. During highly visible and polarizing public squabbles such as these, it is important to reflect on the value that an institution such as Brown provides to our city and state. . . . Brown pays $4 million in voluntary and property-tax payments annually to Providence. Even more valuable to our city and state are the activities taking place inside these buildings—scientific research and technological innovation, the search for treatments to conditions from autism to Alzheimer's, and the hope for future economic growth and jobs. Brown is an engine for growth. . . . While elected officials have sought to quantify Brown's value to Providence—with taxation as the motivation—Brown's contributions offer tremendous value, from the community it supports to the people it attracts to our great city. Burdensome taxation, from the city or the state, could be counterproductive.

Brown's story was not unusual, however. In anticipation of concerns over university contributions to the public good, university administrations typically have data on how universities contribute to the proximate economy (Brophey and Godsil 2009). In fact, Brown drew on a consulting firm to develop a systematic representation of how it stimulates the economy, develops human capital, contributes to both research and development and community, all with an eye toward Rhode Island's economic future.[27]

In this portrait, Providence and environs benefit principally from Brown's work in derivative fashion. Public engagement can also be a major source of focus, as Philadelphia has become for the University of Pennsylvania. That university conceives itself as an "anchor institution." In fact, it hosts a broader network with that ambition. The Anchor Institutions Task Force is premised on the following:

New Institutions have stepped forward as the "anchors" of their communities, particularly institutions of higher education and academic medical centers— "Eds and Meds" . . . these institutions, "by reason of mission, invested capital, or relationships to customers or employees, are geographically tied to a certain location." As such, they have a strong economic stake in the health of their surrounding communities and—due to the scale and scope of their operations (over seven million employees and $1 trillion in annual economic activity) the resources to make a genuine difference. (Brophey and Godsil 2009, 148)

Their network is composed of an intriguing variety of university representatives from presidents to center directors, across a wide range of schools. It makes proposals for federal, state, and local government partnerships with universities and medical institutions and also demonstrates the kinds of things that universities can do on their own to make a difference. For example, it outlines the ways in which the University of Pennsylvania, by changing its purchasing strategies, had substantial effects on West Philadelphia local economies. It discusses how the University of Cincinnati joined four other nonprofit employers to create new affordable housing in the city's Uptown neighborhoods. And it talks about how Syracuse University has become a cultural catalyst for new kinds of collaborations between the university and the city's arts and cultural institutions.

Before becoming chancellor of Syracuse University, Nancy Cantor was one of the most ardent supporters of the publicness of the University of Michigan during her time as its provost. At Syracuse she redefined that university's soul, some would say, in her effort to admit more students of lesser means, making grades rather than SAT scores more important along the way. As one commentator noted, under her leadership "Syracuse's spending on need-based aid increased to $131.5-million from $49.9-million between 2004 and 2011. Meanwhile, the proportion of minority students in each incoming class has risen to 31.7 percent from 18.5 percent; and the proportion of Syracuse students who qualify for Pell Grants has increased to 28.3 percent this year from 19.7 percent" (Hoover 2011). Diversity clearly mattered for Chancellor Cantor, and if diversity enhances collective learning, as the University of Michigan advocated, Syracuse opportunities came to be much greater than they were previously.

Even while this commitment to collective learning was apparent, those who make the argument face recurrent challenge, evident in the dilemma Cantor (2007) spelled out:

> On one hand, in the global knowledge economy, the return on investment for education has never been greater or more important to future health and prosperity. On the other hand, the fierceness of individual competition for a leg up in the knowledge economy has, at least in this country, weakened the collective will for social justice and social mobility, just at a time when access to education for, and economic empowerment of, an increasingly diverse population looms most paramount.

Chancellor Cantor went well beyond the defense of diversity within higher education to argue that excellence is also elaborated in public engagement.

Her effort to link Syracuse university capacities to its local environs was exemplified by the way in which she inaugurated her term at the university. She made a year-long inquiry, "University as Public Good: Exploring the Soul of Syracuse," in which she emphasized "neighborhood revitalization, education in the community and partnering in economic development, past and present" (Cantor 2007). Through it, she laid the groundwork for a public mission view private universities could imagine, and that many public universities typically consider. And that mission continued over her tenure as chancellor.

Although other universities and leaderships have endeavored to make public engagement a hallmark, few have realized so much, so quickly, as Syracuse University. Not everyone praised this effort. Some argued that this public engagement came at the same time as a drop in the rankings Syracuse enjoys. The *Chronicle of Higher Education* channeled some of that sentiment:

> Syracuse is slipping relative to its peers, at least according to the rankings by *U.S. News & World Report*. Syracuse fell from a high of 40th among national universities in the late 1990s to No. 62 this fall, and earned a place on the magazine's list of "A-plus options for B students." The average SAT scores of Syracuse's students are lower than those at the public flagship universities in the state, including the State University of New York campuses at Binghamton and Stony Brook—both of which admit a smaller proportion of applicants than Syracuse does, yet cost less than half the price for out-of-state students. Syracuse's incoming freshmen also have lower SAT scores than do students at urban institutions like Boston University, the University of Pittsburgh, and George Washington University. (R. Wilson 2011)

Here, then, the discourse of excellence becomes the neutral index from which to judge the value of public engagement. Indeed, much as these rankings are used to undermine the public quality of UK institutions, they were also deployed to challenge Chancellor Cantor's vision and commitment. She replied in powerful ways, elevating the significance of this public engagement:

> At issue here is why Syracuse University should care about our home city, when our scholars appropriately have their sights set on disciplinary questions and professional networks spread across the nation and globe, far away from Syracuse, N.Y., and when popular college rankings disregard the value of scholarly public engagement. And why should SU enroll more students, more diverse students, from more places, when those same rankings actually

reward universities for the number of students they reject, not reach? (Cantor 2011b)

Cantor has been developing this message for quite some time. She has argued that university rankings fail to take into account this very publicness:

> Unfortunately, in our view, most, if not all, of the metrics emphasized (even lionized) in these rankings stand fully to the side of, and sometimes directly in conflict with, the efforts that we and many other colleges and universities are embracing to be places of opportunity that optimize impact and reach and thus serve our country's future. At the very moment when voices are being raised all across our country to ensure our national competitiveness by educating the broadest, most diverse population we've ever had, *U.S. News* rewards institutions for the number of students whom they can reject, not for whom they reach; for keeping their student bodies small and elite; for using merit aid to recruit the highest SAT students, by necessity missing some students whose toughness and resolve will serve them and us well in the test of time. (Cantor 2011a)

This very tension, between public engagement and scholarly excellence, can be portrayed as an "either-or." Precisely because of Chancellor Cantor's leadership, however, the question of how publics matter to the private university came to be central to her university's definition.

Where the mission of the Anchor Institution Task Force, and previous conceptions of local public engagement, seem to differ is in the relationship between publics and universities. Here, rather than posing the university as a contributor to local public well-being, it becomes a conscious and deliberate partner in creating public goods that extend the university's scholarly value.

In most discussions of publics and the university, we remain with the relatively immediate—whether core or proximate, and whether treated as employee, contractor, context, or partner. But for the ambitious university, or perhaps even for the future-realistic university, the public can't be local. It must be global, much as scholarship can't, or shouldn't, remain ethnocentric.

Global Public Universities

Both public sociologists I have discussed—Craig Calhoun and Michael Burawoy—are quite global in their reference. Burawoy's ethnographies have taken him to Zambia, the United States, Hungary, and Russia, and with his work as

president of the International Sociological Association, he regularly articulates how sociology travels. Calhoun's early attention to Britain and France
flowed quite directly from his first book (Calhoun 1982), offering a much more
communicative and community-centered interpretation of the making of the
English, and secondarily, French working classes. His fortuitous presence in
Beijing in 1989 led to a number of publications about social movements and
the public sphere in China (Calhoun 1989b, 1994). Not only did he contribute to the global historicity of that movement. By extension, he enhanced
the range of democracy's meanings produced in social transformations and
helped draw our attention to the global public sphere's very constitution of an
apparently local movement itself.

Calhoun's institutional leadership and concern for universities as knowledge institutions has also led him to be especially concerned for how the
global reach of knowledge production and distribution needs to be considered, leading him once again to pose the problem in sociological terms:

> First, a growing number of academic institutions seek to work effectively on a
> global scale. This raises a plethora of complex ethical and practical questions in
> settings where administrators and most academics face shortages of information.
> Second, nearly all universities and many individual researchers must search for
> new resources in the face of cuts in public budgets and in the context of intensi-
> fied competition. This puts pressure on those who must decide which funds to
> pursue or accept. Third, academic social scientists are rightly concerned to make
> their work useful. But problems arise when this is pursued through arrangements
> that either close knowledge to the public or potentially distort it by harnessing it
> to the projects of specific clients. Public social science is generally preferable, but
> problems also arise when this is approached as a matter of media comments only
> weakly related to scholarly research. (Calhoun 2012a, 10)

These concerns reflect the point of his article about the relations of universities to the kinds of risks that faced the London School of Economics and its
relationship to the wealth and power of Libya's Qaddafi family. While in that
instance we might focus more on elite linkages, it is also important to think
about these global ties in more public terms. And with that, I build on Table
4.1 with Table 4.3.

The core public of every university is most obvious, but the global public
associated with global excellence and rankings follows close behind, especially
for the most ambitious universities. The fourth cell of Table 4.3 is similar to

TABLE 4.3 University publics, proximity, and articulations

Academic values	Public as context	Public as partner
Proximate and obvious		
1. Core publics among campus faculty, students, staff, and alumni	2. University as employer, investor, culture provider, and contractor	3. Service learning and scholarship in civic engagement
Distant requiring justification		
4. Global excellence and global rankings	5. Global problems and policy making	6. Partnerships with publics of choice

the first in that both invoke academic excellence. They are also radically different. The first cell is made up of an active, thick public, whereas in the latter, we have excellence without community. Or at least if publics are invoked, these are typically "thin" rather than "thick," to invoke Michael Burawoy's (2005b) distinction between passive and imagined publics and active publics more engaged in constituting meaning.

Here, whether in providing one's faculty syllabi to consumers across the world or making one's library virtually accessible to scholars elsewhere, universities reach global scholarly publics. They simultaneously enhance communicative rationality in various academic milieus and build their own reputation for excellence to the extent their resources are used well. But this public responsibility, readily identified as global, is without interaction of consequence.

The fifth and especially sixth cells are typically the least populated within universities, but together with the fourth, definitive of the kind of global reach universities enjoy. They are rarely, however, considered in public terms. They could be. After all, many universities already claim to tackle "world problems," but the critical discursive rationale for that selection is rarely evident. Publics are even less frequently apparent in problem choice.

Sometimes, however, the public itself can drive the agenda rather than be found once the research problem is identified. This is more likely to happen when one has the equivalent of the proximate public: when distant publics are themselves contractually or morally implicated in a university's life. I have discussed some of these examples from the University of Michigan previously:

The anti-sweatshop movements that have engaged U-M and other universities for at least the last decade illustrate the ways in which the principles of the proximate public can inspire longer distance solidarities. In response to student movement pressures (Anonymous 1999), U-M created a Labor Standards

and Human Rights Committee composed of faculty and students expert in
these affairs to "provide advice concerning University policies and procedures
to address labor issues in the production of U of M goods (items sold with
the University of Michigan's name, logos, or other symbols)" and to ensure
that corporations engaged in the manufacture of licensed goods, bearing the
University of Michigan name and/or logos, are not engaged in unlawful or
unconscionable labor practices.

Claims to social justice can motivate public engagements even when there are
no existing exchange relationships, but are inspired by historical ties. This is most
powerfully illustrated by the events following charges Patrick Tierney offered in
the winter of 2001, before the publication of his book "Darkness in El Dorado." He
suggested in private correspondence that two US academics, including one U-M
faculty member, "intentionally caused or intensified a deadly measles epidemic
among the Yanomami in 1968." The academic community quickly refuted those
charges, and Tierney modified his book. However, the U-M went further to dismiss the subsequently published book in its entirety. After protest from its faculty
and students, the provost's office then acknowledged that while its concern for the
integrity of its faculty member and his research was important, it was also incon-
sistent with academic practice to settle complex scholarly questions with administrative decisions. With then Provost Nancy Cantor's support, U-M anthropologist Fernando Coronil initiated an extended discussion with faculty and students
from Michigan and Brazil on the production of knowledge and the university's
obligation to those indigenous peoples it engages in that research (Coronil 2001).
In each of the cases identified above, the university did not quite choose its public,
but was, by claims of social justice and its potential implication in an injustice,
obliged to engage certain publics to which the university, as actor, had an obligation. (Kennedy 2011c)

Are there examples in the sixth cell on which we can draw? Of course, and
these tend to be raised by faculty with extended commitments in that world
area. Sometimes these are relatively simple—who would not identify with
the Polish Round Table Negotiations of 1989? And sometimes they are challenging—the horrors of 1915 in Anatolia, and whether we can identify that as
genocide, as Armenians would insist, and the official discourse of the Turkish
state would reject. These were my examples in that piece published in 2011,
finished in 2008. But in 2012, one can draw on radically different examples of
how global solidarity, without obligations of membership, might develop. In
fact, that was already apparent in 2011 in the Madison mobilization.

The Wisconsin Winter was, as the Sagrans (2011) collection illustrates, directly tied to the Arab Spring, at least in the minds of many of its activists. At the same time, Kamal Abbas, the general coordinator of Egypt's Center for Trade Unions and Workers Services, also offered on February 21, 2011, his own statement of solidarity with the Wisconsin movement (Sagrans 2011, 136–37). Alexander Hanna, a sociology graduate student at University of Wisconsin–Madison conducting research on the Egyptian mobilizations found, after returning to his university home from Tahrir Square, that direct comparisons diminished the real significance of what was happening in Egypt (146–49). And certainly the solidarity that might be offered in Madison mattered little for what would happen in Cairo. Nevertheless, that global solidarity promise has developed far beyond what the Madison activists could have imagined.

The publicly engaged global university might figure a way to develop a meaningful solidarity with that distant public. It might develop a real partnership with a public that is not looking to address a parallel problem but to identify how we are variously implicated in chains of injustice and inequality that can be studied, and with greater analytical clarity, perhaps acted upon with greater consequence.

And this is where Burawoy's global public sociology comes in, for it is highly unlikely that knowledge institutions will engage these global issues with distant publics as unmediated partners. Instead, one needs to figure the global intellectual networks that mobilize those public issues into academic questions whose address might make a difference in both academic and public terms. Those networks establish not only what is studied but where it is engaged. Articulation is, after all, also a matter of recognition.

Articulating, and Recognizing, Publics

The elevation of publics in knowledge is revolutionary, not just because it requires that we ask the reflexive question about knowledge for whom and for what but also because it obliges us to consider relationships made in that pursuit. And when we consider those engagements, we are made more aware of the inequalities realized through different validations of knowledge. Consider, for example, Michael Burawoy's global course, "Public Sociology, Live!"[28]

In classes across the world—in Teheran, Barcelona, Johannesburg, Kyiv, São Paulo, Oslo, Berkeley—sociologists watch the course and then summarize each class's discussion on the group Facebook page,[29] which in turn moves discussion across them. Already particular publics are chosen to globalize this public sociology, but this particular intervention has many antecedents, and even extensions. One of them focused on the world region in which I have worked and a knowledge network of which I have been a part.

In March 2012, Burawoy joined scholars from the Academic Fellowship Program to discuss the dilemmas of globalizing public sociology.[30] Drawing on different sociologists participating in his virtual course, Burawoy developed the ways in which public sociology must attend to the very different qualities of publics in different situations. In some places, as in Spain where Ramon Flecha and Marta Soler develop their "critical communicative methodology," power is present but not likely deadly. In other circumstances, like what Nandini Sundar faces in India, or what Cesar Rodriquez-Garavito addresses in Colombia, public sociology must deal directly with how warring militias shape the conditions for public dialogue and the role intellectuals play in bringing scholarship to bear. Different publics thus generate different dilemmas for sociology's development.

In some places, for example, public sociology needs to defend professional sociology's own autonomy and development, Burawoy argued. It's not only in cases where the state intrudes; he also worries that activism itself can smother sociology's realism and distract it from the constraints facing social change. This likely disarms many professional sociologists who equate public sociology with activism. More important, however, is how this public sociology mission shapes solidarity around sociology.

Burawoy's concerns about protecting sociology's intellectual independence and rigor both from elites and from activism provide a clear foundation for developing global solidarity around sociology's cultivation. At the same time, such a formulation could leave the discipline's normative foundations trapped in a professional domain ignorant of the variety of contextual challenges facing scholarly choices.

In conditions where emancipatory movements are clear, and reactionary forces are globally recognized, the normative dilemma hardly appears. In his own case, Burawoy recalled the ease with which public sociology could identify with empowering the anti-apartheid movement. It did not have to worry about convincing reactionary Afrikaners about where truth lay. In the post-communist world, however, choices are rarely so clear-cut. Indeed, choices made elsewhere often lead us to consider only some dilemmas worthy of global engagement, while others are left as particular instances best addressed locally and overlooked globally. However, by rethinking public sociology, we might also rethink this global inequality by foregrounding this problem: What method do we use for recognizing publics beyond the proximate?

That rethinking will also require a new sense of public responsibility that goes well beyond a disciplinary conversation. It will take a reflexive surge, one that has been locally energized by public mobilizations like those discussed in this chapter. Public mobilizations can, after all, change these manners of knowledge management.

Intellectuals are, of course, free and even obliged to ask questions about public engagement, but with the professionalization of knowledge and its purchase through commodification and celebrity lists, the reflexive injunction can be lost. Universities are also free and obliged to pose these questions, but the interlocutors can be put safely into their cubbyholes where academic freedom is preserved and the consequences of discussion managed.

The Occupy movement began to move these questions in powerful ways. It is likely to continue. It probably won't be apparent in its core expression but in various spin-offs. Its descendants may pose new challenges for the relationship between knowledge and change, especially in the address of inequality. That movement will go further if public sociology informs the spirit of civil society and shapes the disposition of institutional leaders in politics and universities. The movement around public knowledge is, therefore, itself transformative. It brings the public value of intellectuality more centrally into the heart of knowledge cultures, in both theory and practice. The very notion of "anchor institutions" reflects the potential for just that synergy. It does little for articulations of globalizing knowledge, however.

At one level, the globalizing university can even make matters worse for cultivating the relationship between knowledge and change. To the extent inequalities within the global system of knowledge production are exacerbated, and knowledge wealth is concentrated ever more in the 1 percent of universities and their most proximate publics, public knowledge actually diminishes. That trajectory is not necessary.

Let us dispense with that notion of the global public as an invisible passive receptacle into which the wisdom of the elite is deposited. Let us pluralize that public and reconceive it as a partner for posing problems, figuring methodologies, and developing knowledge consequences. In that case, the risks of concentrated knowledge might be reduced. That extension is especially likely if the culture of critical discourse recognizes who is part of the conversation and who is not. Thus, we must ask this question: Which publics count in globalizing knowledge?

5   Difference: Recognizing Global Contexts

Publics can exist only in contexts. They are conceived through communication, and thus their histories, institutions, culture, and languages are critical to their recognition. When those publics are proximate to intellectuals and their institutions, the distinctions of context can fade from discursive recognition. Not all knowledge endeavors are public, however. Indeed, not all knowledge is understood in context, even while context affects all forms of knowledge.

This value of context is obviously true for those forms of learning affected by a region's particular histories and institutions, as area studies and history are. Even those endeavors engaging the physical world are affected by their context if only through the languages scientists must use to discover and communicate their ideas. Scholars in science studies have made this point very clearly. To speak comparatively, one might say that different kinds of knowledge are variably affected by the contexts in which they are elaborated. Some scholarly endeavors vary more by national, regional, and local contexts, while others are more clearly embedded in transnational or global epistemic communities.

To recognize the value of context is not quite the same as appreciating the politics of recognition in globalizing knowledge. After all, some contexts are recognized and thus validated, both implicitly and explicitly, more than others. For those who seek to globalize knowledge, this variable prominence of certain contexts over others should be a critical vector of engagement.

In this chapter, I explore the ways in which various global contexts have figured in the English-language-presented social sciences. First, I consider how context shapes the scholarly imagination and then move to consider the positions of particular places in the social sciences. After establishing the relative significance of different places in the world's leading social science journals, I then explore how particular places—Poland, Kosova, and Afghanistan—appear in them. By understanding how events, networks, and prominence in global scholarship shape those patterns of recognition, one might do more than mark enduring structures of inequality in global academic engagement. One might even work to change those inequalities, at least in the terms of recognition. We need to begin this account with the recognition that not everyone values context in knowledge.

Context and the Scholarly Imagination

Some forms of globalizing knowledge can easily overlook context. Researchers working across the world on DNA sequencing will likely be concerned only about those contexts—the qualities of government regulation and conditions of research support—that enable scientific research to proceed. Those concerned about who has the proper historical and philological claims enabling Macedonian identification demand very sophisticated accounts of how context influences knowledge (e.g., Brown and Hamilikis 2003). Such attention to context varies both across and within disciplines. Intellectuals might even be understood as those whose ideas transcend context.

Randall Collins (1998, 19) defines intellectuals as "people who produce decontextualized ideas. These ideas are meant to be true or significant apart from any locality, and apart from anyone concretely putting them into practice." Many aspire to contribute ideas that survive the ages. Piotr Sztompka (2011, 392) was particularly emphatic on the importance of such transcendence for sociology: "Sociological research, as long as it is worthy of the label of science, reflects universal human worries, predicaments and social issues, providing generalized knowledge to diagnose, explain, predict, and hopefully eradicate them, wherever they are." Not all intellectuals seek that kind of immortality in text and scholarly worlds.

Some intellectuals seek greater public consequence, to see how ideas might transform the worlds in which they live, and thus put as much emphasis on the articulation of ideas as in their generalized value. Even when the problem is common—for instance, how the European Union's transformation might be addressed—contexts shape how the object is itself addressed (Lacroix and Nicolaidis 2010). And only some intellectuals are able to find the context that allows them to imagine their ideas transcending context. The claims of many scholars can rarely be transcendent, marked as they are by being recognized only as the African American scholar, the Kosovar scholar, the Afghan scholar.

In short, that tension between grounded and transcendent claims, both academic and socially real, animates enduring and, particularly recent, debates. I find one side of that debate most compelling, and Charles Taylor's (1994, 72–73) presumption worthy as foundation:

> It is reasonable to suppose that cultures that have provided the horizon of meaning for large numbers of human beings, of diverse characters and temperaments, over a long period of time—that have, in other words, articulated their sense of the good, the holy, the admirable—are almost certain to have something that deserves our admiration and respect, even if it is accompanied by much that we have to abhor and reject. Perhaps one could put it another way: it would take a supreme arrogance to discount this possibility a priori.

I see this focus on context as an extension of Taylor's point. Those who disregard the challenge of difference in the presumption that worthwhile information and perspectives will float to the top of a universal pool of knowledge contribute to just that supreme arrogance, even if unintentionally. To extend Taylor's humility, those wishing to develop globalizing knowledge need consider the ways in which knowledges are not only differently articulated but unevenly recognized.

We have already seen how intellectuals' biographies over time and across places shape their arguments, and how their framings of issues imply, and help to constitute, spatial and temporal frameworks. We have seen how universities struggle to articulate the world, especially with thematics that might claim universal, global, or international reference. At the very least, certain regional references imply particular visions of the world. We have seen how much proximate publics shape universities and their sensibilities of institutional responsibility, even while the inequalities within and among those publics are not always articulated. Finally, even when knowledge publics go global, their own grounded sensibilities shape *how* they go global, whose problems they take up, which partnerships they consider, if they consider any at all. Sociology, as a discipline, should be especially attentive to these tensions and problems.

Raewynn Connell (2007) pulls these themes together systematically in her own elaboration of "southern theory." She discusses theory about and from Africa, Iran, Latin America, India, and Australia, with particular attention to aboriginal challenges to modes of northern theory.[1] However, Connell's own work shows the power of context for even formulating the challenge to northern theory.

Her different facilities with various parts of the Global South are apparent. Her Australian grounding, and expertise, is especially evident. The fact that India's subaltern studies and Latin America's dependency theory are so well known and elaborated means that she has a rich literature on which to draw. In some cases, however, that southern theory is more apparent within area studies traditions than in our discipline—as is the case in African studies and the African Renaissance to which she refers. In some cases, her depictions show only how contexts constrain knowledge. For example, Connell's choices around Iran illustrate not only the value of knowing more about Iranian scholarship but also the challenge of identifying who deserves to be recognized. For many reasons, I am somewhat cautious in venturing too far beyond the grounds of my expertise, even while concepts like "Global South" give us license. They should also give us pause.

It may make sense for those who have experienced, in common, the various dispossessions of Western imperialism to recognize one another's similarity. However, formulations grounded on those inequalities don't always resonate so readily for those who have suffered the dispossessions of other imperialisms. Japanese imperialism has historically dispossessed Okinawa, Taiwan, and Korea, but their contests have in much more limited ways informed sensibilities of the Global South (Duus 1998; Lo 2002; Lie 2004). Those limitations are also beyond my regional ken. Other Asian stories are closer to my competence.

Central Asia and the Caucasus today should clearly be part of a Global South in any sense of the term, but it is rarely part of the empirical, much less theoretical, arsenal of social sciences associated with that demarcation. Some work to bring that politics of knowledge into a broader conversation (Amsler 2007), but it has not yet made sufficient impact on how we figure global transformations. Consider, for example, the acronym BRICS in which Brazil, Russia, India, China, and South Africa are joined. Some have argued that this new formulation of global alliance suggests an alternative future for the world (Unger 2005, xvi). For most in the post-Soviet South, to elevate the empire that once ruled them in such fashion shows just how much those anticipating global alternatives do so without their region in mind.

Southeastern Europe has, historically, been the Global South of Europe. Even today, parts of the region clearly identify imperialism as they also invoke their European history and trajectory. Kosova's movement for self-determination, Vetëvendosje, for example, would not make sense in historical and comparative terms were it not for its resonance with other such movements in the twentieth and twenty-first centuries (Knudsen 2014). On the other hand, even as it wages that struggle against other Europeans, Vetëvendosje does so claiming also to be European. While few in Central and Eastern Europe would make such a case for being part of the Global South, especially following their entry into the European Union, or even before (Kennedy 1999a), their subordinate status within Europe shares many qualities with some parts of the Global South Connell identifies (Kennedy 2012c; Zarycki 2014). In short, while Connell and other theorists of the Global South recognize variations, some variations are more recognized than others. Southeastern Europe and the post-Soviet South rarely fit.

To work in the lands formerly ruled by communists, as I have, means that my global sense is less informed by the sense of a Global South. After communism's collapse, I had to engage a transition culture that seemed hegemonic at century's turn. It worked across the region to inform change from dictatorship to democracy and from plan to market by identifying exemplary and problematic places (Kennedy 2002a), with the West as one of the "normal" places toward which change is directed (Eglitis 2002). Although the abiding crisis of capitalism in the core has made that transition seem less golden, geopolitical visions of global change are still, somehow, different when communist dictatorship is part of a nation's history (Chari and Verdery 2009).

Within that context, public sociology has itself been challenged. While it is not so hard, as Michael Burawoy (2005a) puts it, to "provincialize" American sociology, the different places from which that provincializing is done produce different knowledge dynamics. It's not so easy, at least in those initial postcommunist years, to work with Marxism's historical legacy to identify the challenges of public sociology, for example. As the West convulses in financial crisis, and postcommunist capitalisms develop ever more intense forms of corruption and injustice, that legacy might become once again relevant, even if it will require some reconciliation with the 1989–91 revolutions against revolution (Kennedy and Galtz 1996). That is, however, happening in both theory and practice, with quite apparent roots in Poland (Kubik and Linch 2013).

I developed my sociology around an engagement with Poland's professionals, organization of power, 1980–81 Solidarity movement, and sociological tradition. They formed the basis for my dissertation research and first book (Kennedy 1991). This also was more than a case in globalizing my sociological imagination. My research in Poland and my ties to Polish colleagues and friends transformed my vision of the world, and I am not alone. Poland has had a relatively powerful influence on American sociology and its sociological imagination. Figuring how those influences develop is one critical step in figuring how context matters.

In an earlier publication (Kennedy 2004b), I developed a collective biography of American sociology in so far as it has explicitly recognized, and has been explicitly influenced by, Polish history and society.[2] I established that particular story within a more general one that portrays a hierarchy of various national influences on American sociology. I now turn to Kosova and Afghanistan to extend the story. Your first thought on reading that turn is likely to ask why, but that already becomes part of the story we hope to clarify here.

For those who know me, or for those who first heard my paper on Poland in the American sociological imagination, the answer as to why Poland is obvious. It was only respectful that if I were to talk about globalizing knowledge to a meeting of the Polish Sociological Association that I should talk about the Polish-American sociological relationship. The particular story of my draw to Poland is, in the end, peculiar and not based on the familiar narratives of ancestry or elective kinship. Kosova and Afghanistan are different.

Kosova is a critical place in the global social imaginary for one obvious reason: It is the place where a humanitarian crisis inspired what Václav Havel (1999) called the first war launched in the name of human rights. That 1999 attack by NATO on Serbia not only halted ethnic cleansing and genocide in the making but also created a new kind of society. For more than a decade, international agencies have overseen Kosova's political existence, meaning that substantial numbers of people from across the world have lived in Kosova even while, because of its ambiguous international status, Kosovars have found it difficult to travel across the world.

I have also worked in Kosova since 2009 with colleagues at the University of Prishtina. Through these years of collaboration, I have acquired a far richer sense of this society than I have of any other country besides Poland and my own. At the same time, my sense of the place is limited most profoundly by the fact that I do not speak Albanian.

Afghanistan is another critical place in the global imaginary, not least for its significance as a place where some argue the collapse of the Soviet Union began, where Al-Qaeda was born, and where another international protectorate of sorts has existed for more than a decade. I also do not speak any of the languages of Afghanistan. Worse, I have not worked there. However, I have worked with others from and expert on the country in order to figure how to extend Afghanistan's place in scholarship further.[3] Few in my discipline have held that ambition.

Nevertheless, many in other knowledge networks, notably in international relations and in anthropology, have engaged Afghanistan far more than have sociologists. By comparing the same places in international relations and anthropology journals as we do for sociology, we can appreciate just how much disciplines vary in their relationships to places. Recognizing some of the patterns of that variation is another step toward understanding better the articulation of context and the scholarly imagination. That elaboration should begin with my own discipline in my own national context.

Places in the Social Sciences

Most disciplines in US universities have no *necessary* interest in other parts of the world. Other universities across the world may not be able to allow such ethnocentrism, given the global distribution of research and scholarship. However, regardless of position, it is reasonable to assume that the history of a place will disproportionately influence its scholarship. That may play out by focusing on national histories or societies or literatures. It may reflect a colonial heritage that is both acknowledged and resisted in the attention it receives. Or it may even reflect a particular special relationship among nations (e.g., Mearsheimer and Walt 2007). Each discipline, however, has its own particular qualities and internal organization of scholarship with consequence for how the world is viewed and ethnocentrism enacted.

As discussed previously, some disciplines and professions claim no national reference, as medicine or engineering or social work. But in those cases, while they may have global aspirations, they also typically must meet credential boards that have some contextual grounding in power and law.

Some disciplines and professional schools, such as comparative literature and security studies, are by definition international. Even here, however, one can distinguish approaches by the contexts that such approaches elevate in empirical study or intellectual inspiration. A comparative literature that focuses on France and Germany is different from one that addresses Bengal and Tamil Nadu (Shankar 2001).

My own discipline of sociology has struggled long over its ethnocentrism (Hughes 1961), manifested in a number of ways, most obviously in the fact that most of American sociology is about American society, enabled by that society's power, privilege, and diversity. Ethnocentrism is, however, mitigated by the immigration of scholars from abroad. When these scholars enroll as students or join faculties, they bring their networks, cultures, and histories into the scholarly formation. Of course, they also adapt to local institutional practices, even as, we hope, they extend them. It is therefore important to consider the demographic composition of various academic formations.

Nations need not enter a scholarly formation only through the movement of people. Ideas travel too, in potentially different form from the transformations in a society that inspire those ideas. My study of Poland in the American sociological imagination certainly confirmed that, for I was not the only scholar moved by the ideas inspired by the 1980–81 Solidarity movement and the movement itself. More generally, scholarship extends its global vision when another nation becomes important to it. The ways in which a nation becomes important matters, but for that manner of engagement to matter, a place must first be present. And that is where we can begin.

One empirical starting point for recognizing the influence of particular contexts on scholarship is to recognize their relative absence or presence in publications.[4] But already we face a problem. For what places might we search in these publications? When I originally prepared this analysis for colleagues in the Polish Sociological Association, Poland was the obvious choice, as were a few of its neighbors for comparison. Those not so particularly interested in Central and Eastern Europe may not choose Poland, Hungary, and Ukraine. That already illustrates the importance of context and its regional references.

In that original study, I decided not to include Great Britain, given the powerful network connecting US and British sociology, but I did address the other European powers. Every US sociologist would be curious about the relative significance of France and Germany, because of the importance of those nations for our discipline's historical development. Given their power on the world stage, we should expect references to Japan, Brazil, India, the USSR/ Russia, China, and South Africa to be prominent and an object of sociological and broader social scientific interest. We should also expect, to a lesser degree, other regional powers to be significant.[5]

My focus on Afghanistan and Kosova partially derives from my prior engagements. However, those engagements are themselves shaped by my belief that such places ought to be far more central in the American scholarly imagination than they are. Indeed, both Kosova and Afghanistan, as places, are just as important to global scholarship and politics as Poland has been. But certainly they don't receive the same kinds of attention as Poland has between 1890 and 2009,[6] as Table 5.1 illustrates.[7] For ease of reference, in this and subsequent tables, I boldface these three countries.

It is not surprising to see that French, German, Japanese, Soviet, Indian, Chinese, South African, Russian, and Italian references would lead Poland in sociology journals, given their relative significance in global history and knowledge networks. I do find it interesting, if still explicable, that Poland would be more prominent than Australia, Brazil, Hungary, Ireland, Korea, Mexico, Nigeria, Turkey, and Ukraine. It is quite distressing, if not surprising, that for the significance of Kosova and Afghanistan in recent world history they are so infrequently engaged.

It is conceivable that their relative rank is due to the 120 years of reference that this ordering produces. Some places on this list were not independent countries over that period.[8] For that reason, I have included any references to Yugoslavia and Albania in my search for treatments of Kosova. Even with that, it is more attended only in comparison to Ukraine, Afghanistan, and Korea during this time period.

If we were to consider relative attention over the last twenty years, when the wars of Yugoslav Succession grabbed the world's attention, or over the last thirty years when Afghan struggles influenced the Cold War and conflicts associated with what President George W. Bush called the war on terrorism, we might find something different. In fact, the rankings are relatively consistent for sociology (Kennedy 2004b). We should not presume, however, that sociology journals are as relatively stable as others. Consider, for example, publications in journals focused more on international relations over the last thirty years (Table 5.2).[9]

At least in comparison to sociology, there is much more variation in the relative attention places receive in international relations journals. Some

TABLE 5.1 Average number of articles per year in leading
sociology journals engaging particular places

	Average 1890–2009	Rank 1890–2009
Afghanistan/Afghan	**17.1**	**20**
Australia/Australian	49.7	14
Brazil/Brazilian	60.8	11
China/Chinese	111.6	6
France/French	331.5	1
German/Germany	307.5	2
Hungary/Hungarian	44.6	15
India	136.8	5
Ireland/Irish	47.9	15
Italy/Italian	76.0	9
Japan/Japanese	184.6	3
Korea/Korean	30.2	19
Mexico/Mexican	67.5	13
Nigeria/Nigerian	40.7	17
Poland/Polish	**73.1**	**10**
Russia/Russian	96.7	8
South Africa/South African	107.6	7
Soviet Union/Soviet	157.9	4
Turkey/Turkish	50.0	12
Ukraine/Ukrainian	10.5	21
Yugoslavia/Kosovo/Albania	**32.3**	**18**

places remain in position. Note that the Soviet Union remains at the top even
in the decade following its disappearance, and Russia rises in significance
following the collapse of the USSR. Still, several societies change places over
time. Afghanistan, Mexico, and Yugoslavia/Kosova/Albania vary substantially, while Poland and India vary to a lesser degree.

International relations (IR) scholarship can vary in geographic attention
relatively rapidly because the expectation for contextual expertise on places is
smaller. In part, this is because IR often articulates places with perspectives
associated with more general theories or with the foreign policies of hegemonic powers, or both. Thus, one need not speak Albanian or Dari or do

TABLE 5.2 Countries in rank order of article mentions per year in leading international relations journals

	1980–1989	1990–2001	2002–2009
1.	USSR	USSR	France
2.	France	France	Germany
3.	Germany	Germany	USSR
4.	China	Russia	China
5.	Japan	China	Russia
6.	Mexico	Japan	India
7.	South Africa	South Africa	**Yugoslavia/Kosovo/Albania**
8.	Russia	Korea	Japan
9.	Korea	India	Korea
10.	India	Italy	**Afghanistan**
11.	**Afghanistan**	Mexico	South Africa
12.	Italy	**Yugoslavia/Kosovo/Albania**	Turkey
13.	**Poland**	Turkey	Mexico
14.	Brazil	**Poland**	Italy
15.	Turkey	Brazil	Australia
16.	Australia	Hungary	Brazil
17.	Hungary	Australia	Ireland
18.	**Yugoslavia/Kosovo/Albania**	**Afghanistan**	**Poland**
19.	Nigeria	Ireland	Hungary
20.	Ireland	Ukraine	Ukraine
21.	Ukraine	Nigeria	Nigeria

more than be able to refer to the meanings of "loya jirga" or "blood feud" to engage the security questions of Afghanistan or Kosova. Those expectations are radically different for journals associated with anthropology and its commitments to contextual expertise, as is evident in Table 5.3.

Especially in contrast to international relations, but even in comparison to sociology, anthropology's places are remarkably stable.[10] From decade to decade there is very little change in relative ranking, with the most dramatic change in the place of India, moving from fifth to first place over the last two decades.[11] France, China, India, Mexico, and South Africa remain at the top

TABLE 5.3 Countries in rank order of article mentions per year in leading anthropology journals

	1980–1989	1990–2001	2002–2009
1.	France	France	India
2.	Mexico	Mexico	France
3.	China	South Africa	South Africa
4.	India	China	Mexico
5.	South Africa	India	China
6.	Australia	Germany	Germany
7.	Germany	Japan	Australia
8.	Japan	Australia	Japan
9.	Italy	Brazil	Italy
10.	Brazil	Italy	Brazil
11.	Russia	Russia	Russia
12.	Ireland	Ireland	Ireland
13.	Nigeria	USSR	Nigeria
14.	USSR	Nigeria	USSR
15.	Turkey	Turkey	Turkey
16.	**Poland**	**Poland**	**Poland**
17.	Korea	Korea	Korea
18.	Hungary	**Yugoslavia/Kosovo/Albania**	**Yugoslavia/Kosovo/Albania**
19.	**Afghanistan**	Hungary	**Afghanistan**
20.	**Yugoslavia/Kosovo/Albania**	**Afghanistan**	Hungary
21.	Ukraine	Ukraine	Ukraine

throughout these three decades. Poland, Afghanistan, and Kosova remain in relatively stable positions of relative disinterest.

That stability is understandable in fields devoted to contextual expertise and the importance of linking deep study of particular places with theoretical innovation. Beyond the fact that the regional focus of individual scholars changes less over time than that of most scholars in international relations and many in sociology, graduate training in the latter two are likely to be provided by those without the same contextual interests. There is more consistency in anthropology graduate training across thematic and contextual expertise. Those aspiring to study both social anthropology and Romania are likely to choose an anthropology graduate program such as that where Katherine Verdery teaches, for example. In sociology and IR, choices about programs of study are rarely made because of the geographic accents of their faculty.

Beyond variations in pedagogy, these comparisons show something else about how places vary in importance across knowledge cultures. In Table 5.4, I compare the relative rankings of places across knowledge cultures in the first years of this twenty-first century. First, all three knowledge cultures attend to France, Germany, Japan, Korea, Nigeria, Turkey, and Ukraine to a relatively common degree within the hierarchies of their disciplinary attentions. Anthropology and sociology are similar in how frequently they engage Afghanistan, Brazil, China, Poland, Russia, South Africa, the USSR, and Kosova. IR and sociology are similarly attentive to Australia, India, Ireland, and Italy. Anthropology and IR are similar in how they attend to China, Hungary, and Poland. Most interesting for the purposes of this chapter is how Kosova and Afghanistan fare. IR attends to Kosova and Afghanistan, in addition to the USSR, Russia, and Korea, far more than the other two knowledge cultures (and to South Africa, Mexico, and Brazil far less).

Any of these relationships is fascinating to consider in greater depth, but in the sections that follow I focus on Poland, Kosova, and Afghanistan. One cannot understand the dynamics of position in global reference without attending to the networks, events, and recognition for intellectual innovation within and across nations.

Poland in the English-Language Sociological Imagination

While anthropologists have historically engaged "distant" cultures, and international relations scholars have engaged the places with whom their hosts are at war or in trade, American sociologists have since the end of World War II tended to focus on other societies that are "like" it, or increasingly like it. Those societies tend therefore to be amenable to the theories, methods, and concerns developed in the United States. Poland has never been studied because it is *simply* similar to the United States, however.[12]

For nearly half of the twentieth century, American sociologists studied Poland because it represented an important difference: its "socialist" quality. However, because it was more like the United States than the Soviet Union,

TABLE 5.4 Relative attention to places by knowledge cultures, 2002–2009

Anthropology	International relations	Sociology
India	France	France
France	Germany	Germany
South Africa	USSR	South Africa
Mexico	China	Japan
China	Russia	India
Germany	India	China
Australia	**Yugoslavia/Kosovo/Albania**	Mexico
Japan	Japan	USSR
Italy	Korea	Brazil
Brazil	**Afghanistan**	Russia
Russia	South Africa	Turkey
Ireland	Turkey	Italy
Nigeria	Mexico	**Poland**
USSR	Italy	Australia
Turkey	Australia	Hungary
Poland	Brazil	Korea
Korea	Ireland	Ireland
Yugoslavia/Kosovo/Albania	**Poland**	**Afghanistan**
Afghanistan	Hungary	Nigeria
Hungary	Ukraine	**Yugoslavia/Kosovo/Albania**
Ukraine	Nigeria	Ukraine

with the Polish appreciation for scientific sociology and critical theory at the very least, it became the "like" society in the "unlike" camp. It enabled us to discover how general American theories were even as we worked with the society that most reflected American qualities (Lenski 1978; Kohn 1993). That is not the only reason for its importance.

Poland has been powerfully connected to sociology in the United States for more than a century. Its peasant diaspora shaped the work of Thomas and Znaniecki (1958) quite profoundly, and that work has influenced an entire tradition of American sociology. More than one-third of book reviews devoted to Poland or Polish matters between 1890 and 2001 in the sociology journals I have considered are concerned with the Polish diaspora. In fact, Thomas and Znaniecki's volumes inspired seven of the first eleven reviews dealing with

Poland or Polish social phenomena in the *American Journal of Sociology* and *Social Forces* between 1918 and 1941. Even after that most intensive period, work on Polish immigration continues, even if the leading figures of the discipline are not so typically involved.

Poland's academic diaspora has also been critically important, with Florian Znaniecki himself and a host of other Polish scholars in American sociology departments helping make Poland more important in the American sociological imagination. Consider the portrait of Polish sociology Znaniecki's wife offered in the second issue of *American Sociological Review* (Znaniecka 1936). One could only be impressed with Poland's sociological achievements well beyond Znaniecki. But of all the figures in Poland and the United States that made Polish sociology prominent in the first half of the twentieth century, Florian Znaniecki has been the most important. His status as the 1954 president of the American Sociological Society reflected and augmented his importance (Halas, 2000a 200b, 2006). Collaborations count too.

While W. I. Thomas and Florian Znaniecki were central interpreters and promoters of Polish affairs in American sociology for most of the twentieth century, during the 1980s and 1990s Mel Kohn most obviously played that role. In the volume to emerge from his 1987 presidential address to the American Sociological Association, four of seventeen chapters had Polish authors (Kohn 1989). His partnership with Kazimierz Słomczyński is also evident in American sociological publications. These collaborations produce even larger networks of consequence with a number of their coauthors and research collaborators. Kohn and Słomczyński (1990) themselves, however, identify the network's progenitor within Poland, in the person of Włodzimierz Wesołowski. With these examples spanning the twentieth century, we can see the value to American sociology of imaginations and networks born in Poland (Kohn 1993), but not all of Poland's influence can be attributed to the migrations of peasants and collaborations of scholars.

The substantive focus of scholarship and a nation's place in that work can influence the likelihood of a particular nation entering American sociology. And sometimes another nation becomes important because it is important for a larger political story. Poland became a powerful focus in the United States first because of the 1980–81 Solidarity movement and then because of the collapse of communism. There was terrific interest in the United States from all political vantage points on the end to the Cold War division in Europe.

Contemporary global transformations are not the only vehicle that inspires focus; sometimes theoretical arguments make countries newly significant. For example, Poland was important to world systems theory because of its being a "bread basket" for the development of the capitalist world system in the sixteenth century, thereby providing Polish historians and historical sociologists an important opening into American sociology (Wallerstein 1976).

One can attend to these dynamics of knowledge production much more carefully, as I did in that earlier publication. The point in this chapter is to develop comparisons, and I conclude my comments on Poland with one more observation. Already in 1977, the Annual Review of Sociology devoted an article to recent scholarship in Poland. Invited by the editors, Zdzislawa Walaszek (1977), an accomplished sociologist who was also married to one of America's leading sociologists, James Coleman, spelled out how Polish sociology was distinctive. There is nothing equivalent to that article in US sociology with regard to Afghanistan or Kosova to this day.

One might conclude these reflections on Poland with three basic points: (1) the initial establishment of a problem in American sociology legitimates its return later, hence the abiding value of the Polish peasant, civil society, and postcommunist radical change for the Polish ledger in American sociology; (2) the establishment of networks of collaboration are critical, but the conditions for their reproduction over time are not automatic; and therefore (3) the importance of continually inventing new arenas of centrality in both theoretical and political discourse is central to American sociological Polocentrism.

One might hope that the abiding and increasingly innovative *Polish Sociological Review*, founded initially by Florian Znaniecki, could inspire new waves of collaboration. After all, it provides an outlet for Polish scholars and others to read the work of one another in English. The impact of that kind of outreach remains to be seen, especially when Poland has become another "normal" society in the world. Kosova, however, remains quite distinctive.

Kosova in the English-Language Sociological Imagination

Although many fewer articles in these journals engage Kosova, Yugoslavia, and Albania than Poland, especially in sociology, it bears consideration what thematic interests are roused in the academic literature that *do* engage these places. One way to consider that variation is to examine which journals attend

TABLE 5.5 Mentions of Yugoslavia, Albania, or Kosovo in sociology-related journals, 1890–2009

Ranking	Number	Journal
1	890	*Annals of the American Academy of Political and Social Science*
2	279	*American Journal of Sociology*
3	197	*Contemporary Sociology* (all book reviews)
4	150	*American Sociological Review*
5	109	*Journal of Palestine Studies*
6	106	*Social Forces*
7	92	*International Journal of Comparative Sociology* (with book reviews)
8	82	*Public Opinion Quarterly*
9	74	*Journal of Modern African Studies*
10	72	*Journal of Marriage and the Family*
11	67	*Theory and Society*
12	56	*MERIP*
13	53	*Industrial and Labor Relations Review*

to the region. Table 5.5 identifies thirteen sociology journals with the most articles that engage Yugoslavia, Albania, or Kosova.

In sheer numbers, the *Annals of the American Academy of Political and Social Science* is by far the publication most attentive to these southeastern European places, in part for relatively longer run of issues. It's also a matter of substantive focus: Yugoslavia was particularly important for the number of articles addressing communism and international affairs, notably around the nonaligned movement Yugoslavia helped lead. That doesn't explain why the leading journals of US sociology would be so attentive to the region, however.

American Journal of Sociology, Contemporary Sociology, American Sociological Review, and *Social Forces* each attended to southeastern Europe. Yugoslavia was an important site for comparative studies of socialist societies, especially for those who wished to rethink the workplace, given Yugoslavia's leadership in self-management. Yugoslavia was quite often referenced in the journal *Industrial and Labor Relations Review.* Its relatively open research environment, in stark contrast to the exceptionally closed Albania led by Enver Hoxha, also made it an American sociologist's heaven, especially when complemented by the number of outstanding sociologists working in Yugoslavia during the socialist period.

Most of these articles focus on Yugoslavia as such rather than Kosova, Slovenia, or Croatia. Given the equation of "society-ness" with national independence, that makes sense. It is important, however, to see how Yugoslavia as such is portrayed. Consider, for example, one of the portraits of sociology in Yugoslavia from before World War II, before communist rule.

Joseph S. Roucek (1936, 981), a scholar from New York University, began his account in *American Sociological Review* by emphasizing that Yugoslav sociology was "strongly influenced by national problems and history," with "little tolerance and appreciation for the opponent's viewpoint," leading to an unfavorable condition for developing a science of the social. Beyond the import of ideas and sociologies from elsewhere, Roucek emphasizes two things. First, the international socialist movement inspired many Yugoslav scholars and public figures to search for more communal forms of social organization. Equally if not more important, many efforts were undertaken to explain the various identifications held by southern Slavs and the distinction between Slavs and Albanians. None of the sociologists he mentioned were Albanian; the assumption is that Yugoslavia would be a Slav project, even if non-Slavs live there, and might be studied.

Washington University's Dinko Tomasic (1941) offered his own take on Yugoslav sociology just a few years later in the *American Journal of Sociology*. Like Roucek, he emphasized the national differences among sociologies and was a bit more critical and prescient about their racist and imperialist elements, especially of Serbian and Croatian sociologies. Here, Albanians were not even mentioned, for these sociologies were entirely, as Tomasic said, "ethnocentric."

In contrast to what Poland enjoyed with Florian Znaniecki's influence on US sociology, Yugoslav sociology before World War II was perceived mainly as an extension of the country's politics, which seemed to be distant from US concerns. Nevertheless, in the early 1970s one of those Serbian sociologists was reintroduced to the English-language audience.

Tomasic portrayed Jovan Cvijić as a racist and imperialist, but Svetozar Ćulibrk (1971), a scholar from Beograd University, spoke about this former geography professor, rector of Beograd University, and president of the Serbian Academy of Science and Arts, as a most esteemed scholar, responsible for introducing sociology to Yugoslavia and addressing comprehensively

the characteristics of the various peoples of the Balkan peninsula. However, Ćulibrk never named Albanians as such in describing Cvijić's research
agenda. Indeed, the nationalism of both is apparent even here, where Ćulibrk
(1971, 435) spoke of Cvijić's approach to Balkan towns and ways of living in
them "under the backward Turkish system."

Albanians were often prominent in that "backward Turkish system," that
Ottoman system, leading many of the most highly educated and eminent to
speak Turkish in addition to their native languages. After the fall of the Ottoman Empire, this limited identification (after all, Albanians also rebelled
against the Ottomans) moved Serbs to figure ways to force out these Albanians whom they often simply called Turks. Inspired by the ways Nazis treated
Jews, the leaders of interwar Yugoslavia carried out forced expulsion of Albanians to Albania and "back" to Turkey (Malcolm 1999, 285–87). Within pre–
World War II Yugoslavia, then, Albanians were treated at best as residents,
and often enemies, a fact that hardly seems to have reached most American
sociology, even sociologists of race and ethnicity (Bonilla-Silva 1999, 903). This
nonrecognition also has extended to their place in sociological treatments of
the region by Americans better informed by Yugoslav scholarship.

The sociology of the family was one of the major themes to emerge
from Yugoslavia's ethnological studies of peoples. Indeed, the "Balkan family" becomes a major theme in sociology journals. Nevertheless, Albanian
peoples remain in relatively obscure focus. For example, Kaser (1994) critiques most "Balkan family" accounts for their failure to engage properly
the broader comparative study of families. His focus is, as for the scholars
mentioned earlier, the character of South Slav household systems, especially around the *zadruga*. Although there were Albanian households in the
regions under study, and a similar household called *shtepia* might have been
considered (Ehrlich 1976), they are not typically engaged in these studies.
Indeed, Kaser (1994, 253, 264) takes the literature to task for not considering
possible variations in ethnic groups for the likelihood of joint households,
especially of Vlachs, "a mysterious Balkan people." Albanians do not form
part of his critique, given the ways in which they were made invisible in
censuses from those times.

Although Kaser is exemplary for moving us into greater historical specificity, he is still implicated in the larger historiography that even the word *Balkan*
implies. As Maria Todorova (1997, 35) has argued, the term has been historically,
and remains, a "synonym for unreliability, lethargy, corruption, irresponsibility,

mismanagement, blurring of the competences and borders in the order of law and much else." It is, of course, even used within the region itself:

> Despite the fact that some accept, although reluctantly, their Balkanness while others actively renounce any connection with it, what is common for all Balkan nations is the clear consensus that the Balkans exist, that there is something that can be defined as Balkan, although it may be an undesired predicament and region. What they would like to prove is that they do not belong to the repellent image that has been constructed of it. (57)

That imagery changes, to some degree, with the socialist revolution in Yugoslavia. In fact, just a few years after the celebration of Cvijić, the *British Journal of Sociology* again featured Yugoslavia. This time it had a very different take, celebrating the development of historical sociology with Yugoslav sociology at its heart (Allcock 1975). While the discipline's development in articulation with Yugoslav Marxism is now emphasized, once again, the Slavic emphasis is apparent. Even in this article animated by a more critical sociological imagination, inspired by C. Wright Mills himself, Albanians are absent entirely.

Albanians, one should imagine, can't be absent from the question of ethnic difference in Yugoslavia. Indeed, the whole Yugoslav experiment was, like the Soviet one, an attempt to create a new kind of transnational identity. In 1994, the *American Sociological Review* raised that very question (Sekulic, Massey, and Hodson 1994), with scholars from George Mason University (formerly from Zagreb University), University of Wyoming, and Indiana University looking to understand who was most likely to identify as Yugoslav. They compared survey data in 1985 and 1989, before the outbreak of open war.

Sekulic, Massey, and Hodson (1994, 84) note that "apart from Bosnia between 1961 and 1971 and Kosovo, self-identification as a Yugoslav shows a general pattern of increase from 1961 to 1981"; however, "most people in Kosovo" think of themselves as Albanian or Serbian. While this distinction is noted, the difference among majorities and minorities, and their relative power, was not itself highlighted. Albanians were without their own republic and were more persecuted than any others by Serbs, with a new cycle of intensity begun at the very times of these surveys. That condition does not matter for their empirical argument, however, since the data about Yugoslavia came only from Serbia, Croatia, and Bosnia and did not include the data from Kosova. Even in a study of ethnic difference and Yugoslav identification,

Kosova remained relatively invisible. Of course, in the study of war it should be prominent.

Making a case for Yugoslavia's significance in war's study is, perhaps, obvious. In a major *American Sociological Review* analysis of war's dynamics, the wars of Yugoslav Succession appear to bracket the end story and fit the narrative:

> In the first phase of transition (from empire to nation-state), secessionist wars of "national liberation" against the ruling empire are likely to be fought. In the second phase, wars between new states over ethnically mixed territory may break out, and ethnic minorities might rebel against political exclusion by national majorities. The model predicts that such civil wars are more likely where ethnic discrimination is high, where governments are poor, and thus unable to accommodate ethno-political protest. (Wimmer and Min 2006, 876)

This appears to fit Kosova's situation. Sort of. Wimmer and Min (2006, 894) themselves recognize that "the patterns of warfare in the Caucasus and the Balkans in the 1990s resemble those on the Indian subcontinent in the 1940s, those of Eastern Europe during and after World War I, and so on." In this sense, Kosova, for the American sociologist, is just another place in the Balkans, and the Balkans, just another place after empire.[13] And when there aren't good data, whose absence reflected Kosova's very position in socialist Yugoslavia, Kosova's invisibility can appear merely technical and not too consequential. After all, only two million people live there. Yet that omission reflects the very ethnocentrism against the globalizing knowledge grain that is the object of this discussion. It deserves closer scrutiny, especially in light of transition and its culture and sociology.

Transition offered an opportunity for sociologists interested in such general processes to engage post-Yugoslav societies more. Even here, however, Kosova was not so commonly depicted in transition culture, given that it was not only postcommunist but also in the midst of war, or postwar, and thus complicating the typical erasure of violence from transition's study (Kennedy 2001c).[14] However, for those interested in the mobilization of civil society, Kosova offered in the 1980s and 1990s an exceptional place to learn as a result of what its people organized.

Kosova in Transition Culture and
Globalizing Public Sociology

Most narratives of the wars of Yugoslav Succession focus on the 1990s, but one might argue that that dissolution could have been anticipated already in the 1980s when the Milošević regime began its brutal repression of Kosovar society. Gale Stokes (1997, 121) writes, "The road to civil war began in March 1981 when Albanian students took their demands for better conditions at the University of Prishtine to the streets. . . . Their demonstration touched a nerve of Albanian patriotic feeling, and over the next month anti-Serbian demonstrations demanding that Kosovo become a Yugoslav republic became so massive that the federal government sent in troops."

I drew upon Stokes in my earlier work on the wars of Yugoslav Succession and even invoked his own reference to the alternative society made in resistance to Milošević's brutal attack in February 1990. While I noted this self-organized civil society around underground structures in education, health, and taxes, I didn't attend to it like I studied the Polish Solidarity movement of 1980–81 nor have many others in the West, with Howard Clark (2000) the most important exception.

Clark, an activist in nonviolent resistance, worked with Kosovars from 1985 through 1997. Although his volume is portrayed as historical and scholarly, its identification with Kosovar Albanians is apparent. That is a welcome change from most work on the region, especially for his discussion of the "turn toward non-violence," which nobody knows, exactly, how or why it happened (Clark 2000, 46). Sociologists, especially those committed to public engagement, ought to engage this far more.[15] Here are some reasons why.

Comparative studies of workers' significance finds much here. As in many circumstances of workers' rebellion, miners were at the center of the 1988–89 struggle against the loss of Kosova's constitutional autonomy. The 1980–81 worker-led Polish Solidarity movement was an important inspiration for that mobilization (Agani 2012).

Those who wish to explore the articulation of intellectuals and civil society could explore how Ibrahim Rugova, formerly president of the Writers Association and subsequent leader of the Democratic League of Kosova (LDK), worked. His would become the dominant political movement for much of the 1990s. And under his leadership, nonviolent resistance became the principal definition of Kosovar political aspirations and civil society for most of the 1990s.[16]

For those who wish to understand variations of nonviolent resistance and the conditions of its consequence, this is a good case. The Kosovars established referenda to declare independence, elections for a president and parliament associated with that independent state in 1992, and boycotts of Serbian elections in 1990 and of the 1991 census.

One of the most extraordinary efforts associated with their struggle was to create a parallel society. Other communist-led societies enjoyed this kind of self-organized civil society, complete with their own *samizdat* publications. None of the others reached the scale Kosova mobilized. Kosova enjoyed functioning systems of education, with primary, secondary, and university levels; health services; and taxation organized beyond the official state structures controlled by Serbs. This exceptional effort was not without its limitations, of course, but the fact that it could have happened at all is, in retrospect, remarkable and deserving of more historical sociological accounting.

One of its most indigenous and innovative expressions was the campaign to reconcile blood feuds between 1990 and 1992 when campaigners visited villages and stimulated public ceremonies to help turn the sense of honor involving vengeance into a sense of honor demanding national solidarity (Clark 2000, 60–64). Exemplary of intellectual responsibility, intellectuals and their students led this campaign to transform Kosovar Albanian identity (66).

These times are also important for elaborating public sociology itself. One of the most important figures in this movement was himself one of the leading sociologists of Kosova: Fehmi Agani. Although his scholarly work was important, his contributions to the movement, as the LDK vice president, chief negotiator, and strategist, are best remembered. Shkëlzen Maliqi (2000) wrote,

> Agani was, however, more like an independent actor and, in comparison to Rugova—who kept on repeating the same dry phrases and promises—conducted active daily politics and directed the LDK's and the Albanian movement's ideological and strategic policy. . . . He was one of the intellectual ideologues of the demand for republican status for Kosova (demonstrations 1968), who later maintained contacts with a group of communist leaders that led a realistic policy and accepted Tito's compromising formula of a double status for Kosova (equal unit of the federation and, simultaneously, a part of Serbia) and that were removed from the political scene in 1981 (Mahmut Bakalli, Gazmend Zajmi, Pajazit Nushi, etc.). While Rugova played the role of a big

leader and became embroiled with his historical mission, Agani was leading a pragmatic policy and managed the active part of the legalistic policy, balancing the tensions between the governing structures of the movement, informal ideologues (Bakalli, Zajmi, etc.) and centers of power (parliament and government of Kosova).

Agani has since been memorialized in monuments and street names, but the scholarly reflection on the combination of his scholarship and practical action has only just begun (Hyseni 2013).

By 1996 the contest over that parallel society became more vital as Kosovars, especially students, discussed how to move from passive to active nonviolence. The alternative to nonviolence became more apparent as well, and even desirable for many. The Kosova Liberation Army (KLA) offered another kind of practice for defending Kosovar Albanians, a kind of resistance that became especially compelling after massacres in the Drenica region in the spring of 1998. Although a family following nonviolent methods was the first to be killed, the slaughter of one man prominently associated with the KLA and more than forty of his family members inspired a more violent response. "The dead Adem Jashari became a more potent symbol in 1998 than the passive Rugova or the erratic Demaci" (Clark 2000, 174).

Nevertheless, some activists in Kosovar civil society see the delay of war as itself a kind of victory. Mentor Agani (2012, 26) explains:

> This peaceful movement succeeded, however, in postponing the war that Milosevic's regime was desperately seeking to start—a war that would achieve what the regime really wanted, a complete ethnic cleansing of Albanians from Kosovo. Consequently, given the experience that international community had with the wars in Croatia and Bosnia and Herzegovina, when the first armed clashes occurred in Kosovo at the end of 1997, the way was already paved for international military intervention as the only possible resolution for the last in Milosevic's series of wars.

Because war is not typically among sociologists' foci, those in the discipline are likely to cede academic ground to political scientists. One might make the contrarian case, as Wimmer and Min (2006) do, but that distracts us from the problem of recognition. Why has Kosova as such and Kosovar publics in particular not been more central to English-language sociology? I hope to have shown here why Kosova *should* have been more engaged for those interested in power, history, and social change.

Kosova hits the mainstream English-language sociological map only in 2006, and then only as an object of international organizations' engagements. That begins with a book review on networks of democracy in Kosova (Holohan 2005; Polkinghorn 2006). Holohan compares two organizations in different Kosova locales to help us rethink what makes an effective international organization. Indeed, this presence of international organizations is what brings Kosova to the forefront of journals in social scientific studies, most notably around what happens in postwar international regimes (Arzt 2006; J. Wilson 2006; Hagan and Ivković 2006). This kind of attention is not so new (Kennan 1993), for the core of the world system is frequently interested in other societies as a problem of imperial, or global, governance. Sociologists are increasingly interested in this level of governmentality, which can quite readily become primarily a study of international organizations rather than the host society per se. Fortunately, there are scholars engaging the subject who are equally at home in both worlds (Pula 2009).[17]

These observations could lead us to conclude that those interested only need read different publications, to turn to area studies journals and edited volumes focused on regions. It should also be, however, an invitation to consider how sociology is remade when a different context is elevated. And that is happening around Kosova, in part for a reason I already identified around Poland's place in the American sociological imagination. Simply, the status of Kosovars in English-language sociology is changing.

Relatively few in the US academy are proficient in Albanian.[18] There are even fewer Albanian-speaking Kosovars in American universities. And there are fewer Kosovars than other southeastern Europeans. Those who are part of the academy are relatively early in their careers and are mainly people who left Kosova in the 1990s.[19] Kosovars' relative invisibility in global English-language social science reflects the systemic and systematic disadvantage Kosovar Albanians suffered during the socialist republic of Yugoslavia and its aftermath. As these scholars increase their prominence, Kosova's prominence in American sociology can change. Contemporary Kosovar society also can be a critical prompt.

Kosova's rich array of nongovernmental organizations (NGOs), with particularly complicated relations to the international organizations that sometimes sponsor them, make for exceptionally interesting work for those engaging civil society.[20] Some scholars are motivated by the problem created by that very condition. For example, instead of recognizing the parallel state Kosovar civil society made, there was no recognition whatsoever that the war in Kosovo was not a consequence of absence of civil society, but rather a result of its failure. Instead of trying to revive the previous civic spirit—of which Kosovans were still proud—the international mission started with tremendous efforts to create an altogether new one. It was pitiful to see how the same civic activists who under the horrific conditions of Milosevic's dictatorship achieved to organize the entire social and political life in Kosovo through civic engagement, quite often risking their lives in the process, had to undergo a "civil society for dummies" type of education provided by international bureaucrats who had decided that it was civil society that Kosovo was lacking. (Agani 2012, 15)

And with that condition, Agani argues, civil society was faced with impossible contradictions. If it is to counterbalance the state, it must limit the arbitrariness of the very international protectorate, dominant over the existing state, that feeds it while at the same time recognizing that with its mission around "security," the state cares little about democracy (17–19). Ironically, or perhaps consequentially, the movement that has opposed that international administration and not received its support has also been the most vigorous (Kelmendi 2012).

As a movement, Vetëvendosje is exceptionally active and innovative. Able to trace its roots to the late 1990s when nonviolent resistance moved from its relatively passive to its more active stage, most notably through the Student Action Network, Vetëvendosje began its work by supporting families whose members were lost during the war of 1998–99.[21] Its meaning in Albanian, "self-determination," suggests a relatively simple notion, but its politics are much more complex.

Although it does seek clear independence for Kosova, its politics are organized around equality and justice within and across nations. As a social force within the Kosovar parliament and civil society, Vetëvendosje is among the most innovative in its repertoire of movement techniques and political maneuvers (Cardais 2012; Schwandner-Sievers 2013). It is also the most active: it has organized by far the most protests since 2002 in Kosova, even though it was founded only in 2005 (Kelmendi 2012). Perhaps it is most powerful in its self-positioning as a force for "truth" against what it says is the "institutional lie" of the international protectorate in which Kosova's move toward sovereignty is embedded (Kurti 2011). Public sociology as such has resonance in this kind of environment.

Kosova's place in English-language sociology is very different from what we see for Poland, although it is true that Poland's Solidarity movement began when there was not such dramatic change in the rest of the communist-ruled world. Kosova's remarkable social transformation was initiated when there was exceptional change throughout the postcommunist world, thus distracting potential English-language attention. However, that does not sufficiently explain the relative lack of attention.

Beyond the intensity of change in the 1990s, Kosova's location in the cultural politics of knowledge production is exceptionally complex. On the European foreign policy front, the Cold War's end enabled a generation of leftists come of age in the late 1960s to rethink what progressive politics meant in the end of the 1990s. They could worry that pacifism in the face of aggression was no virtue (Berman 2005; Rathbun 2004). That moved them to develop a dialogue with Eastern Europeans liberated from Soviet internationalism to produce a new kind of humanitarian interventionism. Václav Havel (1999) declared that NATO intervention against Serbia in defense of Kosovars facing genocide was the first war launched in the name of human rights. Kosovar Albanians' embrace of NATO intervention has made for a complicated relationship to intellectuals and activists who normally support those who are dispossessed or mobilizing for justice.

Most critical intellectuals readily mobilized around the denunciation of NATO's bombing (T. Ali 2000). Edward Said's (2000) essay, "The Treason of the Intellectuals," is especially powerful for his critique of NATO bombing despite his identification with displaced and dispossessed persons. For their assessment, most depended on a kind of equivalence between NATO and Serbian aggression. Admittedly, the essays to which I refer specifically were early responses and without benefit of the subsequent scientific work that established clearly that Milošević's forces were responsible for the systematic campaign of killings and expulsions Kosovar Albanians suffered (Ball et al. 2002). It's not just a matter of evidence, however, but the broader cultural horizons of the time. Žižek (1999) captures it well:

> Looking back, one has to say that in the debate over NATO's bombing both sides were wrong. Not that the truth lies somewhere in the middle. On the contrary, both sides, the supporters as much as the opponents of the bombing, were simply wrong. Both attempt to take a universal, neutral, and ultimately false standpoint. The supporters of the bombing make their stand on depoliticized human rights. Their opponents describe the post-Yugoslavian war as

an ethnic struggle in which all sides are equally guilty. But both sides miss the political essence of the post-Yugoslavian conflict. And that is why the conflict continues to smolder under the ashes.

Beyond the complication of its social struggles' location in time and space, it's a matter of knowledge institutions and networks. Kosova was subordinated to Yugoslav/Serbian sociology. No senior Albanian scholars were prominent in US social sciences. There were too few collaborations between US and Kosovar scholars. There was no equivalent to Florian Znaniecki among Albanians and has been no equivalent in later generations to Mel Kohn and Gerhard Lenski engaging Albanians. But these conditions are changing as younger scholars develop their capacities, Kosovar knowledge institutions consolidate, intellectual collaborations build, and journals are introduced.

Afghanistan's challenge is, in some ways, even greater.

Afghanistan in the English-Language Academic Imagination

Although many fewer articles in sociology journals engage Afghanistan than southeastern Europe, it bears consideration what thematic interests are roused when they do.[22] Building on Table 5.5, I compare how often Afghanistan and southeastern Europe appear in sociology journals (Table 5.6).

Once again, in sheer numbers, the *Annals of the American Academy of Political and Social Science* is by far the publication most attentive to both Afghanistan and southeastern Europe, in part for the age of the journal. And again, it's also a matter of substantive focus. Just as for Yugoslavia, Afghanistan was particularly important for the number of articles addressing war and violence and the involvement of the leading powers in the Cold War in that country. There are a few other consistencies here.

Afghanistan and southeastern Europe are relatively similarly ranked in many different journals for somewhat similar reasons. First, they are engaged much more often in book reviews than in articles, and for those journals that have that practice, regions like Afghanistan and southeastern Europe are more likely to be addressed, given their comparative prominence in monographs and edited collections. That difference is especially evident in the relative inattention Afghanistan receives in the *American Sociological Review.*

Not surprisingly, Afghanistan does not figure so prominently in journals with particular interests that favored southeastern Europe. It does not have

TABLE 5.6 Mentions of southeastern Europe (SEE) / Afghanistan in sociology-related journals, 1890–2009

Ranking SEE/Afghanistan	Number of mentions SEE/Afghanistan	Journal
2/4	279/90	American Journal of Sociology
4/12	150/32	American Sociological Review
1/1	890/357	Annals of the American Academy of Political and Social Science
14/8.5	42/51	Comparative Studies in Society and History
3/5	197/74	Contemporary Sociology
6/8.5	92/42	International Journal of Comparative Sociology
13/23	53/7	Industrial and Labor Relations Review
10/22	72/8	Journal of Marriage and the Family
5/2	109/282	Journal of Palestine Studies
12/3	56/214	MERIP
6/10.5	106/35	Social Forces
9/6	74/58	Journal of Modern African Studies
8/7	82/46	Public Opinion Quarterly
11/10.5	67/35	Theory and Society

Yugoslavia's self-management to make it the object of *Industrial and Labor Relations Review*, nor does it have a demographically distinctive kinship structure that has made it into the sociological discussions of *Journal of Marriage and the Family*.

Afghanistan should appear much more often in publications associated with the region, an association that is obvious with *MERIP*. But it's also surprisingly prominent in *Comparative Studies in Society and History*, in part because of the relative importance of historians and anthropologists to the journal's production and readership, especially those engaging South Asia and the Middle East.

The biggest contrast between regions, however, is not apparent in the table but in the titles of the journals' articles. Afghanistan is hardly mentioned in the titles and is more likely to figure in an article as a derivative of a larger discussion: of the Cold War between Americans and Soviets, of terrorism and war, or as an example of a developing country or Islamic society. It also figures quite prominently in borderland discussions of, for example, Pashtuns who live both in Afghanistan and Pakistan. This dissonance between state boundaries and sensibilities of peoplehood helps explain Afghanistan's particular place in history, anthropology, and international relations. It is also more than a matter of borderlands (Caron 2007).

Caron (2007) argues that the historiography of pre-1978 Afghanistan was very much caught within the modernization problematic that other South Asian and postcolonial studies escaped. This is curious, given that the West has been involved in the region's wars, but on reflection, he argues, it makes sense. Too much of that history is implicated in imperial statecraft, and imperial statecraft finds in modernization a useful framework to justify imperialist positions. In particular, whether in the hands of nationalist or imperial elites and their various intellectual infrastructures, accounts tend to be organized around elite/mass tensions. Insurgent masses are typically framed as irrational in the face of the modernizing elites. Islam, in that framework, becomes the expression of rebellion and seen only through that lens. The exceptions, Caron writes, are too few in number to mobilize much of an alternative historiography. Modernization remains apparent even when the approach is more institutionalist (Gregorian 1969).

Transformative elites like the early twentieth century's King Amanullah are painted as having "failed" in the face of the overall class balance in society and the place of Islam in securing those traditional relations. Nevertheless, Caron notes a number of works, by David Edwards, Ashraf Ghani, and others, that seek to develop a more complex articulation of class actors, religious forces, and social networks that move us beyond an account framed by oppositions between tradition and modernity.

I don't find Caron's criticism of state-centrism entirely convincing, but that moves beyond my expertise and the point I wish to make. Rather than Afghanistan offering a point of theoretical innovation, it remains caught in a theoretical backwater. Thus, it is unlikely to inspire much more than policy-relevant accounts accepting the underlying narrative of an externally normative modernity seeking to transform an indigenous and backward tradition, which, with the Taliban and attacks of 9/11, becomes even dangerous. This, however, is where intellectual innovation promises broader knowledge transformations.

Ashraf Ghani, discussed earlier, has contributed in a number of ways to the transformation of Afghanistan itself, but his scholarship offers the kind of challenge to the academy that promises more beyond the region.[23] I have already considered Ghani's National Solidarity Program; here, his scholarly work deserves much more consideration.

Afghan Democratic Internationalism

Despite the title, Ashraf Ghani's major theoretical work with Clare Lockhart (2008) is not only about failed states. They look for lessons in success stories, from pre-Euro-crisis Ireland to the southeastern United States, concluding with this point: "These stories of transformation demonstrate the possibility for either creating or recombining existing assets to develop stocks of financial, human and intellectual capital that will enable a country to connect with global economic, financial, and knowledge flows" (50). The Afghan foundations of Ghani's internationalism become apparent with their critique of the global aid complex supposedly designed to channel those connections.

In rich detail, they outline how this complex "creates a cocoon for its own staff, without becoming a catalyst for institution building within the host country that it purports to help" (Ghani and Lockhart 2008, 77). Instead, the aid complex should perform particular functions, "namely, generating prosperity by bringing a global knowledge of stocks and flows to countries without it. . . . In view of the fact that it comprises extractive industries and technical assistance brigades, the aid system—instead of opening countries up to legitimate entrepreneurial activity—epitomizes the side of capitalism that is fundamentally exploitative" (86). Consultants can also be quite problematic, especially because this reliance on external experts can undermine the development of a fully sovereign state (102).

This work has attracted a great deal of scholarly attention and inspired much critique. For some, it has typified the problem of focusing on states rather than on the problems that the post-Cold War unipolar system produced (Halvorson 2010). Others have proposed that their focus on state functions and the importance of fighting corruption has been especially important to those who focus on peace building in postconflict societies (Doig and Tisne 2009). Some have identified their work as emblematic of postliberal theory, one of the major streams of international security theory (Chandler 2010b). In that spirit, Chandler (2010a) has also taken Ghani and Lockhart to task for overestimating what the European Union has done for southeastern Europe: the EU has become rather neocolonial in its stabilization and association agreements for the region. Especially in recent years, few in Kosova would disagree, and this becomes another opportunity. Indeed, Vetëvendosje in particular might appreciate the point Rowsell (2012) has recommended in extending the double compact to a triple. Conditions of effective states should be recognized not only in the relationship between citizens and state, and states with international community, but also directly in the relationship between international community and publics. After all, that last relationship might enable our focus on corruption itself.

Clearly, then, Ghani's work has inspired a great deal of scholarly engagement, but the place of Afghanistan in the broader scholarly imagination remains more limited than it should be. However, one recent publication by Mariam (his daughter) and Ashraf Ghani offers another point of entry. *Afghanistan: A Lexicon* (2012) is just the kind of publication whose original form, engaging format, and lively way invites more interest, even as it lays down certain puzzles. For those who wish to engage universal issues through Afghan experiences, the brief entry on loss is especially compelling. This volume's impact remains to be seen, but it offers for me an exceptionally accessible engagement with a place I should understand more, a society whose trajectory shapes two global transformations: of Soviet power's end and, we might hope, the end to great power wars in central Asia.

In both theory and practice, Ashraf Ghani offers the kind of articulation that should increase reference to Afghanistan in scholarship and globalizing knowledge. However, even as this brief review suggests, most references to Ghani and Lockhart's work treat Afghanistan either as an example of a failed state and why it's dangerous or why the failed state concept is wrong and how the global system is problematic.

However, when local publics themselves become critical partners in advancing theory and practice, whether in the example of the National Solidarity Program or in the struggles against corruption in a triple compact, the qualities of life in Afghanistan figure much more prominently. They are also quite prominent when gender organizes discussion.

Gender in Context

One of the intriguing findings about the National Solidarity Program in Afghanistan has been its effects on gender. Preliminary results from the work of Andrew Beath and collegues (2010) conclude that the program creates councils that complement the authority of village elders, as well as increases the possibilities for women to have influence in these villages. Understanding gender in context does not always flow simply alongside globalizing feminisms, however, especially in postcommunist contexts.[24]

Feminism, or at least the positioning of women in prominent roles, was not so alien to Poland before communist rule. Polish women were assimilated into early North American feminist writings as particular exemplars of emancipation (Filipowicz 1996). During and especially after communism's collapse, gender studies have not articulated easily with Polish intellectual culture, as the earliest feminist engagements emphasized (Funk and Mueller 1993).

There were important scholars of gender in Poland during those communist and early postcommunist days,[25] but the globalized feminist community of discourse didn't resonate as well in Poland as in East Germany, Hungary, Russia, or the former Yugoslavia in the postcommunist world, or in Turkey, India, or China in other parts of the Global South. Some North American feminists explained that dissonance with Polish male chauvinism and the influence of the Catholic Church; some Polish scholars explained it with intimations of feminist unculturedness or Western national chauvinism. The better scholars used more nuanced interpretations (Marody 1993). Those days are for the most part gone, and gender consciousness, in its own vernacular, has developed powerfully. Joanna Regulska's work in Poland and across postcommunist countries more broadly has been especially important in developing that articulation of globalizing knowledge in vernaculars.

As Regulska and Grabowska (2013) suggest, understanding the mobilization of women in postcommunism requires one to move beyond the conventions of women's studies in the West. First and foremost, one can't look for "mass" movements in the region, partly because resistance continues to be expressed in reaction to the forced group identities of the communist era. That, in turn, reflects the particular challenge of the old second world and its articulation with their old first.

While women have successfully mobilized in different domains with various resources, gender equality movements frequently draw on extranational symbolic and material resources. Western foundations channel women's movements in ways that can appear alien to the champions of the "nation," especially when mobilizations challenge patriarchs and their supporters who claim to speak for that nation. Worse, even those who support gender equality in postcommunist places may not be the best allies. Gender equality can function less as a goal of struggle than as part of a larger package and, in those countries acceding to the European Union, as a sign of being European. A particular policy and practice supporting women's rights winds up being subordinated again, this time to larger geopolitical identifications rather than to communist ideology (Gerber 2011).

One of the more exceptional, and publicity effective, movements of women to have emerged in the postcommunist world has been Ukraine's Femen. The ease, or challenge, of its interpretation illustrates in particular the difficulty of figuring feminism in this global context (Zychowicz 2011).[26] Famous for its use of nudity to gain recognition for causes they believe harmful to women, Femen has attempted to globalize its own approach to change by using its naked repertoire in actions in England, France, and Turkey. For some, this has had increasingly bad effect, moving potentially sympathetic feminist intellectuals and activists into even greater disdain for their project.[27] Indeed, their own actions can even feed into perceptions in other parts of the world that feminism is part of a larger imperialist project.

Gender equality has long been a key element legitimating imperialism, whether in its capitalist (Keck and Sikkink 1998) or communist (Northrop 2004) variants. Following Soviet occupation, Taliban rule, and democratic peace building, women's rights in Afghanistan also face challenging reads, to be understood not only in terms of democracy but also in terms of sovereignty and the struggles of women themselves within Afghanistan (Kennedy 2011a). While women are especially prominent in the definition of civil society, the gender politics of the political sphere also seem central to globalizing knowledge about Afghanistan (Heath and Zahedi 2011). Wazhmah Osman (2011, 2012) helps.

Osman's focus on the Afghan public sphere requires that she put gender to the center of her work. On the global scale, "saving Afghan women" became a centerpiece justifying the invasion in 2001. But it was a double cross, as Osman (2012) writes:

> Instead of giving Afghan women the podium from which to speak, as one would presume, this double-crossing discourse actually took what was left of Afghan women's agency in order to aggrandize the power of so called expert individuals and organizations, both governmental and non-governmental. So while "Afghan Women" as a body of imagery proliferated and circulated widely, they made their subject matter a hollowed out empty signifier at best. Their silent over exposure actually made "Afghan Women" a joke, a caricature that was mocked and ridiculed in satirical exposes in magazines and videos, in genres ranging from comedy to pornography.

In order to move beyond the critique of this gender-charged imperialism, Osman (2012) conducted her fieldwork with these notions in mind:

> How are charged issues such as gender/sexuality, human rights, democracy, and religion contested, framed, and negotiated by local cultural producers? How do local Afghan institutions "talk back" to the global circulation of images of Afghan women and other discourses about them? Why is television particularly catalytic in fueling public debates and dissent? In terms of gender, why is the tele-presence of women as compared to their circulation in other mediums particularly problematic to the religious sector?

While the contest is powerful, she argues, the violence makes talk of the public sphere as such difficult. Humor tells. She writes that this is the common sense among Afghan journalists: "you have freedom to express yourself but no more freedom after the expression." When murders, especially of women, are too often the result of such free expression, Osman warns against invocations of exoticizing honor killing, which easily hide the real stories behind violence with all-too-modern, not "traditional," interests in mind. The story is far more complex than the familiar narratives allow, and thus gender clearly does not automatically move a contextual expertise critical of globalizing hegemonies and cognizant of vernacular knowledge.

NATO's 1999 intervention in southeastern Europe, however, was not about rescuing women, even while brutalization of women during the wars of Yugoslav Succession was substantial. In the spring of 2013, Nazlie Bala, a human rights activist, was attacked for leading the struggle to introduce an amendment to a law on the status and the rights of the martyrs, invalids, veterans, members of the Kosova Liberation Army, civilian victims of war, and their families that would "provide survivors of sexual violence war crimes legal recognition, respect and public acknowledgement, as well as the right to receive compensation, rehabilitation and other forms of reparation" (Front Line Defenders 2013). Both civil rights activists and sociologists have mobilized around this issue as a clear indicator of gender's abiding significance in understanding inequalities and civil society's emancipatory role. More generally, gender figures prominently for globalizing knowledge in vernaculars and challenging hegemonic interpretations of war, peace building, and transition (Luci and Gusia forthcoming). One of the most important starting points for this effort develops along the politics of remembrance and belonging.

Drawing on interviews with women who led change in Kosova, Luci and Krasniqi (2011, 170) both reconstructed feminism and meanings of Albanianness in Kosova itself. While the recollections of the inspired and inspiring women in Kosova are moving, the editors' conclusion synthesizes powerfully:

> Feminism is not only a mode of knowledge, but also a potential for transformative politics. The rejection of hierarchies of duality is inseparably bound to our dissatisfaction with the language and practices of resistance. To resist is not enough. While all of the women here were active agents in a politics of resistance to a hegemonic other, almost all become dissatisfied with limits of political and social forms that were permitted and/or made available. They argue for the transformation of the status quo and relations of power. These are related to both their articulation of the "national question" and the "women question." Future research should focus on the possibilities of avenues for feminist intervention, but also research that is sensitive to meanings of feminism. Women in Kosova widely reject the use of the term feminism, therefore it is not in our place to define this as a lack. But, we do strongly insist for de-essentializing feminism as it is used in the Kosovar context. There needs to be an opening of spaces for contestation, of what feminism entails, but also a more imaginative politics for ending the subordinate position of women. (287)

By rethinking gender within and across contexts, the articulations of globalizing knowledge promise much. There is a terrifically rich theoretical literature on which scholars and practitioners from a wide array of contexts can draw to identify the particulars of their place even while mobilizing knowledge about the commonalities of women's subordinate positions, as the work by Luci and Krasniqi illustrates.

Gender scholarship is transformative not only within place but potentially across places. That also depends on gender scholars' knowledge institutional security and the networks that collaborate with them. And all of this depends on the reflexivity born in globalizing knowledge across places.

Articulations of Context in Reflexivity

The reflexivity of each disciplinary and national scholarly tradition is enhanced when it has partners sufficiently distant to make problematic presumptions visible and critical questions central. Reflexivity is thus realized not only through the scientific analysis of the rules, resources, and strategies of scholarship and its fields of practice. It is also developed in practice through collaboration with others beyond, but familiar with, one's assumptions. To the extent any place fails to engage in that transformative practice with its knowledge partners across the world, it loses its ability to recognize its peculiarity, even as it reproduces its ethnocentrism. With sufficient power and influence, some nations like the United States can globalize their knowledge with ethnocentrisms intact, perhaps even reinforced.

It is useful to presume ethnocentrism forms a point of departure in all forms of social life, including knowledge production. It's also critical to recognize that such ethnocentrism is much more likely in higher education when one's institution and intellectual networks are organized around global relations of power and privilege. For this reason so many US educators have historically seen higher education as a means of expanding one's sense of the world by learning languages other than those with which one grew up, and by traveling, studying, and working beyond one's nation. Those in less privileged circumstances manage that by migrating and only sometimes returning.

Knowledge being globalized through these travels does not mean that we learn about the world without imposing our ethnocentric visions on that engagement, which is, in part, what both the Orientalist and the dependency/world systems critiques have been about and what Connell's elaboration of "southern theory" promises. But even those critical interventions fail to help us appreciate which places lead us beyond the reproduction of ethnocentrism within globalizing knowledge itself.

The tradition of area studies, as discussed previously, is part of the answer. Here, questions that are important for a world region are raised, regardless of their status in global theoretical and methodological discussions. These questions can lead more prestigious scholars with global and universalist credentials to dismiss those who know more about what scholars and publics do in Peshawar, Pecs, and Poznan. But when innovations in theory and practice come from those places, that "area studies" knowledge can become more important, and scholarship from those regions more consequential. Globalizing knowledge can develop more profoundly because the power and privilege with which it was previously articulated have just been altered with a new regional sensibility in the mix.

That elevation of knowledge is not just a matter of intellectual entrepreneurship or a region's significance in global powers' affairs. It is both structured and influenced by practice. By analyzing how Poland, Kosova, and

Afghanistan enter the English-speaking academic world, especially through sociology and other social science publications, I hope to have clarified some aspects of that process. In conclusion, I wish to synthesize what I have found in order to move the transformation.

First, we need to recognize that places are unevenly represented in scholarship. That is obvious, perhaps, but the reproduction of that variable prominence astonishes, especially given the transformations in the world. In particular, despite the global transformations that move places to the center of global attention, their academic engagement changes relatively little. The situation is to some extent different for scholars of international relations, whose attention moves with the foreign policies of their states. Wars draw attention, as scholarship engaging the former Yugoslavia and Afghanistan reflects, but even that attention is articulated by the qualities of previously existing knowledge cultures. That is apparent in the different area studies engagements around Poland, Kosova, and Afghanistan.

Although Russia dominated the area studies tradition devoted to the European communist world, Poland was a major site of area studies engagement. Its size, Slavic-language base, and relative intellectual and cultural distinction enabled that prominence. The significant Polish intellectual diaspora also helped. Yugoslavia was also relatively prominent in that area studies tradition, especially because of its nonaligned status. However, due to national differentiation and diasporic contests, it never quite realized the prominence of Poland. Within southeastern European studies, Serbian and Croatian studies were certainly more prominent than Albanian and especially Kosovar Albanian engagements.

That relative disadvantage for Albanians has many sources in the regions themselves—both of Albania's relative isolation during communism and Kosova's discriminated status within Yugoslavia. It also has its sources in American academia, given the relative few who knew Albanian language and engaged its peoples in systematic social scientific ways. And that has been a loss for globalizing knowledge, especially when developments of such world historical consequence around resistance in the 1990s and the international protectorate of the twenty-first century exist. This relative lack of global engagement, beyond the Kosovar Albanians themselves, reinforces the imperialist qualities and contradictions of a European Union dedicated to human rights and the rule of law in Kosova.

Although Afghanistan has enjoyed greater sovereignty and openness to the world than Albanians over the last century, the intensity of wars in the last thirty years has marked its difference. Given the length of engagement by the West, one would have thought that far greater scholarly investment would have been made. It has not, which leads us to, in combination with our observations about Kosova, a fundamental point.

Context does not become more important in the scholarly world without simultaneous attention to the knowledge production process itself. In order for a place to become relatively prominent in globalizing knowledge, not only its people and those devoted to the region need to work in the languages and histories of a place. There need to be better mechanisms that bring those sensibilities into ever more global, and theoretically universal, discussions. The Polish example informs.

One can't duplicate Poland's size or historical privilege, but one can invest in the production of and recognition for scholars like Florian Znaniecki and collaborations like those between him and W. I. Thomas, or between Kohn and Słomczyński. This can happen through normal social science but also might become the object of more strategic investment by those who see globalizing knowledge networks as helping constitute global public goods.

The value of these collaborations can be extended when one has a Znaniecki in-house. In this sense, Afghanistan's Ashraf Ghani offers an invaluable resource for transforming the knowledge culture around Afghanistan's place. And he has to a considerable extent already, even as his scholarly contributions are shifted toward knowledge in practice. Given the value of public social science, it might be enough to draw more attention to what he does than to wish he would offer decontextualized ideas that might find immortality in their purity.

In the end, however, one can't replicate a Znaniecki or Ghani or multiply easily the examples of Kohn and Słomczyński, but one might look to particular areas whose fusions of global and proximate sense promise consequence in globalizing knowledge. And here, gender studies might be a good candidate, especially when we consider the critical fusions of expertise around gender, art, and media that so many gender scholars bring to the table. There are already many examples of just that kind of collaboration at work, and much of it with terrific public consequence. Indeed, gender studies in Poland, Kosova, and Afghanistan might not be as influential within their nations as other fields, but feminism's flow is one of the most powerful currents of globalizing knowledge.

6 Connectivity: Understanding Global Flows

Unlike area studies and the contexts in which they are implicated, global flows have historically been studied with less attention to the broader spaces of their work. They have been more commonly engaged on their own terms, within their own relatively bounded knowledge cultures fixed by relatively delimited theoretical and methodological guidelines, but these approaches can change. Especially motivated by notions of connectivity inspired by globalization and its knowledge cultural politics, flows do more than connect. They reconfigure our worldly imagination.

In what follows, I consider the ways in which intellectuals and knowledge institutions and networks have considered the space and articulation of global flows. Following one relatively explicit discussion of a quite political global flow, I consider how globalizing knowledge articulates the world's energy flows through concentrations of expertise and the cultural political articulation of national energy interests. I conclude with reflections on how an emergent information order might anticipate not only a new global culture and knowledge industry but a new energy order of things. And that moves with a broader sense of intellectual responsibility rearticulating global public goods.

The Space and Articulation of Flows

What do we mean when we talk about flows? Is it sufficient to say that this refers to the movement of knowledge, people, wealth, and weapons?

Studies of people's movement or migration studies have a substantial scholarly pedigree. After all, it was the study of the Polish peasant in Europe and America that anchored Poland in the American sociological imagination. Studies of population movement have expanded beyond their association with demography and sociology. They now address its consequence for the sending country's economic development and the organization of migrants' work, notions of rights, citizenship and nationality, among other arenas. "Digital Diasporas" captures the novelty, and potential consequence, of rethinking the flows of people across boundaries of all kinds with new capacities associated with the information revolution (Brinkerhoff 2009).

Trade has long been a critical field in economics and other social sciences, but it has taken on a new distinction. Given the ease with which new communication technologies have made finances circulate in ever more rapid fashion with new financial instruments their midwife, global finance leads in globalization's definition. Trade in weapons need not be distinguished from other commodities, of course, but they typically are treated separately, given their association with security—whether in the sales of sophisticated warplanes or in attempts to regulate the distribution of plutonium. Crossover analysts are, therefore, increasingly critical. Some, for example, have noted that the proliferation of trade in small arms has a decidedly negative effect on development; the proliferation of small arms increases the magnitude, and likelihood, of violence, which in turn diminishes economic growth (e.g., Collier et al. 2003).

International relations, a subfield in political science, itself enjoys a prominent position in defining international studies in many US universities. While its realist side is unlikely to look for itself in the world of flows, those working with the more "constructivist" articulation are quite important in defining that world. Here, the learning shared among nongovernmental actors is particularly critical, arguably transforming the character of international relations as we know it (Keck and Sikkink 1998; Sikkink 2011; Thomas 2001).

It's not only knowledge that matters in the world of flows, however. The character and implications of global flows of images, symbols, and communications have commanded an exceptional increase of interest in the last several decades, altering our very sense of geography (Appadurai 1996). The global culture industry has probably done more to refashion the sense of flow than any of the other domains in which things travel (Lash and Lury 2007). One might illustrate the point relatively readily by flashing an image to you right now, in order to see how much images matter, and recognition works, in the world of flows (Figure 6.1).

FIGURE 6.1 Pussy Riot's iconic photo. Photograph by Igor Mukhin, Wikimedia Commons.

Although I consider Pussy Riot at greater length later in this chapter, the fact that you should know to what this image refers illustrates powerfully the global culture industry's consequence. This Russian performance art, symbolized by women wearing balaclavas, has acquired a worldwide reputation through Internet dissemination of their 2012 punk prayer in the Cathedral of Christ the Savior in Moscow. That video's message was amplified because of their arrest and subsequent trial by Moscow authorities. That trial would not have mattered, however, were it not for the terrific solidarity artists, feminists, activists, and fans across the world offered in a wide array of forms. While few of their worldly supporters know Russian, or could invoke Dostoyevsky in the same ways as Nadya Tolokonnikova managed in their trial, Pussy Riot already moved beyond the challenge of recognition in globalizing knowledge. Performance art in the world of flows travels and potentially extends solidarity for others and their struggles.

These various flows do come together in some treatments of globalization. For example, Saskia Sassen (2007) has developed her own complex approach to global formations for a broader public by articulating treatments of global institutions and processes and elements of globalization fixed in place. The

World Trade Organization exemplifies the first; global commodity chains, the second; and global cities like New York, London, and Tokyo, the third. In general, however, the location of different global flows is critical for understanding the restructuration of space and the various authorities associated with those different scales of operation (Sassen 2008). Understanding the variety of those flows is important not only for analytical purposes, Sassen argues, but also for those who would seek to regulate them in various emergent global formations.

In a rhetorical flourish, I once proposed that a new international studies mission could be developed around the flows of "knowledge, people, wealth and weapons" where the comparison of these flows, and their interactions, would help us recognize more clearly how global transformations have developed and especially how they might still take place.[1] Of course, that builds on a substantial body of literature that has not yet had either the public or even scholarly impact one might have imagined.

In particular, we face three layers of knowledge challenge in a world of flows. First, we need to build on each flow's knowledge culture so that we recognize not only the dynamics of its movement but its articulation with the various contexts in which it swirls. In particular, we must do this in ways that cumulate our sense about particular flows and places and about how they combine to enable alternative global futures. Second, we need to develop a new way to figure which flows are consequential and why for shaping those global futures. We are too easily drawn to the images that travel rather than the powers that channel them. We notice the most compelling images but not the networks of money and power they address or that may even funnel them. Finally, we need to consider how these articulations of flow/context and priority are themselves influenced by the context from which we argue. In a world of flows, cosmopolitan promise seems proximate, but the dangers of ethnocentrism continue to loom quite large. I approach those challenges, beginning with one of the intellectuals who made the world of flows most prominent in the scholarly imagination.

Arjun Appadurai (2001, 5) wrote this back at the turn of the century: "It has now become something of a truism that we are functioning in a world fundamentally characterized by objects in motion. These objects include ideas and ideologies, people and goods, images and messages, technologies and techniques. This is a world of flows." Manuel Castells (2009) moves that along powerfully. He argues that societies are today fundamentally different

from what they were before the microelectronics revolution. While socie
ties have always been composed of networks, the significance of networks has
grown dramatically with the development of digital communications in what
he calls the information age. For Castells, networks are communicative structures that process flows of information (2009, 20). With the digitalization of
those flows, networks become global if nonetheless selective in their distribution (25). They also produce new forms of space and time.

> The *space of flows* refers to the technological and organizational possibility of
> practicing simultaneity without contiguity. It also refers to the possibility of
> asynchronous interaction in chosen time at a distance. Most dominant func-
> tions in the network society (financial markets, transnational production net-
> works, media networks, networked forms of global governance, global social
> movements) are organized around the space of flows. (34–35)

Although we can think of communication in normative terms that bracket
power, it is more useful to figure how this space of flows made through communication changes our conceptions of power and the rules that validate or
delegitimate it. Intellectuals as such are not the agents of this cultural work.
Those with the capacities to constitute networks with particular goals, what
Castells calls "programmers," are. Their power rests less in ideas or knowledge and more in coordinating the network's action. This is best conceived,
Castells argues, in Bruno Latour's (2005) sense of the actor network and the
theory associated with it, referred to as ANT.

For Castells, networks all depend on the ideas or cultural frames organizing them. They are thus substantively, not just structurally, variable. His
is not formal network theory. Following him, we should not be surprised
that flows of weapons, people, wealth, and knowledge would be organized
in distinct knowledge cultures, each within its own validating and contesting claims about value. Switchers might rearticulate those network cultures,
however. They can reshape networks because they control connections among
them. Castells's (2009, 45–47) "switchers" are both critical for reproducing
what exists and potentially transformative, depending on the articulation of
these networks and flows. That, in turn, suggests an analytical strategy, where
society is analyzed

> first as a global architecture of self-reconfiguring networks constantly pro-
> grammed and reprogrammed by the powers that be in each dimension;

second, as the result of the interaction between the various geometries and geographies of the networks that include the core activities—that is, the activities shaping life and work in society; and third, as the result of a second order interaction between these dominant networks and the geometry and geography of the disconnection of social formations left outside the global networking logic. . . . In the network society, the space of flows dissolves time by disordering the sequence of events and making them simultaneous in the communications networks, thus installing society in structural ephemerality: *being cancels becoming.* (26)

The implications of Castells's work are profound. Not only does his emphasis on communication power reinforce the significance of knowledgeability, articulation, and networks. It also suggests the importance of moving both comparatively across regions and critically across knowledge fields associated with different expert domains. It also changes our sense of intellectuality and its consequence. The notion of Castells's programmers is not so new, of course, as it mainly reassigns expertise to the administration of networks. But the switcher *is* new, and critical.

Consequential knowledge is less about either breadth *or* depth than the capacity to make new connections across weakly articulated but potentially powerful networks in combination.[2] However, some things are more easily rearticulated than others. Energy, for example, is exceptionally weighty because of the wealth associated with its control, its material qualities, and the powerful knowledge cultures organized around it. Some other objects, however, are more subject to the switch and to the transformation of social relations.

For example, Gianpaolo Baiocchi and Ernesto Ganuza have worked extensively on how transformations of political process develop within particular contexts and are translated across the world. Focusing in his first book on the innovations in "participatory budgeting" in Porto Allegre, the process by which local publics obtain control over portions of municipal budgets to allocate according to transparent public discussions, Baiocchi (2005) helps clarify one of the local institutional transformations that made Brazil's Workers' Party so successful. He has developed these notions to consider how these ideas traveled across Brazil and their implications for the local state and its civil society (Baiocchi, Heller, and Silva 2008). However, in his subsequent work with Ernesto Ganuza, he has explored how these ideas have traveled across Brazil and the world (Baiocchi and Ganuza forthcoming).

Now in some fifteen hundred municipalities across the world, participatory budgeting as an idea has taken off. It has become unmoored from its grounding in the Brazilian context and from the ideas around administrative reform and social justice that give its original purpose. By tracing its travel across the world, Baiocchi and his colleagues have explained how this technique adapts to different circumstances and different agents of implementation. This knowledge flow highlights the ways in which things are transformed and can transform. By breaking down participatory budgeting into its communicative "Habermasian" moment, and the Rawlsian administrative one, Baiocchi and Ganuza illustrate that in a world of flows, some things are a bit stickier than others, while other things more easily go with the flow.

One might point to a number of other studies that have engaged the notion of flows to transform our sense of how the world is connected. As we read them, we should also consider the implications of a focus on flows for our conventional understandings of social transformations. But the best way to consider just that problem is to consider a particular flow that rearticulates context. Pussy Riot rocks that invitation.

Performance Art and Pussy Riot's Flow

We all know who/what Pussy Riot is.[3] Well, that may be quite an exaggeration. Nevertheless, I suspect that is more true, especially if you are a digital native, than saying we all know who Lech Wałęsa, Albin Kurti, or Ashraf Ghani is. After all, the Pussy Riot image flowed across the Internet in ways even better than their music. And it was better than their music, but that's not the point.

On August 16, 2012, three Pussy Riot performers were sentenced to two years in prison for acts of religious hatred. The problem? They and their bandmates earlier that year jumped on to a sacrosanct part of Moscow's Cathedral of Christ the Savior for some forty seconds to perform their punk prayer for Putin's removal from power.[4]

By itself, this performance was not in and of itself globally consequential. Had the Russian authorities fined these women and sent them home, the performance would not have been so momentous. But who knows? It was recorded and then distributed on the Internet. However, its significance grew to global proportions only when the women were put on trial and their cause was taken up by a considerable array of organizations and prominent public figures.

Human rights organizations like Amnesty International supported them.[5] Political spaces like the UK Houses of Parliament (Andrew 2012) and the European Union Parliament (Fox 2012) held debates about their example. Arts media like *Art Review* magazine and poets like Sophie Robinson (2012) extended their cultural impact.[6] Well-known performers like Madonna, Bjork, Yoko Ono, and Sting elevated Pussy Riot celebrity with their solidarity. Political officials got into the act, too, with the European Union foreign affairs chief Lady Catherine Ashton joining President Obama in decrying the two-year sentence for an exercise in free speech. That, one might argue, is consequential knowledge work, or at least consequential performance art.

It's easy to view this happening, this event, within the context of the world of flows. Without global media, the global awareness of the trial and the issue would not have taken place. More than a few commentators suggested that this was like Stalin's show trials of the 1930s, even as they would quickly deny the full parallel. After all, the media were all over the Pussy Riot defense. Without the ease of transmitting simple symbols of solidarity, like the balaclava worn by these women and other Pussy Riot performers and sympaticos, the capacity to signal awareness of and identification with the Moscow contest across the world would be lost. Without the global glare of celebrity, the solidarity of Madonna and the others would not have mattered much. But to treat the power of Pussy Riot in terms only of celebrity, symbolism, and connectivity misses the much deeper articulation of knowledge and global transformations hidden in their power of performance. Yekaterina Samutsevich, one of the three Pussy Riot performers put on trial, recognized this too, as the *Guardian* reported:

> The three women were deprived of information from the outside world, but kept informed of events by their lawyers. "One day in court, the lawyers showed us photos. We didn't understand what it was. Then they explained it was Madonna, with writing on her back supporting us," she said. That was when she understood the whole world was watching. Madonna was one of a handful of artists who performed in Moscow, and who came out in support of the jailed band. "All this solidarity meant we were understood in modern cultural society," Samutsevich said. "That was very important to us." (Elder 2012)

Not all celebrate Pussy Riot's influence.

My friends and colleagues, notably Roz Galtz, drew my attention to the growing number of serious Russian expert critiques of Pussy Riot. Some noted that others have suffered so much more by Putin's hands. Others pointed out that these women elicit support only because they are young and attractive. Still others argue that there are so many more serious challenges to power than those who don't get the global media's support, like Julian Assange. These concerns move me back to the previous discussion of Lewis Coser (1973) and his denigration of "celebrity intellectuals." These celebrity intellectuals are not serious, and the media elevated them without proper review, so the argument might go. But then Tania Lewis (2001) reminds us that if public consequence is part of our concern, all the sins associated with celebrity are simultaneously what we need to rethink. We should not allow the flash to blind us from the profundity in what is said, in what actions inspire.

The final statements offered by two of the defendants have flowed along the global networks I inhabit as much as, if not more than, their performance itself. Why? Because they invoke the giants of the Russian intelligentsia, their traditions of dissent, and the importance of recognizing how in Russian culture those high-minded notions can blend with punk to create a culture of critique and consequence that conventional intellectuals might only envy. Sometimes they are called "holy fools," invoking a Russian religious tradition (Eyres 2012), but I'm not so sure that historical references are the best marker. There is something suggestive of the future more than the past in their performance. Maxim Pozdorovkin (2013), co-director of the HBO film on Pussy Riot, puts it this way:

> From the very beginning we knew that the most interesting film would be one that was immersive and present tense while, at the same time, revealing the individuals behind the colorful balaclavas. Whether that film was possible was not at all clear at the outset. Sitting inside the courtroom, I was amazed by the way the women of Pussy Riot managed to gain the upper hand and transform the trial into a piece of performance art. The women's motion to have the proceedings recorded was granted. RIA Novosti, the Russian equivalent of Reuters, filmed the trial. Upon inquiring about licensing material I discovered a treasure trove of never-before-seen rushes, which showed the women interacting, amongst themselves and with their lawyers, before the trial commenced each day. These moments were all the more invaluable for the fact that the three women awaited trial in separate cells and did not have a chance to interact. These moments awaiting trial were a window and everything we dreamed the film could be.

There is a kind of knowledgeability that comes from understanding the cultural schemas of the worlds one inhabits and the power of symbols for their transformation. Genevieve Zubrzycki (2006) has done much in general to explain the particular ways in which the symbolic power of the cross in a Poland inflected by Roman Catholicism goes well beyond its official use.

That cross is saturated in power, and its use, even by a few isolated individuals, can have huge consequence. This happened when dissident Poles planted crosses outside Auschwitz in an attempt to reclaim the concentration camp as a site for martyrdom not only for Jews but also for those beyond the Mosaic tradition in the Polish nation. Strategic use of symbols saturated with meanings might be accidental, as the beheading of John the Baptist symbolized in the desanctification of Quebec's political identity (Zubrzycki 2012). They might even be quite deliberate, reflecting profound awareness of likely reactions. Pussy Riot, based on their background and their otherwise evidenced knowledgeability, suggests just that. That very power depends upon a certain distribution of knowledgeability and material resources in the world of flows. Freedom especially travels.

Nobody owns freedom. Of course, there are transnational organizations like Human Rights Watch that make it their cause. Some political agents, notably the United States and the European Union, lay claim to that moral force in their own expressions of more particular interest. States need to be able to claim legitimate monopoly on the use of force. Religious authorities rely on being able to convince others of their preferred access to the intentions and order of the transcendent, subordinating freedom to the divine. When those like Pussy Riot manage to disturb the conventions of those claims, especially when the force/sacred conjunction is mocked by those whose access to truthfulness, augmented by global solidarity, appears greater than that of those in authority, the potential for consequence knocks. Where the doors to domains housing legitimacy are buttressed with greater claims to knowledge, however, it takes much more than performance to bring the house down. Energy is much different, so I take it up at length.

The Expert Articulation of Global Energy Flows

Energy is the object of an increasingly substantial knowledge network that goes far beyond the one already enjoying that very name at the United Nations. However, this "UN-Energy Knowledge Network" articulates a prominent aspect of the energy field nicely:

UN-Energy aims to promote system-wide collaboration in the area of energy with a coherent and consistent approach, as there is no single entity in the United Nations system that has primary responsibility for energy. Its role is to increase the sharing of information, encourage and facilitate joint programming and develop action-oriented approaches to co-ordination. It was also initiated to develop increased collective engagement between the United Nations and other key external stakeholders. UN-Energy brings together members on the basis of their shared responsibility, deep commitment, and stake in achieving sustainable development.[7]

The United Nations is but a small part of the much larger knowledge network around energy; for example, various nonprofit organizations are interested in extending similar missions. The Global Energy Network Institute comes first to mind, but sustainability is becoming a major theme even of those commercial enterprises whose wealth derives from its antithesis.[8] However, the energy field is not necessarily so focused on the transition to sustainability; energy has other normative and strategic penumbrae (Guidry, Kennedy, and Zald 2000) in the hands of other network programmers.

States, for example, have their own energy information infrastructures, with expert/political actors able to develop the articulation of national need and energy outlook, typically through the frame of energy security. As with other forms of security, energy security can connote many different things, with energy exporters concerned for the security of demand, importers for the security of supply, and most for the security of the mechanisms of exchange and distribution, as experts in the industry remind (Tippee 2012). Most who articulate energy security celebrate some aspect of diversity—whether of source, transit, and/or customer—in this formulation.[9] Energy security can be linked to sustainability and environmental issues, but not necessarily.[10]

The US Department of Energy is arguably the world's leading programmer among states in energy knowledge production, but less so in defining the terms of energy affairs. Here, globally distributed national control over energy resources shapes the terms of energy knowledge. Oil, historically, has been the most important resource in this regard.

In 2010, the largest oil producers in the world were, in the following order, Saudi Arabia, Russia, the United States, China, Iran, Canada, Mexico, the United Arab Emirates, Brazil, Nigeria, Kuwait, Iraq, Venezuela, Norway, and Angola.[11] Proven reserves of oil continue to increase with new discoveries and the development of technologies that allow for newly economically viable forms of production. But that does not change the fact that most of those oil reserves are located in the Middle East (International Energy Agency [IEA] 2011, 119–21). And with that concentration, new articulations of knowledge production have been developed.

The United Arab Emirates is, in particular, transforming its reputation for knowledge and culture with massive investments. Research on energy leads in many ways, with Masdar, and its mission, exemplifying: "We are at the dawn of a global energy revolution that will transform the way we think about power generation, distribution and consumption. The scale and complexity of these changes is almost without precedent, and companies that seek to survive and thrive in this new environment must have the agility, the expertise and the long-term vision to respond to this new and uncertain landscape."[12] This mission is not unusual for those enriched by energy production. The search for reserves, the technologies needed to extract that resource wealth, and the capacities to produce, transport, and consume those energies in ever more effective and efficient ways can inspire substantial knowledge productions. While Masdar illustrates how national interest, energy business, and global futures might be synchronized in public presentation, national associations with energy production are not always so reassuring in the world of energy flows.

Russia has historically been the world's largest gas producer. In 2011 it produced 18.5 percent of the world's total natural gas. With new technologies in gas production, the United States moved ahead of Russia with 20 percent of that total in the same year. The Middle East produced only 16 percent; Iran, Qatar, and Canada produced more than 4 percent of the world's natural gas (BP 2012, 22). This concentration of gas reserves has inspired many in the world to a different kind of energy-associated knowledge production: the quest to understand how energy might become a weapon. For example, those in other nations whose first concern about energy is its security of consumption often identify the Russian state's association with Gazprom as a dangerous linkage of energy and state in a world of global interdependence (Hurst 2010).

That may be an extreme example. Nevertheless, it is difficult to find energy knowledge actors who do not see the world through national prisms, even when there are major consortia organizing investments and knowledge production. Consider, for example, Nabucco, a pipeline once proposed to connect Central Asian natural gas with Europe. In 2012, it was owned by a consortium combining firms associated with national interests: Austria's

OMV, Hungary's MOL, Romania's Transgaz, Bulgaria's Bulgargaz, Turkey's Botas, and Germany's RWE. Having earlier enjoyed substantial support from the United States, this pipeline project was based on a combination of expertise around energy and geopolitics. It made sense only to the extent that energy consumers would see Russia both as a critical energy source and an unreliable energy exporter. By 2013, Nabucco has been downsized and most believed it likely to fail, in part, because Russia had through that year managed to develop trustworthy partnerships and to blunt the charges of its critics. Thus, through 2013 most expected that Russian accents in the articulation of European/Eurasian energy flows were likely to expand, not based on any world evolutionary project but entirely dependent on the cultural politics of energy and the events that might transform them. To read those cultural politics is, however, much more difficult than to read those of Pussy Riot. Energy's cultural politics lie not only in the most visible reaches of public news but also within deep and extensive networks of expertise.

Consider, for example, the ways in which the IEA works to depict energy futures in global terms. One is helped in that reading if one knows the IEA's constitution. The IEA (2011, 2), established in the wake of the 1973 oil crisis, was charged with promoting energy security among its member countries through "collective response to physical disruptions in oil supply, and provide authoritative research and analysis on ways to ensure reliable, affordable and clean energy for its 28 member countries and beyond." The IEA does this by attending to emergency response capabilities, promoting sustainable energy policies, making international energy markets more transparent, supporting collaboration on global energy technology, and finding solutions to energy-related problems by encouraging dialogue. Its report, *World Energy Outlook*, is one of the key texts in defining the state of global energy affairs.[13] Although what follows draws on the 2011 report, one can say with confidence that two major variables dominate the IEA's discussions of energy for the present and the long term.

First, energies vary by source. The major distinction lies between those associated with fossil fuels and those associated with renewable energies. This distinction is critical given their differential effects on global warming. On a more specific level, energies are differentiated among the fossil fuels—oil, coal, and gas—and the rest—nuclear, hydro, biomass, and waste, alongside other renewables.

Renewable energies can dominate optimistic public discussion, and they do play an important role in meeting the increase in aggregate global demand.

Hydropower and wind power especially help account for half of the new global capacity to supply energy. All energy experts, however, acknowledge that fossil fuels will remain dominant, if declining slightly from 81 percent of the mix in 2010 to 75 percent in 2035. Natural gas does become more important over this period, with new sources of gas—what is called "unconventional"— growing to one-fifth of total gas production (IEA 2011, 40).

That new source changes the place of energy power in the world in interesting ways. China will rely much more heavily on it and imports; the United States will, in the IEA's "new policies" scenario, nearly end imports of natural gas by 2035, while the European Union will become even more dependent on sources from beyond its borders (IEA 2011, 93). There is no global shortage of natural gas for the global demand, according to these experts. Indeed, the world may be entering the "golden age of gas" (155). However, the qualities of that age are plagued with uncertainties, not least for the growing disputes about the environmental security of unconventional gas. The IEA puts it this way: "A range of factors needs to be positively aligned before unconventional production can make headway, including suitable geology, public acceptance, well-adapted regulatory and fiscal regimes and widespread access to experience and technology. For a relatively new industry, this points to a future in which the pace of unconventional development will vary considerably by country and by region" (163). Indeed, that variation articulates with other important points about geography, the second major variable concerning energy. The most typical geographic distinction rests in the difference between countries that are members of the Organisation for Economic Co-operation and Development (OECD) and the rest. And here, it appears, the dynamics of the energy system are not dominated by the wealthy.

Although energy consumption in India, Indonesia, Brazil, and the Middle East is growing more rapidly, China often assumes pride of place in these discussions since it will be the world's largest energy consumer by 2035. In fact, analysts expect that Russia will sell more and more of its fossil fuels to China, with the former's export earnings from China growing from 2 percent in 2010 to 20 percent in 2035 (IEA 2011, 44). Investment in energy production will also grow dramatically, but here again, most of the investment will take place outside the OECD countries.

This growth in economies and energy consumption is the most transformative part of the energy system. However, for many in the most dynamic parts of the world system this is the wrong optic to use in accounts of energy futures. Instead, one might focus less on increasing energy consumption and more on the inequalities associated with its use. And here, even in 2035, the United States is projected to remain, by far, the most energy-intensive nation (understood as energy consumption per capita). Although the IEA is designed to be global in reference, the particular composition of its twenty-eight-country membership perhaps skews it toward transformations in overall, rather than the inequalities of, consumption.[14]

Constructing scenarios depends on identifying trends in consumption, production, and inequalities. Recent transformations in the world have made the expert energy community a bit more cautious in its capacity to project futures. After all, energy consumption depends on demand, and the global financial crisis has made it hard to anticipate that demand. It is also hard, these experts say, to anticipate the significance of climate-change policies, for the roles of government in altering energy mixes is likely determinant. One can't anticipate with confidence how the global energy supply will change given the new significance of unconventional gas, and it's hard to anticipate what role nuclear power will play in the future, considering what happened around Fukushima Daiichi. Finally, the "events" in the Middle East and North Africa change the terms of energy affairs. Experts for the IEA write,

> The uncertainty facing the world today makes it wise to consider how unexpected events might change the energy landscape [IEA 2011, 50]. The civil unrest that has swept through some parts of the Middle East and North Africa (MENA) region, which is responsible for around 35% and 20% of the world's oil and natural gas output respectively, since December 2010 has contributed to higher energy prices and any worsening of the unrest or its spread to major exporting countries in the region could lead to a surge in prices sufficient to tip the global economy back into recession. The unrest has led a number of Gulf States to boost significantly public spending, including spending on welfare programmes. While this is likely to lead to greater demand for imported goods (which will reduce the global economic impact of high prices) it also means that oil producers may need yet higher oil prices in the future in order to keep their budgets in balance. (56)

While the primary dependent variable in these scenarios may be energy costs and investment capacities, the independent variables are increasingly beyond the ken of normal energy expertise. For instance, they identify the following "potential causes of lower investment" in energy production:

- Deliberate government policies to develop production capacity more slowly in order to hold back resources for future generations or to support the oil price in the near term.
- Constraints on capital flows to upstream development because priority is given to spending on other public programmes.
- Restricted, or higher-cost, access to loans or other forms of capital.
- Delays due to legal changes or renegotiation of existing agreements.
- Increased political instability and conflicts.
- Economic sanctions imposed by the international community.
- Higher perceived investment risks, whether political or stemming from uncertainties in demand.
- Constraints on inward investment as a result of stronger resource nationalism, particularly in regimes seeking to pre-empt popular uprisings.
- Delays due to physical damage to infrastructure during conflicts. (IEA 2011, 145)

Whereas it is the job of the IEA to help its member countries manage these uncertainties of energy production, when one rearticulates the uncertainties—in terms of trends, their geographic distribution, and the longer-run association with global warming—the knowledge challenge seems extraordinary. It is certainly beyond the expertise of any single discipline, even of energy studies per se. Yet, without a rigorous knowledge base that moves beyond the assumption of the industry itself or of those variously positioned seeking to manage or challenge it, the foundations of a new global energy governance (Goldhau and Witte 2010; Inkpen and Moffett 2011; Stokes and Raphael 2010) seem quite precarious. Indeed, the challenge of understanding a single country in these terms is, by itself, exceptionally difficult. Russia may very well be the most challenging.

The Cultural Political Articulation of Energy Flows

In 2011 Russia had "13% of the world's ultimately recoverable resources of conventional oil, 26% of gas and 18% of coal" (IEA 2011, 284). The IEA recognizes what was indisputable at the time: Russia is the largest gas producer now, and will still be, by 2035 (155). However, because of the shale revolution, the United States is now the biggest producer, but anxieties about Russia still animate because of the European Union's dependence on Russia. The EU, however, also points to Russian dependency on its customer: 80 percent of Russian oil exports, 70 percent of its gas exports, and 50 percent of its coal exports go the EU.[15] Beyond its energy power, the political economy of that power clearly concerns the importers of its energy.

More than 90 percent of Russian oil production is dominated by two state-owned and seven publicly traded or private Russian firms (IEA 2011, 287). A single state-owned firm—Transneft—owns all the pipeline transportation equipment. State-owned Gazprom controls gas through a vertically integrated system of gas production, processing, storage, and distribution (312). The experts offer this conclusion: "Despite intermittent signs from the government of a desire to open the Russian oil and gas industry to foreign investment, history suggests this is likely to be a slow process" (288).

Russia becomes an object of extensive discussion among energy analysts for a number of reasons. Its vast energy resources and close association between commercial and state interests is interesting enough. The IEA also identifies a number of risks associated with Russian energy powers. In the short run, it identifies disruptions in supply and, in the longer run, insufficient investment to keep up with growing demand. It finds risk greater for both the producers and consumers of energy when there is insufficient diversity of supply, transport, or export markets. Energy security, the IEA argues in principle but especially with regard to Russia, depends on diversity. There also are obstacles, derived in part from the "complex set of energy relationships" Russia enjoys with its neighbors (IEA 2011, 337).

On the one hand, Central Asia's independence from Soviet power alters Russia's energy power. Previously, for example, Turkmenistan could ship its gas only through Russian pipelines; Russia would purchase that gas at great discount and resell at world prices. As Turkmenistan develops more direct energy relationships with other countries and draws on other transport infrastructures, Russia loses some energy power. To maintain its centrality, Russia must control transport, not only of its own energy resources but of those formerly associated with it in the USSR. And even for its own national energy powers, it must be assured that transit countries do not use their own transit power to exact rents. Ukraine was central in this debate even before the developments of 2013–14. IEA (2011, 338) describes Ukraine's role in the transit of Russian gas to European markets this way:

Despite some progress towards a more transparent, commercial basis for gas supply and transit, political considerations continue to bear on this relationship, as indicated by the gas supply agreement of April 2010, which provided Ukraine with temporary relief on the price of imported gas at the same time as an agreement was signed extending Russian rights to base its Black Sea Fleet in Crimea. This apparently irreducible element of politics, alongside the slow progress being made by Ukraine in tackling the inefficiency of its own gas consumption (so as to mitigate its high dependency on Russian gas imports) perpetuates the perception of risk associated with this route to market.

The authors present this as if politics does not normally intrude on other energy affairs, but that appearance of a normality embedded within a market-driven system is itself a construct of a preceding global political constellation.

Timothy Mitchell is one of those intellectuals whose work could make a critical difference. He steps well beyond the dominant frameworks of both energy and area studies to develop a new foundational argument for seeing the constitution of modernity in the terms made by energy. Consider, for example, the oil crisis of 1973. This oil crisis is often considered, he argues, as an illustration of market economics disrupted by cartel behavior. It is not so simple as that. Arab producers initiated the oil embargo in protest over US support for Israel against Palestinians, not to recoup greater investments (Mitchell 2011, 185). The reduction in oil production by six states did not affect the overall supply of oil in the world. Consumers and their governments behaved in ways that increased prices and reduced supplies available to consumers. Thus, even in 1973 politics intruded on energy affairs and made the modern energy system, for the knowledge culture associated with energy emerged in the wake of that crisis.

Once oil became subject to the control of producers beyond the militarily dominant in the world system, energy knowledge actors began considering ever more intensively the relationship and substitutability among energy sources. Western oil companies, recognizing that their profitability and status were at growing risk in a conflict between oil-producing nations and their principal customers, also came to appreciate their role in these other energy forms. They thus sought to influence their development. Oil companies realized that their own research domain required much more serious investment, and breadth, moving to include "public relations, marketing, planning, energy research, international finance and government relations" (Mitchell 2011, 193). Mitchell's account of class conflict around coal mines, Churchill's consequent shift to oil use for the British navy, the post–World War II dominance of oil as a global commodity, and petroleum political economic foundations of empire and Cold War is critical not only to energy's story but to the cultural politics of modernity and democracy themselves.

Mitchell makes a huge contribution with his engagement of flows around oil and ideas and his grounding those flows in the material conditions of their production, transportation, and consumption. With regard to energy, Mitchell (2011, 235) proposes that one can better understand the nature of modernity itself by "tracing the connections that were made between pipelines and pumping stations, refineries and shipping routes, road systems and automobile cultures, dollar flows and economic knowledge, weapons experts and militarism." I think he is right. We can have that confidence in part because the intellectual articulation of Western colonialism and postcolonial conditions, especially around energy and the Middle East, is relatively secure. Postcommunist history, especially around the nature of imperialism, is much less obvious, especially if one begins that history in the South Caucasus. Context, after all, matters when you work to understand how energy articulates the world.

The Cultural Political Articulation of European-Russian Energy Flows

Before the actual Russian-Georgian War of 2008, Georgia's president, Mikheil Saakashvili, warned on November 14, 2006, in the European Parliament against appeasing Russia in its energy foreign policy, especially vis-à-vis Georgia. Although Georgia's territorial integrity was central to his speech and to his indictment of Russian interference, he also identified the economic blockade of the region's water and wine exports as further indicators of Russia's imperialist practice (Rettman 2006).

Those seeking to undermine this new Russian empire built pipelines that would take oil and gas from the Caspian Sea through the Caucasus and Turkey, effectively skirting Russian pipeline control. This would, theoretically, increase the sense of European Union energy security by diversifying both source and route. To legitimate such substantial investments, justifications had to go much further than worries about Russian empire. In the first major investment around the Baku-Tblisi-Ceyhan pipeline, scholars explained how this was more than a project in energy diversification. S. Frederick Starr (2005, 11) identifies this pipeline as a vehicle of modernity in civic, political, and economic terms for its host countries:

Development issues have loomed far larger in the BTC project than in most other such undertakings. Their centrality has meant that the process of designing, constructing and managing the pipeline has been no less important to the pipeline's success than the mere putting in place of the steel tube. The heart of this process has been an intensive process of consultation that has already run to several thousand meetings. Virtually anyone affected by the work has been given an opportunity to register his or her concerns. Anyone confused about how and where to do so could consult the Citizens Guide that BP issued and disseminated widely.

The pipeline became operational in May 2005, but as one can see from the publicity surrounding its justification, it was already assumed to be an investment in democracy. It was, clearly, political, designed to reduce Russian influence over the world of energy flows *and* to reconstruct a global context long known for interimperial rivalries.[16]

It was also a sign of the times. The region enjoyed a democratic revolutionary fervor following the 2003 Rose Revolution in Georgia and the 2004–5 Orange Revolution in Ukraine. Western analysts amplified the euphoria. "The orange revolution had set a major new landmark in the postcommunist history of eastern Europe, a seismic shift Westward in the geopolitics of the region. Ukraine's revolution was just the latest in a series of victories for 'people power'—in Poland, Hungary, and Czechoslovakia in the late 1980s and, more recently, in Serbia and Georgia" (Karatnycky 2005, 35). This democratic sentiment also shaped the interpretation of energy flows or, rather, the interpretation of their disruption.

On January 1, 2006, Gazprom cut off gas supplies to Ukraine following months of negotiations over the price of gas and a variety of other matters. It could have been very easily seen as a normal business dispute. In fact, if experts on the energy business would rule, Ukraine would likely be at fault (Stern 2006). With this shutoff for its own supplies, Ukraine siphoned off gas destined for Europe, leaving Europe at risk. Instead of blaming Ukraine, however, the Russians were generally brought to task (BBC News 2006a).

Russians defended themselves in terms of the rule of law and contracts. For some reason, the Europeans, perhaps partly because of the cold they experienced, were unwilling to accept Russian claims. After all, the Europeans had only a year before supported the Orange Revolution, and it was defined in terms of a Ukrainian move to Europe and that nation's embrace of democracy. Solidarity demanded that exceptional narratives be introduced and that

Russia be identified as a source of instability, which brought, one might argue, new meaning to a Cold War II.

The matter was provisionally resolved but gave new impetus to the Energy Charter Treaty proposed by the Europeans after the Cold War's end (Selivanova 2010). The treaty was also political, even if more "legal/rational," in its attempt to diminish Russian energy power. By the time of writing, Russia has still not ratified this treaty. Most if not all Russian actors see the treaty as positively disadvantaging Russian interests. While global gas interests and especially Europeans see the Energy Charter Treaty as a neutral regulatory device, Russians see it as undermining Russian power. And it does.

Instead of transforming the legal/rational foundations of energy flows, Russians have done much to transform their material conditions by creating new transits. One of the first initiatives was the Blue Stream pipeline connecting Russia with Turkey. In 2006 the Nord Stream pipeline was proposed, dedicated to connecting Germany and Russia directly under the Baltic Sea. That same year, the Italian firm ENI signed a memorandum of understanding with Gazprom to develop ties with it to construct a South Stream line moving from Russia under the Black Sea to Bulgaria, from there north through Serbia and Hungary to Austria, and through Greece to Italy or perhaps through Slovenia to the north of Italy. New gas fields also were being developed in Shtokhman, where the French firm Total was involved. In short, Russia preferred to create a world of energy flows bypassing the European Union as such and some of Russia's most challenging EU neighbors.

Those challenging relationships are, of course, formed in politics and diplomacy, not through energy relations. The relationship between the current prime minister of Poland, Donald Tusk, and the Russian authorities is notably better than the relationship of his predecessors, even while Poland's foreign minister, Radek Sikorski, has been a prominent figure in those ties throughout. Nevertheless, there is a certain cultural momentum in these relationships, one that two European Council of Foreign Relations authors have tried to illustrate with their construction of national characters in relation to Russia:

"Trojan Horses" (Cyprus and Greece) who often defend Russian interests in the EU system, and are willing to veto common EU positions;

"Strategic Partners" (France, Germany, Italy and Spain) who enjoy a "special relationship" with Russia which occasionally undermines common EU policies;

"Friendly Pragmatists" (Austria, Belgium, Bulgaria, Finland, Hungary, Luxembourg, Malta, Portugal, Slovakia and Slovenia) who maintain a close relationship with Russia and tend to put their business interests above political goals;

"Frosty Pragmatists" (Czech Republic, Denmark, Estonia, Ireland, Latvia, the Netherlands, Romania, Sweden and the United Kingdom) who also focus on business interests but are less afraid than others to speak out against Russian behaviour on human rights or other issues; and

"New Cold Warriors" (Lithuania and Poland) who have an overtly hostile relationship with Moscow and are willing to use the veto to block EU negotiations with Russia. (Leonard and Popescu, 2007, 2)

In mid-2013, one might have argued that the prospects of the relatively frigid were melting and were most evident in the success of Nord Stream itself.

On April 30, 2006, then Polish defense minister Sikorski likened the Nord Stream pipeline to the 1939 Molotov-Ribbentrop Pact, saying that this was mainly conceived to threaten Poland and Belarus, not increase energy security (Voice of America [VoA] 2009). That could mobilize Poles, but to stop the pipeline, Sikorski and his allies had to mobilize other Europeans, which meant drawing on other knowledge cultures, not just Polish national memory, for critique.

Rather than try to divine Russian and German intentions, Nord Stream's other critics depended on the science of unintended, or irresponsible, violations of the environment. The Nordic countries, Sweden in particular, along with Poland and Latvia, called for environmental impact tests that addressed the likely effects on marine flora and fauna as well as what digging up seabed with buried Soviet chemical weapons from World War II might do. Finland also initially withheld endorsement of Nord Stream on ecological grounds (Rettman 2009). Russian authorities met the challenge.

Russian authorities have the capacity to practice an energy politics that recognizes public concerns and looks to be visionary in its environmental practice. One need only recall Vladimir Putin's response in 2006 to the big debate over the location of a pipeline near Lake Baikal shipping oil from Taishet to Primorye. Despite Transneft's economic arguments, Putin came down on the side of academicians' arguments and Greenpeace protest to move the pipeline twenty-five miles north (BBC News 2006b). While different actors likely have their own preferred accounts—Greenpeace (2006) then might have attributed Putin's decision to its pressures and *Vladivostok News* to reasoned reflection by President Putin—the more general point is compelling: Russia can practice what appears to be environmentally responsible energy distribution. And it managed just the same in the Baltic Sea.

Had the environmental threat posed by laying a pipeline on the Baltic seabed stuck, that might have turned the tide against the Russian-German collaboration. Those who opposed Russian designs did not articulate their networks in consistent and coherent fashion. This was especially apparent in Estonia, where objections to the Russian-German venture should have been applied as well to the Finnish-Baltic-Estonian interconnector pipeline (Aalto et al. 2013). In this sense, Castells's switchmen were asleep on the job.

By 2013, Nord Stream triumphed and came to be celebrated. President Putin honors former KGB operatives and Western energy executives with special Russian state honors (Moscow Times 2012) while Western EU heads of state hail the triumph of energy security through Nord Stream. Angela Merkel said, on the completion of the second trunk of the pipeline, "Our long-lasting and equal partnership is obviously beneficial for both parties. Europe gets more security in energy supply as gas remains the most important energy source in our countries. Russia secures a stable demand and profitable sales of its gas. The Nord Stream project showed that state and business can build an efficient unit across national borders" (RT 2012).

In this light, prospects to halt Russian pipelines along the southern rim looked dimmer and dimmer. South Stream did not inspire as much conflict as Nord Stream for several reasons. First, Russia has better historical relations in the southeast than it does in the northeast of Europe. Second, the South Stream pipeline brings in additional nations as transit sites, making additional allies rather than excluding nations from transit or weakening their historic role. Third, laying pipelines in the Black Sea is not as dangerous as in the Baltic Sea, prompting less environmental protest. Nevertheless, the smooth extension of 2012 expectations has been interrupted. Even before the contentious politics around Ukraine in 2013–14, the European Commission charged that those bilateral negotiations violate EU law (EurActiv.com 2013).

South Stream indicates the eventfulness of EU-Russian energy cultural politics. There are no clear evolutionary streams in figuring energy trade between the EU and Russia. That was certainly evident in 2009 when Russians turned off the gas again to Ukraine, for nineteen days. This time, however, the Europeans blamed *both* Russia and Ukraine. Business rhetoric came to dominate the discussion. One expert said this:

"Most EU energy firms have contracts with Russian state gas supplier Gazprom or intermediaries. But the Ukrainian side may bear the brunt of attacks due to Gazprom's powerful market position. . . . They will not sue Gazprom because they have signed supply contracts until 2030 or 2035. And you don't want to get into trouble with your partner if you have that kind of contract," European Council on Foreign Relations' (ECFR) expert Pierre Noel told the European Observer. (Runner 2009a)

At the same time, Russian media experts were shaping the European press, inflating a measure of Ukrainian political incompetence:

The European Commission on Friday (16 January) threatened to take unspecified sanctions against Russia and Ukraine unless gas flows to the EU resume after the weekend. "It's a situation the seriousness [of which] goes beyond the specific issue of gas," commission spokesman Johannes Laitenberger said. "As of next week, if the gas does not flow again, we will have to look point by point at our relations with Russia and with Ukraine and assess in each case whether we can do business as usual." (Runner 2009b)

But Russian foreign minister Sergei Lavrov was powerful when he argued,

"If someone's not interested, we won't force them to come to Moscow," he said at a press conference in Russia. "This is a case when the EU should show their famous solidarity and explain to their Ukrainian colleagues the inadmissibility of not fulfilling a contract." (Runner 2009b)

Ironically, perhaps, Ukrainians were in a worse position because they signed the Energy Charter Treaty and were contractually violating international law. The Russians had not ratified it and thus were in some ways less illegal. Regardless of who was worse off in this crisis, the critical point is that the Europeans lost solidarity with Ukraine in this moment, led, in part, by Hungary and its legal actions against Ukrainian business.

What changed? Certainly the Europeans had longer to evaluate the political culture of Ukraine after the Orange Revolution, and the democratic bloom had been replaced with an assignment of incompetence. The stench of corruption, not distinctive to Ukraine but newly prominent in European discourses given the problems of corruption that Romania and Bulgaria brought to the EU 27, made Europeans more sympathetic to Russian claims: while the Ukrainians might look democratic, they are just as corrupt as, if not more than, we Russians.

In light of the discourse of Ukrainian corruption and unreliability, now a new notion for Europe, a wholly Russian version of energy security could become dominant: the need to diversify energy routes, not energy sources.

Europe displayed incredible solidarity in 2006 against Russia in support of Ukraine. This required an assumption that Ukraine was democratic and European, and that Russia was fundamentally different and dangerous. It also assumed that Europe could wield enough power to assure that Russia could be chastised. None of these assumptions was sustainable. Russia could also help make, through its own cultural politics, a stronger case that Ukraine was not democratic and that its government was not competent and trustworthy. Europeans could be split apart with this charge, and solidarity ruined, not only with Ukraine but also with one another in relation to Ukraine. And at the end of 2013, the story changes again with Euromaidan, a subject to which I return in Chapter 8.

The story about energy cultural politics illustrates something critical about the world of flows: it is not as "emergent" as some proponents of an associational sociology might suggest. Timothy Mitchell can manage a compelling story in those terms but only because there is a well-developed metanarrative organizing his story. Over many years, historians and others have elaborated the ways in which dominant Western powers exploited Middle East oil resources, how nationalists took those resources to use them to build state power in a Cold War system, and how the Organization of the Petroleum Exporting Countries (OPEC) transformed those cultural politics by elevating the power of producers. Mitchell could remedy key elements in that narrative, but he had a relatively coherent narrative with which to contend.[17]

In the world of energy flows affecting the EU and Eurasia, the story about energy security and disruption is not so coherent. Prospects of new data collection do not resolve. To understand the trustworthiness of Russia as an energy producer and the procedural rationality of an Energy Charter Treaty are not expert knowledge projects. Rather, they emerge from the articulation of flows shaping global public and policy makers' dispositions around energy production, distribution, and consumption, and their implication in other flows of resources and knowledge associated with global finance, security, and human rights. The cultural politics of those dispositions need be treated as seriously as the technology choices and public policy options typically animating energy research institutes.

Public Knowledge and the Articulation of Energy

Public engagements of energy in today's world reflect a time long past and a planet that cannot survive. Too often energy choices and debates are implicated in debates about other things—national security, economic outcomes, and even the environment. Their articulations too rarely allow them to be explicitly addressed beyond the ideological frames dominating discussion. Those frames are, in turn, defined by concentrations of power and expertise that can defy and deny challenge. In the world of flows, especially with new mobilizations of knowledge for the public good, transformations are more than ever possible. And necessary.

To engage that emergent knowledge around energy requires a different kind of intellectuality, one that moves well beyond both existing domains of expertise and the state and commercial practices organizing energy knowledge. It demands a new articulation of knowledge and public good based on the emergent qualities of information and wisdom in a world of flows, a challenging situation if existing practice is any indication.

One of the best examples of an interdisciplinary energy knowledge institution within the academic world is the Oxford Institute for Energy Studies (OIES),[18] which describes itself this way:

> Its unique multidisciplinary expertise allows it to examine the economics, the politics and the sociology of energy with a focus on oil and natural gas. Its research spans the international relations between producers and consumers of energy; the economic development of producing nations and the geopolitical aspects of all these issues alongside the economics and politics of the environment in relation to energy, including climate change. The Institute's intellectual independence places it firmly at the centre of the dialogue between consumers and producers, government and industry, academics and policy makers. The Institute serves a worldwide audience with its research on all major energy issues of the day.[19]

That it is unique is disturbing; one should imagine, given energy's importance, that most universities would be engaged in such address. Many research centers *are* so focused, but they are typically dominated by knowledge cultures closest to the producers of energy themselves. If social sciences are involved in such centers, they are likely economists or political scientists whose embrace of consumers through markets and policies through states is indicated, as in the language in the quotation.[20] The absence of citizens and publics from these mission statements is striking. Perhaps it is only a rhetorical difference. It depends, of course, on how knowledge works and how OIES and its kin knowledge clusters operate. The leadership of OIES and its kin in the field thus deserves more extensive study. The OIES public presentation offers a starting point.

It is not so much the structure, amount, or even publicity of their research that matters. Their working papers, for example, are organized in conventional fashion—around country and regional studies, forms of energy, and energy studies associated with particular disciplines or institutional conjunctions, as in the relationship between energy and the environment. This is not very different from the transnational agencies, energy corporations, and state ministries so focused and described earlier. However, it is their independence, their autonomy, that matters for producing the kind of trustworthy knowledge one expects of intellectuals more than experts in the employ of states and corporations. Indeed, their publications are explicitly marked against ideology. For example, in his foreword to one such publication, Jonathan Stern (2012) celebrated an author's work for remaining "distinct from the ideological and political commentary which characterizes most of the literature on these issues."

As indicated previously, however, independence from the knowledge cultural power of the energy world is difficult (Gustafson 2012), or at least it is difficult to prove one way or another. The institute's sponsors include firms like the BG Group (UK), ENI (Italy), E.ON Ruhrgas (Germany), Gazprom (Russia), Delta Energy Institute/Gasunie (the Netherlands), Shell (Anglo-Dutch with headquarters in the Hague), Statoil (Norway), and Total (France). Scholars and their institutions are typically able to deflect charges of obvious bias moved by the philanthropic support of commercial and state interests. However, that maneuver is especially difficult to manage in energy when "ideological and political commentary" characterizes the dispositions of those beyond the responsible world of energy experts.[21]

The discussions about energy I have engaged earlier—its expert assessments, implications in security, regional variations, and association with commercial and state powers—reflect a particular kind of globalizing knowledge. Diane Stone's (2005, 936) observations about the "global agora" are especially suitable here:

With its diversity of both actors and activity, the agora may be an unequal environment. Rather than organizational density and diversity disrupting hierarchies and dispersing power, they can also represent new constellations of privatized power. Instead of being civil society manifestations of bottom-up, non-statist globalization, networks and other formations may be viewed as "mutually implicated" in the affairs of states and international organizations.

Given the incredible financial investment and intense knowledge accumulations involved in assessing energy, it is hard to imagine a public sphere where rational/critical discussion produces an emergent consensus about global public well-being.[22] It could be better than it is if one were to compare it to the global agora around global warming.

As Timothy Mitchell (2011, 234–46) points out, both are very complicated subjects and expert driven in analysis, but energy futures are made more challenging by their complicated energy measurements, their relatively nontransparent assessments (in private corporate and nondemocratic state offices), and massive shifts in the relationship between price and technology. By more sustained public social scientific engagements, one might do better. Lessons can be taken from a number of places.

Figuring ways to link movements concerning the environment with more rational/discursive public discussions of energy investments themselves is important. Environmental movements under communist rule were critical in the struggle for democracy and national independence (Dawson 1996), and how movements now struggle across the world, especially in Japan, around alternatives to nuclear power remain the most prominent articulation (Saito 2012). There have also been mobilizations around hydraulic fracturing to promote the technology's reputation for safety as well as to prevent its deployment in particular regions. While most of those globalizing knowledge trumpet the significance of "fracking" for changing the distribution of energy wealth and power in the world (Kaplan 2012), mobilizations of knowledge and movements around its environmental security have begun.

In the United States, especially in Pennsylvania, Florida, New York, and Colorado, activists have become prominent in the debates over the technology's deployment, while universities in those areas have become increasingly receptive and supportive of the technology's monitoring or even opposition. That mobilization has also developed in Europe, although quite unevenly, with France and Bulgaria among the least supportive of fracking. Poland and

Ukraine were among the most receptive. The opposition has, however, begun in Poland (Khazan 2012).

That mobilization, especially in Poland, faces difficulty. Cold War logics of knowledge production reappear in the fusion of competencies around foreign affairs and energy. Its exemplars will highlight the ways in which Russia supports anti-fracking environmental movements (Tucker 2012) while overlooking how corporate influence limits inquiry into its possible dangers (Schiffman 2013). Some innovative journalists are linking the discussions in Pennsylvania and Poland with their reporting, hoping in that fashion to undermine the ease with which fracking worries are tied to Russian energy imperial interests.[23]

Corporate influence is not limited to engagements beyond the United States. It's quite palpable around coal and other carbon-energy dependencies in this country. The debate intensifies when knowledge institutions engage the fray.[24] Perhaps in those university explorations one might find new inspiration for developing more critical intellectual and institutional responsibility in the address of energy's production, distribution, consumption, *and* effects in the world.

Articulating Knowledge in the World of Flows

It is no surprise that those who theorize the world of flows are typically animated by flows of things that can be digitally constituted. It is surprising, however, that the implications of the world of flows for transforming knowledge production and learning themselves are considered in such limited terms.[25]

One can begin by considering the implications of digital information for knowledge production and the importance of developing infrastructures that make knowledge sharing possible and codes interoperable. Digital libraries and cyberinfrastructures for research sharing are good examples. Putting digital information in the legal terms of commons becomes one of the ways in which this can be conceived, motivating substantial rethinking of the scholarly infrastructure and the place of universities therein. The characters of authorship and publishing change, too, where scholarship becomes less individual and more collaborative in nature (Borgman 2007).

While the character of scholarship is being changed in knowledge institutions, the implications for learning are being transformed more slowly.

Especially for those who are not digital natives, the new "culture of learn-ing" that accompanies this digital revolution is slow to be incorporated in institutional practice. Today's culture of learning, Thomas and Brown (2011) propose, flows more, relying less on preexisting stocks of knowledge or fixed cultures of intellectual authority and more on a passion for learning that itself is a form of play. With virtually unlimited information resources, learning becomes almost of necessity designed around the personally meaningful; knowledge cultures become something that emerge in, rather than adapt to, change, where knowing becomes less a command of information than the capacity to acquire information critically and nimbly without sanctioned authorities guiding that consumption. Some of that spirit might be evident in one attempt to globalize knowledge through digital media.

The MIT Media Lab,[26] and Ethan Zuckerman in particular, reflects that sensibility. Zuckerman (2013, 5) develops it most extensively in his own intel-lectual networks, which might be reflected in his latest volume:

> As we enter an age of ever-increasing global connection, we are experiencing vast but subtle shifts in how people communicate, organize themselves, and make decisions. We have new opportunities to participate in conversations that are local and global, to argue with, persuade, and be persuaded by people from our borders. And we have much to argue about, as our economies are increasingly intertwined, and our actions as individuals and nations affecting one another's climate, health, and wealth. And as these connections increase, it should be no surprise that we will also experience a concomitant rise in mystery.

To which he argues that we need to rewire, to reconnect, by building new tools of communication:

> We can make it easier to understand conversations in other languages, and to collaborate with people in other nations. We can take steps toward engineer-ing serendipity, collecting insights that are unexpected and helpful. With a fraction of the brainpower that's gone into building the Internet as we know it, we can build a network that helps us discover, understand, and embrace a wider world. (7)

He does this fully recognizing that the world is not flat but "lumpy," in the increasingly popular parlance describing connectivity. He also sees that homophily, love of the same, might characterize our global networks. That's not inevitable, he argues. It could be changed by serendipity, which itself might even be a matter of design.

His own work, together with Rebecca MacKinnon's, on developing a global blogging network reflects the achievements, and challenges, of just that effort. Global Voices continues to this day, with some nine hundred contributors from more than one hundred countries, representing a powerful and emergent global knowledge network.[27] Zuckerman (2013, 127–28) acknowledges its limitations:

> Both of us hoped that by offering a global perspective through the eyes of a specific individual on the ground, readers would have an easier time connecting with unfamiliar stories. Instead, Global Voices has become a go-to source for information on the infrequent occasions that countries rarely in the news suddenly burst into the headlines.

It's also a matter of attention, not just information's supply from around the world. Even that, Zuckerman argues, can be improved with some attention to design and the bridges that can be built across structural holes in networks of information flow and the pathways that make serendipitous discoveries of value more likely. We might also think about how this kind of attention might address the more material flows connecting our world.

We could see the importance of digital activism around those social movements concerned for the environmental impact of hydraulic fracturing. We might even see it as universities debate divestment from coal and other carbon-energy production systems. Mobilizations to protest violations of environmental security, while important, are hardly sufficient, much less reflective of the ways in which knowledge can be mobilized and channeled in shaping alternative global futures. Indeed, in contrast to the saturated knowledge cultures organizing the flow of energy across the world, episodic associations through social media, or even celebrity endorsements of right causes as we saw in Pussy Riot, are hardly adequate. The juxtaposition of performance political art and energy suggests some leading questions about the comparative study, and engagement, of global flows.

Need the difference between the deep materiality of energy and apparent ephemerality of performance art be reinforced by their accompanying knowledge cultures? The concentration of and investment in energy expertise, with responsibility to funders with particular interests in its interpretation, shape disproportionately how we approach energy. The dispersion of performance art critical expertise, and the perceived capacity to judge its quality, increases the value of whatever captures the attention market. While one might argue about Madonna's sophistication in Russian human rights discourse, the fact that she scrawled support for Pussy Riot on her back during a Moscow performance was enough to validate Pussy Riot's struggle for millions.

Might there be an analogous refiguration of energy expertise? Student movements challenging the prerogative of fossil fuel influence in their universities must, in order to change policies, develop scholarly accounts that trump the energy industry's own knowledge network. It is difficult to manage that trump using the energy industry's knowledge rules around expertise and ideology.

Although one cannot underestimate the amount of specialist knowledge that goes into figuring how to make cleaner coal or to develop pipelines that minimize risk to the environment, one should not overestimate just how much ideological work goes into making energy knowledge appear beyond politics. This visibility varies considerably, and so do the scholarly foundations for its identification.

Energy's implication in developing the great power politics of the world in which we live is apparent, but often naturalized and made invisible. In this, Mitchell's (2011) work to clarify how political choices shape apparently neutral market mechanisms is invaluable. A work like Mitchell's is difficult to imagine in the European/Eurasian sphere, given the intensity of commercial and political interests in defining the question of Russian trustworthiness. This challenge persists even when Russian interventions defy the conventions of the post–Cold War global order.

Politics become most readily apparent when alternatives are clear. Europe and Eurasia's contentious energy politics have become starkly evident because geopolitical and cultural political contests over the borderlands move energy's political nature to the center of public awareness. Entire expert cultures rooted in national foreign ministries and corporate cultures work to securitize energy and, with that interpretation, point to the inadequacy of expertise in defining energy's proper flow. It becomes a political contest where knowledge is subordinated to the mobilization of resources in pursuit of a particular interest beyond commerce.

Mitchell's work is political, too, but not in the sense of pursuing a particular interest. It is political because he shows how global flows have constituted a sense of legitimate politics and the necessary knowledge to assure its reproduction. We clearly need more than that knowledgeability, however, to assume intellectual and institutional responsibility when energy's flow is interpreted through a market lens. In this, Pussy Riot's example might be instructive.

Art in general, as I proposed in Chapter 3, but performance art in particular, is critical for engendering public discussion. Already, upon release from prison, Masha Alyokhina and Nadya Tolokonnikova have used their celebrity to mobilize world attention on prisoners' well-being within Russia. They build on their own recent experience and their more general challenge to human rights abuses to move global public attention. And in that effort, these former exemplars of Pussy Riot draw on a knowledge culture around human rights made by a knowledge network that has sanctified its form. Energy has no such expression, leading to this conclusion.

Global flows vary not only in terms of their materiality and virtuality and the qualities of the accompanying knowledge cultures. They also vary in terms of the cultural landscapes in which they are embedded. Those landscapes vary, too, in terms of their articulation with emancipation and sustainability. To some extent, knowledge networks help establish those landscapes with their own expertise. They also should be recognized within the cultural politics that form them and the social interventions that might rearticulate them.

Energy's flow may be the most critical in these terms. Knowledge about energy is thoroughly embedded in commercial interests and in state interests, which are themselves variably syncopated. Energy production and distribution also can inspire public engagement, but these mobilizations can take very different forms. Commercial interests touting the economic benefits of the energy business can fill the airwaves of thin publics' media. States can move slogans like "energy independence" to justify new kinds of investments. Publics also can be mobilized based on more horizontal communicative action, most notably when communities feel their ways of life threatened by the production and transportation of energy in their space. There may be knowledge network ties that connect those local publics, and they can grow in power and potential with the revolution in information and communication technology. But those network ties, and their knowledge culture foundations, appear quite thin in comparison to those motivated by commercial and state interests. Universities might pursue their notion of public good quite effectively by concentrating their resources in the address of the landscapes shaping views of energy alternatives. That, however, is a matter of design.

7 Design: Knowledge Networks in Transformation

Networks have long been a result of intellectual practice (Mews and Crossley 2011), but they have become more important in the last decades. That is evident in our everyday discourse as we discuss how "networking" might advance a career. It's especially apparent for how we now conceive networks as information maps (Kadushin 2012). Knowledge is not the same as information, however, just as networks are different from intellectuals and their institutions.

As we consider knowledge networks, we focus less on what intellectuals do and what knowledge institutions are and more on how intellectuals and their institutions are related to one another in various webs. Although there are many different forms of knowledge networks, they are ontologically different from knowledge institutions. They are both emergent and potentially more subject to design's intellectuality.

In what follows, I consider the main outlines of design intellectuality and its suitability for thinking about knowledge networks. I consider a number of knowledge networks I have engaged in a variety of ways. I focus on four kinds of networks with various cultural schema and resources organizing their work—those that lead with scholarship, those that lead with policy and consensus, those that lead with struggle and vision, and those that, to my mind, combine them in the struggle for democracy's extension. These comparisons might also allow us, in the end, to consider more productively how switchmen and programmers can mobilize different networks for realizing alternative, and better, futures. It's also possible that these networks might simply emerge. We should, however, consider whether they could also be a matter of design.

Network Formation and Design Intellectuality

Networks are different from knowledge institutions and organizations in a number of ways. They depend much more on secondary collegial ties than the primary ones characterizing an employing knowledge institution. Thus, one needs to consider why networks attract participants at all. These commitments are, in a sense, much more voluntary—while wages might embed an intellectual in a knowledge institution, affinities are much more significant for the network. As such, networks are both easier to shut down and harder to start up but, once mobilized, are potentially redirected in less costly fashion. They are typically based on commitments to more particular knowledge cultural elements than are universities: disciplines, substantive concerns, particular regional studies, and normative frames all provide these guiding commitments. In this sense, networks might reflect better than universities the identities of their members and the visions of knowledge and change those network participants embrace. After all, knowledge networks can focus on transformation more than either a pursuit of excellence or reproduction of the status quo because networks need not prioritize their own survival. And for all these reasons, knowledge networks are much more suitable for extending design's impact than are knowledge institutions with all their contradictory and contending logics.

Those who study knowledge networks emphasize their variety. Some may consider more formal network properties (Moody 2004; Funk 2013). Others focus more on historical and comparative differences (Charle, Schriewer, and Wagner 2004). Still others may highlight network variations around organization, issue, space, openness, and ideology, both in terms of specific political orientations and in relation to the ideologies of disinterested knowledge itself (Maxwell and Stone 2005). For academics, matters like "i) the initial cultural gap; ii) the configuring of the internal cultural model; iii) the types of mediators that intervene; iv) the problems aroused by the language used and by the translation of basic notions; v) the specificity of the cultural field under consideration; and vi) the particular situation of a given disciplinary field within the general cultural setting" might shape network variations (Charle 2004b, 198). In the more policy-oriented world, these mediators can serve as research brokers, interlocutors facilitating media attention, and distributors of the things that often accompany the spread of knowledge: norms, best practices, and so on. Nevertheless, knowledge networks in general cohere, at least in distinction from other transnational networks, for they are typically composed of "professional bodies, academic research groups and scientific communities" mobilized around particular issues whose associations are developed in order to share and spread knowledge more effectively (Stone 2005, 91).

It helps to imagine these networks in very concrete terms, as we might see in the ways in which the Annales School generated its own transnational network of historians (Schottler 2004). It's even more productive to imagine how variously structured knowledge networks produce different kinds of outcomes. For instance, the global knowledge networks of Berlin and Paris organized around German pluralism and French centralism produced very different outcomes in the beginning of the twentieth century:

> The resources and exchanges on offer to the small group of Sorbonne professors conferred a worldwide prestige on their university that was not to be seen elsewhere. One effect of this was to create an insuperable hurdle for the younger generation of innovative academics who worked in provincial universities in their efforts to become active on an international level. . . . Conversely, the custom of working on several fronts at the same time established by the Germans was far more productive and creative, because there was no self-elected and aging elite who abused their dominant position. However, the German academic model also (suffered) the interference of politics in the academics sphere, the dispersion of academic activities, and the dependence on extra university resources, thus leading to specific geographical and thematic orientations. (Charle 2004a, 450)

It's unlikely that these very different outcomes for the knowledge networks of Berlin and Paris were a matter of design intellectuality, but for those working in the field today, they very well might be.

In Chapter 1, I referred to those extending the meaning of design as perhaps the most exemplary of intellectuals in the world today. One of my students, Julia Thompson, was particularly emphatic about this in the fall of 2012, but I was resistant. Somehow, the notion of design didn't grab me. In a class dedicated to intellectuality, design didn't seem to belong within its penumbra. After all, if design is a means to optimize the form of products for others' use, it seemed quite distant from the open-ended qualities of a culture of critical discourse associated with intellectuality. As I listened to her more, and met others who embraced the concept, I can see why I had the wrong connotation. Pendleton-Jullian and Brown exemplify this point.

Their work, at the most abstract level but filled with examples, is less, one might say, about designing products or even understanding change than about understanding and shaping change simultaneously. Their approach is rather ecosystemic, based on insertion into the problem rather than strategic adaptations from without.[1] This is exactly the blend of theory and practice I had in mind in casting intellectuals in Chapter 2. Consider, then, Pendleton-Jullian and Brown's presentation of design's distinction.

> *Design has always been a visionary pursuit* and a visionary practice,—one that projects the future while remaining deeply grounded in the past and the present. The link between vision as a mental activity—imagining a future—and its accomplishment in the world—the building of the imagined future—is design. Design's principal focus is the making of things, whether material entities, virtually produced material entities, or fully virtual entities. Because design's principal enterprise is the making of things that operate in the world—a world unfolding—design is an agent of the future.

> Design is *optimistic*. It brings new things into the world. Designers take on problems, model them, frame them, and create responses through the distribution of material, real or virtual, in space. Designers are by nature *opportunistic*. They create openings from which to make things. When there are no clear and present problems defined, they go out and find them embedded in the intricacy of everyday life. By problems, we do not mean only things problematic, but also opportunities for working on the questions, puzzles, and enigmas that are inherent to human existence.

> The beauty of design as an approach to life is its creative opportunistic tendencies. The entrepreneurialism associated with these tendencies has always been a driving force and one that has been effective in negotiating change at all scales. From elegant objects to infrastructure, design has the distinct capacity to affect the context in which it sits.

> Visionary, optimistic and opportunistic, design is different than instrumental problem solving. Instrumental problem solving works to solve defined problems. Design works within a rich mental space in which problems are the impetus for work that converts ideas into things that are integrally linked to human behavior, perceptions, values and desires. As such, design may or may not *solve* problems *directly*. It engages the life around problems. This distin-

guishes design not only in its focus, but also in the methods and practices it engages. It requires a different set of skills and capacities, a different disposition, and a different set of instincts. Quite simply, *design has a different DNA.*

The optimism associated with design is a *skeptical optimism.* It is an optimism shaped by questions that arise. It is not abstract or naïve. As a process that interweaves thought with action, one receives feedback from the action and the feedback leads to new questions that expand understanding of the problem space. Thought is grounded through the test of theory hitting the real world. Trying out ideas leads to failures and unexpected new questions, and ultimately to greater depth, breadth and sophistication of the responses. Design activity relies on *perpetual* skeptical optimism. Optimism that is called into action again and again, as one faces new questions, limited successes, and things that do not work. Optimism drives design forward, leveraging learning and insight from action that is integrally associated with questions.

Design's skeptical optimism is aimed at the world. It serves to translate and mediate change. It serves to assimilate and shape the ongoing disruption and evolution of culture, society, and technology. Further, design *makes things* that participate in the evolution of culture, society, and technology. Think about the iPod to iPhone to iPad revolution and its impact on how we express ourselves, how we connect to each other, and how we work with new platforms of information. (Pendleton-Jullian and Brown forthcoming)

In many ways, their approach to knowledge and change exemplifies this volume's quest to clarify the articulations of globalizing knowledge. Their roots in architectural design and the social life of information are apparent, as the transformational qualities of interventions take pride of place over the contexts that define the conditions of their consequence. Their association with the world of flows, especially of information, is manifest. They exemplify Castells's switchmen. They cross many domains of intellectual life in the physical and social sciences and humanities. Their own knowledge networks appear, as reflected in their substantive topics and references, quite diverse.

In some ways, Pendleton-Jullian and Brown are the ultimate cosmopolitan intellectuals, seeing context without binding national borders. Indeed, it's unclear from their approach how they are connected with social forces in general. Their ties are more contingent, perhaps accidental, maybe even serendipitous. And with that focus on the emergent, the normative has less obvious anchors.

Normative questions have bedeviled most critical intellectuals, alongside the search for the more enduring qualities of structures denying equality and justice. Those deep resonances fade before the complexity and indeterminacy of living through the Cambrian moment in which the authors argue we live. In this sense, their approach to design focuses more on the emergent qualities of change and their associated networks.

Such a disposition bears affinities with an approach to knowledge and change that celebrates networks over institutions, especially if those networks are a matter of design for change, developed for and disappearing with goals' realizations. Not all networks are so fleeting, however. One needs to figure the relationship between networks and these more enduring structures of power and privilege to understand the relationship between network knowledge and global transformations.

Convening Institutions in Global Knowledge Networks

Universities themselves are increasingly articulated in global knowledge networks, defining this form of association critical for remaining relevant in the globalizing knowledge-based world. These networks change the qualities of the institutions belonging to the network, making them much more open to the global environment of which they are a part. One recent meeting so dedicated identified the following subjects critical for "research institutions in developing and middle-income countries":

> the role of research universities in the global knowledge economy; the international networking of higher education institutions through consortia; the rising mobility of researchers via international knowledge networks; policy-making regarding academic knowledge and output; and the global growth of institutional research . . . the potential of partnerships, whether for research capacity building in developing countries or between universities on a North-South basis; the impact of rankings systems and methods on rising universities in middle-income countries; the role of learned societies in bridging research, policy-making and funding; and the nexus of research universities, technology transfer, and job creation. (Stanfield and Lincoln 2012)

These concerns are important for all universities, not just those on the middle and lower rungs of national power. Universitas 21 (U21) is one example mentioned earlier.

U21's very existence is about redefining the whole of the global education field of which it is a part. Its network is composed of twenty-four research universities and seeks "to facilitate collaboration and co-operation between the member universities and to create opportunities for them on a scale that none of them would be able to achieve operating independently or through traditional bilateral alliances."[2] U21 indicates the success of its venture by marking improvements in university rankings and the ease of student travel across the network's universities.[3] This university network is but one of very many of varying scales, powers, and reaches.

For the most part, networks made by universities and their constituent units are focused primarily on how to meet their own institutional needs in global fields and markets. They have knowledge institutional goals such as facilitating research and learning, but the increasingly integrated global market for students and for power and prestige drives their mission (Verger 2009). Rankings figure increasingly in dominating that market, which in turn have an increasingly important role in defining excellence.

As we increase our reliance on university rankings to define our ideas of academic excellence, we are even less inclined to think about the varieties of knowledge institutions in the world. We are much more likely to see how they sit on these imagined but carefully measured hierarchies of achievement. While few serious intellectuals embrace such rankings wholeheartedly, many nevertheless act as if they are truthful representations of how knowledge is distributed across the world.[4]

In his depiction of the great American university to which I referred in Chapter 3, Jonathan Cole helps reproduce that ranking's sense of excellence. Referring only to the United States, he says that in 2007 there were "roughly 4300 institutions of higher learning (that) offered one kind of degree or another. Most offer undergraduate degrees only. Perhaps 600 or so offer master's degrees, and about 260 can be classified as research universities. Within this group of 260, *only about 125 contribute in meaningful ways to the growth of knowledge*" (Cole 2009, 6, emphasis added). That italicized throwaway comment clearly demarcates universities, a demarcation that is itself associated with a particular organizational membership. Within the United States, that top group is more or less defined by membership in the Association of American Universities (AAU).

The AAU defines its membership as the "leading edge of innovation, scholarship, and solutions that contribute to the nation's economy, security, and well-being."[5] And that definition of membership is not taken for granted; if quality falters, universities can be voted out of the association, as the University of Nebraska–Lincoln learned.[6]

The membership of this group is composed of a roughly equal number of private and public universities, but at the very top of the rankings, private universities dominate.[7] That dominance also has an effect on a global scale. Hotson (2011) spells out the implications of this system for the United Kingdom. He argues that the rankings produced by Times Higher Education and Quacquarelli Symonds, known as THE-QS World University Rankings, helped create a compulsion to augment certain parts of UK universities:

> Every year since 2004, these tables have appeared under some variation of the headline "US Universities Dominate World Rankings." And every year the picture has been more or less the same: on average, US universities have occupied 13 of the top 20 positions, while British universities have occupied four. US universities outnumber their UK rivals further down the league table too, and no other country remotely challenges America's effortless supremacy.
>
> It isn't difficult to see how these tables have helped push government policy towards its current infatuation with markets. All but one of the 13 American universities which have routinely topped the tables are private institutions and those inclined to neoliberal ways of thinking are unlikely to see this as a coincidence. If the global supremacy of US private universities is the product of their exposure to competitive markets, then the sooner such markets are introduced into UK, the sooner we can begin to watch their magic "driving up standards." The government's zeal to marketise UK higher education, to emulate American universities and to invite US corporations to set up private universities in Britain are all of a piece. Because the dominance by US universities of the upper end of these tables is thought to be so absolute, their role in informing the political consensus underlying government policy is rarely discussed.

Michael Burawoy (2012b) continues Hotson's theme and puts it into a broader sociological focus. First, when one focuses only on the leading institutions of higher education, one leaves out the bigger story of growing inequality within the higher education system itself. Cole (2009) notes Harvard's wealth, for example, but Burawoy argues that the bigger story is in the growing inequality between that top 125 and the other 4,200 within the United States and in relation to the rest of the world.

It's not just that US higher education is good, but it is increasingly dependent on students from the rest of the world enrolling to earn advanced degrees (Burawoy 2012a, 145). Then relatively more and more resources are focused on US elite universities and their elite counterparts across the world. And that system is defined in large part by the priorities and values of the universities at the top. This is the source, Burawoy might argue, of the homogenizing trends in higher education found in the world society: not voluntary emulation but knowledge/power institutional coercion.

What could be wrong, one might argue, with those universities at the top defining higher principles? After all, the universalism Cole celebrates does not exclude any university.[8] Indeed, the top universities do train the faculty who go on to work in the rest of the higher education system. Burawoy argues that the problem is that the US ruling classes define the terms.[9] It's not *whose* ranking systems dominate but a question of the commercialization of the university system and the commodification of knowledge itself. Cole might argue that a university ethos defines university excellence. But Burawoy (2012a) argues that markets increasingly intrude into the university as rankings affect revenues and the jobs their students get, which in turn inspires tuition hikes or industrial support for research.

This market intrusion bears real, negative impacts for those valued principles. External actors thereby shape university priorities with commercial considerations. Burawoy (2012b, 147) argues that we should move beyond the innocence of the Mertonian ethos Cole embraces, toward values "that pay close attention to the accountability of the university to society, that recognize the movement toward the contextualization of scholarship and teaching, and that oppose the destructiveness of markets."

We could think about other purposes rankings can serve, as efforts around sustainability suggest. In the last twenty years, we have seen the growing importance of ranking universities on their environmental curricula and greening initiatives.[10] Kennedy et al. (2012) elaborate:

> The pioneer was the Sustainable Endowments Initiative (SEI), ranking schools on nine criteria in its College Sustainability Report Card.[11] The SEI "grades" sent shock waves (of variable size) through low "green GPA" schools, especially as the *Princeton Review* incorporated environmental criteria and *Sierra* magazine (widely read among college-age demographic groups) began ranking universities. This also reinforced a conceptual shift.

"Sustainability" has become a central institutional goal for higher education (e.g., American College & University Presidents' Climate Commitment 2013). It is a major theme of universities as well as their programs devoted to the environment.

In our study (Kennedy et al. 2012) of various Luce Foundation–funded projects on the environment and higher education, we found that sustainability was one of the most effective themes for moving ahead the environmental agenda in higher education, due in part to the fertility of the concept itself.

> Sherman (2008) argues that "sustainability" as a term has almost exclusively been implemented as a series of "prescribed practices" rather than through a broader ideological framework. He has proposed instead that sustainability can become more significant when faculty colleagues from across the university, in a variety of disciplines, work together in figuring how sustainability might come to the heart of their various disciplinary/departmental research and teaching cultures. In fact, as a consequence of that strategy, his own University of Puget Sound is in the process of putting sustainability to the heart of its higher education. The results are impressive, contributing not only to the formation of a Sound Policy Institute but also to sustainability, as a big idea, becoming a core part of the Puget Sound curriculum (Sherman 2010).[12] Ideas can mobilize knowledge networks of consequence, especially when they are part of a social network sharing best practices the Luce initiative itself facilitated. (Kennedy et al. 2012)

There are, no doubt, potentially perverse effects even in these sustainability ranking systems. Given the wide array of meanings associated with sustainability, one could well imagine this as an important site for exploring how universities contribute in meaningful ways not only to their own students' education but also to longer-term transformations in social and biophysical environments.

Rankings also shape education markets influenced by internationalism. Universities and their networks invest substantially in how to think about rankings and collaborate to devise metrics by which to assess progress (e.g., Osborn 2013). For example, the American Council on Education (ACE 2012) has devoted great effort to thinking about how to map the internationalization of US universities.[13] Another higher education association, the National Association of Foreign Student Advisers (NAFSA), began offering in 2002 the "Senator Paul Simon Award for Campus Internationalization."[14] These maps and awards are designed to reinforce recognition for internationalizing scholarship. Recognition is designed not only to enhance best practice but to provide symbolic resources for internationalism's advocates in elevating their place within universities and elevating the place of internationalism in ranking universities.

Rankings can also become the object of immanent critique. Consider, for example, the work by Universitas 21 on global rankings of universities. U21 challenged the practice of ranking from within the logic of the ranking system itself. It focused on national educational systems rather than on universities in U21's work to affect students' school choices. In so doing, the United States does not look so obviously dominant. Finland, Norway, and Denmark are ranked better when one considers government funding of higher education as percentage of GDP. Denmark, Sweden, and Switzerland have the greatest investment in research and development. Sweden also leads on research journal articles *if* one views it as a percentage of articles per capita. Singapore and Japan join Scandinavia in having a higher ratio of researchers in the economy. International collaboration is also greater in Indonesia, Switzerland, Hong Kong, SAR, Denmark, Belgium, and Austria, while the United States, China, India, and Japan are at the bottom in this category (Williams et al. 2012).

Universitas 21 thus offers an alternative vision of the global university and its network according to criteria in which the United States does not so obviously lead. In many ways, they offer the most radical challenge: to step outside the individual institution and to consider it as part of a broader field of learning, one that attends to the networks associations facilitate. Indeed, scholars working in the global field of higher education struggle to remake their own institutions, but sometimes against quite traditional, and parochial, foundational senses of what that knowledge and change are all about. It's not all transformational.

Knowledge networks, like Universitas 21, represent a complex blend of design and institutional reproduction. U21 is, first and foremost, organized to improve the institutional capacities of its member universities, especially for students and the leading faculty and qualities of learning that recruit them in the global marketplace. Knowledge networks can, thus, primarily extend the qualities of their member institutions per se. They can also struggle to tilt the balance of academic power in the world, as U21 seeks in its effort to move university powers away from North America, or even change the terms of struggle with the ranking criteria used to assess excellence. For example, the Global University Network for Innovation (2014) has recently argued that universities should become more active agents in creating a more just and sustainable world. One might even go further and work to challenge the language of the criteria themselves, as Chinese cultural linguistics could recommend (Schulte 2004). Networks need not mobilize institutions, however. Transformative network intellectuality might be greater when intellectuals, rather than institutions, are its nodes.

Convening Scholars in Global Knowledge Networks

Jadaliyya, one of the newest and most consequential critical knowledge networks, has assembled diverse intellectuals commonly tied to public engagement in the Middle East. That, however, is one of the newest knowledge networks. One of the most foundational such networks is much older, even if similarly committed to public engagement. The Social Science Research Council (SSRC), especially since the turn of the century, has defined much of its distinction as a network of networks dedicated to the mobilization of knowledge for the public good. Considering its trajectory thus can illustrate some critical vectors of network power convening scholars rather than their institutions.[15]

SSRC has always had something of a public mission guiding its work. Even at the start, it stood for the idea that better knowledge could make better public policy. For example, in the 1930s it organized research that facilitated the development of the US Social Security system. In 1942, SSRC began its international mission by working with the American Council of Learned Societies (ACLS) to develop expertise within the United States on Latin America. After World War II, SSRC publications helped provide the intellectual rationale in universities for developing area studies (R. Hall 1949). SSRC wound up creating committees dedicated to various world regions so that America would no longer be so ethnocentric in its scholarship or its policies. That mission, however, would only last through the Cold War.

With the fall of communism in Europe, foundations appeared to lose their interest in area studies. During the 1990s, SSRC and ACLS, its partner in this venture, thus began to lose the foundation support they needed to carry out their mission, and both shifted away from area studies. At the same time, they also began to more deliberately develop international collaborations in which it was less a matter of training Americans to be more international than of reconfiguring the humanities and social sciences to be more globally collaborative.[16]

This shift was difficult and contentious, for area studies was one of the great success stories SSRC could name. It was also biographically meaningful for many individual scholars. They would develop a lifelong partnership with SSRC for all the SSRC support they earned—from dissertation fieldwork fellowships to committee work defining the cutting edges of the fields of which they were a part. Too, many of these scholars were themselves deeply embedded in international collaborations, often in the languages of the region. In this new global order, where English could offer the language of collaboration and more particular competencies the foundation for research, many area studies felt a great loss. SSRC seemed to lose its commitment to contextual expertise and thus the support of many formerly defined as key constituents.

The organization struggled to figure ways to retain that commitment, looking, for example, at how new thematic issues could emerge from the civilizational concerns of other world regions. This was difficult to sustain for reasons that go beyond this chapter's scope. It was not, however, for lack of interest and sympathy for the issues that area studies itself inspired. Consider, for example, how SSRC presented its profile in the summer of 2012:

> For the last decade, the SSRC has focused on conflict and peacebuilding, development and social change, the public sphere, knowledge and learning, and strengthening global social science, with close to thirty major programs within these five program areas. Topics past and present include academia and the public sphere, American human development, digital media and learning, the environment and health in China, international migration, media reform, the privatization of risk, religion and international affairs, scholarship in Eurasia, and the challenges posed by HIV/AIDS in Russia, Africa, and around the world. We also offer a number of prestigious fellowships for researchers doing promising work in the social sciences and related disciplines. Our largest fellowship program, the International Dissertation Research Fellowship (IDRF), funds graduate students for research across the globe.[17]

As is evident, SSRC worked hard to globalize its networks while simultaneously respecting the importance of contextual expertise. Its knowledge and change program developed a project explicitly dedicated to figuring how research universities across the world face common, and different, public challenges (Rhoten and Calhoun 2011). While it has supported efforts to bring together religion scholars and international relations scholars from US universities and to figure how spirituality affects public life in the United States,[18] SSRC has also worked to internationalize even that discussion.

SSRC's most obviously global work, however, has happened most readily through the United Nations.[19] SSRC's physical proximity to that global organization, in its global city, has made many of its international efforts not only viable but consequential. In particular, its work around conflict/peace building and development/social change is tied heavily to the UN contracting organizations that can mobilize knowledge quickly and beyond institutional limitations to address both long-standing and urgent needs.[20]

SSRC's international commitments are even more apparent with its commitment to capacity building in the social sciences across the world, most notably in Vietnam and Cuba. That could be argued to be one of the organization's most consequential initiatives undertaken for increasing social science value in the world. That effort has had its most dramatic expression recently in the creation of the Arab Council for the Social Sciences (ACSS).[21]

Drawing upon SSRC expertise and personnel in its establishment, the ACSS sought its own grounding in the region. It established its base in Beirut and developed its membership-based organization around a conception of Arab identity. For individuals, membership is open to those holding "Arab Nationality or [who] are originally from an Arab country regardless of their current country of residence. This includes Palestinians residing in the occupied Palestinian territories." In this sense, the organization is itself, although regionally based, organized around global networks, especially if one looks to those who participate in its first paradigm-forming conference.[22] These younger scholars have Arab origins but are working in educational institutions across the world. ACSS's grounding in the region and its cultural politics are also apparent, as the sense of values and scholarship develops an appropriate resonance in a region defined by profound change.[23]

In the end, no matter how international the reference groups of SSRC, the organization has been located in New York City and most of its leading academic supporters have been in US universities. Scholarly reference has most easily taken the American context as point of departure. And when it has mobilized knowledge for the public good, it has been much easier to do so in US contexts. Over the last decade, some of the most prominent manifestations of public social science drew on networks within the United States, dedicated to figuring how social science could inform US problems from emergency responses to Katrina to the privatization of risk. Sometimes SSRC focused on mobilizing knowledge itself, whether in public (how more accessible data about evaluating American inequalities and accomplishments might enhance public discussion) or in universities and primary and secondary schools. Indeed, one of its greatest public engagements was quite local—in the effort to improve New York public schools.[24]

SSRC's example illustrates both the potential and challenge for knowledge networks. SSRC has been critical in developing new fields of scholarship— from area studies and comparative politics to recent articulations of religion and international affairs and policy implications following the privatization of risk. It has also played a critical role in social science capacity building, whether in Southeast Asia and the Arab world or in New York City public education and US disaster relief.

To be successful, both institutions and networks need some kind of legitimation deriving from the histories they can claim, the recognition their members and supporters can inspire, and the resources they can utilize in carrying out their work. Those resources can be infrastructural—the qualities of a room and its building for face-to-face engagements are critical—but the resources are often less tangible. Resources can rest above all in the quality of knowledge work and its spread across its own and adjoining networks. Sometimes it's difficult to distinguish the qualities of discussion from the different kinds of capital individuals bring to the discussion, however. Quality is not only based on intellectuality as such but the networks beyond knowledge that can define consequence.

Policy Leading Global Knowledge Networks

Development work has, like most fields, matured in a number of ways. It leads some to argue that it already needs to be superseded by new paradigms of global economic integration and exclusions organized around the multiplicity of flows and powers shaping change. However, a substantial number of scholars and organizations still work in that framework with a variety of important consequences. Important for this volume, some have thought critically about the distinctive qualities of knowledge work in development, for example, Simon Maxwell and Diane Stone (2005).

Their focus attends to the ways in which knowledge is more or less available, how policy makers more or less seek it, and how various contexts make different kinds of networks more and less valuable, with a fundamental interest in enhancing the value of these networks. Some of their contributors discuss how various ideas become more or less powerful, how different mechanisms enhance that consequence, and how this reflects various interests and powers in the world.

Their work also helps us think about the varieties of networks—as transmitters of knowledge or as interlocutors for different communities, which in turn helps us consider different designs of these networks—as hegemonic research organizations, as franchise organizations, and as competitive collaborations (Maxwell and Stone 2005, 13). This framing also enables us to consider how the translation of ideas works across different domains, as, for example, how the "idea" of the "barefoot doctor" can work in a different sector (animal health) in a very different regional context from that of the original conception (Court and Young 2005) and what the conditions of increasing impact might be.[25]

Although I find this focus on global knowledge networks around development intrinsically interesting, I find the analytical shift for thinking about knowledge networks particularly instructive. By focusing on the link between knowledge and policy, something SSRC would only sometimes undertake, we are moved beyond the definition of networks by their issue, or their discipline, toward a more abstract account that links the practice of knowledge production and dissemination with its impact on policy. The relationship between disciplines and global transformations is therefore profoundly mediated by more general questions of the relationship between scholarship and the world beyond the academy.

Although there remain some who find material foundations determinate, I can't distinguish in categorical terms networks made by intellectuals and networks made by their funders. The networks made by the development world described previously are clearly dependent on their moneyed foundations for motivation, but scholars' control over the terms of engagement is relatively great. Indeed, one might generalize to say that the longer a network is in operation, the more likely it is that the intellectuals employed by it control the terms of its reproduction, ceteris paribus. However, some networks are clearly *not* controlled by intellectuals, with the World Economic Forum (WEF) first among them.

Why would we consider the WEF in these terms at all? Pigman (2007, 5) makes the case: "The Forum is fundamentally a knowledge institution:

it affects its field of operations by causing the thinking of its members and interlocutors on problems and solutions to change and develop. The Forum's story is a story of the power of words, ideas, and discourse." It seems wrong to emphasize the institutional qualities of this organization more than its network. As an organization, it has only two hundred employees (33) and is thus so much smaller than most universities by far. Its effect, and articulation with global transformations, is so much greater.

Any singular characterization of WEF is likely to be insufficient, especially over time. Sam Huntington likely gained currency in the progressive world with his dismissive account of the "Davos Man," whose cosmopolitan pretensions put him well out of touch with those people whose vistas remained national and much more immediate (Arasu 2013). From this skeptical standpoint, the Davos vision depended not on being grounded in global transformations but on having a privileged view of them from afar, and above. Pigman (2007, 48, 26) describes it as a kind of *Lebenswelt* for the global elite that includes representatives of nearly one thousand firms, stratified by levels of contribution.[26]

WEF has, however, changed over time. In particular, it has sought to include more voices beyond its characteristic elite. Its evolution from a primarily European discussion club to a more global organization began quite notably with its invitations to the Chinese communist government authorities at the end of the 1970s. In response to the protests against Davos at the turn of the century, it became decidedly more open to the voices of civil society itself. The Forum specifically identifies three groups from civil society that it elevates: labor leaders, nongovernmental organizations (NGOs), and thought leaders (Pigman 2007, 32). There are also programs dedicated to enhancing women in leadership (28–30). And then there are its "knowledge networks" among "young politicians, business leaders, academics, arts and media figures (initially known as 'Global Leaders for Tomorrow' later 'Young Global leaders'), cultural and arts leaders ('World Arts Forum'), and business and academic leaders in high technology sectors (industry summits for 'Global Growth Companies')" (16–17).

WEF has been called, and has called itself, a kind of private club. And certainly, no matter what the intellectuality of participants, it is difficult to call even the most erudite club a knowledge institution or network when it emphasizes exclusive sociality over merit-based scholasticity. WEF does have many attributes commonly associated with knowledge networks. It organizes a number of regular and focused reports on the most critical global issues of the day (Pigman 2007, 41–48). Its products are also quite refined. Pigman describes their increasingly generalized methodology originating in their annual competiveness reports:

> A blend of quantitative indicators and perceptual indicators based upon surveys of business leaders is assessed and measured to generate league tables that rank countries in terms of competitiveness. The competitiveness findings are explained discursively in text that is accessible, compact but not superficial, and intended for the general public. Scholarly articles reflecting upon the findings and different perspectives on the implications are a major component. Detailed quantitative data on competitiveness in each country are also included, with accompanying textual explanation. (104–5)

This general method around competitiveness has been extended and now includes a variety of initiatives with three common characteristics: public/private partnerships, multiple stakeholder approaches, and the WEF as a catalytic agent for their address.

One might, then, think of WEF very much as a knowledge network more akin to the professional knowledge networks Stone and Maxwell engage. It is also much more academic than one might think. WEF brings universities explicitly into this Forum in a variety of fashions. For example, it develops a Global University Leaders Forum (GULF) to help shape the agenda for the WEF mission.[27] That group has recently "contributed to advancing the agenda on a number of other top university-related issues. One example relates to the topic of campus sustainability, which the GULF took on in collaboration with the International Sustainable Campus Network (ISCN), setting a standard for the implementation of sustainable practices and the measurement of performance of academic institutions in reducing their carbon footprint."[28] Through my university's association, I was invited to join its Regional Agenda Council for Europe and Eurasia and attend a related meeting in Vienna.[29] The meeting itself was organized around three pillars: global competitiveness, the resource equation, and risk resilience, with its regional emphasis on Europe and Eurasia prominent.

The elite emphasis was there, to some degree. While certainly not of the Davos level, it did enjoy prominent participants. At the concluding session, organizer Stephen Kinnock celebrated that membership by noting that the meeting included 13 heads of state and government, 140 CEOs, and 30 leaders from civil society, including those from the trade union movement. Although not the diversity one typically encounters, even this level certainly enriches. Our discussion of corruption illustrates this principle.

I was one of seven who served as a facilitator for a discussion of corruption among some seventy people at the conference. In that session, one leader from the corporate world elaborated in some detail the methods his firm took to make his firm cleaner; a head of state rehearsed with pride the efforts his state has taken to reduce his country's corruption. We broke into smaller groups for more intense discussion.

Given the CEO weight of discussion, the primary focus of most corruption talk was to discuss the interaction between an organizational culture and its rules with the broader sociopolitical and economic environment. It was difficult, they say, to simply transport one organization's culture to another environment. Thus, one must develop new rules to cope with the pressures toward corruption. It is easier to resist those forces of corruption when one's organization is bigger, but even then, one should develop networks of collaboration across organizations to reinforce the professional behavior resisting that external pressure to pay bribes and so forth. According to the official WEF summary, business should lead:

> Business has an important role to play in fighting corruption, which often takes the form of sales employees paying bribes to procurement officers of public or private customers to obtain orders. Businesses seeking to fight corruption should adopt and require their employees to sign codes of ethics and enforce the codes consistently with zero or near zero tolerance. Top management and boards of directors must lead by example. Large businesses can help small businesses resist demands for bribes by creating umbrellas of protection, for example, by adopting codes of conduct for subcontractors. There are four pillars in the battle against corruption: criminalization, prevention, cooperation and education. An interdisciplinary approach is needed and anti-corruption educational problems should be introduced at an early age. (WEF 2011, 15)

Russia is a particularly challenging environment, they said, for avoiding that corruption, and the spotlight on Russia in the event's official summary said as much:

> Russia's economy is lagging behind other large emerging BRICS and is facing multiple challenges but has the potential to grow. There is a serious lack

of institutional trust in Russia—corruption is the number one factor deterring investors. However, in its push to secure membership in the World Trade Organization and OECD, Russia has introduced new regulations to combat corruption. (10)

In many ways, the discussion followed the script of the day—corruption is a serious problem because it is a major burden on business development and diminishes the responsiveness of government to citizen needs. It's a complicated subject, of course, because organizations like the World Bank and World Economic Forum don't want to be "political," so attacking corruption is a way of being political without claiming to be partisan: one is simply in favor of transparent and reputable business and political practices (Myers 2002). It also becomes an important NGO kind of effort, where monitoring can have effect; in fact, during this assembly, a new memorandum of understanding was signed in which World Economic Forum's Partnership against Corruption Initiative was connected to the new Anti-Corruption Academy in Vienna.

Alena Ledeneva (2013), whose own critical take on that global knowledge culture is so important, is a part of this broader global network of corruption expertise. It is, however, among the most complex cultural formations. Its definition, while appearing transnational, is designed to mark the inferiority of certain places without prejudice, and certainly without recognizing the vernacular knowledge of those charged with corruption. At the same time, the engagement of corruption is, potentially, transformative itself if the diversity and expertise of participants are right. This was evident at the WEF meeting.

Following public discussion, one civil society activist long engaged in the struggle against corruption approached the CEO who discussed his firm's successful struggle against the corrupting influence of the surrounding society. The activist asked whether it was possible for a company to be clean in a corrupt society. The corporate leader of course said yes. What else could the person say? The activist said that such innocence was impossible. The conversation, unfortunately, stopped and is not apparent in subsequent publications even while a blog so dedicated continues the effort to incorporate a wide array of voices in moving the analysis and engagement of corruption ahead.[30]

That halt does not mean that the insight did not travel, did not carry. It is difficult to assess the WEF as a global knowledge network in part because so much happens offstage; as one WEF employee told me, the effects of these assemblies are often "subliminal" rather than explicit. By putting together participants as they do, they hope that innovative knowledge emerges to address the problems they identify. And perhaps the discussion between the activist and businessperson carried forward. We do not know, but we do know that this civil society activist is part of other global knowledge networks rooted more in organizations that monitor governments and business than are part of them.

This concern for representation and difference is apparent in a number of ways and is illustrated quite powerfully by more recent statements on challenges facing the world. In particular, the WEF is quite concerned about "shaping the values of our connected world." In one of its blogs, Tim Leberecht (2012), chief marketing officer of Frog, a global design and innovation firm, argues that dialogue based on a new social covenant across various layers of difference in the world is critical:

> In light of the financial crisis, growing social divides in many countries and deepening mistrust in business, a multistakeholder dialogue on values is more important than ever. In our hyperconnected world, the consequences of our actions are more transparent and dramatically amplified, and the gap between values and behaviour is increasingly open to public scrutiny and subject to systemic effects. . . . Consumers and citizens demand more transparent, collaborative and inclusive models of value creation that produce well-being, happiness and meaning as much as profits. However, it appears that even well-articulated and broadly supported moral principles are difficult to translate into day-to-day decision-making.

Critical to that gap is, in fact, to move beyond the common and recognize the challenge of difference. Leberecht develops the point:

> Identifying and promoting shared values is important, but the real litmus test for a moral economy is the respect it can afford for the values of others. This is particularly true for our ever more connected world where the other is just one click away and we are all neighbours.
>
> If the Global Agenda Council on Values can help articulate what we have in common while appreciating what distinguishes us, then we will have made a small but meaningful contribution to improving the state of the world.

The humility is striking, even while the ambition is remarkable. The quality of members on that particular subgroup of the council was impressive, including prominent scholars like Homi Bhabha, Anthony Appiah, and Jim

Wallis.[31] The problematic they take up depends on the assumption that differences mainly need respect and that transcendence can be realized through dialogue rather than transformations of power. Not all global knowledge networks presume such potential consensus as starting points.

Struggle Leading Global Knowledge Networks

The World Social Forum (WSF) developed in part as a critique of the World Economic Forum. Their class bases and relationships to power are fundamentally different, but there has also been overlap. As a sign of the very world in transformation with which both networks grapple, Lula da Silva, Brazil's president, participated in both WEF and WSF meetings in 2005. Elected as a representative of the people WSF is meant to organize, and as a leader of one of the increasingly influential world powers WEF is supposed to host, Lula mediated the knowledge networks associated with each world (Pigman 2007, 129). They typically don't flow together, however, as the WSF is the second incarnation of antisystemic movements, at least in Wallerstein's sense of global trajectories.

Immanuel Wallerstein (2012) recently rearticulated two classic dilemmas facing the world Left. On one side stand those who resist the compromise and systemic legitimation electoral participation makes. On the other stand those who embrace electoral contest to offer either the pragmatic win or the symbolic contest within the electoral process. While most antisystemic movements—both socialist and nationalist—from 1850 through 1970 were animated by tension between state-centric and anarchist visions, the state-centric clearly won in that period over those emphasizing more individual or cultural transformation (Wallerstein 2002). That changed after 1968. While individual rebellions had local grievances, they all shared two things: opposition to the hegemony of the US/USSR contest in defining global alternative futures, and a common alienation from those who once claimed the antisystemic mantle. According to Wallerstein, 1968 was a global rebellion against actually existing power. And it spawned a multiplicity of Lefts—Maoist, Green, human rights, and antiglobalization. They found their meaningful assemblage in the WSF:

> WSF seeks to bring together all the previous types—Old Left, new movements, human-rights bodies, and others not easily falling into these categories—and includes groups organized in a strictly local, regional, national

and transnational fashion. The basis of participation is a common objective—struggle against the social ills consequent on neoliberalism—and a common respect for each other's immediate priorities. Importantly, the WSF seeks to bring together movements from the North and the South within a single framework. The only slogan, as yet, is "Another World is Possible." Even more strangely, the WSF seeks to do this without creating an overall superstructure. At the moment, it has only an international coordinating committee, some fifty-strong, representing a variety of movements and geographic locations.

That multiplicity is part of its strength, relying as it does on organizing different networks, with intellectuals prominent among them. Geoffrey Pleyers (2010) explains that formation.

Pleyers identifies "engaged intellectuals" as the critical actors behind this alternative network defined in opposition to neoliberalism, especially in the first stage before the WSF meeting in January 2001 in Porto Alegre, Brazil. After that meeting, the number of intellectuals and activists recognizing and performing their connectedness grew substantially. Pleyers identifies the coherence of the movement through its common meanings and opposition to neoliberalism, resting above all on their "knowledge and expertise" in opposition to the neoliberal Washington Consensus. An embrace of diversity complemented that definition through a common enemy (Pleyers 2010, 28). At the global level, this works as a kind of valorization of the modes different forms of resistance register in what Pleyers calls the way of subjectivity. He emphasizes, however, that this activist identity is also completed by "the way of reason" "founded on technical and abstract knowledge, expertise, and popular education" (109).

This dialogue is very different from that in which the WEF organizes its version. In the latter, Reason among the most talented and resourced actors in the world is assumed to be able not only to divine proper responses to the world's challenges but to recognize their real foundations. For the WSF, however, there is a much more vital sense that the various interests in the world limit the range of conversation about the character of problems and their sources, with Reason itself being one of the casualties of the global elite's purchase of both property and knowledge.

A key concept can distinguish these organizations effectively. For WEF, a "multiple stakeholder" approach defines the network's principal methodology, drawing together states, corporations, and representatives of civil society to figure problems. For WSF, such a definition of stakeholder is itself a problem, as it presumes those without such power have no stakes in the game, nothing to lose by others' definition of their problems, and nothing to offer in the way of devising alternative futures. This is profoundly wrong, at least for those who are part of the WSF network and its ripples.

Pleyers challenges the assumption that the WSF and alter-globalization activists are less likely than those of the WEF to be associated with "expertise." Notably with a number of scholars expert in international law or in more specific fields like genetically modified organisms or financial transactions, this broad movement for a more just and sustainable globalization mobilizes considerable knowledge in support of a vision of transformation more explicitly attuned to those without power. Too, the way in which they mobilize expertise differs from that of the WEF.

While both might claim to wish public debate, the WEF seems to privilege dialogue, while the WSF would rather focus on elevating indignation through its emphasis on transparency and more fundamental alternatives (Pleyers 2010, 118–21). Additionally, the WSF is more likely to recognize, and suffer, the contradictions between experience and expertise in more open and passionate fashion (123–29). At the same time, to go global, it also relies on the status some of its engaged intellectuals bring to the movement (130–53). However, precisely because of the movement's recognition of the contradiction, different things are possible within it than in the more scripted occasions that take place within the WEF.

Sometimes, as in London's European Social Forum 2004, dialogue becomes all but impossible. Those tensions also can prove productive, as happened in 2005 according to Pleyers. In that year's WSF, while the way of reason held sway, a new more decentralized form of organization enabled a wider array of subjectivities to be expressed and to inform subsequent action (Pleyers 2010, 194–98). With the end to the Washington Consensus around neoliberalism, some might argue that the alter-globalization movement has realized some success. David Graeber, one of the major intellectuals associated with the movement, at least thinks so.

In the introduction to his collection of essays written between 2004 and 2010, Graeber (2011) characterizes the major challenge of emancipatory movement theory. In 2007 he and Japanese colleagues were developing a "strategic analysis of the global situation from the perspective of capital, and the movements against it," which they had dutifully managed. But the G8 meetings themselves never came up with such a strategic plan. They had something different in mind, he writes:

> Those bigwigs assembling at their various summits were probably more aware than we were that the entire system—based on a very old fashioned alliance of military and financial power typical of the latter days of capitalist empires—were being held together with tape and string. They were less concerned to save the system, than to ensure that there remained no plausible alternative in anyone's mind so that, when the moment of collapse did come, they would be the only ones offering solutions. (Graeber 2011, 3)

The global justice movement, as he calls it, one based on direct action and direct democracy, did have its successes, he argues. It ended structural adjustment policies, blocked new global trade agreements, and halted the growth and blunted the power of neoliberal governance institutions like the International Monetary Fund (IMF) and World Trade Organization (WTO). Consider, he offers, how the Argentine public, so outraged by the 2001 economic crisis brought on by following IMF advice, so threatened their ruling classes that Nestor Kirchner, a social democrat, defaulted on that debt on taking power. Chase and Citibank took their losses when the IMF would not bail them out. And that was the beginning of the end of global influence for the Washington Consensus and its instruments (Graeber 2011, 22–23).

Graeber's theoretical practice has been more than a celebration of neoliberal failures, however. He, along with many others, has argued that success is to be found in the movements themselves, a kind of "prefigurative politics" (Graeber 2013, 23). In light of the failure of revolutionary insurrections to produce greater justice, the revolutionary movement has gone in reverse: to produce in immediate communities the qualities of life they wish to see writ large for the future. Direct action, direct democracy, speak to these (41–65), because the transformative moment lies not in their institutionalization but in the transformation of imagination that takes place when those administrative grips made in injustice are loosened and the beginning of improvised change happens (61).

It is tempting to make gross generalizations with these examples of the WEF and WSF and the intellectuals and knowledge products and practices associated with them. One might distinguish them simply on the basis of their explicit political identifications and visions alongside the various forms of capital at their disposal to validate knowledge claims. In that, we would find a traditional sociology of knowledge (Camic, Gross, and Lamont 2011, 6), one that finds a fusion, or at least ready articulation, between social position and epistemology.[32] We also know that knowledge practices are much more nuanced and can carry within them quite unintended consequences even with the best of intentions. Knowledge practices associated with democracy's extension are especially powerful illustrations of this point.

Democracy Leading Global Knowledge Networks

Of all the globally engaged knowledge networks of which I have been part, I have been most involved with the extension of democracy, beginning with the struggles of the Solidarity movement in Poland in 1980–81 (Kennedy 1991, 2013b), through various engagements with "transition" in the postcommunist world (Kennedy 2002a). I have conceived my role in much the same terms as Trotsky considered his: as being part of a movement while at the same time trying to elaborate its theory and practice so that it would realize more of its critical potential (Burawoy 1989).

I undertook this work initially innocent of the scholarship surrounding democracy assistance.[33] When I became the principal academic guide at the University of Michigan establishing a center devoted to extending democracy across the world, my sensitivity to the larger global network, and not only to domestic political differences in democracy's local expression, grew substantially.[34] First of all, context matters a great deal. In that center's initial work, we kept the focus on places formerly ruled by communists; the implication of American power did not figure so problematically as it would in, for example, Iraq. American scholars in Poland and Georgia were part of the emancipatory fusion of knowledge and practice, at least for most.

To allow context to lead too much can also be a mistake in figuring democracy's network knowledge power. Graeber draws a line that few would acknowledge but deserves more careful study. Recalling some of those discussions immediately preceding Occupy Wall Street, Graeber (2013, 10–11) recounts the unusually mediated trail from Seattle to Tahrir, prompted by Otpor!'s support for the Tahrir occupation in 2011:

> The tactics that Otpor! (the Serbian youth movement that helped to bring down Milosevic) and many other of the groups in the vanguard of the "colored" revolutions of the aughts—from the old Soviet empire down to the Balkans—implemented, with help from the CIA, were the ones the CIA

originally learned from studying the Global Justice Movement, including tactics executed by some of the people who were gathered on the Hudson River that very night. . . . It was difficult not to notice that back around 1999, right around the time that a loose global network of antiauthoritarian collectives began mobilizing to shut down trade summits from Prague to Cancun using surprisingly effective techniques of decentralized direct democracy and nonviolent civil disobedience, certain elements in the US security apparatus began not only studying the phenomenon, but trying to see if they could foster such movements themselves.

Such a focus on particular movement techniques associated with democracy's extension might be more generally associated with the movement to extend the culture of critical discourse in the world today. And perhaps the most powerful network associated with that mission is one animated by the Open Society Foundations (OSF; Sudetic 2011).

George Soros is the single most important figure behind the movement to build open societies. Both his ideas and his money matter, but it's his money that is most exceptional even as the range of issues OSF addresses rivals in importance. Unusual among philanthropists, Soros's commitment is guided by his own scholarly training and orienting theory of reflexivity, in which he emphasizes the importance of recognizing the difference between knowledge and change. With that principle, he set up a foundation to move ahead a mission in three moments: "(1) opening closed societies, (2) making open societies more viable, and (3) promoting a critical mode of thinking" (Sudetic 2011, 12).

The history he tells—failing in South Africa, succeeding in Hungary, and then moving to China, Poland, Russia, and beyond—is quite illuminating even for those of us who have worked with various parts of this organization for some time. His pragmatism and the significance of establishing knowledge networks were critical through all of these ventures. His organization was also intriguing—a matrix of national foundations combined with network programs that cut across places, without, at least in the early years, strict economic planning. This created a project of terrific consequence, especially in Central and Eastern Europe. His foundations' work has also focused on knowledge institutions and networks, with one-third of the budget dedicated to education in different forms, from Central European University in Budapest to the Higher Education Support Programme (Sudetic 2011).

The OSF have clearly moved beyond the regions in which their influence was initially felt. Soros concludes his own contribution to Sudetic (2011) by focusing on the United States; the conclusion of Sudetic's volume addresses the foundations' work combating drugs, especially in Baltimore, and help following Katrina. This particular volume discusses how transparency in resource-rich countries besides the United States enables civil society to hold governments more accountable; how criminal justice on a global scale might be approached; how alleviating poverty through economic development occurs (in which Albania and Moldova are featured); and how failed states (notably Haiti and Burma) and drug-resistant tuberculosis should be addressed. The struggle against tuberculosis began in Russian prisons in order to gain access to the prisons themselves. Because guards were equally subject to infection, prison authorities welcomed OSF help.

Despite this diversity of interests, Soros's general commitment to civil society, regardless of region, abides: "On the one hand, we help civil society to hold governments accountable. On the other, we try to work with those governments who are willing to accept our help to meet their obligations better" (Sudetic 2011, 35). That niche—civil society holding governments accountable—is what makes Soros anticipate the enduring influence of his foundations.

Although Sudetic's volume is exceptionally interesting, it is also curious: it hardly addresses the ways in which Soros's philanthropy has made a difference in knowledge institutions and networks,[35] one of the principal objects of his philanthropy. But then that's also the place where I have worked the most between 2005 and 2013.[36] The Academic Fellowship Program (AFP) was articulated with a larger initiative called the Higher Education Support Programme in which other programs have also been developed.[37] I draw upon that, as well as publicly available documents, for the following observations.[38]

In a major conference organized in March 2012 in the Hungarian Academy of Sciences to reflect on AFP achievements and challenges, OSF board member Leon Botstein (2012), Central European University board chair and Bard College president, challenged the conceit of universities with their presumptions of impact and association with freedom.[39] Even more critically, he proposed that universities fail to the extent they prepare their students to resemble their teachers instead of anticipating future challenges. One might find terrific resonance in this lament for the kinds of design intellectualities with which I began this chapter (Pendleton-Jullian 2009).

While all attendees at the conference, and in the network AFP organizes, recognize that their association can help universities build better curricula, develop more rigorous and visionary research, and elaborate more appropriate forms of university governance that reflect dynamic rather than conservative institutions, those in that large hall were also wondering whether the network might itself be more than a vehicle facilitating the flow of knowledge. Could it not also generate the vectors of knowledge production themselves? For the attendees were not just sharing best practices and developing transnational collegialities. They were, we were, refashioning, through our practice and our affinities, the point of higher learning in a world transformed. AFP was already conceived in just that condition.

Established in 2004–5, building on a program associated with civic education motivated by a kind of academic idealism, AFP was a more realistic project. It focused on fewer people in fewer units, recognizing that change doesn't come through the spread of ideas by itself. It develops through investments in particular people, and units, over a longer time period in order to realize consequence.

AFP supports a couple hundred individual scholars each year who, in turn, are presumed to transform the knowledge institutions of which they are a part and then, indirectly, to extend the openness of the societies in which they live. This support operates with the assumption that integration into global, especially Western, knowledge networks facilitates scholarly development and, indirectly, institutional change. These are the particulars (Shavarshidze 2012):

- The program focuses most of its resources on "returning scholars," those with degrees in the "West." Between 2005–6 and 2012–13, the program has supported 607 fellows, with annual totals growing each year. More and more of the returning scholars have already earned, or are working on, their PhD degrees, whereas at the start, a majority had a master's degree only.

- AFP also has supported 230 "international scholars," typically EU European or North American, to work with the returning scholars and their units for a year or more. Over time, these international scholars are increasingly citizens of the European Union rather than of Canada or the United States.

- AFP also helps university departments through its Partnership Program, supporting about forty-five to fifty-one units per year. It additionally facilitates electronic collaborations through its Academic Webfolio Project, an especially valuable resource for returning scholars and partner departments as it provides access to JSTOR and EBSCO. It sponsors discipline groups and their meetings and manages an alumni program.

- This Academic Fellowship Program also has a powerful symbiotic relationship with another Soros venture—the Central European University, for many of the returning scholars have earned their degrees at CEU and many international scholars teach at the Budapest institution. Nearly one-fourth of AFP fellows are affiliated with CEU.

The initiative has changed over the near decade of its existence. Most notably, the particular concentrations of expertise supported have shifted. While conventional academic disciplines were the principal focus of its earlier work, more professional programs concerning, for example, human rights, public health, and social work, have joined the list. And the regions enjoying support have also changed; as countries joined the European Union, their scholars and institutions could no longer be supported. Rather, these "alumni" often offer support to others, as Bulgaria's sociologists now do. Additionally, OSF began support for Palestine, for the West Bank, in 2013–14 and is scheduled to increase that investment substantially in the following year. Table 7.1 shows the constellation of countries and academic units enjoying support in 2012–13.

Many of the principles and practices underlying OSF are apparent in this table. First, OSF clearly responds to places and organizations that are themselves responsive—beyond the overt antipathy Russia has increasingly held for Western NGOs, other places, including those not even on this list, are even more unwelcoming. However, look at how Georgia and Kyrgyzstan and secondarily, given size, Ukraine, Kosova, and Mongolia, embrace the possibilities of partnership.

Of course, these partnerships are not distributed across all higher education institutions within countries. In some places, notably Ukraine and Krygyzstan, the privately organized Kyiv-Mohyla Academy and American University of Central Asia are among the most successful in developing OSF partnerships, even while they are simultaneously publicly engaged. For the most part, however, OSF has worked to support and transform the public universities struggling to escape their communist pasts. Transition culture does indeed thrive in the life of postcommunist knowledge institutions.

Were we in the rankings business, we might simply end with this distribution and discuss how it reflects global knowledge engagements. We might remark that Georgia and Kyrgyzstan are ahead of the game in developing their

TABLE 7.1 Distribution of academic fellowship programs by discipline/country

	A	B	C	D	E	F	G	H	I	J	K	L	M	Total
Albania						1					1			2
Armenia						1						1	1	3
Azerbaijan						1					1			2
Bosnia & Herzegovina				1							1			2
Georgia		1		1		1		1	1	1			2	8
Kazakhstan										1				1
Kosova							1	1				1		3
Kyrgyzstan	1	1	1			1		2	1			1		8
Macedonia								1		1				2
Moldova					1	1					1			3
Mongolia	1		1	1						1				4
Russia						1		1.5				.5		3
Serbia		1						1	1					3
Tajikistan				1										1
Ukraine	1	1			1	1						1	1	6
West Bank													1	1
Total	2	4	4	2	3	8	1	7.5	3	4	4	4.5	5	52

A   Anthropology
B   Communications/Journalism
C   Economics/International economics
D   Gender
E   History
F   Law
G   Philosophy
H   Politics/International relations
I   Psychology
J   Public/Population health/Social medicine
K   Social work
L   Sociology
M   Other

knowledge cultures, and politics and law are among the most dynamic (if not also in greatest need) in knowledge cultural change. Of course, this is not so simple. Russia, for example, is developing some global university capacities in extraordinary ways toward some of the same ends. But if that were our final ambition, then we would miss the greater point of AFP and OSF more generally. We would overlook the more foundational efforts of the initiative in the transformation of knowledge institutions and extension of public goods in civil society. The program's designers, leaders, and participants are well aware of that challenge and work in both formal and informal ways to figure how to assess and extend those effects.

It's hard to figure the independent effect of the AFP initiative, however. AFP certainly supports some of the most ambitious and talented scholars in these different regions and thus can only complement, rather than determine, what these individuals might achieve in their teaching, curricular reform, research, or institutional leadership within universities. For example, AFP fellows have led in the work to develop library programs in several universities, developed more than a few new degrees (including the development of a PhD program in "Social Transformations" associated with both sociology and political science in Kyiv-Mohyla Academy in Ukraine) and some new academic departments and new research centers, including the Institute for Social Studies and the Humanities and a Center for Cultural Studies within it at the University of Prishtina. Likewise, when some AFP fellows become prominent in policy advice, civil society, or in governance itself, it is difficult to say that AFP enabled this public engagement. It's also hard to overlook that many contributions AFP associates offer, especially around human and children's rights and health issues, are facilitated by AFP support. Indeed, Kyiv-Mohyla's journal of social criticism, *Commons*, is associated with two Returning Scholars supported by AFP who were, in turn, participants in AFP International Scholar Michael Burawoy's global public sociology initiative.[40] As discussed in Chapter 4, that global knowledge network affects the quality of public sociology's debate (Kennedy 2012a).[41]

More substantial and systematic work would be necessary to parse these effects. One might argue, however, that AFP has developed a relatively successful model for attracting and retaining Western-educated scholars in AFP region universities (about 80 percent of them remain within the academic sector). And even when those individuals leave university life, they usually leave units better off than before. However, AFP can succeed only when the home units are hospitable. Clearly we can't talk about the "independent" effect of AFP work but rather its "interactive" effect: AFP empowers those predisposed to make change. Therefore, terrific burden falls on AFP to recognize who are so inclined and what kinds of changes are important to render.

In this recollection of AFP's work, I'm struck by how much of its network intellectuality might be conceived in terms of Pendleton-Jullian and Brown's (forthcoming) ecosystemic design. First, the conception of higher education was transformed: to borrow their words, AFP was very much an enterprise of "making things that operate in a world unfolding." However, like most of transition culture, it relied on an imagined future based on what already existed in the West with its institutionalized culture of critical discourse in universities (Eglitis 2002). Second, AFP was fundamentally optimistic in its practice, assuming that by bringing new scholars into existing institutions, things could change, which in turn would change the context in which institutions were embedded. Of course, by working with those scholars over time, the network figured new elements for its strategy. When that proved insufficient, AFP would actually withdraw its support from those individuals and their institutions. In this, AFP's optimism was indeed skeptical, a disposition years of communism certainly facilitated. It was not, however, cynical, which is perhaps a more likely product of the combination of communism with postcommunism. Finally, while design typically focuses on things, one might say that these things could extend to knowledge networks and the nodes of their transformation. For AFP, there are some remarkably clear moments of this change.

AFP has been especially important for those areas, like gender studies, that are less likely to have important bases of power within the already-existing knowledge institutional cultures. It's also important in those traditional bastions of university power, like history, where nationalisms antagonistic to critical inquiry can be preserved and nurtured. One might look to Moldova's network of AFP historians to find one of those exemplary effects, to see where a new kind of critical history actually found public footing. However, I need to return to a context more familiar to make the case about the value of AFP knowledge networks.

In the fall of 2012, the University of Prishtina celebrated the founding of the sociology and philosophy departments forty years earlier. Most of the scholars were from the University of Prishtina. More than a few others joined the occasion from other places in Europe and North America to reflect on the character of knowledge and change in Kosova, and its relation to the rest of the world. And the results of that assembly, and more, are now available because colleagues at the University of Prishtina produced the second volume of *Njohja*,[42] which in Albanian means "Knowledge" (Kennedy 2013a).

Available in English and funded by a US embassy grant, this issue of *Njohja* elaborates the trajectory of Kosovar sociology. In particular it explores human and social transformations within Kosova and across the world. The issue includes articles on the place of Hindu culture in Kosova (Halimi 2013) and on articulations of Africana philosophy (Limani 2013). It includes accounts of how changes in southeastern Europe end the modern myths of democracy and development (Katumaric 2013) and how Internet activism changes political discourse (Tahiri 2013). David Weberman (2013), from the OSF-supported Central European University, explored the many ways in which philosophy can shape change, distinguishing how the search for truth might improve the soul, enlarge our vision, sharpen our reasoning skills, or actually shape how we change the world or ourselves. If it might realize some of the influence that its cousin *Polish Sociological Bulletin*, then *Polish Sociological Review*, had on a broader global sociology and human sciences, Kosova's place in English-language globalizing knowledge will be consequential. But already, as the journal suggests, the quality of discussion and knowledge production has grown dramatically. *Njohja* has become much more important for the rest of the world figuring how to relate knowledge production to a world in crisis and in need of transformation.

Before turning to the penultimate chapter that last sentence anticipates, I conclude with some reflections on the various forms and implications of the knowledge networks considered here.

Networks in Transformation's Articulation

It is much easier to generalize about knowledge institutions than networks because of the homophilizing tendencies sociologists have identified in the former. Networks don't have that quality. The substance of what they do, the people populating their interactions, and the rules guiding their missions define much more what knowledge networks become. Some networks do much the same work as knowledge institutions, especially those networks composed of knowledge institutions. In those circumstances, transformation is primarily the work of reproduction, that is, trying to preserve the space of knowledge institutions in the midst of profound change. When we focus more on networks connecting individuals from very different kinds of institutional and contextual circumstances, we may see network knowledgeability's transformative power. Contrasting SSRC, the WEF, the WSF, and the OSF directly can help us clarify the relationship between knowledge and change and the place of design in its articulation.

SSRC is by far the oldest of these networks, and controlling for that age, has changed, one might argue, the least. Its abiding commitment to knowledge for the public good remains, and its three accents—around encouraging interdisciplinary scholarship in new areas, building scholarly capacities, and figuring their value for policy and practice—continue. The way it does internationalism, the particular interdisciplinary projects it identifies, and the modes of public engagement change with the times, its presidents, and scholarly media. Nevertheless, this particular quality of reproduction and transformation depends first and foremost on the brand that SSRC has earned and works to preserve. Its design intellectuality walks a careful tightrope between the need to innovate and the cultivation of academic distinction, between the quest for autonomy and the importance of demonstrating value to funders and to promoters.

There are no other scholarly networks like SSRC, although ACLS might come closest for its place in the humanities. It would be exceptionally difficult to build an SSRC in these times, at least in the United States. Interdisciplinarity is not something alien to most knowledge institutions; in fact, every knowledge institution presents that practice as if it is unusual but distinctive to itself. Every knowledge institution is global in its aspirations. And most have some kind of public mission. Because of SSRC's history of accomplishment, and its elevation of knowledge consequence over the promotion of its own faculty and students, it has a distinction, a kind of convening power that marks it as special. Because it can mobilize scholars from anywhere to address a problem, and because those scholars know that SSRC's distinction lies in assembling the best to develop the innovative, SSRC can do something different, only because it is not beholden to any faculty that it owns or students it must promote above others. SSRC's value rests in its reputation, itself organized around its capacity to convene the best of the best in the address of any social science problem or any problem in the world social science might improve with its engagement.

At the same time, SSRC is not a wealthy organization like the WEF or the OSF. Especially as the philanthropic world shifted toward its own search for efficiency in awarding grants, the kind of funding that allowed SSRC an operational infrastructure and autonomy in problem selection faded, at least in comparison to its own past. SSRC had to become much more interactive with its foundational partners and philanthropists, convincing them of the value of the ideas SSRC brings to the table even as SSRC would work to move foundation and philanthropic interests into the kinds of projects it would like to carry forward. And here, then, we see the first challenge of knowledge networks: they depend not only on mobilizing scholarly resources but on finding material resources with which to generate knowledgeable change, requiring a certain resonance with those of means.

The WEF and the OSF have very different models for assuring that financial base. OSF is not replicable, given that one man's resources define its capacity and autonomy, relative autonomy at least from forces beyond George Soros himself. The organization's internal structure and Soros's philosophy do, however, shape what is feasible and what is not. Although there is a certain amount of loyalty—OSF's award of $60 million to Bard suggests that—the organization itself is hardly bureaucratic in its logic and much more consequentialist and reflexive in its allocation of resources.

OSF is, one might argue, a pure knowledge network of consequence, so long as that knowledge and consequence are in tune with the sense of Soros. And that resonance happens through a mixture of personal ties and intellectual rationales that leads the organization into a wide variety of endeavors. Extending critical thinking is, after all, needed everywhere. Prioritizing according to a deductive script has no place in a philosophy that celebrates innovation and reflexivity. However, OSF has also changed far more over its shorter life than SSRC because its core mission is so flexible and its resources so ample; it could continue to support higher education even as it moved more toward public health, drug policies, and disaster relief. To the external world, the business of priorities and tough choices is not apparent in OSF logic.

WEF's business plan is more replicable if no less remarkable in its achievement. Klaus Schwab developed a model that has grown dramatically over the years, redefining itself in response to challenges without losing its own core sense of assembling a global elite to meet the world's challenges. The organization is, however, more rational and deliberative, one might argue, than OSF because power is far more dispersed and dependent on Schwab's abilities for persuasion among very powerful actors whose continued engagement depends on their finding value in the association. And here we can see that the knowledge cultural elements fade. Its power depends far less on the knowledge public goods it can produce than in whom one might meet. It's not just a social club, however; the idea that this is a kind of Habermasian public / private sphere for the world's elite is not wrong. WEF does provide a setting where less public, and less "interested," conversations can take place. And even as civil society's representatives join the conversation, the rational critical discourse is extended. It is also disciplined by the weight of the elite's presence and the dependence of the organization on their continued support, much like the WSF depends on the mobilization of alter-globalization activists.

WSF has no financial base equivalent to its consequence, partially because it is even more a network of networks than is the SSRC. WSF depends entirely on its capacities to mobilize activists and intellectuals and on its reputation as a network respecting the diversity of life experiences that neoliberalism and its successor ideologies and political economies deny. Its fractious and fragile qualities reflect that very experience, even as it mobilizes more "free labor" in policy work than what WEF or OSF would ever imagine. At the same time, in this very fashion it operates on similar principles as SSRC, for both depend on the donation of knowledge work to the tasks set out in the network of networks.

With this juxtaposition of cases, we are now prepared to see transformational knowledge networks in a new light, even if with conventional 2x2 tabular form, as shown in Table 7.2.

As we have discussed, OSF and WEF are on relatively sound financial grounds. While they each mobilize free knowledge labor, the relative importance of that labor to the money flowing through their networks, both formal and informal, is quite insubstantial in comparison to what SSRC and WSF mobilize. SSRC and WSF depend relatively more on the reputational capital associated with each of their networks. Of course, OSF and WEF have their own prestige, which depends to a considerable extent on the money reinforcing it. SSRC and WSF don't have that measure of backup. But the kinds of knowledge associated with SSRC and WSF are very different.

Both SSRC and WSF are concerned for public goods. SSRC cannot define itself by its association with a certain part of the global struggle in ways that WSF must. If that rational critical discussion leads SSRC or OSF down a path WSF networks have already blazed, they might just follow, or accompany. Democracy's extension around the colored revolutions and beyond is a good illustration. But they cannot begin with the same assumptions that WSF entertains. It is much easier for SSRC to begin with the same assumptions as WEF, especially to the extent one must rely on similar financial foundations that WEF has mobilized so effectively. Here, then, lies the quandary.

Knowledge institutions have developed substantial mechanisms to assure that wealth does not corrupt their mission. Knowledge networks typically don't build that kind of insulation. Unless they depend on an ideological

TABLE 7.2 Rules and resources of transformational knowledge networks

	Reflexive knowledge	*Interested knowledge*
Finance capital resourced	Open Society Foundation	World Economic Forum
Knowledge capital resourced	Social Science Research Council	World Social Forum

foundation that demands it, as WSF does, they can't afford that distance. But then we should not overestimate the distance knowledge institutions have from such power, as we found in Chapters 3 and 4. To understand how resources of various sorts shape knowledge networks' foci, memberships, and impacts is one of the most critical transformational questions in these times.

Times they are a changing, and the powers of intellectual connectivity are beginning to outpace even the more agile if still conventional knowledge networks. Various emergent knowledges, not only those designed in and through already-existing networks, are potentially of increasing importance. Whether those new networks can bring the cosmopolitan intellectuality that universities and the networks associated with them seek is another question. It's even a greater question with which publics one might build a knowledgeable and consequential solidarity.

8 Framing: Cosmopolitan Intellectuality and Consequential Solidarity

By focusing on articulations of globalizing knowledge, we can explore the resources that enable certain kinds of knowledge to pass for wisdom while others appear as ideology, some to appear as parochial while others universal, some to look anachronistic while others visionary. We also can assess the cultural schemas that move intellectuals, knowledge institutions, and networks to anticipate global transformations that could make the world better. We can think about the articulations of worldly theory and practice by intellectuals and their institutions and networks around different global contexts, flows, and publics. And with that, we can focus on refining schemas of intellectual and institutional responsibility and the frames that mobilize and legitimate them. However, while we might pose these issues in abstract analytical time, transformations of knowledge and the world happen in real historical time.

In what follows, I refine the conceptual tools necessary for recognizing those schemas likely to be productive of such responsibility in these world historical times. I am especially attentive to figuring frames that bind subjectivity and system, scholarship and public engagement, worldliness and grounding. By considering the various forms of knowledge attending these conjunctions, we might be better prepared to articulate the qualities of cosmopolitan intellectuality and consequential solidarity that animate intellectual, institutional, and global responsibility for a world in crisis.

Framing, Cultural Formations, and
Sense-Making in Time

Framing is an obvious and important perspective in the social sciences and has become increasingly common in the discourses connecting intellectual work and the worlds of policy and practice.[1] Its literature is substantial, but I find it useful, in the end, to consider frames as those devices that encapsulate the principles, themes, memories, or symbols that agents use to organize information about an object (Snow et al. 1986; Fiss and Hirsch 2005).

Sometimes, however, an issue does not have clear and salient agents elaborating explicit and competing frames. When this is the case, it is especially useful to think about "cultural formations." As elaborated by Raymond Williams (1977, 117), these are "effective movements and tendencies, in intellectual and artistic life, which have significant and sometimes decisive influence on the active development of a culture and which have a variable and often oblique relation to formal institutions." Here, I don't presume one can identify the agents and their frames; interests are often, if identifiable, only theoretical.[2]

One could tie cultural formations and cultural frames together through this concept of sense-making: "how the identification of patterns of meaning depends on salient cues from the environment" (Fiss and Hirsch 2005, 29). Sense-making "stresses the internal, self-conscious process of developing a coherent account of what is going on," thus focusing on why such frames come into existence in the first place and how they are connected to structure (31). Its analysis also helps explain how meaning is contested and how structural factors bind the discourse.

In short, I would propose that there are three degrees of "coherence" in shaping the interpretation of global transformations: (1) frames, where one can clearly identify a relatively coherent articulation that resonates closely with an identifiable actor or interest; (2) sense-making, where clearly identifiable actors and interests struggle to figure out how an object relates to their concerns or position; and (3) cultural formation, where the discussion is sufficiently opaque that it shapes, rather than reflects, the location of the actors themselves. I am especially interested in the last circumstance, for cultural formations offer new identities and possibilities through cultural politics and are especially likely to appear in crisis.

To engage crisis means not only to appreciate real historical time. It's also about recognizing identities and possibilities that the moment offers. It's a hermeneutics that's not only historical but critical in its anticipation of alternative futures. To write in the wake of 2011–13 is, in this sense, a world historical blessing. In Sewell's (2005) sense, those years were most eventful. They also require us to rethink intellectualities themselves.

Beyond engaging the historical conjuncture of a world redefined by social movements and uprisings, we need to learn from the resonating scholarship within regions in crisis and their movements of transformation. It's not just a matter of scholarly collaboration but of recognizing the conditions of knowledge resonance with publics, patrons, and the knowledge institutions and networks in which those articulations form.

I have referenced throughout the intellectualities enabling and implicated in the Arab Uprisings of 2011 and the Occupy movement that followed. Given the diversity of these mobilizations, I find it intellectually irresponsible to address these movements in terms that only assimilate them to past cultural politics. They are novel expressions and in their contexts transformative, at least potentially. Elaborating their practice to refigure a world in need of transformation is intellectual responsibility.

Articulation is again the keyword. As noun, it emphasizes properly the importance of location within and among the tendencies defining the crisis. As action, it properly signals the importance of figuring linkages that redefine the whole. Intellectual practice engaging real transformation may also require a different concept. *Rearticulation* seems right. It properly signals the importance of recognizing the novelty and power of these years of transformation and their implications for refiguring the culture of critical discourse around responsibility.

One cannot now declare the intellectual currents emerging from 2011–13 in the same fashion we could identify liberalism, conservatism, radicalism, and populism to have come from 1848 (Calhoun 1989a). It is, however, appropriate to recognize that there are two very different emphases to have emerged in these years. They reflect the dualities of structure that continue to animate our thinking. One emphasizes alterations in subjectivities; the other, alterations in the structures shaping them. By clarifying those distinctions, we might articulate more adequately the sense-making globalizing knowledge requires.

Intellectualities in Search of Subjectivity

Before 2011, a terrific amount of sociology addressing global transformations focused on the structural contradictions and inequalities of a neoliberal world system. Those struggles pointing beyond the binary were present but were overlooked in favor of figuring subjectivity as expressions of systemic contradictions. Eastern European resistance, for example, challenged that derivative logic with the defense of public goods institutions against neoliberal desecrations (Szelenyi and Wilk 2013). That resistance could have been critical to transforming our sense of alternative futures given Eastern Europe's prior role in assuring neoliberalism's 1990s triumph (Kennedy 2002a).

Many in 2011 in fact tried to use 1989 to contain the radical implications of the Arab Uprisings. They failed to recognize how 1989's revolution in the name of normality depended on identifying salvation's place as already existing and innocent of the injustice against which the oppressed rebelled. That 1989/2011 identification could not last. The West has been deeply implicated in the injustices against which the uprisings of 2011 were defined (Kennedy 2011b). As that 2011 inspiration has traveled, it has also met a knowledge culture relatively unprepared for the new subjectivity these uprisings and their descendants across Europe and North America represented.[3]

During the first decade or more of the new millennium, intellectuals were hard at work developing their arguments about cosmopolitanism with a relatively structural account of a globalizing world. Even if that was a world of flows, subjectivities were much more responsive than they were transformative. They were agentic only in seeking ways to redirect the flow in more intellectually responsible and globally sustainable and just fashion. As is often the case, social and global transformations can change sociologies and broader intellectual currents. Indeed, since 2011, we can see a new kind of intellectuality emergent, one that promises even more radical transformations.

Because my expertise lies mostly in North America, Europe, and Eurasia, I focus my remarks on the main currents evident there. But first, I acknowledge someone whose contextual expertise lies in Southeast Asia and whose insights on the state and resistance span the globe. He has recently come to anarchism's celebration and the subjectivities and intellectualities apparent in it (Scott 2012).[4]

Jim Scott acknowledges the kind of knowledgeability that typically goes unrecognized, the everyday intellectuality that recognizes what's wrong and surreptitiously goes ahead and does what's right.[5] In the unrecognized, he appreciates how local knowledge defines roads by their destinations, not by the numbers remote geographers assign them. For the subterranean just, he celebrates, along with those German anarchists who made a papier-mâché

monument to their resistance, military deserters who refuse to kill innocents. However, it is through more enduring monumentalities that we come
to appreciate the knowledgeability Scott cheers.

In contrast to the lock-step interpretation of war that the Iwo Jima monument inspires, where the image of soldiers planting the US flag on a rock in
the war against Japanese imperialism legislates our association of heroism,
triumph, and patriotism, Maya Lin's memorial to Viet Nam's war does something different. It depends on each person bringing his or her own knowledgeability, memories and sense of loss, and recognition of comrades missed
alongside loved ones remembered to the monument's completion. This kind
of knowledgeability need not be cumulated, organized, and disseminated. It
is localized, personalized, and identified with particular individuals and contingent lives. It is human, just as it is limited.

In an offhand remark but with obviously profound feeling, Scott noted
that while the monument is beautiful, it only marks American losses. He
writes, "A truly cosmopolitan monument to the war would, of course, list all
Vietnamese civilian and war dead, together with Americans in the order in
which they have fallen" (2012, 62). But that is hard to imagine given the ways
in which nationalism dominates our moralities. And that is why cosmopolitanism is so critical to develop, one that can't come from the celebrations of
locality anarchists offer. Or might it?

As discussed in Chapter 7, David Graeber has articulated the ties between
anarchist sensibilities and the global justice movement. These ties are also
apparent in the WSF mobilizations. This sense of global solidarity is broadly
distributed among anarchists and deserves more elaboration as a cultural
formation itself. Slavoj Žižek is no anarchist but he does focus on subjectivities in ways that are not distant from anarchism's emphasis. He is, however,
identified with a kind of communism that seems to me more provocation
than intellectually genuine. That, however, is Žižek's oeuvre, which itself has
sincere, and abiding, philosophical roots (Kennedy 1994; Kennedy and Galtz
1996). Žižek is also something of a celebrity intellectual in ways that neither
Scott nor Graeber is.

Žižek is known for his approach to ideology and is often celebrated by
those who embrace the prospects for radical change across the world (e.g.,
Zabala 2012). He is constantly showing us how what we think is true is not
really true and how ideology functions differently than we believe. He shows
us by using not only various philosophical currents but also popular cultural

elements. His is a very different kind of intellectuality, positively disdaining any system-type thinking. After all, that very administrative rationality blinds one both to the emancipatory hope beyond its grasp and the structural impossibilities that define system engineers' work and make it so unstable.

Žižek (2012) focused on 2011 itself. He argues that media and dominant ideologies denied the emancipatory potentials of this moment. He dedicates his work to recasting what these rebellions represent and cannot represent. Although he gives each their due, he accounts for them in two basic ways.

There are rebellions that are but expressions of impossibilities. In the United States, the populist rebellion apparent through the Tea Party signifies a moral contest masking a class struggle, but one that functions to preserve vested economic interests (Žižek 2012, 31). The London Riots of 2011 represent more purely the impossibilities of voice for many within the system; its performance signifies only the impossibility of acknowledging their own contradictory and impossible lives. Its only possible expression is a kind of "acting out" ostensibly without political meaning but loaded with it simultaneously (53–55).

Žižek exemplifies a kind of intellectuality that works to make the nonsensical sensible. He points to what the real contest, the unacknowledged but fundamental fight, is all about. He typically does not find the Real contest expressed properly in any real social conflicts. However, he is clearly enamored of the Arab Uprisings, finding in them real radical left emancipatory hope. Alas, it only becomes apparent in the movement's suffocation (Žižek 2012, 74–75). Žižek clearly can't be expected to understand the intricacies of the Arab world's contests, and one might fault him in a number of ways for his account of the Arab Uprisings. There might be less ground to fault him in Europe, for here, his own positions find deep resonance with actually existing struggles. He finds the Greek contest most compelling (81).

First, all the dominant ideological positions are meaningless in capturing the contest. Those positions are designed to cover over that which each side won't acknowledge. Second, and in response, the emancipatory struggle has moved appropriately to remain outside power. Like Occupy Wall Street, they have not offered concrete demands. This, he feels, is a critical kind of politics. By refusing to engage issues on the terms of the dominant, they wind up creating a space that cannot be dominated. At the same time, you can see that Žižek is no anarchist—his Leninism comes out.

Žižek appreciates how the Greeks are prepared to think about the political party that needs to lead, to be disciplined, to take decisions. He has no real advice here, except to say that movements like these should "insist on a particular demand that, while thoroughly 'realistic,' disturbs the very core of the hegemonic ideology, that is, which, while in principle feasible and legitimate, is defacto impossible (universal health care for example)" (Žižek 2012, 84).

Žižek's intellectuality in theory is very much for those who would wish to extend the movement's critical distance from the system and anticipate a future that is not yet known. He writes,

> Instead of analyzing them as part of the continuum of past and present, we should bring in the perspective of the future, taking them as limited, distorted (sometimes even perverted) fragments of a utopian future that lies dormant in the present as its hidden potential. . . . One should learn the art of recognizing, from an engaged subjective position, elements which are here, in our space, but whose time is the emancipated future, the future of the Communist Idea . . . even as we retain a radical openness to that future. (128–29)

Though one may be anarchist and the other communist, Graeber and Žižek both stand with the revolution "because the notion of a redemptive future remains the only way we can possibly make sense of the present; we can only understand the glue of what surrounds us from the perspective of an imaginary country whose own contours we can never understand, even when we are standing in it" (Graeber 2011, 9).

The American Sociological Association can also stand with the revolution. At least many of its presidents have. While subjectivities may be part of it, sociologists typically find the social structures and relations binding those possibilities. Frances Fox Piven's (2008) presidential address takes that structural starting point but then asks whether power from below can change the world. That is a more sociologically responsible, if not radically comfortable, question.

Given her abiding focus on poor people's movements, one can already anticipate her answer. She believes that globalization extends the significance of interdependent power that in turn augments transformative capacities from below. It is, however, more a matter of strategy, less of subjectivity. It's a matter of figuring the new scripts of interdependent power that move change. She is especially attentive to how breaking rules can change perceptions of grassroots contributions. To realize that change, movements require solidarity and endurance, and that solidarity depends on linking the multiple ties that define social life to a kind of moral judgment about the value of sacrifice and the evil of reigning authorities or systems. Piven's sociology offers a concrete strategy and sociological sense that complement the subjectivity Žižek, Graeber, and Scott celebrate.

Piven, Scott, Graeber, and Žižek, each in their own ways, represent a genuine intellectuality of consequence. All are highly regarded, at least in their own networks. Most of those working to understand a world in transformation will know their names. In this, they are conventional intellectuals, even if they eschew the dominant strands of recognition those in their disciplinary practices might celebrate. Estimation of their intellectual value should rest less in their publicity. They more likely find validation in changing how we understand, and perhaps even engage, a world in transformation.

They each celebrate, and work to discover, intellectualities and knowledge-abilities that cannot be recognized within existing hegemonies. Their contributions, their own example, stand as the most radical challenge to hegemonic knowledge practices: how we connect our deep expertise with the world that is becoming, and might still be, emancipated. But they may not be the best examples of transformative intellectuality if only because of their distance from the systems that dominate and empower us. Jürgen Habermas might be a better example.

Intellectualities in Search of Systemic Transformation

Habermas is the exemplary traditional critical intellectual in these times (Freedan 2010, 83; Calhoun, Mendieta, and VanAntwerpen 2013, 23). His intellectuality is unquestioned, for his scholarly depth and range, as well as his ability to move between scholarly and public worlds, are exceptional. He is usually near the top of any list of world thinkers, especially if European inflected. He even manages to influence American newscasters with his work on communicative capacities (A. Williams 2012). Habermas also directly addresses the crisis of our times, especially in the European Union. Although of course he has written far more, I focus my remarks here on his *Crisis of the European Union* (2012).

His response to the European Union in crisis should be familiar to anyone who knows his work. He continues to address both the EU system and life-worlds, working to figure their relationship through a public, constitutional, and social democratic lens (Muller 2010, 99–104). Habermas (2012, 52) is concerned primarily with the growing power of a core of the European Council as it seeks a kind of executive federalism that is a "template for a post-dem-ocratic exercise of political authority." This growth of administrative power depends on political elites pandering to their national constituencies, gaug-ing public opinion moods, and failing to take real leadership in building a coherent, more democratic all-Europe policy. Beyond the opportunism, he also speaks of various "mental blocks" that prohibit this shift (13). One of his principal concerns rests on breaking the erroneous assumption that popular sovereignty depends on state sovereignty.

Habermas's hope rests in an evolving civic solidarity among Europeans (2012, 29). While different issues and policy arenas require different kinds of legitimations, he does find growing possibilities in the "flows of ideas circulat-ing through the communication networks of civil society," primarily within the nations of Europe but potentially across them too (68). As they realize potentials through the European Union for the exercise of their rights, they will in practice become more European (49).

His hallmark in the simultaneous engagement of system and lifeworld con-tinues to inspire my own approach. He takes seriously that system but does not pretend to explain beyond the legal domain and its constitutional reference. Overall, he regards "the graduated integration or different speeds of unification as the only possible scenario for overcoming the current paralysis of the EU" (Habermas 2012, 116). However, political leaders fail to offer the political will and decisive leadership needed to realize this function. Germans are in particu-lar abandoning their historical moral responsibility, acting more and more like a "normal nation," which they are not (124). Ultimately, the leading political figures of the dominant nations must address the basic problem of "aligning levels of economic development within a currency area" (121).

In fact, this basic problem stands in the way of the EU's proper economic administrative function and of bringing about that EU lifeworld sensibility criti-cal to moving the EU's development to the next stage. Integration cannot happen without popular participation (Habermas 2012, 132). He writes, "A Europe-wide civic solidarity cannot develop if social inequalities between the member states become permanent structural features" (53). This inequality, among others, is, however, deeply embedded in the European Union itself (Kennedy 2012c).

Many diagnose the problem in the same way. George Soros (2012) said it starkly, with an appropriately unnerving historical comparison:

There is a close parallel between the euro crisis and the Latin American debt crisis of 1982, when the International Monetary Fund saved the international financial system by lending just enough money to the heavily indebted countries to enable them to avoid default. . . . Today, Germany is playing the same role as the IMF did then. The setting differs, but the effect is the same. . . . As a result, the eurozone has become divided into creditors and debtors, with the creditors in charge of economic policy. There is a center, led by Germany, and a periphery, consisting of the heavily indebted countries. . . . The innocent, frustrated, and angry victims of austerity provide fertile ground for hate speech, xenophobia, and all forms of extremism. Thus, policies designed to preserve the financial system and the euro are transforming the EU into the opposite of an open society.

Like Habermas, Soros can bring his particular expertise and broad intellectuality to bear on the system crisis through which the European Union muddles. Both celebrate civil society and the lifeworld's role in resolving the crisis. Both have elaborated in intellectually responsible fashion the forms of reflexivity and publicity democracy requires. But neither inspires transformers focused on the lifeworld as such. While one might find many challenging Soros on this dimension given his wealth and power, there are also many who challenge Habermas. Balibar (2012) exemplifies this, even while he acknowledges Habermas's intellectual distinction and contribution to recognizing the crisis:

> It comes after a series of brave views where Habermas hit out at the "new nationalism" of German policy and the "unilateral" prejudices that it conceals (we find ourselves wishing that French intellectuals would show the same independence). It makes a remarkable effort to hold together the political, economic and social aspects, and provides an idea of what Europe's contribution could be in finding a global crisis exit strategy, in which must be factored the need to protect social rights (which does not mean their immutability) and the need to regulate credit mechanisms that increase rapidly above the real economy. It clearly shows that a politically unified Europe (whether or not we call it "federal") is only possible under the condition of substantial democratisation of Europe, that affects the very nature of its powers and their representivity, therefore their legitimacy.

Balibar goes on to offer a familiar critique of Habermas's position: that his democracy remains too formal and that "something like a movement must emerge." Of course, Balibar is much more elaborate elsewhere and is far from being alone (Lacroix 2010). But one need not be moved by anarchism or communism to recognize the need for new social movements to change the debate. There are a number of other kinds of intellectual articulations just in Europe along these lines. Mary Kaldor and her colleagues (2012, 30) summarize brilliantly:

> Many cultural, religious and intellectual figures have issued appeals that call for a different conception of Europe beyond the market. For example, Mikis Theodorakis, the renowned songwriter and composer, and Manolis Glezos, politician, writer and World War II resistance fighter, issued the "Common Appeal for the Rescue of the Peoples of Europe" last October, which invoked the cultural and democratic legacy of Europe and opposed it to the "empire of money" which has come to dominate. This appeal formed the basis for the later solidarity campaign for the people of Greece that spread throughout Europe. In France, Alan Badiou, together with others, wrote the manifesto "Save Greece from its Saviours!" It likewise summons the ideal of European democracy which is threatened by a neo-liberal onslaught, and it calls on a community of intellectuals and artists to "multiply articles, media appearances, debates, petitions, demonstrations" to save the people of Greece from imposed impoverishment. Ulrich Beck and Danny Cohn-Bendit call for a "Year of Volunteering" in order to reconstruct European democracy from the bottom up in "We are Europe! Manifesto for re-building Europe from the bottom up." While British Chief Rabbi Sir Jonathan Sacks, in "Has Europe lost its soul to the markets?" calls on religious leaders to reassert the role of religion in society to act as a bulwark against untrammelled markets—invoking the story of the Golden Calf to remind us why the Sabbath was established in the first place: to preserve a day for things which do not have a market value.

It is really worth examining each of these initiatives on their own, and comparing them, so that we have a better grasp of their variety and existing and potential articulations. And this already sets the stage for the most consequential transformation of intellectuality apparent in this crisis. It is no longer enough to have brilliant individuals opining on the pages of newspapers about who is intellectually responsible and who is not. It's not even satisfactory to get many signatures expressing solidarity with wrongs done elsewhere. Action is much more direct, and intellectuality much more networked, in these times. This third way is not a matter of design but of rearticulation, of emergent alternatives made by sometimes anonymous intellectuals in practice. That transformation has happened very quickly, and by the time these words are published, they should be seen more as a matter of historical record than of theoretical projection.

Networked Intellectualities in Sense-Making Practice

Many political intellectuals are working to take advantage of what Habermas (2012, 116–17) acknowledges: that this crisis provides "the opportunity to break out of their national cages and gain new room for manoeuvre at the European level." Among the existing political elite, Alfred Gusenbauer and his Next Left project are likely to be the most realistically ambitious in figuring that moment, which was conceived both as an opportunity and a necessity: this was a chance for the social democratic Left to redefine its political strategy, not just a matter of choice. For this Left to find its place in a world marked by a crisis in which they were implicated, that social democratic Left *had* to redefine itself.

This Next Left project emerged in the wake of the disastrous defeat of European Socialists in the 2009 European Union elections. Although some were initially motivated to figure only why those affiliated with the Party of European Socialists did so badly in elections, those associated with the Next Left research program moved toward a deeper consideration of the causes of what they would call "the crisis of social democracy." Some in that old democratic Left considered this mainly an electoral failure. Gusenbauer and his network sought deeper accounts for social democracy's decline. They were motivated by a different sense of responsibility, both intellectual and political.[6]

To some extent, Gusenbauer grounded that Next Left project in the very challenge Tony Judt (2009, 2011) raises about social democracy's contemporary failure (Gusenbauer 2010a). Gusenbauer (2011) also identified his commitment to renewal, in working to redefine progress. He identified the future in the history of the social democratic movement itself, as it experienced its own evolutionary development through various epistemic breaks, each responding to the challenges of its own era (Gusenbauer 2010b). In this era, Gusenbauer identified globalization, postindustrialization, and individualization as the principal challenges even while equality ought to be elevated as a core value.

The social question, he wrote with Ania Skrzypek, must be restored to the center of politics alongside linking the world of finances with the real economy (Gusenbauer and Skrzypek 2013). Gusenbauer (2012) emphasized the primacy of politics over markets as the means to get there. That primacy is not hard to emphasize, given the ways in which financial markets came to dominate the world, and then to ruin it, he argued. He sought, in the end, to imagine "the next left as a formula that can both frame and establish one" (23).

To do that, Gusenbauer proposed moving beyond old constituencies that defined the social democrats while not alienating that traditional base. He proposed that one could learn from the parties that have gained ground in recent times by highlighting a problem rather than pretending to offer a solution. Additionally, he proposed that social democratic parties not even try to absorb the new movements but rather ride their wave and embrace their spirit. He identified the spirit of that new narrative around equality and inclusion, the market economy's democratization, social solidarity in practice, and enhancement of popular participation. In short, he sought to reinvent social democracy by simultaneously working inside and outside it, which meant working with coalitions of progressives as a matter of fact, and of principle, for the new system (Gusenbauer and Skrzypek 2013).

Although some believe Gusenbauer, given his stature, was critical to assuring the impact of the Next Left project, one can also find evidence of its achievement in the organization and consequences of this Next Left movement itself. This Next Left project was developed through the social democratic movement's think tank, the Foundation for European Progressive Studies (FEPS), with particular and recurrent support of Austria's Renner Institute. The Next Left project is tied with the Party of European Socialists and the many European national parties of the social democratic Left. Because it is tied to all of them, it is obliged to no single one of them. The Next Left movement has nonetheless engaged all of them through conventional intellectual practices. They have organized and participated in joint meetings, in workshops organized around particular publications, and in various national round tables, some thirty in all as of the summer of 2013.[7]

This project has also organized the FEPS Young Academics Network, formed in 2009 out of a call for papers around the FEPS journal *Queries*. In 2012, approximately thirty young scholars, those studying for their PhDs and those who had recently earned them, were mobilized to discuss the questions animating social democracy's past and future (Figure 8.1).[8] These academics, distributed across various working groups, focused primarily on youth

FIGURE 8.1 FEPS Young Academic Network, 2012. The scholars and their places of work or study: Lorenza Antonucci (UK), Laura Ballarin (Catalan/Spain), Janna Besamusca (Netherlands), Giacomo Bottos (Italy), Laura Caroli (Italy), Carlo D'Ippoliti (Italy), Isil Erdinc (Turkey), Marc Esteve I Del Valle (Catalan/Spain), Nicola Genga (Italy), Jeremy Green (UK), Jeroen Horemans (Belgium), Alvaro Imbernon (Spain), Jesper Dahl Kelstrup (Denmark), Scott Lavery (UK), Pim Paulusma (Netherlands), Piotr Plewa (Poland), Denis Preshova (Macedonia), Davide Ragone (Italy), Danilo Raponi (Italy), Teodor Slavev (Bulgaria), Iulian Stanescu (Romania), Ben Taylor (UK), Dragan Tevdovski (Macedonia), Michael Weatherburn (UK), and Benjamin Wilhelm (Germany). From Lorenza Antonucci, Rémi Bazillier, Pim Paulusma, and Michael Weatherburn, "Fixing the Broken Promise of Higher Education in Europe," June 10, 2013, FEPS Young Academics Network, http://www.feps-europe.eu/assets/257fff38-96e0-4359-aa4b-eed1607b97ef/fixing-the-broken-promises-of-higher-education-in-europe.pdf.

unemployment; economic governance; education, labor, and skills; migration/integration; social Europe; and public support. They also developed network ties with young academics from India.

The network itself is one of the leading achievements of the Next Left initiative, committed to creating a genuinely European identification in their work. However, even the photograph itself suggests some of the challenges, with the relative dominance of men over women. And there is certainly a clustering of representation, and relative absences, on national terms. There are relatively few Scandinavians and Eastern Europeans, while Italians are the most apparent in the group. Those involved recognize the problem but also find the challenge in its transcendence. Their work product injunction is, however, explicitly European.

Through its work, this Next Left research program theoretically created an intellectual space that not only allows but demands intellectual innovation with practical consequence. Its academic production is considerable—over a little more than three years, it has produced six edited volumes, produced nine issues of *Queries*,[9] and developed the European Observatory on Social Democracy, an Internet platform committed to extending a European public sphere.[10]

Its most obvious policy effect to the date of writing can be seen in the Party of European Socialists Fundamental Programme produced on June 22, 2013. Although the calls for a Social Union do not appear strikingly different from the visions of a Social Europe now some four decades old (Skrzypek 2013), the rhetorical shift is apparent in highlighting the dangers of financial capitalism. The intellectual shift is, however, in the new social deal for Europe, where the efforts of the Next Left around a different vision of what that social deal means are apparent. Their affirmation—"We will empower all people thanks to meaningful employment, quality education, health, access to culture and a sustainable living, and by enabling all to take part in society"[11]—may be appealing on its own terms. However, the scholarship behind it is readily apparent in previous Next Left publications, notably in the volume *Next Left: For a New Social Deal* (Stetter, Duffek, and Skrzypek 2013).

The Young Academic Networks have also made their mark. For example, the Young Unemployment Working Group developed an intellectual/political agenda that ultimately led to a new, more creative thrust for a European socialist campaign with its "youth guarantee," "a guarantee that ensures that every young person in Europe is offered a job, further education or work-focused training at the latest four months after leaving education or after becoming unemployed."[12]

All of its affiliated parties share a common agenda around increased electoral power. However, as the nature of the debates illustrates (especially in the volume *Next Left: Building New Communities*), the trajectories of change suggest that such short-term ambitions are wholly inadequate to a Next Left that is more than a poor reflection of a past self. I wrote in the introduction to that particular volume, "Given that different left parties and their constituencies are variously located in these global transformations, and that these transformations demand a new sense of Left that anticipates change instead of merely reacting to it, FEPS represents a new kind of knowledge network that helps to shape change with critical analysis. Indeed, the point of FEPS interpretations is to change the world, by changing the sense of the Left in it" (Kennedy 2012e, 15).

Baiocchi and Ganuza (2012) elaborate one of the exemplars of the alter-globalist movement in that FEPS collection. Although much of the innovation can take place around movements, it can also change around policies. Consider, for example, how a movement for reduced working hours could address unemployment and carbon emissions directly, as Schor (2012) argues.[13]

It would be easy to see the social democratic part of the Next Left as wholly antagonistic to the movements who distrust all parties and elites. But that very point is part of the project's effort to reach out beyond actually existing parties, to see something more than a social democracy of the past. Skrzypek (2013) argues that a completely different kind of social contract is critical for these times, especially as there is not much consistency in expressed values across these parties anyway.

Europe's Next Left, rooted as it is in already well-institutionalized parties themselves, struggles to move beyond the sense of politics as usual. Slavoj Žižek (2012, 20) does that all the time, especially in his disdain for social democracy as the political agent representing capitalism above its factions. But Žižek is rather like Habermas, allowing his intellectuality to move him beyond real politics. David Graeber is much more like Gusenbauer in his embeddedness in intellectual practice, even if he shares Žižek's disdain for the system.

In some ways, Europe's Next Left, just as America's, might learn more from Latin America's transformative Left symbolized first by Chile and Ricardo Lagos. In Chapter 2, I considered Lagos's example of intellectual responsibility and public consequence, but it's also critical to see him in more cosmopolitan terms. After all, he is one of those former national executives most committed to bringing political sense to global warming discussions. Equally important is his abiding work in developing a more cosmopolitan and consequential social democracy.[14] In this expression of cosmopolitanism, one does not look only to Europe for leadership but might find inspiration in Latin American transformations for social democracy's rearticulation (Lagos 2012a). Indeed, Oscar Landerretche (2012), one of Lagos's younger colleagues, marks the fourth way Chile's experience suggests.

Through this "dialogue of dialogues," a new kind of networked intellectuality around social democracy's transformation can be found. But it must work within the structure of Left traditions and Next Left potentials. Consider that structure on a global scale. The Socialist International, while claiming global articulation, is dominated overwhelmingly by Europeans. Within Europe too, various national traditions of social democracy hold sway, which in turn mirror national influence within the European Union (Kennedy 2012c). Germany is on top (and increasingly ascendant with the eurozone crisis) alongside France, with the United Kingdom off to the side, followed by other nations with various claims to power and status. The social democratic tradition is not entirely dissimilar to this structure of power and privilege, although Sweden and Austria may be slightly more powerful because of the strength of their parties. One would expect the UK to be less influential given the distance most European parties have for its "third way" (something Labour has trouble shedding), but UK-based scholars are quite prominent in Next Left debates and even the Young Academic Network. Spain's Left influence has certainly declined over the last years with the eurozone crisis, and Italy's center Left traditions are in deep need of reconsolidation. Voices from the periphery, no matter how articulate (exemplified by Michael D. Higgins [Fox 2013]) or how critical their mobilization against austerity (the complicated relations between Syriza and the Next Left come to mind), may not be enough to make up for the relative weakness of those national traditions in the articulation of a European Left.

At the same time, the very nature of knowledgeability in transformative practice illustrates the limitations of such structural determinations. For example, by virtue of its size and long-standing socialist tradition, one would imagine Poland to be more at the center of that Next Left, something it very much tries to be in these times with its attempt to reorganize the political spectrum by assembling a new alliance around the Congress of the Polish Left. However, the problematic legacy of the dominant Left party's association with a communist past and, just as important, its own organizational difficulties, have prevented it from enjoying a more prominent role in the Next Left's European articulation, much less in its own national contests.

Alfred Gusenbauer (2013) is sober in his assessment of European parliamentary elections, as well as in his judgment about the Next Left Research Programme. After rehearsing all the fractures within the European socialist movement, and the electoral strategies that might enable PES victory, he acknowledges that it's hard to envision a new mobilizing narrative beyond one that opposes austerity and supports particular initiatives like the youth guarantee mentioned previously.

With this particular case, one can appreciate the possibilities and challenges of *designing* a knowledge network that seeks social transformation. No matter the intellectuality at the helm, sense-making in times of crisis is ultimately constrained by the position one inherits. That is not a limitation limited to the Next Left. One might argue that Habermas, Žižek, Graeber, and Gusenbauer are all embedded in a process of sense-making more than rearticulation as such.

Of course, Habermas and Žižek are worlds apart ideologically, just as Graeber and Gusenbauer are distant on ideological terms. Clearly the latter two develop their intellectuality in practice far more than the first two, who address changes from an intellectual's perch. That perch may allow wider range of expression and acknowledgment of past sins in the search for more adequate intellectual expression than those also obliged to a movement or party. It is also, ultimately, shaped by the intellectual oeuvre, and corresponding networks, in which the intellectual is himself located. However, not all intellectual positions are so circumscribed, especially when intellectuality is embedded in transformative moments and movements like those in 2011–13. Mary Kaldor's work with scholars across Europe suggests just that direction, especially in their recognition of a new practice they call "subterranean politics."

Although the movements that Kaldor and colleagues (2012) explore across Europe have little in common with each other ideologically, or in terms of their issues, they are clearly alienated from the political system as such. And they pose the problem clearly: "We need to be open to understand the (potential) cultural dimension of these current public displays of subterranean politics; the absence of a specific demand need not be dismissed as a shortcoming, but rather as a manifestation of a different, 2.0 culture that (potentially) transforms (the idea of) politics and the nature of political actors and that is about processes rather than outcomes."

Beyond recognizing their coherence, their movement consequence is not at all clear. Gitlin's (2012) account of the Occupy Movement illustrates one approach to figuring that effect. Gitlin not only elaborates the qualities of the movement but figures its articulation with other elements of change, especially those that remain tied to the political system. This, it seems to me, is one of the most critical issues for intellectuals to engage in these times of transformation.

TABLE 8.1 Intellectualities in transformation

	Theory	*Practice*	*Rearticulation*
System/Policy	Habermas	Gusenbauer	Kaldor
Movement/Ideology	Žižek	Graeber	Gitlin

One way to recognize the distinction of rearticulation as approach is to compare some of intellectualities I have considered, facilitated in Table 8.1. Each of these positions represents a critical point of articulation for an even broader rearticulation in these times of radical transformation.

In the exercise of intellectual responsibility, individuals do need to take on the task of understanding the meaning of the crises and transformations through which we live. They must figure pathways beyond them. Habermas and Žižek are theorists in this moment, reflecting the different addresses—in systems and in subjectivities—toward which critical intellectuals need channel their energies. But this, in the end, is a most traditional kind of intellectuality: the scholar explaining what is really going on and what really needs to be done.

Not all intellectuals stand on the theoretical sidelines, of course. Gusenbauer and Graeber are both enmeshed in moving their intellectualities to practice, albeit with very different accents. Graeber can write massive tomes of scholarly wisdom about debt, but he is also very much embedded in the movements of transformation themselves. He refines our sense of anarchism as he goes. Gusenbauer is embedded in the social democratic side of things. His intellectual practice is far more institutionalized and far more attentive to making the system work better through different policies. Like Graeber, he searches for how to mobilize knowledge and practice in the transformation of foundational ideas and modes of political change. They exemplify sense-making from their own relatively clear political locations just as Habermas and Žižek illustrate it from their own relatively coherent intellectual positions.

Žižek and Graeber have many more affinities politically speaking, for they stand with the revolutions in progress even while they each have clear ideas about which ideas and practices extend the revolutions. Habermas and Gusenbauer also recognize systemic problems but search within the constraints of the system the best paths to move ahead. They might seek, in Andre Gorz's (1967, 6) old terms, "non-reformist reforms."

Todd Gitlin (2012), whose work I discussed extensively in Chapter 4, and Mary Kaldor represent something different, that rearticulation of intellectuality in cultural formation to which I previously referred. They are much more the analysts of others' actions. They systematize the movements' contradictions, anomalies, and potentials with a sympathetic eye toward including alienated voices into a process of systemic change. They look for points of and barriers to connection within, and beyond, the social and political landscape. In analyzing others' actions, and in finding potential articulations systems and subjectivities might repress, they create new sensibilities for what is possible, enabling others to refigure what is newly feasible in change. They are also different from each other.

Gitlin engages a movement that more or less coheres and, in this, stands with Žižek and Graeber in his relatively clear identification with the revolution. However, his intellectuality does not stand so far above the movement but in dialogue with it, questioning more than explaining the alternative futures that face Occupy. Kaldor and colleagues work to identify an emergent identification now grounded in systemic alienation but potentially, through mutual recognition, something else entirely. Nevertheless, Kaldor and Gitlin share a common commitment to rearticulation in both theory and practice, facilitated by their method and focus on transformation.

I also find rearticulation powerful, and critical in these times when intellectualities are as emergent as they are traditional or organic in the Gramscian sense. However, different moments of transformation suggest different kinds of dialogues among the six qualities of intellectuality described earlier. Two transformational movements in these eventful years of 2011–13 illustrate clearly the importance of globalizing knowledge with these differences of intellectuality in mind.

Emergent Intellectualities in Digital Transformation

Following the United States, Japan, and others, on January 26, 2012, representatives of most of the European Union's countries, as well as the European Commission's representative, signed the Anti-Counterfeiting Treaty Agreement (ACTA).[15] After earlier contests over kin legislation, most in the know expected electronic protest of some sort. In the United States, for example, Wikipedia went dark on January 18, 2012, to challenge the Stop Online Piracy Act in the US House and Protect Intellectual Property Act in the Senate. But the European protests against ACTA went far beyond what happened in the United States. And this mobilization has gone far beyond what most of those promoting ACTA and other elaborations of intellectual property revisions anticipated.

Most thought these disputes would be business-world battles over how to define intellectual property, with content providers and Internet service providers taking the lead opposing positions in the contest (Baker 2012). But it became something quite different, redefined as a contest over threats to freedom and the conditions of creativity in a digital world (Barker 2012).

Drawing on a new generation, what might be called "Web Kids" (Czerski 2012),"civi-digital society" hit the fiber networks and streets across Poland in January 2012.[16] Anonymous Poland ACTA posted on January 22, 2012, its own video identifying the threat ACTA posed and the hackers' normative claim: "Chcemy wolności słowa" (We Want Freedom of Speech).[17] Their declarations were also more powerful than words: they said they wanted the government to hear them, and thus they blocked access to a number of government sites (Kluz 2012). A few weeks later, on February 11, more than thirty thousand people across more than one hundred cities of the European Union marched to demand that their fundamental rights stay protected and that their interests as citizens take precedence over the rights of content providers worried about losing money because of copyright infringement (Kirschbaum and Ivanova 2012).

While the different pirate parties might readily stand with this mobilization, and benefit politically by it, various Liberal and Left political parties in the European Parliament followed that mobilization to move against ACTA. They focused primarily on questions of democracy, transparency, and rights. Following this mobilization, the European Commission vice president responsible for the digital agenda, Neelie Kroes, anticipated the death of ACTA and its defeat by a "strong new political voice" (Kroes 2012). Finally, on July 4, 2012, with only 39 votes supporting ACTA and a whopping 479 votes against, the European Parliament killed ACTA.

Across the Internet, civi-digital society and its activists celebrated like I have never seen before. On Twitter, La Quadrature du Net declared this a "Total Victory for Citizens and Democracy"; David Hammerstein called it "Epic Victory for Human Rights and Access to Knowledge!"; StopActa offered congratulations to everyone, changed its name to PostActa, and toasted, "Long Live the Future." It is quite possible that this extraordinary movement could fade, but that seems doubtful. Its success is too great, and its mobilization potentials quite sustainable. This is evident in a number of domains.

After hours of actual and virtual public discussion, Poland's prime minister, Donald Tusk, whose party was part of the European alliance that led on ACTA, declared that the "concept of property rights—the Internet has turned this traditional reality upside down" (Tusk 2012). By drawing on refined policy documents (Karaganis 2011), a new political vision could mobilize civi-digital society across Europe and the world, not only to defend what exists but to develop a vision of the future that reframes the relationship between property and the public good.

The mobilization against ACTA has shown that popular mobilization, in alliance with new business models, has made traditional defenders of property rights an anachronism. The movement itself, in its own exceptional and digitally enhanced reflexivity, offered its own account of this struggle's implications for transparency and new models of property and of European and global solidarity. IP (2012) argued that this struggle inspired recognition of the importance of transparency, international civil society synergy, unity in diversity, Europe from the bottom up and from the East, and a divided business community for the Internet community being able to defend itself.

This civi-digital society mobilization offers much to whoever seeks to understand the articulation of knowledge in public mobilizations. "Web Kids" reflects a European movement that might wear the Guy Fawkes mask as a symbol and have its own music,[18] but it digs deeper in its challenge to those who define injustice. This was not only a mobilization against constraints on private file sharing but also protest against the ways in which this legislation risked access to generic drugs and public health in poorer regions (Reichman 2009).[19] This kind of mobilization is now inspiring other global knowledge networks to extend their engagement on intellectual property and on digital rights.[20] It promises even more.

In contrast to the Next Left and its party base and recognizable intellectual tradition with luminaries and debates, the civi-digital social movement is not nearly so codified. It is emergent alongside the global flows of information and culture discussed in Chapter 7. These global flows manifestly rearticulate issues and contexts when their cultural products are recognizable and symbolically powerful.

Both Pussy Riot and the ACTA mobilization drew upon masks to signify their alienation from powers that be. They develop solidarity around a common anonymity that authorities impose on subjects yearning for more, knowing that those authorities can't recognize them for who they are. Their

immediate consequences were variable—while two of Pussy Riot were impris-
oned, the Web Kids stopped a law on intellectual property that had the back-
ing of the most powerful governments in the world. We can't now anticipate
the longer-term impacts of either movement, but one thing is certain. They
signal a new kind of cosmopolitanism cresting in the world of flows and an
emergent intellectuality that rides its current.

Castells's (2009, 38) hypothesis is compelling: "The common culture of the
global network society is a culture of protocols of communication enabling
communication between different cultures on the basis not of shared values
but of the sharing of the value of communication." This was true for Pussy
Riot and the Web Kids, but it was also something more than recognizing
communication's value. This was a cosmopolitanism based on an emergent
resemblance crossing national boundaries found in global cultural digital
practice.

Luminary intellectuals like those discussed in the previous section were
not very visible in this struggle, even while its dimensions promised profound
transformations in European identification, property relations, and notions
of freedom and justice. The struggle abides, too, as trade agreements are
negotiated behind closed doors, reflecting anachronistic propertied interests
more than digital cultures of critical discourse. It could be that the Internet is
an arena that celebrates specialist intellectuality more than the general currents in which luminous intellectuals live. But the latter should find a new
home in this world of flows. This world promises to transform even those
most traditional of structures otherwise known as nation-states. At least this
is what has become apparent in Ukraine at 2013's end.

Euromaidan Emergent

During the weeks in which I concluded this volume's revision, Ukraine moved
into a crisis born of systemic contradictions and met with new subjectivities
difficult to recognize. That difficulty is not evident in much discussion, however, for many were eager to identify, rather simply, what the struggle is about.

Some might date the start of the conflict to November 21, 2013, when the
Ukrainian authorities declared that they would not ratify an association
agreement they had long negotiated with the European Union. Many had
already debated the costs of that agreement for the Ukrainian population,
especially for the effects it would likely have on the manufacturing industry

in the east. For those who assembled in Kyiv's Independence Square, renamed Euromaidan by the protesters, it was not a matter of economic policy; it was a statement about values and whether Ukraine belonged in Europe or to Russia.

Because Ukraine has been defined by a difference between "West" and "East" (Darden 2014), there were many pundits and intellectuals ready to say that the Euromaidan protest was simply a regional movement. And while it was indeed the case that the earliest and largest demonstrations opposing the government's withdrawal from the agreement were held in the west, and were much less prominent in the south and east, many intellectuals worked hard to demonstrate something different.

In the early days, scholars like Mykola Riabchuk (2013) argued that youth were at the center of the movement, reflecting a *generational* mobilization more than regional division. Yaroslav Hrytsak agreed and argued further that they identify as much with those in Rome or Warsaw as anywhere else but have no prominent job prospects. They have become, he argues, an "intellectual proletariat" (Rachkevych 2013).

The movement, while likely inspired by students at first, grew far beyond it. Sociologies of participation note many surprises. Onuch (2014) began researching the movement on November 27 and drew five principal conclusions:

> 1) Protesters are older than expected. 2) Protesters are more diverse than expected. 3) Social media are important, but not simply as a provider of information about existence of protests. 4) Social-networks—both within and outside of social media—seem to be highly influential in bringing people out into the streets. 5) Social media and Internet news sites seem to have been successfully used as key framing devices for protest themes.

Social media have been quite powerful too in developing a broader movement for global solidarity. They include Global Voices Online, the initiative supported by MIT Media Lab. Tetyana Bohdanova communicated globally the issues animating protest, with an interactive map of Euromaidan protests provided already on November 24. She continued through other developments, including the violence rained on protesters and the authorities' introduction of legislation to prohibit protest.[21] She also offered one of the first accounts of how the Internet turned Euromaidan into a movement (Bohdanova 2013). Live-stream television, most notably through Hromadske TV, has also been critical globally, but especially within Ukraine (Balmforth 2013).

Those without such global platforms have also realized considerable effect. Among the more notable was another student, Kataryna Kruk
(@Kateryna_Kruk), whose informative, frequent, and witty English-language
tweets brought her some celebrity even in the more conventional media world
(U. Friedman 2013). Other kinds of celebrity were also brought to the Euromaidan stage.

Those who study, and extend, Occupy types of movements recognize the
importance of men and women who provide the protest's social infrastructure from food to health care (Kharchenko 2013). However, in this case, performers have enlivened the square, most notably with music that animates.
Ruslana, the most regularly and prominently associated with Euromaidan,
even moved from stage invocations of peace. Her transformation from pop
star to moderator of the revolution sparked substantial Western attention,
leading some even to call her the "soul of the revolution" (Orr 2013). Others
with more institutional authority in defining soul find it in the square itself.

Much as Pope John Paul II argued that the unification of Europe after
communism's collapse might bring a certain spirituality to the West from
the more religious in the East, Ukrainian theologians have also argued that
Euromaidan brings a kind of renewal to the rest of Europe as it has already
transformed Ukraine. For example, Borys Gudziak (2014), bishop in Paris for
Ukrainian Catholics in France, Benelux, and Switzerland and president of the
Ukrainian Catholic University in Lviv, proposed that the movement offers to
Europe and the rest of the world a message in human dignity, a "new Ukraine
emerging before our eyes—hope, fellowship, solidarity, and authentic joy."
Cyril Hovorun (2013), associated with the Ukrainian Orthodox Church Mos-
cow Patriarchate, wrote something similar.

> The Maidan is giving or has given birth to a community which represents a
> classic instance of the civil society, almost its pure substance. This commu-
> nity identifies itself on the basis of shared values, including dignity, honesty,
> non-violence, solidarity, and readiness for self-sacrifice. Civil society in the
> form currently present at the Maidan can hardly be found even in Europe,
> where for the most part people nowadays are united on the basis of common
> interests, but not common values. I cannot personally imagine any contempo-
> rary European country where people would be freezing and risk being beaten
> or even killed for 24 hours a day for weeks, for the sake of values that seem
> quite abstract. The Ukrainian Maidan that gathered "for the sake of Europe,"

has become more European than Europe and its politicians. The Ukrainians see how the European politicians betray the European Maidan, but they do not betray the European values they stand for. The Ukrainian Maidan actually brings back to many Europeans confidence about Europe; it cures what can be called "the European fatigue."

Euromaidan appeals to the secular intellectual community for many of the same reasons. Those associated with the Polish journal *Krytyka Polityczna*, notably Sławomir Sierakowski, organized a petition among prominent intellectuals in support of Euromaidan and its wish to associate with Europe. This was not just an act of gentile solidarity, however; they argued too that the struggle offers the European Union a means by which it might return to the idealism motivating its founding (Sierakowski 2014).

In these acts of recognition and global flows of information and communication, one might argue that we see the formation of a genuine cosmopolitan intellectuality and consequential solidarity, one that recognizes and embraces the challenge of difference and looks for means to provide support. Some, however, find profound limits in that declaration.

Among the most challenging issues in recognizing Euromaidan has been its association with a far right movement called Svoboda (Freedom). Svoboda's heritage can be traced to the Bandera movement allied with Nazis in opposition to the Soviet Union and could also be tied to more militant youth prepared for violent confrontation and eager to destroy monuments, notably of Lenin, that memorialize the USSR they so oppose. Svoboda's leader is one of three politicians often claiming to speak for Euromaidan. Critical intellectuals, notably Volodymyr Ishchenko (2014) and Andreas Umland (2013), pose these discomforting associations for a movement that appears to embrace European and cosmopolitan virtues. They are right to do so, especially in a cosmopolitan milieu that values the culture of critical discourse.

Among the issues Ukrainian intellectuals and others debate as I conclude this volume is how to interpret, and explain, the slogans and symbols deployed that associate Euromaidan with a nationalism Europe itself struggles to shed. Even more challenging, they struggle over how to represent the violence that threatens to overwhelm the dominant spirit of nonviolence Euromaidan has represented. One open letter from Ukrainian intellectuals illustrates:

> The government in Ukraine is trying to frame the situation as programs initiated by the extremist, radical rightist organizations, . . . We are moderate

people, peaceful professionals, of varied ethnic origin, from various regions of Ukraine. We do not sympathize with the right-wing radical organizations . . . , [or] think that throwing Molotov cocktails or stones can serve as adequate instruments for protecting one's values. [But] we declare our solidarity with those, who have been forced to use these instruments today. . . . The attempts to portray the protesters as fascist-like extremists is nothing but a ruse, a manipulation and a falsification on the part of the government, designed to absolve itself of responsibility for the clashes in center city Kyiv and to form the corresponding public opinion about the anti-governmental protests. (Zakharov et al. 2014)

These intellectuals were not alone. In fact, a transnational network of scholars expert on Ukrainian nationalism also wrote an open letter to the global media asking them to refrain from the irresponsible representation of Euromaidan in terms that give the far right too much prominence. Such reporting was not only factually wrong, they argued, but it was also irresponsible, for it played into certain geopolitical forces seeking to undermine this "liberationist" movement (Umland 2014).

Understanding the movement in terms of the demography and repertoires of the citizens' participation is important, but recognizing the movement's purpose is quite another, and perhaps even more important. Among others, Mychailo Wynnyckyj, chair of the PhD program on social transformations at Kyiv-Mohyla Academy in Ukraine, has been Facebook posting alongside the movement's development. He offers among the most innovative and thoughtful contemporaneous accounts of the movement's meaning and possibilities. He identified the movement's evolution through four stages—from a student movement, through a movement based on an innocent hope that its voice might be recognized, to a self-organizing movement for civil society, and finally, a movement of diverse expressions (Wynnyckyj 2014).[22] As violence escalates, however, the challenge of finding meaning beyond preserving dignity challenges. Wynnyckyj wrote on January 25, 2014,

Ukraine's revolution is not over yet. It is clear that we are witnessing the final days of the Yanukovych regime, but the actual format of the climax of this winter's events and their denouement is still unknown. Although I have primarily written here about misinformation and negative "memes," I should note that the video footage of Mykhailo Havryliuk—the Kozak who was stripped naked and abused by Berkut riot police this week—has served to galvanize the Maidan demonstrators, and has spread the protests well beyond Kyiv. Images of Havryliuk's dignified behavior under extreme stress, and his simple modesty after having been rescued (during and after the press conference) have "gone viral" in Ukraine. They demonstrate the values of Maidan better than any slogan, and I would argue (in addition to the multiple deaths and injuries resulting from police brutality) have served as a catalyst for regional rebellions across the country. His message needed no packaging, nor was there anyone available among the protesters to package it. I guess, that's both the strength and the weakness of Maidan.

It is certainly beyond my capacity to do more than the intellectuals I have identified, although I mention them here because it is through their networks that we might learn more about Euromaidan and figure the best ways to support it and the aftermath this transformation yields. At the same time, one should not overlook the ways in which many of these intellectuals have already been networked in a national and cosmopolitan fashion with an eye toward consequential solidarity itself.

Most of the scholars I have mentioned know each other, and while not coordinated in any formal way, they are connected through their organizations and networks. Hrytsak, a professor at both Lviv State University and Central European University, and Riabchuk, an independent cultural analyst, are both editors of *Ukraina Moderna*, one of the country's most distinguished intellectual periodicals.

Ishchenko, Umland, and Wynnyckyj are all professors at Ukraine Kyiv-Mohyla Academy, itself one of the leading knowledge institutions in Ukraine and additionally acknowledged by the Academic Fellowship Program described in Chapter 7. Their students were among the leaders mobilizing Euromaidan: "'Better to skip a few lectures than to miss our whole future' is the general message among students out on the streets" (Spolsky 2013). The academy's rector, Serhiy Kvit (2014), was among those celebrating what Euromaidan stood for and its fusion of knowledgeability and protest. He argued Euromaidan to be an expression of civil society itself, with its organizations of "writers, students, journalists, sports people, experts, show business representatives, ecologists, medical workers, lawyers, military veterans, trade unions etc." Other rectors support the protest, and several joined it as institutions: Borys Hrinchenko Pedagogic University in Kyiv, Kyiv Polytechnic University, Kyiv-Mohyla Academy, and Ukrainian Catholic University in Lviv.

In short, although Euromaidan was "spontaneous," it was grounded in a knowledge culture that has been networked and cultivated over time. It is an emergent intellectuality just as the anti-ACTA movement was. Like the Web Kids, it was grounded in a culture of critical discourse that sought to establish its distinction from what oppresses their sense of dignity and right. That distinction is both too simple to recognize and too hard at the same time.

Many in the West are eager to see Ukraine's struggle as a confirmation of their own superiority, a quality transition culture readily bestows but one that is increasingly insufficient and inappropriate when geopolitical contest rather than transition cultural hegemony looms (Kennedy 2008). Those critical of the European Union's terms of association deserve to be heard, just as those who challenge the European Union for not doing enough to win Ukraine need to be acknowledged (e.g., Fischer 2013). However, instead of seeing this as a failure of political will and imagination, which it no doubt has been in part, one should, as Habermas and Gusenbauer suggest, look for its roots in the structure and system of the European Union itself.

Beyond that quest to understand systemic deficiencies and policy lapses, this is an opportunity to look for the emergent subjectivities Žižek and Graeber would highlight. They are not, however, so likely to embrace Euromaidan. Its wish to be part of Europe seems to legitimate the hegemonic system they are most comfortable in deconstructing. Those associated with the WSF are also much less likely to embrace Euromaidan even while those in the WEF might see Euromaidan's attack on corruption as confirmation of WEF disposition in public discourse. But that easy assignment is wrong too, for this genuinely powerful struggle on behalf of human dignity does not likely find so much in common with the Davos man, at least as popularly portrayed. Instead, the popular struggle on the streets of Kyiv has much more in common with the horizontalist movements that have defined the spirit of Occupy from Wall Street to Rio de Janeiro (Baiocchi and Kennedy 2013). Or at least they might, depending on the rearticulations that develop and the senses of cosmopolitanism and solidarity they generate.

Comment on Ukraine beyond the Time of Composition

I concluded revisions for this book a month before the Russian invasion of Crimea and the subsequent violence in the south and east of Ukraine. I review this book manuscript for final editorial revisions in the first days of July 2014, following the election of a new Ukrainian president, Petro Poroshenko, and his signature of a European Union agreement whose late 2013 refusal sparked the formation of Euromaidan. Poroshenko has also launched an Anti-Terrorist Operation seeking to take back control over some Ukrainian territories from those who have asserted the independence of those territories. Questions of energy security become newly urgent in light of this violence, but it remains to be seen how my assessments in Chapter 6 might be affected. What is clear, however, is that my account of Euromaidan demands more immediate comment.

Poroshenko's use of force leads many who celebrated the nonviolence of Euromaidan to applaud his defense of Ukrainian territory from those who seek union with Russia. Naming those who resist the Ukrainian authorities in Kyiv is no simple analytical enterprise but, rather, part of the cultural political and military struggle itself. Are they separatists or terrorists or something else? We might treat empirically the question of whether they are citizens or foreigners, but there are no methods in conditions of war to determine the answers to such questions safely and with rigor. It is clear, however, that the cosmopolitan intellectualities animating Euromaidan appear to have little place in these times. War flames nationalism, and internationalism in such conditions means defining the allies and enemies of one's nation.

To be intellectually responsible in these times and around the extension of Euromaidan's cosmopolitan potential, one must take up matters of empire and forms of war that were relatively distant concerns in the Euromaidan struggle of civil society against a corrupt state. Even dignity and human rights, matters so central to that struggle, now frame new problems, most apparent with refugees from violence and the fate of Crimean Tatars in the Russian state's occupation of their homeland (Office of the United Nations High Commissioner for Human Rights 2014).

One must also go beyond typical sociological themes. The intellectually responsible need engage, as the Latvian Ministry of Defense has elaborated powerfully, the forms of asymmetric warfare apparent on the Russian/Ukrainian borderlands (Bērziņš 2014). Responsibility also goes beyond recognizing methods of war's prosecution. Intellectuals, not just pundits and ideologues, need to figure Russia's intentions and Putin's power and logic. I have found the work of Lilia Shevtsova (2014) most compelling, but she is surrounded by exceptional debate that is shaped not only by nationalisms of various sorts but also by disciplinary and methodological differences. Cold War intellectualities are reborn in these times.

Some resurrect the spirit of détente, leading us to theorize how Russian and Western cooperation and mutual interests might survive differences over Ukraine, diminishing the struggle and wishes of Ukrainians in the process. Others find echoes of 1980–81 in these times because of the resemblance between Poland's Solidarność and the spirit of Euromaidan. I myself find in these different decades' struggles anticipations of an emancipatory, and more cosmopolitan, condition deserving consequential solidarity. Some insist, like my student Juho Korhonen, that there must be another path beyond these choices originally cast in different world historic times. In conditions of war, intellectual responsibility is even more challenging to articulate, but one thing is clear. One must understand more adequately how Russian, European, and North American intellectuals, political figures, and economic elites are implicated in one another's interests and how these ties and affinities shape the alternatives facing Ukraine and, by extension, the world.

My brother and I have worked to combine our different intellectual competencies and political dispositions to articulate those pathways for immediate public consumption (Kennedy 2014c; Kennedy and Kennedy 2014). We are certainly not in a position, nor is anyone else prepared, to fully recognize the new world the revolution in Ukraine and Russia's invasion have made. But we need to be. We need to figure how to engage the rearticulations of theory and practice demanded by a world in crisis and transformation. And while I formulated the need for cosmopolitan intellectuality and consequential solidarity before anticipations of World War III came readily to anxious lips, I do believe that those guidelines may be more important than ever, especially when nationalisms stir passions and righteousness beyond that culture of critical discourse we might readily embrace in more peaceful times.

Sometimes cosmopolitanism is identified with the disposition of states to "protect helpless foreigners from the abuses of their own governments, distant wars and global crises" (Brysk 2009, 3). One might have seen in Western support for Euromaidan evidence of just such disposition. Some sympathetic to Putin's account of ethnic Russians in Ukraine's east and south might find evidence of a Russian version of that cosmopolitanism. I think it an abuse of the term to consider Putin's interest in co-ethnics evidence of cosmopolitanism and not only for the national limitations of this articulation. Ethnic Russians were not at risk in Ukraine's transformation, but this judgment, too, is a matter of cultural political and military struggle. I find their danger was rather made real in the information war, which in turn helps cause real violence, which in turn led to death and destruction.

To recognize cosmopolitanism in the execution of war is more challenging than I am now prepared to address, but it is important to figure under what conditions cosmopolitanism, in its most critical sense, might be found in the articulation of violence that we have seen in 2014 Ukraine. It is challenging enough to consider cosmopolitan intellectuality in times of relative peace.

Cosmopolitan Intellectuality

For the most part, political philosophers and policy makers approach the cosmopolitan question as an extension of governance beyond the nation-state. They may consider it in terms of the extension of international law or the development of more integrated global governance institutions. Specialists on particular flows, for example, around energy (Goldthau and Witte 2010) or information (Mueller 2010), also work hard on this question. In general, global governance addresses particular kinds of issues, from the formal organization of such governance to the norms that might underlie such coordination. It also produces many anxieties, whether in terms of the concentration of state power or the scale of problems associated with democratic procedure, demos's and citizenship's recognition, or pluralism's meaningful preservation.

Theorists of cosmopolitanism typically don't engage more specific domains like energy or even information, given the density and distinction of expertise in these fields. They attend more publicly prominent arenas, around the assurance and extension of environmental security as well as of human rights, the latter of which raises questions over the conditions of military intervention. This kind of discussion worries over the constitution of such cosmopolitan governance, in the making of transnational civil societies and social movements, and the cultural frames that could attend such formations (e.g., Archibugi and Koenig-Archibugi 2003).

When sociologists today speak of cosmopolitanism, they typically ground their approach more in global transformations than in regulatory dilemmas. Ulrich Beck (2000) is among those who find it hard to imagine the world without that cosmopolitan consciousness. Consider the global networking of markets, the transformation of information and communication technology, universal demands for rights and democracy, the stream of images from the global culture industry, the emergence of a polycentric world polity with many more actors, and the articulation of truly global problems like poverty and environmental destruction alongside transcultural conflicts. This is not just a philosophical disposition, he argues. Threats create society, and global threats create global society (28). When threats, like mad cow disease, depletion of ozone or of tropical rain forest, or weapons of mass destruction, are issued and know no political boundaries, our everyday consciousness is transformed, economic issues become politicized, and questions about layers of governmental accountability are raised.

Accountability's shift is important to mark. As Sassen (2008) suggests, there is a tendency in globalization's development to assign more power to executive decision and to expert bodies well beyond democratic oversight. While one might attempt to restore a more political engagement to that address, Beck also suggests that new notions of risk be introduced into all of these processes. In particular, there could be a movement to push those with power to introduce "new standards" "for adequate proof, truth, and justice in the face of dangers likely to affect everyone" (Beck 2000, 99–10).

Formulating these risks helps us move, in concrete ways, beyond the most manifest problems of ethnocentrism into a scientifically grounded formulation of dangers for the world. That science is linked directly to a kind of cosmopolitan passion (Beck 2000, 67) even as morality is becoming more individualist. As individuals are exposed to a wider variety of cultural, political, and economic stimuli, ethical choices come to be grounded more in networks than in communities, which, in turn, are more partial than enveloping. That, additionally, can generate less certainty but also more search, as dialogues produce additional reinforcement for moral dispositions (77–86). The WEF illustrates that very sensibility. In anticipation of its 2013 Davos meeting, for example, WEF founder Klaus Schwab (2013) invited his network to think about "resilient dynamism" in the address of global risks.

Cosmopolitanism can too easily imply commonality based on similarity before universality. Sometimes that reflects the class consciousness of the frequent traveler. It may be a response to real global risk. It might even, as the Web Kids suggest, not only reflect rejection but be an act of projection about new identities, issues, and processes that embrace the world in newly connected fashion.

For cosmopolitanism to be progressive and critical, it needs to develop a sensibility beyond the similarities on which civi-digital solidarity relied and resilient dynamism implies. It needs to develop a deeper cosmopolitanism that engages differences in meaningful connections developed through an appreciation for historical trajectories and thus cultural peculiarities of those who articulate global issues. Craig Calhoun (2007, 25–26) is especially good on this:[23]

> Cosmopolitans do not simply fail to see the cultural particularity and social supports of their cosmopolitanism, but cannot fully and accurately recognize these without introducing a tension between themselves and their social world. And here I would include myself and probably all of us. Whether we theorize cosmopolitanism or not, we are embedded in social fields and practical projects in which we have little choice but to make use of some of the notions basic to cosmopolitanism and thereby reproduce it. We have the option of being self-critical as we do so, but not of entirely abandoning cosmopolitanism because we cannot act effectively without it.

As I have argued throughout, the foundation for globalizing knowledge rests in the ability to recognize those and their knowledges beyond the worlds we comfortably inhabit. It goes beyond the serendipitous moments when we discover that we like something on first glance or find something valuable, despite our originating presumption. The challenge of difference goes beyond resolutions through encounter, and rather relies on engagements demanding transformations of selves and their articulations.

Sometimes those transformations take place within our nations, as Appalachian struggles recurrently remind too many, or perhaps too few, Americans (Waggoner 2014). More conventionally, those challenges rest beyond one's nation, notably in those places to which markets and wars don't draw the globally minded. Even when so drawn, recognition does not always imply cosmopolitanism, for the concept depends on transcending the limits ethnocentrism and its interested knowledge chart.

Such a cosmopolitan intellectuality obliges globe-trotting thought leaders to move beyond their all too common airport cultural formations. Calhoun (2003a, 90) reminds us that cosmopolitanism can easily become the class consciousness of frequent travelers, "easily entering and exiting polities and social relations around the world, armed with visa-friendly passports and credit cards." Complemented by a culture of critical discourse, where the ethnocentrisms informing cosmopolitanism are highlighted, one might appropriately envision a cosmopolitan *intellectuality* rather than cosmopolitanism as ideology or sociological disposition.

As I have proposed earlier, this intellectuality need not be the province of only the most prominent and celebrated intellectuals. It's a capacity, as Gramsci remarked, of all that need only be cultivated. Indeed, it's especially important for social movements with global aspirations to have that disposition. Recent developments in Europe reinforce that general point. While the Greek challenge and its complexity inspired Žižek, it also suggests another challenge in building alliances across Europe and the world.

The Greeks certainly have little patience for German rescues, but this disposition didn't begin in the financial crisis. They don't have their only historical antecedent in World War II. It's also more recent, as Pagoulatos and Yataganas (2010, 200) explain:

> The implosion of the former Yugoslavia in the 1990s re-energized anti-Western, anti-European reflexes. A large section of the Greek public felt a sense of brotherhood with the fellow Orthodox Serbs, who had suffered at the hands of common enemies under Ottoman rule and, later, the Axis invasion. Sympathy persisted despite the war crimes committed by the Milosevic regime in Bosnia, and a section of the Greek public . . . regarded Karadzic and Mladic as Christian-Orthodox heroes recalling the Greek war of independence against the Ottomans. Consequently the majority of the Greek public viewed with hostility what they perceived as the unfair treatment of the Serbs by the EU and the US culminating with the 1999 NATO bombardment of Serbia over the Kosovo issue.

This account is especially powerful in reminding us of cosmopolitan intellectuality's limits. While its challenge can rest in places unknown, even greater barriers can be found in proximate places. That happens when understandings of the past put firm obstacles in the way of future collaborations.

When I explored with Albin Kurti the possibilities for consequential solidarity across Europe in these times of crisis, he made it clear. No alliances can be made without knowing how potential comrades would understand Yugoslavia's end, he said. Too many understand that implosion as simply a matter of Western imperialism without appreciating, as Kurti put it to me, its dependence on an existing second world to give Yugoslavia's alternative socialism meaning, and the internal contradictions and imperialisms defining Yugoslavia itself. This is where the virtuous nexus of global universities and transformational networks becomes apparent.

The virtue of the critical global university *in statu nascendi* is that it creates the conditions for the limits of cosmopolitans to be marked. We can see
this most clearly in some regions, most notably around South Asia, and in
the efforts of historians and others to elaborate alternative vernacular cosmo-
politanisms that link differently to those made in other terms. For example,
Sugata Bose (2011) invites us to consider Tagore's universalism alongside more
recent articulations by Appiah, Ho, and Bhabha. With that example in mind,
one could very well imagine not only those critical examples where scholars
join to write common histories of those recently, or even decades ago, at war.
One might also work to articulate how visions of the future might stand lessons about that past. In this, cosmopolitan intellectuality is not only about
recognizing global threats but also about explaining how conflicted histories
shape interpretations of those threats in very different ways. It's not only about
the presumptions of connectivity but about the histories of dispossession that
can be so readily overlooked in any global commons (Saito and Wang 2014).

Cosmopolitan intellectuality not only should but can reside within global
universities, and we should figure ways to mark its presence and reinforce
its influence. Indeed, by implicating those academic discussions directly in
transformational knowledge networks, we might find ways to imagine the ties
that bind us, or at least associate us, anew. We might even think about the
terms of consequential solidarity.

Consequential Solidarity

Associations, networks, publics, and solidarity are different.[24] They are obviously related to each other, for they each imply some kind of secondary tie
beyond the familiar and familial, but they do have different connotations and
analytical emphases.

Associations are a common organizational form in modernity, and intellectuals and their institutions are as likely as any to form them to extend their
interests. And these associations are increasingly global in reference if not also
in membership. Defined by formal membership, they are more enduring and
centrally governed than the networks analyzed in Chapter 7.

Networks are based on mutual recognitions of commonality based on
interest or approach and motivated by some kind of exchange. As discussed
in the previous chapter, networks can be fleeting, dependent as they are on
voluntary affiliations with relatively little entry and exit costs.

Publics are also voluntary but differ from networks in the sense that they are typically constituted through communications of various sorts, often in disagreement rather than through coordination as networks suggest. For publics to be enduring, they must be based on some kind of identification with one another, recognition of common membership in some collectivity, or commonly shared stakes in some outcome.

Solidarity takes it one step further. Solidarity is both more substantial in terms of commitment and less dependent on direct connection and interaction. Solidarity depends on the capacity to recognize affinities of some sort and to embed part of one's identity in the fate of others. In this sense, it involves a willingness to bear the burden of others. That last phrase suggests a Catholic affinity, and solidarity can be so rooted. My own respect for the term clearly derives from the Polish Solidarity movement of 1980–81, which was itself influenced by Catholic social doctrine. Some work to rekindle that ethic in both Catholic (Beyer 2010) and more postmodern theological discussions (Min 2004).

The Polish Solidarity movement and its associated concept are also quite rooted in the traditions of labor mobilizations and the social and sociological sense that such collective action represents. For some time, but especially in the age of globalization, labor activists and those associated with the alter-globalization movement have worked to figure the conditions of solidarity generated through what has been called "globalization from below" (Brecher, Costello, and Smith 2002).

One of the most striking expressions of such solidarity comes, however, in the civil rights movement in the United States. Martin Luther King Jr., in his 1963 "Letter from a Birmingham Jail," wrote, "Injustice anywhere is a threat to justice everywhere. We are caught in an inescapable network of mutuality, tied in a single garment of destiny. Whatever affects one directly affects all indirectly. Never again can we afford to live with the narrow, provincial 'outside agitator' idea. Anyone who lives inside the United States can never be considered an outsider anywhere in this country." King marks the problem quite clearly, even as his eloquence was driven to and by solidarity. Networks of mutuality are much more easily conceived within the bounds of citizenship, even if quite unevenly experienced. Thus, when we seek to blend cosmopolitanism and solidarity, we might very well need to move back to foundational principles. Calhoun helps.

More than any other theme, solidarity has been the key problem for Calhoun from the time of his focus on class struggle and reactionary radicals.[25]

Rather than view groups in formation as derived from larger systemic principles, Calhoun has sought to understand the meaning made by actors in their world. He works to elaborate how those meaning-making efforts and consequent actions affected the qualities of community apparently lost in the movement to larger-scale forms of action and association.

Calhoun (2002) puts the question of solidarity into the problematic of public spheres. It is misleading to focus on decision making as such, and rational debate, he argues, without first considering the constitution of the identities and interests that come together in any collective project. What, in other words, produces the solidarities that enable communities of discourse to form? What constitutes peoplehood? It is certainly not a derivative of constitutional experts fashioning rational documents. It is far more a matter of imaginaries of solidarity constructed, and motivations made in its wake. Unfortunately, while Habermas spells out the problem of the public sphere, he is particularly problematic on the subject formation associated with it. As Calhoun (2001b, 155) writes,

> Habermas hopes the public sphere will produce a rational agreement that can take the place of pre-established culture as the basis for political identity. He works, however, with an overly sharp dichotomy between inherited identity and rational discourse. He identifies voluntary public life entirely with the latter, and thus obscures the extent to which it is necessarily also a process of cultural creativity and modes of communication not less valuable for being incompletely rational.

Instead, Calhoun recommends, we should ask whether the discourse of the public sphere can produce the solidarities that enable different kinds of decisions and consequent state action to reflect a superior kind of integration and democracy. This is, in a sense, the difference from most nationalist views as nations being inherited, and different from civic nations with their thin identities. Calhoun asks how thicker identities can themselves be produced by the public sphere itself and whether these can be better or worse.

Moving beyond Durkheim's categorical mechanical solidarity, or the functional interdependence of his organic solidarity, or even the direct social ties associated with classical understandings of community, Calhoun wants to know whether we can envision a solidarity that is less imposed and more intersubjectively realized and best identified with what is public. To speak of publics as I have throughout this volume is, in a sense, to speak of potential solidarity in the making. Publics may be deliberative, but solidarity is something more: it is about, as Calhoun reminds us, the promises people make to one another, those that bind them together.

Calhoun has considered whether through the social relations animating cosmopolitan intellectualities bonds of solidarity might develop beyond those generated by capitalism's privileges and nationalisms' hegemonies. In particular Calhoun asks that we consider (1) the conditions under which solidarities of various kinds of groups are formed; (2) to assess the ways in which these groups, internally, replicate the conditions of open and free public discussion elevated by Habermas, but whose performative and formative dimensions are noted by Arendt; (3) to consider the ways in which these groups might, on the basis of their own reflexive dispositions and communicative competencies, move more independently from systemic needs; in order (4) to consider how well these various publics might, in articulation with various powers, recognize and address needs near and far (Kennedy 2006). While I formulated that synthesis of Calhoun's work nearly a decade ago, it seems like the right set of questions with which to move into consequential solidarity's consideration, especially its articulation with globalizing knowledge.

The global information infrastructure on which so much globalizing knowledge depends plays a double role, making an increasingly wide swath of the world aware of conditions elsewhere, even as it makes globalization, not only as a process but as a cultural transformation, appear increasingly inevitable. As a consequence, "traditional" solidarities, rooted in religious or national communities, are sutured to technological transformations. In that tie, those claiming enduring wisdom must find articulation with those recognizing the power of the information and technological revolution. This familiar linkage is not the only kind of globalization/community relationship on which we should focus. Precisely because Calhoun moves us to understand better how groups are formed through engagement over issues, the idea that enduring communities merely extend themselves through new means seems far too limited. It is especially limiting if we wish to consider the conjunction of cosmopolitan intellectuality and consequential solidarity.

We are beginning to learn, for instance, how the politics and aesthetics of hacking, enabled by the global information infrastructure, changes social movements and the very notion of subjectivity in a globalizing world (Coleman 2013). Here, the very notion of solidarity is transformed. Even while networks like Anonymous clearly act in solidarity with mobilized publics, from

the Occupy movement and the Polish Web Kids to those who would challenge sexual violence in a town organized to hide its crime,[26] the hackers' very
anonymity denies us one of the typical vectors along which publics work to
establish trustworthiness, which in turn is itself an important foundation for
truthfulness, itself the anchor of intellectuality.

At the same time, one of the truths their very action makes apparent is
the development of a new kind of surveillance capacity by authorities, limiting the very notion of privacy and freedom critical for intellectual autonomy
and a culture of critical discourse to thrive (Diebert 2012). Consequently, one
of the most important collective intellectual engagements of our time is to
rethink the meaning of hactivism and to prevent it from being demonized
in lexical warfare (Ludlow 2013). For those who embrace the value of knowledge as such, this statement, issued in the wake of hactivist Aaron Swartz's
prosecution-induced suicide, is telling: "Knowledge is free. The corrupt fear
us. The honest support us. The heroic join us. We are Anonymous."[27]

To mark these transformations and to spell out their implications clearly
reflect an intellectuality of consequence. To the extent it affects transnational
relations, it also marks its global importance. And when hackers work to
extend a movement's effect, as Anonymous did in the beginning of the Web
Kids' resistance to ACTA's implementation, one can clearly see their consequence. Anonymous's work is often an example of consequential solidarity,[28]
even if it can't be identified with an expression of cosmopolitan intellectuality
for the limitations its own secrecy imposes, necessary as they may be for their
own practice.[29]

Their example, and the response of the state to them, illustrates Calhoun's
emphasis on the importance of considering the properties of the Internet
for its public expression and intellectual responsibility. These technologies
might offer alternative means for individual or group economic success and
public constitution. Calhoun suggests higher education institutions can use
their own commitments to learning and publics, along with their capacities
for technological innovation, to think about ways to facilitate the making of
solidarities and publics that move beyond liberalism's thin assumptions about
citizenship and capitalism's generation of owners, producers, and consumers.
Because Calhoun now leads the London School of Economics and Politics,
we can see in practice how such theoretical visions might be developed. And
one can imagine variously consequential solidarities rooted in cosmopolitan
intellectuality in the process. These are frames worth considering, especially

in light of the alternative intellectualities and transformations already addressed here.

Articulations

Intellectuality is rarely conceived in terms of solidarity or other social relations, and it has often been defined in opposition to power and authority. It is sometimes recognized in association with non-intellectuals if the principal power abusing reason and knowledgeability is authorities intellectuals must resist in order to act responsibly. With that formulation, solidarity becomes obvious, for one is either, in Gramsci's terms, a traditional or organic intellectual. But in these times of transformation without telos, it's hard to figure who is traditional and who organic, and sometimes even who is responsible and who is not.

To apply such labels is partly performative. Žižek, the master of such performance, would put all social democratic intellectuals into a traditional camp were he obliged to go Gramscian for a moment. Habermas would land there, just as Gusenbauer, Lagos, and others discussed here. However, because of the systemic complexity of the world in which we live, and the multiple structures and normative valences and possibilities of those structures, I am skeptical of such codes. I am also skeptical of easy assignments of solidarity with the subordinate or with publics at large. At the same time, without struggling to figure those solidarities, intellectual responsibilities seem too easily articulated with the mass of complexity and value of publicity without thinking about any publics at all.

This dilemma is replayed within academic worlds too. In the debate about public sociology, its articulation as the standpoint of civil society is much simpler than figuring and recognizing its expression in academic authority. But finding solidarity with publics among those with different measures of intellectual and administrative capital, to use Bourdieu's sense, is something worth considering at length. To find the practices that extend its public value is something worth doing. Indeed, that is why I consider Ashraf Ghani's case to be so illustrative and informative.

Ghani has been in the halls of academe as both professor and administrator. His exercise of intellectual responsibility within think tanks and governments, even in association with the US military as he works to both redefine and realize Afghan sovereignty in a world of flows and threats (Ghani 2013), deserves critical engagement and extension. It's especially important in this endeavor to move beyond the global flow associated with celebrity lists. His 2014 candidacy for president of Afghanistan inspires even more interest and challenge in representing the fusion of intellectual, institutional, and national responsibility.

To recognize celebrity intellectuals within one's nation or across the world demands little. One is part of an audience, and the listed intellectuals part of some publicists' concoction of *prominenci* in the world of ideas. By expressing familiarity with an esteemed one hundred, or even by being part of it, one might obtain useful cultural capital. Celebrity in association can be consequential, but not all professional associations and other organizations of the highly educated do more than struggle to reproduce the interests of their body's members in a rapidly changing global environment.

Solidarity is rarely used in these articulations, as the group's work is more an expression of common interest, involving little sacrifice for others. Indeed, the American Association of Universities or Universitas 21 hardly seems to work in the world of solidarity. This can change, of course, as the Postsecondary Education Network (PEN) illustrates quite often when prominent writers express their support for their fellows whose freedoms or lives come to be at risk by the actions, or inactions, of their own governments.

Sometimes these associations are less formal. They are based more on participation in more loosely organized networks that are themselves made even more readily given the revolution in information and communication technologies. Here, identifications become more important and can sometimes extend to those beyond the category itself. I think in particular of the ways in which *Jadaliyya* has mobilized intellectuals in the engagement of the Middle East in a way that respects the dynamics of the places it analyzes as much as, if not more than, the interests of those who employ those intellectuals or who would use their expertise beyond the interests of the publics under view. For this reason I identified that network as really a networked public intellectuality, something I would expect others moved by intellectual responsibility to emulate.

In many ways, the Academic Fellowship Program associated with the OSF is like *Jadaliyya* with its self-definition through regional foci and emphasis on knowledge networks. AFP is, of course, better resourced but also more focused on knowledge institutional capacity building. AFP is also more intellectually diverse given the range of scholars it supports but, like *Jadaliyya*, resting on a philosophy that is critical. The latter might be more Marxian than Popperian in inspiration, but both inspire a reflexivity in theory and practice and a knowledge-based public engagement with an emphasis on the former. The SSRC might be closely aligned with both in theory and practice, but not by definition; it depends on the foci of the intellectuals that lead it. In the Calhoun era, it certainly could resonate with both theory and practice, evident in the collaborations SSRC stimulated.

Knowledge and norms are sometimes difficult to disentangle. Some authors do so to distinguish knowledge networks from transnational advocacy networks, for example, or universities from other organizations (Stone 2005). Some organizations base their norms on more knowledge-based grounds than others, as *Jadaliyya*, SSRC, and even OSF do (Sudetic 2011); thus, it is critical to distinguish degrees of ideology or knowledgeability in these practices. Still, we can appreciate that these three are more knowledge grounded than the three that follow.

The Next Left, WSF, and WEF are also knowledge networks but with more emphasis on policy and practice. They lead with their definitions of cosmopolitanism and solidarity, but constituted in very different fashions. WEF defines its cosmopolitanism in the terms Beck would emphasize, with accents on global risks like climate change, false information spreading across the Internet, and bacteria resistant to antibiotics. These issues require little differentiation among elites and the rest. And that suits the principal membership of WEF. Cosmopolitanism and global solidarity without consequential differentiation define WEF knowledge projects. WEF is informed by the virtues of dialogue more than the pains of struggle.

Those associated with WSF, however, come together because of their sense of consequential difference in the world. While the principal axis of difference that drives their association may be between authorities and those without, there is also a greater emphasis on the challenge of difference across the world in other terms. Subjectivities are formed not only by global inequalities and risks but also by the histories and cultures that form the sense of the world of the 99 percent. While a certain disposition toward those articulations might be critical for WSF identifications, the heterogeneity and loose organization of the network also makes the realization of solidarity a challenge.

Žižek may not be WEF's favorite intellectual, but the difference between his ideas and those articulated by President Obama's in Cairo in 2009 shows why. Žižek (2012, 69) said that we don't need dialogue but rather "solidarity between those who struggle for justice in Muslim countries and those who participate in the same struggle elsewhere." To define radically different movements and struggles as one and the same may be only symbolic, but that may itself be a consequential enough solidarity to lead to the rearticulation of so many layers of difference.

Gusenbauer's Next Left is somewhere in between WEF and WSF, comfortable enough with the powers that be but at the same time working to figure how justice and sustainability might be redefined to inform policies that have driven the world into crisis and made social democracy's heyday in the past rather than future tense. Indeed, its hesitation to find common ground with the Arab Uprisings is good indication—after all, Mubarak was a member of the Second International as are all the parties supporting the Next Left. Under those conditions, solidarity is not easily rearticulated if pasts are complicated and not reconsidered.

Even if the past does not intervene, intellectualities defined by existing institutional interests more than cosmopolitan affinities anticipating global transformations can lag. Structures of power and privilege in defining the European Left can interfere with casting the Next Left's future. While the Occupy movement and its kin might be noxious for some social democrats, given that those socialists are also part of the elite that alienates, there was no reason why the Next Left took so long to embrace anti-ACTA mobilization if the world of emergent and networked intellectualities were their constituency as much as welfare states and labor aristocracies.

In the end, however, those emergent networked intellectualities might be the most cosmopolitan and produce the most consequential solidarities we could anticipate in the world in formation. After all, because of ACTA's poorly conceived plan to consider intellectual property in entertainment and pharmaceuticals together, Web Kids have been moved to consider the linkages between global health and patents. To borrow Castells's (2009) terminology, what agent might be the switchman moving them into another global flow, perhaps even into an engagement of energy beyond designing smart grids? There are many well ahead of me in this world of theory and practice, rethinking these very ties.

Dustin Steele is a young activist committed to transforming his native Appalachia.[30] Dedicated to direct action, he is also informed by an anarchist sensibility in which the struggle of all against concentrations of power and expertise is enough common sense to guide consequential solidarity's formation. He is also exceptionally well informed about the history of class struggle in his region and of the alternative futures the energy business and its employees' livelihoods and environmental conditions might face. As I discussed his example in a lecture at the Hungarian Sociological Association, a Central European University student remarked how impressed he was by Appalachian anarchist activism. He then put me in touch with another scholar studying Serb movements in this vein. Comparisons are likely to emerge, but so might a newly networked and increasingly cosmopolitan intellectuality in search of consequential solidarity around clean energy. As I write, university students are increasingly dedicated to campaigns to divest their universities of investments in carbon-based technologies and the firms defined by them.

To struggle over energy is much more difficult than to struggle over Internet freedom. Expertise is not so widely distributed in the energy world. It is concentrated in knowledge networks far beyond public reach. In order to figure the connection between the virtual world of knowledge sharing and the deeply material world of energy flows, we need to understand better the actually existing world articulating global energy flows, as I proposed in Chapter 6. One need not start there. One need only identify the undocumented and indefensible in particular contexts to move the conversation, the knowledge network, and solidarity that might be consequential.

While the debate over fracking in the United States might be over the cost of energy and its environmental risks, in Poland and Ukraine fracking promises emancipation from their nations' energy dependence on an old imperial master whose energy wealth enables abiding geopolitical dominance. Euromaidan's rebellion is manifestly about dignity, freedom, and European association, but it was made, in part, by the kinds of energy dependencies Ukraine still has with Russia. That articulation, regardless of Euromaidan's outcome, will have to be addressed in the years to come.

We can't expect all issues to develop such ready and consequential solidarities as the struggle for Internet freedom yielded, in part because knowledge is not always so broadly distributed and context is not always so unimportant. But then consequential solidarity can be imagined even when expertise is concentrated and differences quite radical. One conversation stimulated that vision for me.

As I sought to understand the possibilities for global solidarity through the Occupy movement (Kennedy 2011d), I sought out my colleagues' expert in Tahrir's mobilization to ask how they considered the various "statements of solidarity" activists in New York and Cairo offered one another. Atef Said, a sociologist and human rights lawyer from Egypt, was among those mediating and mobilizing around solidarity with Tahrir Square.[31] His November 21, 2011, Facebook posting identified explicitly how solidarity might be developed:

> A bloodbath is taking place now in Egypt in Tahrir Square, the icon of all justice seekers and activists of the occupy movement worldwide and the symbol of liberation from all oppression and exploitation of capital and dictatorship (Tahrir in Arabic literally means liberation). Most of the weaponry used against protesters, especially tear gas containers, is U.S.-made. Egyptian military is dependent on the U.S. military aid, as $1.3 billion goes yearly to the Egyptian military.

On November 22, the occupiers of Tahrir Square asked the world for the following actions of support:

- Occupy/shut-down Egyptian embassies worldwide. Now they represent the junta; reclaim them for the Egyptian people.
- Shut down the arms dealers. Do not let them make it, ship it.
- Shut down the part of your government dealing with the Egyptian junta.[32]

Actions became even more specific and targeted. For example, in those same postings about calls for solidarity with Tahrir, activists proposed to assemble on December 1, 2011, outside the gates of the Combined Systems International (CSI) plant in Jamestown, Pennsylvania, to protest sales of the tear gas canisters used by the Egyptian military to repress protesters in Tahrir. Such actions are more difficult given the relatively isolated location and the dependence of the local community on the plant's employment, making the twenty-four-person turnout not altogether surprising (Majors 2011). But rather than focus on numbers, one should consider the object's example for consequential solidarity.

That CSI protest was not a simple affirmation of support for Tahrir by Americans but a direct protest by Americans against the Egyptian government's violence. It focused attention on the ways in which US government policy and US corporate practice facilitate that violence. It was an expression of solidarity that with sufficient mobilization, public recognition, and policy response could have altered the geopolitics that connects Egypt with the

United States. That was, perhaps, what Tahrir's call for solidarity was about and why its call extends beyond its immediate importance. Another statement of symbolic solidarity for Occupy Wall Street offers for me the theoretical key and the reason that cosmopolitan intellectuality and consequential solidarity must be linked.

Vetëvendosje offered a letter of solidarity with OWS, but it goes beyond many expressions of global solidarity in an important way. I found this passage particularly significant for extending solidarity beyond resemblance and toward focus on how we might think more about consequential solidarity: "Your fight at the core of global financial power marks a crucial moment of resistance in the long chain of demonstrations and actions carried out by people in different countries; people that are facing oppression from the same repressive system of illegitimate power."[33]

As I argued in Chapter 5, there are too few who might recognize Vetëvendosje and the implications of this act of solidarity. It is the most substantial opposition movement in Kosova, calling not only for "self-determination," as the name in Albanian implies, but also greater equality and justice within nations and across them. Within the Kosovar parliament and also a social force in civil society, Vetëvendosje is among the most innovative in its repertoire of movement techniques and political maneuvers. But perhaps its most powerful force lies in its self-positioning as a force for "truth" against what it says is the "institutional lie" of the international protectorate in which Kosova's move toward sovereignty is embedded (Kurti 2011).

Identification with Kosova's struggle for sovereignty is not a simple point around which global solidarity might be realized, given the ways in which that movement is itself embedded in a geopolitics overdetermined elsewhere. The idea that there are great institutional lies around which global regimes of power and inequality are organized is a point around which a cosmopolitanism from below might be developed, a cosmopolitanism grounded in claims about justice and equality. It can't be based on a cosmopolitanism of resemblance, however. In the end, we should turn to one of the great intellectuals of the twentieth century for one path toward cosmopolitanism and solidarity.

Ludwig Wittgenstein (1953) suggested that commonality is not conceived best by looking for the common trait but rather a set of overlapping similarities he called family resemblances. One cousin might not look at all like another, but she might share the nose of a third cousin while that second might have his eyes. As consequential solidarity develops in the reflections of cosmopolitan intellectuality, we might not find the common trait that links all of its expressions and transformations. But we might find enough similarities if we trace the chains of injustice and risk, and perhaps even exercises in reflexivity, that bind us.

We can start with eleven theses in that spirit.

9 Eleven Theses on Globalizing Knowledge

Knowledge matters, but what kind of knowledge, and for what and for whom?

Science and technology most easily answer the first question. In justifying investment in research, we most readily invoke those discoveries that appear directly to alter the course of our lives. Medical understandings transformed by discoveries around DNA and modes of communication altered by the microelectronics revolution, for example, inspire. They also can move the economically resourced to support the knowledgeable.

Of course, these great scientific discoveries don't proceed without enabling and consequential transformations in our institutions and social relations. One cannot ask how knowledge comes to matter without inviting a social scientific dialogue. Sociology and its kin disciplines should inform how we think about the purest of science and the most pristine intellectuality and the institutions that support them.

Research universities associate those scientific revolutions in life and computer science with their halls, but we can't easily transpose our valuations of intellectuality into the sociology of the university. It is hard to recognize the intellectual without being assured of her autonomy from power's coercion, but we also know that the most consequential scientific revolutions in our time could not have happened in universities without massive government and/or corporate support. The idea that universities are independent from the state and/or the private sector is a myth, but that myth is absolutely critical to reconstruct in order to assure universities their proper place.

Independence is the wrong word. *Autonomy* is much better. The freedom underlying efficacious knowledge production assures the artist, the intellectual, and the creative team sufficient license to follow the trails genius sparks and dogged dedication brings to consequence. However, many feel that knowledge is too valuable to be left to the direction of its producers. Authorities of all sorts feel the need to steer learning toward more useful applications. Publics also can mobilize to challenge dangerous scholarly learning.

This tension over the independence of the knowledgeable is long enduring, but it also is new. The conditions of knowledge production, dissemination, and consumption are changing so that ownership of their means is no longer so clear, and the sources of critical knowledge no longer so obvious. To understand the place of knowledge in our world today, given the conditions of its transformation, demands far more intellectual engagement if only to understand better what we mean by autonomy for its producers.

This sociology becomes even more challenging and important when we talk about *globalizing* knowledge. This knowledge necessarily marks the challenge of difference and raises the question of identification. At least implicitly, globalizing knowledge demands that we ask for whom that knowledge is developed. And when we ask for whom, for what can more readily follow. Answers to either question, however, have become more difficult because of the changing articulations of knowledge and global transformations themselves.

No intellectually responsible person can address knowledge for whom and for what in general. In some instances, intellectuals and their institutions and networks should attend first and foremost to their most immediate publics; in other circumstances, envisioning a global public is critical. Intellectuals have made the case that they should use their learning to develop weapons of mass destruction, while others can argue that this is the greatest violation of intellectual responsibility. Even those who are not rocket scientists have to exercise intellectual responsibility in figuring their proper course of action.

Edward Snowden judged that his knowledge of state secrets through his contractual assignment and his Internet intellectuality demanded his slow release of National Security Administration information. Global publics, not only American, debate the ethics of this action. Pussy Riot's violation of a sacred space to protest Putin's appropriation of religious authority in his own legitimation of power might be understood only in terms of their music's quality or one's faith in particular patriarchs' access to the divine. To understand the cultural political meaning of their performance art demands, however, that we also figure how Dostoyevsky and Madonna are fused in the struggle for human rights and political responsibility through celebrity.

In short, the more responsible approach to figuring the conditions and consequences of changing articulations of knowledge and change is to consider them first in their own contexts, to recognize them on their own terms. We might then work to compare them to others, by contrasting those contexts through their mutual translations. We thus fuse their horizons of understanding. These dyads are never sufficient, however, for they are always implicated in broader conversations and conventions. By marking this final articulation, we increase our capacities to ask why a particular, or dyad, is embedded in our more general accounts of the world. To figure that object's implications for more general syntheses organized around notions ranging from individual dignity to global sustainability is critical. This is important only in so far as we propose to globalize knowledge in an intellectually, and institutionally, responsible fashion.

Throughout I have explored the dilemmas and implications of these changing articulations along particular vectors. I have considered different kinds of knowledge agents among intellectuals, institutions, and networks along with their media. I have addressed their foci and partners in publics, contexts, and flows. I developed these explorations with an eye toward making explicit the schemas extending cosmopolitan intellectuality and consequential solidarity, particular expressions of intellectual and institutional responsibility.

There are, however, broad trends in the articulations of globalizing knowledge that these more particular accounts ought to engage. In what follows, I synthesize this volume's discussions using an intellectual convention that has worked before in linking knowledge and change. I offer eleven theses on globalizing knowledge in the spirit and genre, if not tradition, of Marx's (1845) final thesis: "The philosophers have only *interpreted* the world, in various ways; the point, however, is to *change* it." I might say this instead: "The knowledgeable have transformed the world with their process and products; the point, however, is to understand how that has happened so that change might itself be more knowledgeable." These eleven theses could help.

1. Globalizing knowledge not only spreads information across a world wide web but also reflects and causes profound institutional, intellectual, and other transformations.

Most obvious for the academically inclined, the field of knowledge institutions has changed in globalization's wake. It's not just that faculty and students are better connected with the increasing mobility of students and scholars and the possibility of making connections through websites like Academia.edu or Facebook. It's also that higher education has become something of a global business itself.

Clearly the global game in ranking universities has reinforced those homophily trends built earlier on emulation, now buttressed by indicators informing patrons about how good, or not, the object of their largesse is. And it's not just a matter of shaping elite taste. Universities and those designing national economies work to recruit students from abroad to make up for the declining support their own states provide at home.

This global recruitment reflects both short- and long-term financial thinking. These students do not only pay out-of-state tuition. As wealth accumulates and concentrates in China, India, Russia, and elsewhere, universities want to ensure its students' parents and alumni are part of that global elite with ideally philanthropic dispositions. Universities thus are increasingly in the business of building markets and inspiring donations in a global field. That global shift in resources has terrific implications for the world of higher education. It increases dramatically the inequalities among universities themselves. Their relative local value decreases before the escalation of global competition, which also makes invocations of the "global university" increasingly common and all too often crudely considered with the lens of the lowest common denominator.

It's frankly striking how often universities modernize old scripts about leaving behind parochialism in the search for global awareness or maybe even citizenship. Lovely liberal arts lullabies sing students to sleep dreaming of worldly sophistication. They ideally dream in the second language they are learning from poorly paid graduate students in the relatively impoverished building next to the newly constructed life sciences building. If we were to end the story about globalizing knowledge with these familiar tabloid tales, we would miss the more profound transformations at work.

Intellectual transformations accompany these institutions globalizing knowledge. New collaborations generate increasingly global knowledge networks rooted in all sorts of arenas, from specific research problems to broader intellectual affinities. And with that general pattern, English-language use has realized a terrific hegemony in practice if not in ideological veneration. That dominance is declining as the Internet becomes a site for both consumption and production of information. Chinese speakers don't write in English for one another. In this sense, the importance and value of working in more than one language has only grown if we want the bridges that make intellectual innovation possible. It's not obvious, however, that we know how to design those bridges.

Ambitiously global universities work furiously to recruit academic elites from elsewhere, but without revolutionary consequence in the meaning and purpose of higher education itself. The best universities are well suited to reproducing themselves and building excellence within their conventions, which includes recruiting scholars and students in a global market. They are not well suited for thinking across their institutions and their broader field.

It is time to refigure the purpose of globalizing knowledge through institutions and networks, especially one that builds on synergies between new articulations of intellectual and knowledge institutional responsibilities. That is difficult because of increasing struggle over the allocation of resources in higher education itself.

2. Global shifts in resources and attention have moved struggles over higher education to the forefront of public life.

The distribution of resources and struggles within and around knowledge institutions is quite uneven. That struggle has also become more broadly consequential. Of course, the neoliberalism associated with the Washington Consensus long ago left the global economy station. The BRICS command attention, and G7 economies falter as they work to figure the source of economic crisis. Neoliberalism leaves its residues, however, even as it becomes the object of protest within universities themselves.

The university's most proximate public, made of faculty and students and occasionally their colleagues in the non-instructional staff, increasingly demand that rationales be made in a culture of critical discourse around truth, beauty, and intellectual responsibility. That core academic public does not respect academic decisions made in the language of accountants, organizational feasibility, and rankings from elsewhere. Reason requires financial calculation and measures of excellence, but for these mobilized publics those indicators cannot adequately encompass intellectuality. The subtle hegemony of the balance sheet and lists of excellence are expressions of the transformation of knowledge begun much earlier.

Knowledge has become increasingly specialized, but the triumph of experts over intellectuals as its individual expression was only realized in the United States in the 1970s. For some, the victory of university administrators over faculty and students is the next step in the march of specialist reason, augmented by administrative power, over intellectuality as such. Those who might invoke these and similar concerns have also become increasingly marginal to articulating knowledge.

They are replaced by the celebrity machine made in markets and publicity and by universities privileging depth in particular fields of expertise over breadth and cultivation in their promotion of and search for faculty excellence. Anxieties over the disappearance of intellectuals, manifest in the search for their public expression, inspire a certain revival. Even that quest enjoys much less authority than its ancestors enjoyed. Knowledge is no longer so concentrated, and intellectuals can no longer even pretend to legislate.

However, those conclusions are both mighty ethnocentric and backward looking. The decline of public intellectuals is pretty much an American problem, and the search for a twenty-first-century Sartre is an anachronism.

3. Globalizing knowledge typically proceeds on ethnocentric terms spelled with freedom.

More than laments about the decline of public intellectuals, ethnocentrism actually animated the first two theses. Of course, such ethnocentrism is not unusual. Most tales of globalizing knowledge begin in the United States and sometimes include Canada, Europe, and Australia. Brazil, China, and India are occasionally motivating the story, but in global tales the subject is typically American in accent. At least in these tales English could appear to be a first language. University leaders and some world society theorists justify the tale by arguing that that's just the way it is. University excellence is concentrated, and it is focused in the United States, which can buy the best intellectuals across the world with the terms of the appointment—not just salaries but with other amenities too. They include concentrations of terrific colleagues, no mandatory retirements, and relatively appealing work conditions, not least of which is academic freedom alongside the ability to continue learning from outstanding colleagues from across the world right there on campus. Inequalities can enable consequential freedom. They can work against consequential solidarity.

Solidarity is often used in stories of social movements and labor unions. It is occasionally found in more theological discussions in which to bear the burden of others is considered sacred. It's implicit in the formations of national identity: to sacrifice one's life for the nation is the most sacred act, inspiring tombs of unknown soldiers across the world. Knowledge, however, is typically seen as something far more precious and distinctive, an expression of intellectual freedom first and foremost. While freedom is critical, to conceive of knowledge primarily in its terms limits the articulation of knowledge with global transformations and public value. By itself, freedom hardly mitigates an ethnocentrism, or racism, that so diminishes intellectuality's transcendent claim. It needs solidarity.

4. Knowledge is a public good around which solidarity could, and should, be mobilized.

Most understand public goods to be things that are not diminished by others' use and from whose use one can't be easily excluded. Of course, intellectual property and exclusive learning opportunities in universities do limit learning in different fashions. However, the schema organizing knowledge production itself depends on sharing and recombining existing knowledge stocks to make more adequate and insightful ones. For that reason, one might find reassurance in some of those more optimistic accounts of university futures. Their competitors, whether in private firms or in think tanks, are limited because their institutional logics demand skewed and limited circulations of their knowledge products. Universities are defined if not by their open source, then at least by their open results.

Invoking open source, however, shows the limits of the knowledge schema legitimating universities and their ideological associations. Universities, by their logic, are devoted to their own individual promotion, just as their subunits struggle to extend their turf and their scholars work to magnify their own individual reputations. Knowledge practices depend on reputations made within an ideology celebrating individual, team, or institutional brilliance less than network effect. That self-centeredness can be out of sync with how knowledge is produced to become more valuable public goods.

Nevertheless, as the fields of knowledge production, distribution, and consumption become increasingly and globally competitive, the ideology of university knowledge compels leading agents to form associations of similarly distinguished universities to burnish one another's reputations and to distribute their products in increasingly open fashion. In that latter gesture, they move increasingly and directly toward treating knowledge as a more public good. Providing syllabi on university websites and even massive online courses free of charge are expressions of this trend, but so are massive public relations campaigns turning some faculty into stars.

These latter efforts are formally public goods, but when laced with celebrity logics, they are also problematic expressions of intellectual and institutional responsibility. On the one hand, they help revitalize that public intellectuality whose loss is lamented. On the other, the public intellectuals and their institutions become increasingly prey to commercial conventions, figuring what kinds of speech might sell, be newsworthy, make sense to the target audience. More than ever, we need to parse the competing, and complementary, logics of public relations and public intellectuality.

The status of universities depends on their reputation for intellectual integrity. Arguments for making knowledge even greater public goods can thus find fertile ground, even while this search for public patronage can lead to the university's capture by particular interests. Thus, working with ever more sophisticated and critical notions of publics is invaluable for developing knowledge of consequence and long-term value.

5. The articulations of publics and knowledge change the value of each.

For most, public has implied something that authorities invoke after God's death in political legitimations to justify their visions of past, present, and future. Notions like "the public interest" illustrate that rhetorical use. They provided not only political leaders but also intellectuals ample room to articulate their visions of right with popular notions of the fair and just. There is less room today for that kind of articulation, however. The technological transformations of media mean that there is much less space for authorities' tales to go unanswered. Television and radio might transmit information in one direction, but social media are interactive and recast the stories others tell.

The very sense of public has changed. Public is unlike any other sociological conception, for its constitution is made by communication among its members, not determined through ascribed or achieved status within some larger preexisting structure. Of course, public has its origins in classical thought, but philosophy and social and cultural theory have caught up to the changes in the world by acknowledging the importance of groups formed by their own public engagement with one another about interests, identifications, and ideas. Because publics can form around those ideas, they can be made more and less knowledgeable and intellectual and thus can also change the practice of knowledge itself.

For knowledge institutions and networks, not only intellectuals, engaging publics becomes the foundation for developing an appropriate intellectuality for our times.

6. Mobilizing publics has already transformed knowledge practices.

Mobilizing universities' proximate publics has at least challenged if not already potentially transformed academic worlds by stripping neoliberal visions of their commonsense articulations, but the transformation goes well beyond that. The Occupy movement's global expression highlights that shift and manages that for reasons beyond its geographical spread. It is also apparent with its dedication to learning, manifest in tent city libraries. It can be seen in its ability to create new visions with which to anchor refined understandings of global transformations. Instead of inequality being the dominant theme of a single discipline in a university, questions about how the 1 percent define the terms of success and failure for the 99 percent are now part of public discourse in consequential ways. The Occupy movement changed public knowledge, but recognizing those transformations is still limited.

A number of scholarly disciplines, most especially sociology, have embraced *public* as adjective and carry out research with its terms. However, the challenging relationship between public in opposition to authority, and public responsibility in the repertoire of those in authority, has hardly been elaborated sufficiently. The intellectual grounds of public knowledge both in authority and without administrative power need address. In particular, it is critical to figure mechanisms translating public sense across layers of power and knowledge. While this might be considered in theory, its elaboration in practice is immediately important.

A number of universities have become increasingly aware of the value of linking with their local publics in ways that go beyond the latent functions of having higher education provide jobs and graduates to its environs. Much more active conceptions of universities as public partners, or in the expert parlance, anchor institutions, have developed in consequential ways. How that resonates with universities' quests for excellence is not resolved. In fact, it is poorly understood.

One reason for that inadequacy rests in how poorly we recognize, much less articulate, the value of that relationship between knowledge and publics. For instance, the academy places great value on publications that few read.

There is relatively little appreciation for translations of how knowledge and its investment, distribution, and coproduction might enhance the well-being of those beyond the academy. Translational research has its place, even if not especially lordly, in the medical field and other basic science centers. However, it seems especially important in these times to figure a way to approximate such ventures in the human sciences. In fact, public sociology and its kin across the disciplines might be just that vehicle. To engage globalizing knowledge in those terms is not so simple, however.

7. Knowledge institutions have poorly articulated relations to global publics.

When universities and their publics are addressed, we will always consider the local environs and, if publicly funded, those sovereigns that help pay the bill. What about those who are distant? Practice again suggests a path.

Expressions of solidarity are most easily found in line with hegemonic nationalisms, but they also can be realized when global connections are discovered or crafted. Universities can justify addressing needs and interests not only of those who share in the global academic life or who live in the same community. They also can, and should, find reason to recognize the lives and well-being of those who are part of the production chain that makes the goods sold in university stores. They might recognize those who join the academic chain of scholarly collaborations. In the exceptional case we find those partners when they become victims of academic research gone bad. To find ways to enhance the identification of research subjects, recast as partners, and to identify their association with knowledge production rather than as data points, are a first step.

Universities can even go well beyond their familiar zones to figure how their knowledge could produce public goods for those elsewhere, even without the mediation of professional peers. Indeed, when universities justify their missions with claims to do research to solve global problems, they do just that. It might be even better if in addressing those global problems, global publics become the partners that both help resolve the problem and formulate the question. Professional peers can mediate and extend the network power of knowledgeability in the process. That could even mitigate the negative effects of global rankings.

Although global rankings have earned the appropriate enmity of those more committed to the culture of critical discourse than to the culture of celebrity, it can be a noble quest to consider how we might compare institutions on their capacities and commitments to deliver public goods on different scales. Assessing universities on their commitments to environmental sustainability has shifted university priorities somewhat in the United States and elsewhere. One could imagine similar effort in assessing commitment to different kinds of publics realizing similar good. It should, however, not only control for capacities and mission but also weight the challenge of global difference and the relative value of different public partnerships in its measure.

8. Globalizing knowledge needs to articulate the variable challenge of difference.

Although most who think about globalizing knowledge recognize the challenge of difference in its articulations, it is exceptionally easy for differences to be homogenized by celebrating all kinds of diversity equally for their contributions to learning. We don't know, frankly, what kinds of diversity are more valuable, and for what purposes, because, in part, of the complexity of the problem. However, it is also a political problem. Those historically disadvantaged can be rightfully suspicious of wishes to complicate the story of diversity at their expense. At the same time, there are few guidelines about who should be at the knowledge table when public reference extends beyond the nation. These are not simple ethnocentrisms but complex articulations deserving more critical engagement. Sometimes, however, ethnocentrisms are more obvious, as when we seek out those whose mirror improves our own reflection.

One of the reasons 1989 could be celebrated and its anniversaries marked in so many universities was that those revolutions against the revolutionary tradition seemed in their goals to sanctify the normal that North America and noncommunist Europe embodied. Those transformations were also realized in a fashion that the knowledgeable should endorse—in mostly, and manifestly, peaceful fashion. As a student of those transformations, I think they deserve even more engagement, especially for silences marked and futures unrealized. I also recognize that embracing Poland is not hard for those not of Polish descent. After all, there is much to admire in what the spirit of *Solidarność* represented and realized in the 1980s. At the same time, it's shocking how much Americans don't know about the spirits of Afghanistan.

The United States has been at war in Afghanistan longer than it has in any other country in America's history. However, US knowledge institutions hardly teach about the place, especially in ways that reflect contextual expertise. Of course, Afghanistan is objectively harder to know than places like Poland—there is no single language that suffices, its historiography is not as developed and is less nationally bounded, and war makes ethnography and other research on the ground not only difficult but dangerous. At the same time, there is greater need to understand this region, especially so we do not fall into the traps that interested knowledge designed to win wars, or to pull out of wars, or to justify lives lost, demands.

Some of the most important knowledge about Afghanistan may also be about the relationships, and global flows, that have constructed it. Here, intellectuals can make a difference, but it is critically important to analyze how. In these terms, Afghanistan's Ashraf Ghani might be the exemplary intellectual for our times.

He is unlikely to be venerated for his success in conventional terms, but he should be recognized for his range of knowledge and practice along with the challenges of intellectual to practical responsibility he has undertaken in the address of both context and flow. Few, of course, have that capacity to replicate his trajectory. Too few even know his story. Even fewer might be able to analyze the conditions of his work and consequences of his practice. In a world of celebrity, we are more likely to recognize those whose expressions inform our own lives, real or imagined. Why is Ghani apparently distant?

Until 2013, top publications explicitly dedicated to identifying "top thinkers" across the world didn't mention Ghani. If they are published in the United States, they might recognize Arab activists in their year of uprising. They will identify scholars and intellectuals from a range of national backgrounds, which likelihood increases dramatically if they are already embedded in networks or featured in media organized through North America and maybe Europe. In short, we should not only trace the dynamics by which celebrity intellectuality is made but also work to constitute alternative forms of recognition that capture revolutions in public intellectuality and the opportunities to extend intellectual integrity beyond global powers.

9. Globalizing knowledge needs different grounds to realize intellectual integrity.

Jadaliyya is one of those transformations. It links critical scholarship in knowledge institutions across the world about the Middle East to Arab- and English-speaking audiences in real time in fashions relatively autonomous from institutionalized powers and interest. With very few resources, previously uncelebrated young scholars have made a knowledge network of great academic allure, if not also public consequence. Established before the uprisings of 2011, the network has been informed and transformed by that region's critical changes. Its website remains important, if not even more important, because of the intellectual and political challenge of understanding those rebellions, revolutions, and invasions and their interactions.

As others emulate *Jadaliyya*'s example, more easily accomplished than following Ghani's example, we might find through new media ways to supplement, if not also challenge, hegemonic narratives that claim the mantle of globalizing knowledge as extensions of the hegemonic self. However, not all regions have that capacity because of the dynamics of globalizing knowledge itself.

Kosova was, at one time, the object of global attention. When Serbia's leader, Slobodan Milošević, launched a major campaign of ethnic cleansing and genocide against the region's Albanian residents, and when, in turn, NATO intervened in what a deservedly celebrity intellectual called a war in the name of human rights, scores of books and articles were written in English and other world languages to talk of Kosova and its struggles. In the preceding decade, however, the place hardly merited attention, even by those focused on southeastern Europe. This was tragedy, especially as nonviolent resistance to Serbian domination had developed in the most creative and generative fashions.

Maybe the reason was that too much was going on in the 1990s. Too, the Albanian diaspora, distinguished as it was, did not hold positions of influence within the knowledge institutions and networks of the West and other global powers to move public discourse in recognition. And that problem remains, as misrecognition and scant engagement of Kosova by global publics of all sorts allow internationally abetted corruption and injustice to prevail in a quasi-independent country problematically subject to EU and US oversight.

Regrettably, Kosova is not the exception to the rule. The problem of recognition extends broadly and reflects enduring patterns of inequality in scholarly and political engagement. Globalizing knowledge rarely makes up for that lack. One reason is that there is no scholarly field set up to address scholarly attention-deficit disorders.

10. Globalizing knowledge needs schema beyond national security.

In the US tradition, area studies partially made up for those attention deficits. It was justified mainly in the language of national security. It was conceived in an era when any kind of knowledge about the "other" could complement the nation's foreign policy and security practices. That kind of worldly knowledge, however, has fallen by the wayside in an illusorily global-ized world connected by the Internet and English.

Ironically, increasing connectivity has led many to depreciate the value of learning about others' languages, histories, institutions, and cultures in the excitement made by growing capacities to internationalize our presumptions through collaboration. Invitations to join in international research teams seem genuinely multinational in theory and practice. Even terminological shifts—like the move from national to human security—signifies globaliza-tion's embrace.

That framework may not be all bad, especially if it leads to more enduring collaborations. After all, the more extensive the relationship over time, the greater the potential, ceteris paribus, for amending the ethnocentrisms of the better resourced. Collaborators brought onboard for their data and greater cross-cultural abilities can become those who challenge knowledge agendas, as Florian Znaniecki illustrated.

However, in a world where collaborations are made quickly and easily, and past commitments dissipate in the search for new grants with new partners, globalizing knowledge will likely proceed on the terms of the dominant. Part-nerships will endure among those who best suit the visions of collaboration's hosts. Human security is nominally better than national security for global-izing knowledge because it does not privilege, automatically, the host nation's well-being. Funding's source, however, may reproduce that privilege in col-laboration. One challenge for globalizing knowledge rests, then, on how to move the origins and terms of partnership.

Violence appears to be one answer. When its threat, or its practice, grows, the presumptuous in the world of knowledge are more likely to listen to those it previously overlooked, if not always in the guise of partnership. The trag-edies of 2001 were a stark moment in a lesson that is unfortunately far too general. Threats are multiplying, for physical and immediate violence is not the only challenge those defining the terms of knowledge production face.

Most dramatically, threats to planetary survival around changes in the biophysical environment ought to move those with responsibility of all sorts to a kind of action that is hardly apparent. Here, we see that scientific con-sensus around biophysical changes is not enough to counter the political and ideological mobilization of ignorance to derail action. Island nations, so attuned to the dangers of this global transformation, hardly have the influ-ence to redirect global resources. A public sociology inspired by those nations' knowledgeabilities, alongside climate science marshaling concentrations of expertise, is one of the most critical intellectual alliances that ought to be cultivated in knowledge institutions and networks.

Tragically, the major threat to globalizing knowledge lies with institutionalized ignorance among the world's most privileged. It's hard to assess that problem in the language of security. At least, one needs to complement environmental security with a cultural politics that makes responsibility more than a slogan and to mark willful and instrumental ignorance an assault on the global public good.

Although the knowledgeable will agree with such stark statements in private, public indictments of ignorants can't be uttered. All sorts of justifications for inaction can be found, not least of which is the claim that this is but one problem of many, and there are many more immediate intellectual problems to be addressed. That's the response of the typical university administrator who has learned to reproduce university convention. These university officers are not alone.

Scholars and experts have become exceptionally adept at defending their turf using the terms of critical discourse's culture without extending themselves beyond it to the terrains where priorities are made in broader intellectualities. Some knowledge cultures can inspire just that movement, however.

Art often functions well in such an environment, especially when it can be linked not only to the celebration of universal beauty and harmony but to the cultivation of vision that obliges us to consider the world as it is and is becoming. Its aesthetics can cut through the veils of ideology that enable our comfort with existing positions in the world. Pussy Riot exemplifies. While Snowden's intervention was hardly artistic, its mode of presentation, drip by drip into global media, also represents the significance of aesthetics and power of performance for moving our awareness.

These interventions have changed the terms of our discussions across the world about the sacred and profane, about privacy and safety, about the public good. They suggest just how important it is to move beyond security in the search to globalize knowledge. They at least suggest the importance of complementing that quest with other schema about the world in order to figure what's good and what's not. Justice, dignity, sustainability, and many others can animate, especially when they ask us to take recognition, translation, and articulation more seriously. For in that process, the frames used to justify action might actually be subject to more critical scrutiny. An intellectuality embedded in cultural formations can redefine the interests, ideologies, and identities of the implicated.

We have seen these cultural formations of intellectuals, networks, and publics in these last years of transformation. In the previous chapter, I focused in particular on the ways in which an attempt to legislate intellectual property generated a solidarity of consequence that promised to redefine the terms of business and politics, not only halt the offending legislation. I considered an extraordinary transformation in Ukraine, coterminous with this volume's final revision, that was not only developing new repertoires of protest but expressing new public sensibilities of dignity and identification in Euromaidan. Intellectuals within the movements were redefining their terms. Too few beyond those movements were rearticulating their importance for a world transformed until war engulfed Ukraine. And when war rains, cultures of critical discourse and cosmopolitan intellectualities are among the first casualties.

It could have been different.

11. Globalizing knowledge changes the world, but how?

Fortunately, knowledge production and consumption are being distributed ever more widely. In their wake, new subjectivities and publics are in formation. We can see this especially in the proliferation and value of knowledge networks. They are of widely varying characters, and their overall effect on global transformations is hardly apparent. What does seem obvious is that they have terrific potential consequence even as they lack the intellectual clarity and organizational sense with which to develop their full value. And this is where I move toward projection and this book's implications for worldly theory and practice.

First, although knowledge networks emerge to affect publics around critically important issues, these networks can often be more ephemeral than enduring in their attention. While some might celebrate that freedom, without our capacity to institutionalize focus on issues that are of critical importance in these networks, the value of knowledge for shaping global transformations is diminished. At least knowledge in the public good, if not in the interests of the already vested, too easily dissipates from one crisis to the next.

One might help these emergent intellectualities find more enduring and consequential institutional homes. Universities should be not only the repositories of wisdom and midwives of intellectual innovation for profit but leading investors in the articulations of knowledge and transformations for global public goods. MIT's Media Lab and its global conversation are clearly examples, but there should be more.

Second, knowledge networks build on distributions of capacities among existing knowledge institutions and intellectuals. Transformations in media do allow for unforeseen possibilities. However, to figure how to implicate the unrecognized and relatively less capacious into network action to address issues is vitally important. Diversity and consequence combine. Not only can diversity supplement what is already understood but it can mark presumptions that anchor any vision's originating ethnocentrism and derived limitations.

Knowledge capacity building beyond privileged knowledge cores is critical to globalizing knowledge. In this, global universities need seek not only to build their brand in other sites but to extend their range of institutional partnerships in ways that encourage mutual learning more than homophily's expression. In short, beware the easy partner and build respect for the challenge of difference into collaboration.

Third, knowledge networks are not typically built to dig deep but to refine prejudices of those funding and animating them. The more radical implications of the culture of critical discourse often cannot adhere because these networks are much more voluntary than those institutions and publics in which membership is more obligatory, tenure more enduring, and conversations longer lasting. How one can invest in the intellectual solidarity that obliges continuing dialogue, even when the foundations of that engagement are shaken by inquiry with integrity, is critical. In short, invest in deep and enduring collaboration, into "networks of mutuality" that might lead to a "single garment of destiny." Martin Luther King Jr. should inspire on many more occasions than his birthday.

Finally, knowledge networks can more easily go with the flow than swim against the current. Of course, the flow is not always wrong, especially if the knowledge flow is generated under conditions of relatively independent scholarship. It's a problem when concentrations of state and economic power, especially in conditions of radical political and economic inequality, define the terms of knowledge. That inequality is most evident in the production, distribution, consumption, and consequence of energy and its dominant knowledge flows. It's difficult to imagine more important knowledge networks of consequence than those around energy, especially ones that are independent of vested interests in their most dangerous forms. But it's critical.

The energy question is a specific example, which in turn reflects the world of knowledge. There are no general intellectuals whose pronouncements on truth, goodness, and beauty can satisfy the needs for expertise in those judgments. At the same time, we need more than ever to develop capacities to figure ways of assigning priorities that go beyond the influence of wealth and power and of specialized intellectual interests and ethnocentrisms of all sorts. It's good to have the culture of critical discourse in our discursive repertoire, but it's perhaps more important to figure how we can develop knowledge networks in cultural formations that put intellectual and institutional responsibility at the core of those formations' constitutions.

In the Preface, I asked us to imagine how much poorer the world would be if racism, class privilege, and art music arrogance had managed to repress the globalization of jazz music. In the end, I invite you to consider what cultural formations are now being suppressed that might not only enhance our lives but enable our survival.

That quest might start by looking for rearticulations of globalizing knowledge among intellectuals, universities, networks, and publics in transformation.

Notes

Chapter 1

1. For those who are interested more in the particulars of this volume and its applications, you might wish to review the Preface and then move to this chapter's final section to read the book's organization to consider which particular engagements you might wish to read first. For those interested only in the implications and consequences of these various explorations, the final two chapters should suffice. But for those who wish to understand the scholarly context of my study, you should continue on and think more about what we mean by knowledge and its relationship to global transformations.

2. I generally learn a great deal from my students, but in this instance, I am particularly indebted to the work of Lucy Bates-Campbell, who drew my attention to these works seeking to measure just that consensus. See Oreskes (2004); Oreskes and Conway (2010); and Shwed and Bearman (2010).

3. Some might have called this a golden calf rather than a straitjacket. Hopkins (2001, 11), for example, identified globalization as a religious system itself with the World Trade Organization, international banks, and monopoly capitalist corporations its trinity.

4. The Leading Global Network of Research Universities for the 21st Century, accessed July 8, 2014, www.universitas21.com.

5. This individual focus may be quite appropriate, but Bhargava (2002) also cautioned that to miss the collective misses an opportunity to halt further cycles of violence.

6. When I began this work at the turn of the century, as far as we could tell, my research assistant, Lisa Fein, and I found only one other publication using the term "globalizing knowledge" (Cornwell and Stoddard 1999).

7. Whenever I use this term now, I can only think about how my colleague Greg Elliot (2009) has developed a research program around mattering.

8. I especially appreciate, therefore, how Kumu (a Hawaiian term of respect) Ramsay Taum (2013) works to make those connections not only in his native Hawaii but elsewhere too, as seen at his website, "Ancient Wisdom Future Knowledge," www.ramsaytaum.

9. Reading Mannheim as the founding father against whom subsequent generations rebel provides one kind of reading; another is to read him in his time, most notably in his difference with György Lukács, as King and Szelenyi (2004, 42–44) do.

10. In his prodigious contributions to sociology one might find resonance with a great deal that is today quite important in this field of sociology, notably in explorations of semantics, rhetoric, and ideas (H. Zuckerman 2010; Camic 2010; Simonson 2010).

11. Their debate shaped the conclusion to Kennedy (1991).

12. Thanks to Marilyn Rueschemeyer for organizing the collection in which that essay appeared and which moved me to think more explicitly about my thirty-year-old approach to knowledge and change.

13. "Communism's Negotiated Collapse: The Polish Roundtable of 1989, Ten Years Later," a conference at the University of Michigan, April 7–10, 1999, http://webapps.lsa.umich.edu/ii/polishroundtable/program.html.

14. Thanks to Keith Brown for the suggestion I review Marcus's work.

15. I named this list for the first time in Kennedy (2013a); I draw on that piece for the elaboration of Sewell that follows.

16. Taylor (2009) uses this frame to explain Habermas's importance.

Chapter 2

1. This elevation of wittiness over truthfulness seems augmented with social media and online journalism, as Balaghi (2012) suggests. Those like Slavoj Žižek in the older generation and Evgeney Morozov in the younger, each of whom might be accused of harboring more than a little intellectual ambition, are frequently derided by critics for being too absurd to be serious (Hari 2007; Meyer 2014).

2. It is especially difficult to find the right qualifiers to express the value of moving beyond local, regional, and national reference. Global, international, and cosmopolitan all have their limits. While I had worked with "worldly" before, even during graduate school, it was only during Nick Dirks's (2012) presentation that it finally clicked as the most appropriate descriptor for this chapter's ambition.

3. Eric Hobsbawm passed away as I worked on later versions of this chapter. Reminiscences of him reinforce many points here about the Marxist intellectual—praised for his erudition but disturbed by blind spots around communist rule in the USSR, he embodied the complexities of this kind of intellectuality. Later in 2012 another intellectual giant passed—Albert Hirschman. In reminiscences about him, there were no

ambivalences registered, only laments that his breadth was a likely reason for his not winning the Nobel Prize in Economics.

4. Kennedy and Suny (1999) elaborate many of this section's themes with greater bibliographic reference.

5. See Znaniecki (1986, 91–163) on religious intellectuals more generally.

6. As usual, Ivan Szelenyi is an exception that proves the rule. King and Szelenyi (2004) argue that the history of the twentieth century can be read as a contest by different kinds of intellectuals over access to power. In typically ironic fashion, they propose, "While there is good reason to be skeptical about whether the New Class is a class at all, the application of the method of class analysis to intellectuals—or to put it more generally, to those who have claims for power and privilege based on the grounds of knowledge monopoly—is at least insightful" (xii).

7. Of course, these neat sociological categorizations can be challenged through the prism of life stories (Franklin 2009).

8. Including Berkeley; Chicago; Harvard; Wisconsin–Madison; Michigan; Yale; Duke; North Carolina; UCLA; UC, Davis; UC, San Diego; Northwestern; University of Pennsylvania; New York University; Columbia University; and Washington.

9. Kennedy wrote in emails to prospective respondents the following between June 10 and June 19, 2004:

> Together with Miguel Centeno, I am writing a chapter for the ASA Centennial history of sociology in America on international dimensions of American sociology. You can imagine the challenge, and therefore we seek your help, given your prominence in defining American sociology's extra-US scholarship. Improvising on Contemporary Sociology's question nearly a decade ago, we are asking you and several others the following question:
>
> Beyond your own contributions, which five books or articles, published in the last fifty years by those working in American sociology, are the most important contributions to scholarship in your field?
>
> Of course we recognize that you might define your field in several different ways thematically and regionally, but we also hope you might humor us, and suggest the best work in American sociology whose data and/or perspective are grounded outside the US, whose scholarship has been important in its own field, and whose value might be recognized even more broadly.

10. That challenge is also evident in the Arab Council of Social Sciences. Consider their own initial formulation of new paradigms at "New Paradigms Factory," ACSS, accessed July 19, 2014, http://www.theacss.org/pages/new-paradigms-factory.

11. I am especially reminded here of the ways in which the Egyptian military in 2011 prohibited mention of their own property-based power. See Abul-Magd (2011).

12. Verdery (1991) elaborates the communist counterpoint clearly.

13. Jürgen Habermas (2009) extends this tradition of disdain for the celebrity intellectual nicely and, more positively, suggests what sets her apart:

What is ultimately supposed to distinguish intellectuals from clever journalists is less the mode of presentation than the privilege of having to deal with public issues only as a sideline. They are supposed to speak out only when current events are threatening to spin out of control—but then promptly, as an early warning system.

With this we come to the sole ability which could still set intellectuals apart today, namely an avantgardistic instinct for relevances. They have to be able to get worked up about critical developments while others are still absorbed in business as usual. This calls for quite unheroic virtues:

• a mistrustful sensitivity to damage to the normative infrastructure of the polity;

• the anxious anticipation of threats to the mental resources of the shared political form of life;

• the sense for what is lacking and "could be otherwise";

• a spark of imagination in conceiving of alternatives;

• and a modicum of the courage required for polarizing, provoking, and pamphleteering.

That is—and always has been—more easily said than done. The intellectual should have the ability to get worked up—and yet should have sufficient political judgment not to overreact. What their critics—from Max Weber and Schumpeter to Gehlen and Schelsky—reproach them with is the persistent accusation of "sterile enthusiasm" and "alarmism." They should not let themselves be intimidated by this reproach.

14. For Ferguson's location in a particular political trajectory, see Balaghi (2011a).

15. Losing intellectual rigor is an especially serious crime when accused by someone with generally superior scholarly credentials as Paul Krugman (2012). Ferguson's rant about John Maynard Keynes, suggesting that his sexuality could have explained his intellectual limitations, drew even more outrage in public commentaries (e.g., Yglesias 2013).

16. Exemplified by the MacArthur Fellows Program (http://www.macfound.org/programs/fellows/).

17. "Mark Blyth on Austerity," September 30, 2010, http://www.youtube.com/watch?v=go2bVGioReE. When I came to direct the Watson Institute for International Studies, one of its distinctive capacities resided in its relatively advanced use of new media for getting out the scholarly message. Given my commitments to public engagement, I enthusiastically supported that use; Blyth's success on video and its effect on his book's reception reinforce the wisdom of that decision back in the fall of 2010. But he was a hard act to follow. Celebrity is made not only with media but with performative capacities alongside. He is unusual among scholars for his Scotsman wittiness.

18. This was the cover of the October 2005 issue of *Prospect*. Twenty-five thousand people voted in the poll. "The Prospect/FP Top 100 Public Intellectuals," http://www.infoplease.com/spot/topintellectuals.html#ixzz1vvNMNDpt.

19. The following section on *Jadaliyya* draws on Kennedy (2012b).

20. *Jadaliyya*, 2014, http://www.jadaliyya.com/pages/about.

21. Julia Elyachar's observation that *Jadaliyya* publishes work associated "with the best of anthropology—in the moment, grounded in theory, capturing historical transformation through engagement in events as they unfold" is a compliment to the ezine as well as to the kind of anthropology of which she is a part (Haddad 2012).

22. The "hits" are based on the number of likes/recommendations. Those numbers might have been compromised for some posts because of updates and earlier changes to the sites. Thanks to Bassam Haddad for this information (pers. comm., February 2, 2012).

23. "Slavs and Tatars: Work About," accessed July 22, 2014, http://slavsandtatars.com/bio.php.

24. Judt (1998) discusses Blum's example at length.

25. One normally finds juxtapositions of such figures in discussions of "political leadership." For example, it is not surprising to find Presidents Lagos and Havel joining Cardoso, Brundtland, Gorbachev, de Klerk, Musharraf, Barak, Clinton, Carter, Schmidt, Goh Chok Tong, and Paul John Keating in Till (2011). One would not attribute intellectual reference to most names on that list.

26. I draw upon Kennedy (2000c) for my account of Havel.

27. The number of his plays, including *The Garden Party* (1963), *The Memorandum* (1965), *The Audience* (1975), and some dozen others, defies simple summary. However, I would suggest that his plays invite us to see normal life with a different eye, to recognize its absurdity and the dangers posed by simple resolution to the problems Havel's plots, and our lives, suggest. Both *The Memorandum* and *The Garden Party* remind us that clichés can organize life (Havel 1990, 193–95).

28. Ricardo Lagos's life has been the object of some critical studies, including that by Peter Winn (2007). I expect, however, that his 2012 autobiography will likely produce more extensive engagements. I draw on that 2012 volume, as well as the conversations I had with him as he composed it, for the paragraphs that follow.

29. Lagos, pers. comm., October 7, 2013, elaborating on Lagos (2012b, 22).

30. Some identify it as more cautious than other parts of the Latin American Left. Although Roberts (2011, 342) contrasted Lagos's approach with a more traditional socialism's concern for property relations, his account of Lagos's accomplishments indicates his intellectual roots: "In sharp contrast to Socialist Party practices in the past, then, Lagos's strategy for improving the welfare of workers did not rely on organizational power and collective action. Instead, it promoted individual worker rights, mobility, and capacitation. This strategy was designed not only to position workers more favorably in Chile's market driven economic boom, but also augment the contribution of human capital to the nation's economic development."

31. Recognition shifted in 2013. Ghani was identified as the second most important "world thinker" by *Prospect* magazine. "World Thinkers 2013," *Prospect*, April 24, 2013, http://www.prospectmagazine.co.uk/magazine/world-thinkers-2013/.

32. Nermeen Shaikh of the Asia Society, "Ashraf Ghani on the Prospects for Peace in Afghanistan," accessed July 19, 2014, http://asiasociety.org/policy-politics/strategic-challenges/us-asia/ashraf-ghani-prospects-peace-afghanistan.

33. http://ashrafghani.af/campaign/archives/5. [no longer available, accessed June 10, 2011]

34. The World Bank, "Community-Driven Development," 2014, http://www.worldbank.org/en/topic/communitydrivendevelopment.

Chapter 3

1. Thanks to Ira Katznelson for telling me about this report.

2. For example, the National Center for Public Policy and Higher Education, July 20, 2012, http://www.highereducation.org/.

3. For a subtle critique and alternative view of this process, see Schriewer (2004).

4. University-Discoveries.com, "Discoveries & Innovation That Changed the World," accessed July 22, 2014, www.university-discoveries.com.

5. I draw on Kennedy (2011c) in parts of the following sections.

6. The methods undertaken for that internationalization vary and have consequence (Charle, 2004b).

7. Among the insider accounts most worth reading on this era, see Biddle (2002) and Hudzik (2011).

8. Bowen (2004), Walder (2004), Szanton (2004), and Dirks (2004) emphasize the importance of particular places for specific area studies developments—Columbia and Harvard for Russian studies, Cornell for Southeast Asian Studies, University of Pennsylvania and University of Chicago for South Asian studies, and the University of Michigan and Harvard for China studies.

9. As is evident from his scholarly production, Richard Nisbett has been developing this theory in association with East Asian colleagues and students for years (e.g., 2007a, 2007b; and T. Masuda et al. 2008).

10. For the following section, I draw on Kennedy (2010c).

11. T. Anthony Jones guided me down this path at the start of my academic career. See, for example, Connar, Powell, and Jones (1991).

12. See the International and Foreign Language Education / International Resource Information System, accessed July 22, 2014, http://iris.ed.gov/iris/ieps/.

13. In the following section, I draw on Kennedy and Weiner (2003).

14. This section benefits considerably from the Ford Foundation–sponsored May 2002 Seminar on Expertise at the University of Michigan. For some of the results of that seminar, see Cohen (2001). I also drew very much on my own collaborations with various professional school colleagues: Doug Kelbaugh, then dean of the Taubman College of Architecture and Urban Planning; and Scott Campbell, from the faculty of the Urban and Regional Planning Program, Taubman College of Architecture and Urban Planning; Rosina Bierbaum, then dean of the School of Natural Resources and Environments, University of Michigan, and with other faculty colleagues in the

School; Sioban Harlow of the School of Public Health, and then also associate director of the International Institute; David Stern, then director of the Global Reach Program at the University of Michigan Medical School; Linda Lim of the Business School and then associate director of the International Institute; and Brad Farnsworth, director of the Center for International Business Education. I also drew from the various articles we published in the International Institute's journal.

15. These rankings are always problematic; we didn't necessarily endorse the accuracy of these rankings by using them. We used them only to reflect one set of conventions apparently operating in the establishment of quality. We might have considered a number of other professions, e.g., social work, nursing, agriculture, journalism, and education. We chose these professions simply because they represented an important range of fields whose focus might be international, whose resources are sufficiently limited, and whose field is sufficiently close to area studies that they might be influenced by a new area studies strategy for the professions.

16. http://loohooloo.mit.edu/vision/index.html. [no longer available, accessed March 1, 2003]

17. http://www.yale.edu/forestry/about/message.html. [no longer available, accessed March 1, 2003]

18. http://www.yale.edu/forestry/about/message.html. [no longer available, accessed March 1, 2003]

19. http://arch.ced.berkeley.edu/people/faculty/faculty_intro.htm. [no longer available, accessed March 1, 2003]

20. http://www.jhsph.edu/globalchange/. [no longer available, accessed March 1, 2003]

21. http://www.law.stanford.edu/international/courses.html. [no longer available, accessed March 1, 2003]

22. http://www.law.yale.edu/outside/html/Centers/cen-schellctr.htm. [no longer available, accessed March 1, 2003]

23. http://www.law.nyu.edu/programs/globalpublicservice/. [no longer available, accessed March 1, 2003]

24. http://www.law.umich.edu/curriculum/externshipsandindependantstudy/. [no longer available, accessed March 1, 2003] See "Measure of America," SSRC, accessed July 5, 2014, http://www.ssrc.org/programs/moa/.

25. http://www.law.umich.edu/CentersAndPrograms/cicl/international/center.htm. [no longer available, accessed March 1, 2003]

26. Yale Law School, "The China Center," accessed March 1, 2003, http://www.law.yale.edu/intellectuallife/ChinaLawCenter.htm.

27. *Bulletin of Yale University*, accessed March 1, 2003, http://www.yale.edu/bulletin/html2002/law/lecture.html.

28. Michigan Law, University of Michigan Law School, accessed March 1, 2003, http://www.law.umich.edu/centersandprograms/pral.

29. http://www.law.nyu.edu/magazines/autumn01/nylsm68–87.pdf. [no longer available, accessed March 1, 2003]

30. Wharton, University of Pennsylvania, homepage, accessed March 1, 2003, http://www.wharton.edu/.

31. This section benefits substantially from conversations with David Stern, director of the Global Reach Program at the University of Michigan Medical School.

32. http://www.hms.harvard.edu/hmi/about/index.html. [no longer available, accessed March 1, 2003]

33. http://www.uphs.upenn.edu/oimp/. [no longer available, accessed March 1, 2003]

34. http://www.med.umich.edu/obgyn/resdir/research.html. [no longer available, accessed March 1, 2003]

35. Some fields have always been international, e.g., naval architecture and marine engineering, given the business for which they work and the global locations of their clients. Korean, Russian, and other national schools of engineering have made this field global in its epistemic community.

36. http://www2.sis.pitt.edu/aboutSIS/missions.html. [no longer available, accessed March 1, 2003]

37. http://www.si.umich.edu/about-SI/mission.htm (emphasis added). [no longer available, accessed March 1, 2003]

38. The Center for Research on Collaboratories and Technology Enhanced Learning Communities, accessed June 30, 2003, cotelco.net.

39. Of course, historians and others explore more satisfactorily the complexities in Russia's relationship to Islam (e.g., Yemelianova 2002; Crews 2006).

40. I draw on a much more extended treatment of her play for this section (Kennedy 2004c).

Chapter 4

1. This section draws substantially on my account for a Ukrainian sociological audience (Kennedy 2009).

2. I rely on the reprinted and adapted version for citations here: Michael Burawoy (2007a).

3. Burawoy's early work focused on social relations on the shop floor, but he reports, wryly, that his fieldwork is in the university now that he can no longer serve as a factory worker. See www.burawoy.berkeley.edu.

4. Burawoy is able to do this in part because he teaches in one of the most prominent sociology departments in the United States. They present an intriguing history of public sociology at Berkeley here: http://publicsociology.berkeley.edu/. His students are also among the most successful in American sociology job markets. See Burawoy et al. (2000) and Burawoy et al. (1991), featuring the work of his contemporary students.

5. This section draws on several earlier pieces: Kennedy (2012b, 2012f, 2011c).

6. http://futurechallenges.org/in-focus/this-is-how-the-occupy-movement-spread/. [no longer available, accessed February 2, 2012]

7. Possible Futures: A Project of the Social Science Research Council, accessed July 10, 2012, http://www.possible-futures.org/.

8. For example, Occupy University, accessed July 10, 2012, http://university.nycga.net/.

9. Tent City University, "Anyone Can Teach, Everyone Can Learn—Occupy London," accessed October 1, 2012, http://tentcityuniversity.org/.

10. And was exemplified at this symposium: Public Knowledge—"The Public University in the 21st Century," a conference at Rutgers University Center for Cultural Analysis, February 24, 2012, organized by Meredith McGill and her colleagues, http://cca.rutgers.edu/events/icalrepeat.detail/2012/02/24/124/23|28/public-knowledge-qthe-public-university-in-the-21st-centuryq.

11. MSNBC, *The Ed Show*, "The Ed Show for Tuesday November 22, 2011," http://www.nbcnews.com/id/45418070/ns/msnbc-the_ed_show/t/ed-show-tuesday-november-p/#.U85nuajTM7A.

12. In the following section, I draw upon portions of Kennedy (2006).

13. *Minerva Controversy Essay Forum*, contributors: Robert Albro, Thomas Asher, Paul Bracken, Victor P. Corona, Faisal Devji, David C. Engerman, Saad Eskander, Conor Gearty, Hugh Gusterson, Alain Joxe, Ronald R. Krebs, Catherine Lutz, Tom Mahnken, David Nugent, Ron Robin, Ian Roxborough, Priya Satia, and John Tirman, Social Science Research Council, 2008, http://www.ssrc.org/publications/view/minerva-controversy-essay-forum/.

14. "The Minerva Controversy," Social Science Research Council, 2008, http://essays.ssrc.org/minerva/.

15. This is especially true when there are real proximities, not only ideological affinities. Consider, for example, the extensive engagement at the University of Kansas with the army, given the forty miles that separate it from Fort Leavenworth (Diepenbrock 2012).

16. I draw upon Kennedy (2011c) for the following section.

17. The *Brown Political Review* obtained the transcript of that talk, which is available at http://www.brownpoliticalreview.org/2013/12/ray-kellys-leaked-brown-university-speech/.

18. This was also distributed on Facebook: https://www.facebook.com/notes/elizabeth-castelli/letter-to-christina-paxson-president-of-brown-university-on-ray-kellys-appearanc/10152069041869180.

19. Although the episode in James Hynes (1997) on Captain Cook's conference is fictional, it is only slightly masked, referring to a conference on culture one of my colleagues organized at the University of Michigan. Hynes misses the major drama in that conference, however: one of the university's clerical staff challenged the organizer's representation of race and gender in using a Benetton poster to promote the conference. That clash illuminated the typical presumption of faculty superiority in articulating cultural representations of university life, and the exceptional quality of staff resistance to that practice.

20. This assumption can break down to the extent that geographic mobility is likely, and quality of education allows graduates to move beyond state borders. This

definition of public seems anachronistic on an academic level, but it remains absolutely critical to the definition of the public university in real politics, especially to the public university that is both dependent on state expenditures and primarily focused on training students for state civic and economic futures.

21. The University of Michigan was exceptionally explicit on this with its Public Goods Council made up of museums, libraries, performance programs, experiential learning, and other programs serving constituencies within and beyond the university. See The Public Goods Council, "Promoting Academic Collaboration," University of Michigan, 2006, http://www.provost.umich.edu/publicgoods/promot.htm. [no longer available, accessed July 25, 2007]

22. The shame Pennsylvania State University has faced in light of its failure to respect the law and to honor human dignity in order to preserve the power and privilege of its football team illustrates the dangers to institutional legitimacy and integrity this kind of public engagement can bring. The ensuing debate about NCAA sanctions and the posthumous demotion of the football coach Joe Paterno illustrates the centrality of sports to US public culture and its complex articulation with knowledge institutions. Sociologists have taken this instance as an opportunity to discuss sexual assaults and institutional protection of assailants (e.g., Goswami 2012; Mattheau 2011).

23. Beat the Streets—Providence, accessed July 22, 2014, http://www.beatthestreets-pvd.org/.

24. I am especially grateful to my students Billy Watterson and Phil Marano for all they have taught me about the program and the grit it inspires among their wrestlers.

25. Swearer Center for Public Service, Brown University, accessed July 22, 2014, http://brown.edu/academics/college/special-programs/public-service/.

26. Perhaps for her background or as a result of the past challenging relations between the university and the city, or both, Brown University's new president, Christina Paxson, made integrative learning and connections across the city, state, and the world central to the university strategic plan she presented in the fall of 2013: http://www.brown.edu/web/documents/BuildingOnDistinctionOct262013.pdf. The regularity of her apparent collaboration with Providence mayor Angel Tavares symbolizes that shift (Paxson and Tavares 2012).

27. "The Economic Impact of Brown University," Brown University, 2014, http://brown.edu/about/reports/economic-impact/.

28. "Public Sociology, Live!," International Sociological Association, accessed July 22, 2014, http://www.isa-sociology.org/public-sociology-live/.

29. "Public Sociology, Live!," International Sociological Association, March 8, 2012, https://www.facebook.com/groups/259654060772916.

30. Michael D. Kennedy, "Burawoy and Public Sociology at Central European University: A Video with Summary," Academia.edu, 2012, http://www.academia.edu/3762795/_2012_Burawoy_and_Public_Sociology_at_Central_European_University_a_Video_with_Summary.

Chapter 5

1. Her discussion of the rootedness of knowledge in her Australian lands reminds me of how Ramsay Remigius Mahealani Taum (2013) has explained to me the rootedness of indigenous knowledge cultures in Hawaii (interview, September 1, 2012) and how Osorio (2002) emphasizes dispossession rather than societal development as history's dynamic.

2. It is true that there are many eminent Polish sociologists whose recognition is not principally associated with the study of Polish society and whose Polish inspiration remains implicit. Consider, for example, that Florian Znaniecki's (1954) only publication in the *American Sociological Review*, his 1954 American Sociological Association presidential address, mentioned Poland only with reference to his publications in Polish. It is also obvious, however, to those who know something of Polish history, that his interpretation of world society and his concern for the iron curtain's effect on sociology most obviously reflect his Polish experience.

3. Most evident in the project at www.engagingafghanistan.org, initially conceived by Shiva Balaghi, whose support I recognize for extending my sociological imagination in a very particular way.

4. In this, I pursue a similar method to that of Schriewer (2004), discovered only after the fact.

5. The journals consulted in this search included *Academy of Management Journal, Administrative Science Quarterly, Annals of the American Academy of Political and Social Science, American Journal of Sociology, American Sociological Review, British Journal of Educational Studies, British Journal of Sociology, Comparative Studies in Society and History, Family Coordinator, Industrial and Labor Relations Review, Journal of Black Studies, Journal of Health and Social Behavior, Journal of Human Resources, Journal of Marriage and the Family, Journal of Modern African Studies, Law & Society Review, Public Opinion Quarterly, Social Forces, Social Problems, Sociology of Education, Sociometry, MERIP Reports, Sociological Methodology, Contemporary Sociology, Journal of Health and Human Behavior, Social Science History, Social Psychology, Social Psychology Quarterly, Political Behavior, Family Relations, European Sociological Review, Theory and Society, Annual Review of Sociology, Academy of Management Review, Journal of Palestine Studies, Sociological Theory, Sociological Forum, Journal of Educational Sociology, Marriage and Family Living, Family Life Coordinator, MERIP Middle East Report, Gender and Society, Middle East Report, Journal of Social Forces,* and *Academy of Management Journal.* In this chapter, I added the *International Journal of Comparative Sociology.*

6. Time is not the only structure limiting scholarship. Because my own grounding rests primarily in the US academy, and English-language scholarly world secondarily, my journal reference group is guided by those conventions. I am not alone in this, given how, even here, "international" journals are often identified as those published in English in Western countries. That, by itself, needs to be analyzed further, but I put aside that problem here.

7. My research assistant Steven Damiano built on my earlier method and improved it, following this approach:

> Through JSTOR's advanced search function, which allows users to look for words that appear in electronically stored issues of journals, I searched through a selected list of sociology-connected journals for instances where the words *Afghan* or *Afghanistan* appeared between 1890 and 2009. To increase the number of journals I used, I took advantage of SAGE Journals' search feature to look for mentions of Afghan or Afghanistan in the *International Journal of Comparative Sociology* (*IJCS*) between the journal's first year of publication, 1960, and 2009. I then added the results from the JSTOR and *IJCS* searches to get the total number of journal sections (articles, reviews, comments, front matter, back matter, intros, new book lists, etc.) where my search terms were mentioned. To understand the significance of these results, I performed the same type of search with other nations and nationalities.
>
> To capture potential turning points where I thought Afghanistan's place in American sociology might change, I divided my search results into five eras: 1890–1946, the post–World War II era until the start of the Soviet Union's disintegration (1947–1989), the Soviet Occupation of Afghanistan (1980–1989), the long decade when the international community abandoned Afghanistan and the Taliban rose to power (1990–2001), and post-Bonn Conference Afghanistan (2002–2009).
>
> In order to compare Afghanistan's place in American sociology compared to Poland's and Kosovo's, I exported to Refworks the citations for all the articles in my JSTOR and *IJCS* searches where Poland, Polish, Afghanistan, Afghan, Yugoslavia, Albania, or Kosovo was mentioned. Through Refworks, I ordered the citations for each nation by publication in order to see the degree to which each journal paid attention to these three nations.

8. Lenski, Noland, and Lenski (1995, 9) even defined societies according to political autonomy and broad range of cooperative activities.

9. The journals consulted in this search included *Foreign Affairs, Global Governance, International Affairs, International Security, International Studies Quarterly, International Studies Review, Journal of Peace Research, New Perspectives Quarterly, Political Science Quarterly, Review of International Studies, Third World Quarterly, World Affairs, World Policy Journal, Foreign Policy, International Organization, World Politics,* and *Journal of Conflict Resolution.*

10. The journals consulted in this search included *American Ethnologist, Anthropological Quarterly, Anthropology Today, Anthropos, Asian Folklore Studies, Cultural Anthropology, Ethnology, Human Ecology, Man, Southwestern Journal of Anthropology, American Anthropologist, Annual Review of Anthropology, Anthropology and Education Quarterly, Comparative Studies in Society and History, Current Anthropology, Ethnohistory, Medical Anthropology Quarterly,* and *Medical Anthropology Newsletter.*

11. In my previous study of Poland in the sociological imagination, I did not include India as a place sociologists study, nor did I consider how Yugoslavia/Kosovo/

Albania or Afghanistan fared. While the latter cases might be explicable because of their relative scarcity of attention, India's absence is, frankly, inexplicable given how much the India example shaped international studies and informed my own engagement of Poland, evident here in Kennedy (1999b). Thanks to work with Steve Damiano, this was rectified.

12. However, it has become increasingly like the United States, at least in comparison to Ukraine (Kohn et al. 1997). On the other hand, Galasinska and Galasinski (2010) argue that Eastern Europe, and Poland in particular, is still terra incognita for other Europeans to their west.

13. Not all sociologists treat it that way. In an article dedicated to recognizing and understanding the unprecedented, Baehr (2002, 824) wondered whether the war in Kosova fell into that distinctive category.

14. Many English-language volumes were addressing the war around Kosova. Many Kosovar colleagues will mention Mertus (1999), but volumes like hers hardly affected the American sociological imagination.

15. This scholarship is more apparent in journals associated with area studies or in publications connected to international development assistance in the region. These alternative outlets thus make available scholarly discussion and public engagement. However, their influence on more globalizing scholarly knowledge is limited by the regionally limited audience of most area studies and development studies publications. For an example of that important scholarship in area studies, see Pula (2004).

16. Although external causes are most commonly used to explain the ultimate failure of the nonviolent movement, some fault the quality of Rugova's leadership itself. Maliqi (2000), for example, argues that his commitments were less elaborated than they ought to have been and were more pragmatic than philosophical and thus more easily eroded. He also writes, "In strengthening his position as a leader, it was not his personal capacities, the depth and power of his thought, nor his leadership and political skills. Of the greatest significance for Rugova's political position and authority among the masses was the support that he gained—from the very moment he stepped into (the) political scene—from international factors, primarily from the US and from European powers."

17. I appreciate what I have learned from Gezim Selaci in this regard. He is working on this subject for his Central European University dissertation.

18. Albanian speakers do number among linguists and linguistic anthropologists, including Victor Friedman at the University of Chicago and Frances Trix at Indiana University. Their scholarship does not appear in the publications I surveyed because they tend to publish in linguistics or area studies journals and edited volumes, and their monographs are not typically reviewed in the journals I considered. In this exception, therefore, my point is extended: the social sciences and international affairs hardly attend to the area studies expertise of those even with exceptionally distinctive abilities. Consider, for example, how valuable V. Friedman (2012) could be.

19. Besnik Pula is one of the most prominent in sociology; he is, however, joining the Virginia Polytechnic Institute and State University political science department in 2014.

20. Its cultural terms are among the most interesting, too, especially concerning how social issues and artistic work blend (Heta and Osmani 2011).

21. University of Prishtina sociologist Shemsi Krasniqi (2010) has conducted extensive research to understand the social dynamics of this flight to safety during 1998–99.

22. I am indebted in this section to Shiva Balaghi for being my co-principal investigator for the project "Engaging Afghanistan" and to Steve Damiano for providing exceptional research assistance that made this section much better than it would have been otherwise. Finally, the SSRC provided the support for both the broader project and the research assistance itself. I am enormously appreciative of all.

23. The following selection draws on Kennedy (2011a).

24. In what follows, I draw on Kennedy (1999b).

25. Małgorzata Fuszara, Renata Siemińska, and Anna Titkow were the Polish sociologists of gender who most often appeared on the global stage in those days. See Gal and Kligman (2000) for one of the most important volumes to facilitate that conversation in those times.

26. I initially learned about Femen from my friend and colleague Tatyana Bureychak, whose analysis remains among the most powerful I have seen.

27. I learn a great deal from my students, but I am particularly indebted to Julia Ellis-Kahana, whose engagement of Femen in my course on knowledge and change altered how I thought about celebrity and positive change. Indeed, her sense of the movement's increasingly destructive ways bears reflection (Ellis-Kahana 2012).

Chapter 6

1. I suggested, "The Watson Institute is a leading center for research and teaching on the most important problems of our time, especially issues of inequality and insecurity in an increasingly complex world. Understanding the conditions and consequences of the flows of knowledge, people, wealth, and weapons across global contexts, the Watson works to improve policies and the public's contributions and media to making a better world." See Office of Global Engagement, The Watson Institute for International Studies, Brown University, accessed June 30, 2014, http://www.brown.edu/about/administration/global-engagement/programs/watson-institute-international-studies.

2. Some of those who seek to transform universities in line with the emergent organization of knowledge recognize this (Page 2012).

3. If you don't, see Gessen (2014).

4. One can find the video in a number of places. See "The 'Punk Prayer'" (2012).

5. "Pussy Riot: A Punk Prayer," Amnesty International, 2013, http://www.amnestyusa.org/our-work/campaigns/individuals-at-risk/pussy-riot-punk-prayer.

6. *Art Review* magazine put Pussy Riot at number 57 on a list of the 100 most influential figures in the art world for 2012; of course, naming them also put *Art Review* in the mainstream press (Associated Press 2012).

7. "UN-Energy Knowledge Network," The United Nations Inter-Agency Mechanism on Energy, accessed July 22, 2014, http://www.un-energy.org/.

8. See GENI: Global Energy Network Institute, 2013, http://www.geni.org/globalenergy/about_us/mission/index.shtml, for a view that links energy security to sustainability; for a way to see energy security in relationship to additional values, see ExxonMobil Perspective, "Energy Security," accessed July 22, 2014, http://www.exxonmobilperspectives.com/category/energy-security.

9. In the wake of the Gulf of Mexico oil spill disaster, on March 23, 2010, BP's Tony Hayward offered a speech on energy security through diversity. See Tony Hayward, "Energy Security through Diversity," Peterson Institute for International Economics, Speeches and Papers, March 23, 2010, http://www.iie.com/publications/papers/paper.cfm?ResearchID=1521.

10. The debate about the Keystone XL pipeline exemplified the importance of environmental issues and an occasion when those interests could become more important in energy security's definition. At the same time, the political debate relied on a complex mix of rhetorical excess and knowledge claims. See Levi (2012).

11. See US Energy Information Administration, Independent Statistics and Analysis, accessed July 22, 2014, http://205.254.135.7/countries/.

12. See the Masdar: A Mubadala Company home page, accessed July 22, 2014, http://www.masdar.ae/en/Menu/Index.aspx?MenuID=42&mnu=Pri.

13. One might consider this publication to be a principal public artifact of energy culture, much as I treated the World Bank's publication *From Plan to Market* as a key artifact for transition culture (Kennedy 2002a). For a discussion of the International Energy Agency (IEA), see Kohl (2010).

14. The members include Australia, Austria, Belgium, Canada, Czech Republic, Denmark, Finland, France, Germany, Greece, Hungary, Ireland, Italy, Japan, Luxembourg, Netherlands, New Zealand, Norway, Poland, Portugal, Republic of Korea, Slovak Republic, Spain, Sweden, Switzerland, Turkey, United Kingdom, and the United States. The European Commission participates in the work of IEA.

15. "Energy from Abroad," European Commission, March 22, 2013, http://ec.europa.eu/energy/international/russia/russia_en.htm.

16. To understand its politics in these conventional terms is only the most evident dimension of its qualities beyond energy; for a substantial discussion of its material qualities, see Barry (2013).

17. We are fortunate that more scholars are considering Russian energy not only in geopolitical terms but also in more cultural political frameworks. See, for example, Rogers (2012).

18. I generally learn a great deal from my students, but in this instance, I am particularly indebted to the work of Hannah Braun (2013). Her analysis of this institute and its network ties moves and informs my own account.

19. The Oxford Institute for Energy Studies, 2014, http://www.oxfordenergy.org/.

20. I have recently learned about a most promising development, the founding of the first center to connect the human sciences to the energy question at Rice

University: Jeff Falk, "New Rice University Center Is First to Connect Human Sciences, Energy, Environmental Research," Rice University News & Media, April 30, 2013, http://news.rice.edu/2013/04/30/new-rice-university-center-is-first-to-connect-human-sciences-energy-environmental-research/.

21. It would be important to analyze the networks of energy expertise, especially in order to recognize their resemblance to those networks that characterize energy corporations' boards of directors in the emergent global order (De Graaff 2012).

22. Although there are other examples, Public Citizen: Protecting Health, Safety and Democracy does have a climate and energy campaign, but it is focused mostly on its environmental, not its economic, impacts (accessed July 22, 2014, http://www.citizen.org/cmep/).

23. To develop this public engagement, print journalist Dimiter Kenarov and video journalist Steve Sapienza traveled across Pennsylvania and Ohio talking about their work and comparisons between the United States and Eastern Europe in this regard. See Dimiter Kenarov and Stephen Sapienza, "Shale Reporter Launches Shale Gas: From Poland to Pennsylvania Project," Pulitzer Center on Crisis Reporting, January 28, 2013, http://pulitzercenter.org/blog/shalereporter.com-launches-shale-gas-poland-pennsylvania-project-calkins-media-fracking.

24. Brown University was among the early mobilizers; it is difficult to anticipate the movement's trajectory based on Brown Divest Coal's experience, but it is illustrative. See Brown Divest Coal, accessed July 22, 2014, http://browndivestcoal.org/campaign-history/.

25. Consider, for example, just how much further ahead the World Bank is in its institutional engagement of social media than are most universities. See Jim Rosenberg, "How the World Bank Learned to Stop Worrying and Love Social Media," May 2013, http://www.slideshare.net/jerotus/world-bank-social-media-summary-jim-rosenberg-may-2013.

26. MIT Media Lab, accessed July 22, 2014, http://www.media.mit.edu/.

27. GlobalVoices, accessed July 22, 2014, http://globalvoicesonline.org/.

Chapter 7

1. I very much appreciate informal communications from Ann Pendleton-Jullian and John Seely Brown on this matter, as well as their willingness to share not-yet-published materials with me.

2. Universitas 21: The Leading Global Network of Research Universities for the 21st Century, accessed July 8, 2014, www.universitas21.com.

3. "The World University Rankings Show U21 Members Are World Class," Universitas 21, October 9, 2012, http://www.universitas21.com/news/details/74/the-world-university-rankings-show-u21-members-are-world-class; and "Students Making the Most of U21 Opportunities," Universitas 21, September 14, 2012, http://www.universitas21.com/news/details/72/students-making-the-most-of-u21-opportunities.

4. One of the most important research projects in this domain is to consider how rankings become more and less important in different fields and how they realize that importance (Sauder and Espeland 2009; Espeland and Sauder 2009a, 2009b; Marginson and Ordorika 2011).

5. Association of American Universities: An Association of 62 Leading Research Universities in the United States and Canada, 2014, http://www.aau.edu/about/default.aspx?id=58.

6. A good illustration of this tension could be found in the recent decision to vote the University of Nebraska–Lincoln out of the AAU. Michigan and Wisconsin voted for their Big Ten partner's exit (Smith and Abourezk 2011). I am grateful to my colleagues at the conference at Rutgers University Center for Cultural Analysis for the discussion that led me to consider the importance of this shift. See Public Knowledge—"The Public University in the 21st Century," a conference at Rutgers University Center for Cultural Analysis, February 24, 2012, organized by Meredith McGill and her colleagues, http://cca.rutgers.edu/events/icalrepeat.detail/2012/02/24/124/23|28/public-knowledge-qthe-public-university-in-the-21st-centuryq.

7. One might argue that it's not only private universities but the ways in which private wealth channeled through foundations helps keep universities on the cutting edge. For an especially insightful account of that foundation world, see Fleishman (2009). For example, he notes that "molecular biology (originally seeded by the Rockefeller Foundation), computational neurobiology (the Sloan Foundation), area studies (the Ford Foundation), international security and arms control (the Rockefeller Foundation) and alternative dispute resolution (the Hewlett Foundation)" (131) were all fields enabled by foundation support.

8. However, even the academic market within the United States suggests a more closed system based on social exchange than what an open market might imagine (Burris 2004).

9. Burawoy also marks alternatives: Brazil's emphasis on treating its own journals as world class, and evaluating faculty there in those terms, is a reminder of how alternatives could work.

10. This section draws upon the wonderful collaborations and learning I gained through a project on the environment and higher education (Kennedy et al. 2012).

11. The College Sustainability Report Card's (http://www.greenreportcard.org/media.html) "Green Report Card" was suspended on March 30, 2012.

12. University of Puget Sound, Sound Policy Institute, 2014, http://www.pugetsound.edu/academics/academic-resources/sound-policy-institute/.

13. "2012 Mapping Internationalization on U.S. Campuses," American Council on Education, 2014, acenet.edu/go/mapping.

14. "Learn About NAFSA," NAFSA, 2014, http://www.nafsa.org/about/default.aspx?id=16295.

15. I limit most of my reflections to the period coincident with the presidency of Craig Calhoun, concluding on June 30, 2012. I draw on documents as well as my association with the council in a number of capacities, including service on its board

of directors (2006–14) and its Regional Advisory Panel for Eurasia between 1996 and 2008.

16. Different area studies initiatives were internationally integrated in various ways. Latin American studies was especially effective not only for its mobilization of scholars across both sides of the equator but also for being able to move across languages in their own cosmopolitan linguistic expression.

17. Social Science Research Council, "Overview," accessed June 3, 2012, http://www.ssrc.org/about/.

18. Social Science Research Council, "Spirituality, Political Engagement, and Public Life," accessed June 3, 2012, http://www.ssrc.org/programs/spirituality-political-engagement-and-public-life/.

19. Social Science Research Council, "Religion and the United Nations," accessed June 3, 2012, http://www.ssrc.org/programs/religion-and-the-united-nations/.

20. Social Science Research Council, "Conflict Prevention and Peace Forum (CPPF)," accessed June 3, 2012, http://www.ssrc.org/programs/cppf/; and Social Science Research Council, "Migration and Development," accessed June 3, 2012, http://www.ssrc.org/programs/migration-and-development/.

21. Arab Council for Social Sciences, accessed July 22, 2014, http://www.theacss.org/.

22. Arab Council for the Social Sciences, "New Paradigms Factory," accessed July 22, 2014, http://www.theacss.org/pages/new-paradigms-factory.

23. I thank its first director, Seteney Shami, for sharing insights about the organization's development; see also Shami (2011).

24. Social Science Research Council, "Research Alliance for New York City Schools," accessed July 22, 2014, http://www.ssrc.org/programs/research-alliance-for-new-york-city-schools/.

25. Ryan and Garrett (2005, 52) offer a list of outputs, outcomes/influences, policy responses, and impacts that is especially useful for subsequent comparative studies of knowledge interventions' consequence.

26. Among its earliest leaders was Thomas Watson Jr. (Pigman 2007, 12).

27. In 2011, GULF included seven university leaders from Europe: École Polytechnique Fédérale de Lausanne (EPFL), Switzerland; London School of Economics and Political Science, United Kingdom; ETH Zurich, Switzerland; University of Oxford, United Kingdom; University of Cambridge, United Kingdom; INSEAD, France; London Business School, United Kingdom. There were five from Asia: Tsinghua University, People's Republic of China; University of Tokyo, Japan; Keio University, Japan; National University of Singapore, Singapore; and Peking University, People's Republic of China. Also included were one from University of Cape Town, South Africa, and one from Monterrey Institute of Technology and Higher Education (ITESM), Mexico. Eleven were included from the United States: Columbia University, Carnegie Mellon University, Johns Hopkins University, Georgetown University, Harvard Kennedy School and its broader Harvard University, University of Pennsylvania, Stanford University, Massachusetts

Institute of Technology (MIT), Yale University, University of Chicago, and Brown University.

28. World Economic Forum "Universities, Think Tanks, Research Organizations," accessed July 22, 2014, http://www.weforum.org/academic-networks.

29. We are obliged as a consequence of participation to follow Chatham House rules, and thus the contributors to discussion go unnamed in what follows. "World Economic Forum on Europe and Central Asia: Expanding the Frontiers of Innovation," Vienna, Austria, June 8–9, 2011, http://www3.weforum.org/docs/EU11/WEF_EU11_Report.pdf.

30. Susan Côté-Freeman, "Perceptions of Corruption in Emerging Economies Persist," *World Economic Forum Blog*, December 7, 2012, http://forumblog.org/2012/12/perceptions-of-corruption-in-emerging-economies-persist/.

31. On December 7, 2012, they also included Daniel Malan, Daniel Shapiro, Dina Shoman, Tayatri Chakravorty, Guo Jianmei, Joel Rosenthal, John DeGioia, Michael Gerson, Michelle Gadsden-Williams, Sandeep Dadlani Seiichi Kondo, Steart Wallis, and Tim Leberecht. See World Economic Forum, "Global Agenda Council on Values 2012–2014," accessed July 22, 2014, http://www.weforum.org/content/global-agenda-council-values-2012.

32. But it's sometimes hard to read positions. Consider, for example, how the Ford Foundation has positioned one of its recent efforts. Its International Fellowships Program (IFP) was made deliberately to link higher education to social change (see Ford Foundation International Fellowships Program, "A Decade of Advanced Study Opportunities for Social Change Leaders Worldwide," http://www.fordifp.net/), and for its final assessment, see Ford Foundation International Fellowships Program, "Linking Higher Education and Social Change," May 2013, http://www.fordifp.org/portals/0/IFP%20PDF/IFP%20Final%20Publication.pdf.

33. Thomas Carothers (1999) has written one of the most insightful accounts of this work in association with his engagement with the problem through the Carnegie Foundation. For a more anthropological sensibility, see Keith Brown (2006).

34. As evidence, I developed in consultation with many colleagues a substantial document (no longer publicly available) on the intellectual rationale behind the project so that it would not fall prey to subsequent political manipulations by others. This is that document:

> The Ronald and Eileen Weiser Center for Emerging Democracies (WCED) is a constituent unit of the Ronald and Eileen Weiser Center for Europe and Eurasia (WCEE) at the University of Michigan International Institute. WCED supports the study of how democracies have emerged and the conditions necessary for assuring and extending freedom.
>
> Freedom is not a simple matter, especially when considered across societies, cultural traditions, and institutional sites. Economic freedom, political freedom, social freedom, and other freedoms must be understood in relation to one another and in relation to other goods such as security, prosperity, national sovereignty, or other principles that highlight independence,

interdependence, justice, and other values. That understanding also requires analysis of the contested meanings of freedom and democracy themselves, and how their meanings translate over time and across cultural traditions shapes their implication in social transformations. Part of WCED's work will be to encourage a richer understanding of freedom in comparative and historical perspective, especially as it affects real political change.

Emerging democracies have been one of the most important manifestations of this articulation of freedom and political change. The study of historical, contemporary, and prospective democratic transformations will constitute the core of the WCED's work. Among issues WCED will explore are the processes by which democracy and democratization become the goal and means of transformation. The Center will also address electoral and governance procedures that might better assure the stabilization and success of these democratic trajectories. More broadly, the Center will support the study of processes and conditions that allow for the public to meaningfully choose their leadership, and the laws that govern them and their elites. By drawing lessons from transformations of authoritarian regimes and dictatorships into more open societies, WCED will support the study of ongoing and future efforts to assure and extend freedom and democracy.

New forms of political organization are not of themselves sufficient for the assurance and success of democracy and freedom. Civil society—the development of legal private economic initiatives; voluntary associations that enhance pluralism, social integration, and the public good; and a public sphere where issues of common importance are communicated and discussed—is critical to the Center's mission. The Center will support study of conditions under which civil society flourishes and the relationship of civil society to freedom and democracy.

Although most research on democratic governance is focused on the national level, WCED will include support for scholarship on the local, regional, transnational, international, and global dimensions of emerging democracies. For example, in what ways have transnational democratic initiatives by states and from civil society affected these emerging democracies? In what ways does the spread of democracy affect the conditions for peace?

WCED is committed to historical approaches to understanding the development of democracy after familial states and polities, colonial rule, fascism, or communism might advance the development of subsequent emerging democracies. WCED is likewise committed to studying variations in the dynamics of democracy emerging from dictatorship depending on the level and types of violence within a society; measures of prosperity and well-being and their distribution across regions and social groups; ways to recognize past injustices and a means for assuring effective rule of law; the spread of political participation and civic engagement; and forms of artistic and cultural expression.

WCED's intellectual framework is therefore broad and diverse in theoretical, substantive, and contextual references. Initially, WCED will focus on freedom and democracy in Europe and Eurasia moving farther afield as conditions and resources warrant. Attention to democratic governance and civil society in contemporary policy and practice may suggest certain disciplinary foci, but this framework is also intended to be a living document, one that evolves through WCED's engagement with faculty and students from across the University of Michigan and the world whose scholarly focus is on freedom and democracy and the conditions of their extension.

35. However, Fleishman (2009, 198–205) focuses primarily on the good realized in Central and Eastern Europe.

36. Between 2009 and 2013, I was a Non-Resident International Scholar at the University of Prishtina, Kosova, and before that, for a year with Lviv National University, Ukraine, in their respective sociology departments for the Open Society Foundations' Academic Fellowship Program. Before then, I also reviewed the Lviv National University MA Programs in Cultural Studies and Sociology, and in 2005, I reviewed the Center for Social Studies and Graduate School for Social Research of the Polish Academy of Sciences for the Higher Education Support Programme of Open Society Foundation. Finally, in 2011–12 I also worked with the internal reviewers, and been a respondent, in the AFP's own review. I draw upon this experience to build my argument, but I do not use any information in what follows that compromises the contractual relations to which I have agreed.

37. http://www.opensocietyfoundations.org/grants/academic-fellowship-program.is. [no longer available, accessed June 30, 2012]

38. The Regional Seminar for Excellence in Teaching (ReSET), for example, is focused on improving the capacities of individuals to teach undergraduate students in the social sciences and humanities mainly by enhancing their network capacities. Most of its work has taken place in Russia and Ukraine.

39. Botstein's Bard College is one of the few US-based knowledge institutions to receive OSF support; in 2011, the college was awarded $60 million in endowment, pending other successful fund-raising (Foderaro 2011).

40. Reflections on that initiative can be found here: Lidia Kuzemska, "Prospects for Public Sociology in Ukraine," *Global Dialogue: Newsletter of the International Sociological Association* 3 (1), November 2012, http://isa-global-dialogue.net/prospects-for-public-sociology-in-ukraine/.

41. Michael D. Kennedy, "Burawoy and Public Sociology at Central European University: A Video with Summary," Academia.edu, 2012, http://www.academia.edu/3762795/_2012_Burawoy_and_Public_Sociology_at_Central_European_University_a_Video_with_Summary.

42. *Njohja*, Hasnije Ilazi, chief editor, with Astrit Salihu, Nita Luci, Stephanie Schwandner Sievers, Besnik Pula, Bekim Baliqi, Valdrin Prenkaj, and Gyjlshen Berisha, Prishtina: Institute for Social Sciences and Humanities, April 2013. Available at http://

www.academia.edu/3630827/_2013_Articulations_of_Transformation_Subjectivities_
and_Structures_in_Crisis.

Chapter 8

1. My colleagues and I have developed this in particular around energy politics
(Aalto et al. 2012, 2013). I draw upon those discussions and my contributions to
their energy politics seminar leading up to it for the formulations on framing that
follow.

2. Given the significance of these "theoretical interests" in the development of
postsocialist market economies, I analyzed postcommunism's transition culture as
just such a formation precisely because the articulation of those various coherent cultures were not yet fully formed (Kennedy 2002a).

3. Although Baehr (2002) focused on the unprecedented qualities of radical evil,
it might be useful to consider the ways in which these new subjectivities have been
domesticated by existing paradigms and not recognized for their unprecedented qualities. Approaches inspired by Alain Touraine (e.g., 2007, 2009) could have been one of
the avenues of inspiration, as Pleyers (2010) illustrates.

4. In what follows, I draw on Kennedy (2013a).

5. Of the scholars I discuss in this section, Scott is most generally recognized for
his intellectual distinction *and* integrity (e.g., Schuessler 2012).

6. Ania Skrzypek, pers. comm., June 24, 2013.

7. The last one at the time of writing took place in Portugal. In 2012, they took
place in Riga, Barcelona, Edinburgh, London, and Sofia.

8. With national backgrounds from across Europe, having undertaken studies
often outside their national homelands, the network produces European identification. See Antonnuci's comments at "Lorenza Antonucci, rapporteur at the FEPS
'Call to Europe' Conference in Brussels, 21–22 June 2012," http://www.youtube.com/
watch?v=CuBF7Mf4ba0.

9. *Queries: The European Progressive Magazine*, accessed July 22, 2014, http://www.
queries-feps.eu/ http://www.feps-europe.eu/en/news/cat11_publications-latest-queries.

10. Foundation for European Progressive Studies, "Pan European Observatory,"
2013, http://www.feps-europe.eu/en/news/cat16_studies-pan-european-observatory.

11. "PES Fundamental Programme," June 22, 2013, http://www.jozefkollar.sk/
wp-content/uploads/2014/03/pes_fundamental_programme-22-06-2013_en.pdf.

12. "Your Future Is My Future–A European Youth Guarantee Now!," accessed July
22, 2014, http://www.youth-guarantee.eu/.

13. This sense of the Next Left also connects directly with different notions in
North America, most evident in the work around the *Jacobin* and its editor, Bhaksar
Sunkara (Blumgart 2012).

14. The volume in which his essay appears is built on the recurring visits of Alfred
Gusenbauer and Ricardo Lagos to Brown University, where a series of public events
around the meaning and future of progressivism took place. In particular, the fall

2010 meeting explicitly brought together those who worked on Europe and those who worked on Latin America to explore the policies, strategies, identities, and affect of the Next Left and the globalized world of which it is a part. See "The Next Left: Globalized Social Democracy in the North and South," Watson Institute for International Studies, September 29–30, 2010, http://watsoninstitute.org/events_detail.cfm?id=1586, available on video at http://vimeo.com/30755687.

15. For this discussion of ACTA, I draw on Kennedy (2012f).

16. I introduced the term "civi-digital society" on twitter during the ACTA protests in Europe, while also anticipating the significance of the Polish mobilization (Kennedy 2012g).

17. "Anonymous Poland ACTA," January 22, 2012, http://www.youtube.com/watch?v=sBqLR_G2T2s.

18. "Bacefook—Stop Acta," YouTube, February 24, 2012, http://www.youtube.com/watch?v=LtEj_nomhcc.

19. Much more critical work remains to be done on this agenda, but I am indebted to one of my students for pointing the way. Olivia Petrocco's work explores why there is not more mobilizing interaction between those who are concerned for intellectual property problems around pharmaceuticals in the Global South, especially India, and the concern for other kinds of intellectual property that animated protest in Europe.

20. The WEF also invests much in this discussion, not surprisingly. See David Kappos and James Moody, "Can We Invent a Better Future?," *World Economic Forum Blog*, July 6, 2012, http://forumblog.org/2012/07/can-we-invent-a-better-future/. The Electronic Frontier Foundation monitors and supports digital rights movements globally, identifying the European anti-ACTA movement as one of the leading cases in 2012. See "Digital Rights Activism across the World in 2012," IFEX: The Global Network Defending and Promoting Free Expression, January 7, 2013, http://www.ifex.org/international/2013/01/07/digital_rights_activism/.

21. Tetyana Bohdanova, GlobalVoices, accessed July 22, 2014, http://global-voicesonline.org/author/tetyana-bohdanova/.

22. I find most innovative "AutoMaidan," an expression captured by William Risch, an American historian of Ukraine studying Euromaidan, and shared over the Internet: "They won't let us govern, we won't let them live in peace." This stage of the movement drives to the homes of Ukraine's elite and protest on-site.

23. For some of the discussion of Calhoun, I draw on Kennedy (2006).

24. Portions of the following draw on Kennedy (2014a).

25. The arc is nice, from Calhoun (1982) through (2012b).

26. For a remarkable discussion of the Steubenville case, see interview with an Anonymous activist and others: "Hacker Group Anonymous Leaks Chilling Video in Case of Alleged Steubenville Rape, Cover-Up," Democracy Now, January 7, 2013, https://www.youtube.com/watch?v=lrtFrXRD7KM.

27. tweet @YourAnonNews, 3:00 a.m., January 28, 2013.

28. Their years of work in solidarity with those who oppose the development of the Keystone XL pipeline to transmit tars ands oil south from Canada to the Gulf of Mexico is a good example of this.

29. They are, however, focused more on public image as I write. In Seattle, people in Guy Fawkes masks handed out roses to passersby, along with a note describing their aims and how to join the movement (Rensink 2013).

30. During his fall 2012 visit at Brown University in support of Brown Divest Coal, he elaborated the conviction that global change can happen most consequentially only when direct actions each happen in their own fashion across the world. One of my students (Cohen 2013) has been especially good at elaborating direct action's ties to other strategic action fields. I am grateful to her for this scholarship as well as her introduction to Steele.

31. For his account of the first wave of Egyptian revolution, see Said (2011).

32. "Answering Egypt's Call for Solidarity," OccupyWallStreet, November 26, 2011, http://occupywallst.org/article/answering-egypts-call-solidarity/.

33. See Vetëvendosje's message to Occupy Wall Street, "A Message of Solidarity," October 17, 2011, http://www.vetevendosje.org/en/news_post/a-message-of-solidarity-5/.

Bibliography

Aalto, Pami, David Dusseault, Michael D. Kennedy, and Markku Kivinen. 2013. "Russia's Energy Relations in Europe and the Far East: Towards a Social Structurationist Approach to Energy Policy Formation." *Journal of International Relations and Development* 13 (1): 1–29.

Aalto, Pami, David Dusseault, Markku Kivinen, and Michael D. Kennedy. 2012. "How Are Russian Energy Policies Formulated? Linking the Actors and Structures of Energy Policy." In *Russia's Energy Policy: National, Interregional and Global Levels*, edited by Pami Aalto, 20–42. Cheltenham, UK: Edward Elgar.

Abbott, Andrew. 2001. *The Chaos of Disciplines.* Chicago: University of Chicago Press.

Abul-Magd, Zeinab. 2011. "The Army and the Economy in Egypt." *Jadaliyya*, December 23. http://www.jadaliyya.com/pages/index/3732/the-army-and-the-economy-in-egypt.

Acar, Taylan, Robert Chiles, Garrett Grainger, Aliza Luft, Rahul Mahajan, João Peschanski, Chelsea Schelly, Jason Turowetz, and Ian F. Wall. 2011. "Inside the Wisconsin Occupation." *Contexts* 10 (3): 50–55.

Agani, Mentor. 2012. "Civil Society by Proxy: The Development of Civil Society in a Protectorate." In *Civil Society in Kosovo since 1999*, edited by Mentor Agani, 13–32. Prishtina: Center for Political Courage.

Ali, Tariq, ed. 2000. *Masters of the Universe? NATO's Balkan Crusade.* London: Verso.

Ali, Wajahat. 2013. "Against the Brahmins: An Interview with Pankaj Mishra." *Boston Review*, May 19. http://www.bostonreview.net/BR38.3/wajahat_ali_pankaj_mishra.php.

Allcock, J. B. 1975. "Sociology and History: The Yugoslav Experience and Its Implications." *British Journal of Sociology* 26 (4): 486–500.

American College & University Presidents' Climate Commitment. 2013. "Higher

Education's Role in Adapting to a Changing Environment." http://www.presidentsclimatecommitment.org/files/documents/higher-ed-adaptation.pdf.

American Council on Education (ACE). 2012. "Mapping Internationalization on U.S. Campuses: 2012 Edition." acenet.edu/go/mapping.

Amsler, Sarah. 2007. *The Politics of Knowledge in Central Asia: Science between Marx and the Market*. London: Routledge.

Andrew. 2012. "Pussy Riot Event Held at UK's Houses of Parliament." Punknews.org, October 19. http://www.punknews.org/article/49385/pussy-riot-event-held-at-uks-houses-of-parliament.

Anonymous. 1999. "Student Power: Sole's Occupation of the U-M President's Office." *Agenda* 12, April. http://www-personal.umich.edu/~lormand/agenda/9904/12.pdf.

Appadurai, Arjun 2001. "Grassroots Globalization and the Research Imagination." In *Globalization*, edited by Arjun Appadurai, 1–21. Durham, NC: Duke University Press.

———. 1996. *Modernity at Large: Cultural Dimensions of Globalization*. Minneapolis: University of Minnesota Press.

Arasu, Akash. 2013. "The Evolution of the Davos Man." *Huntington Post*, January 22. http://www.huffingtonpost.com/akash-arasu/davos-man_b_2529544.html.

Archibugi, D., and M. Koenig-Archibugi. 2003. "Globalization, Democracy and Cosmopolis." In *Debating Cosmopolitics*, edited by Daniele Archibugi, 273–92. London: Verso.

Arrighi, Giovanni, and Beverly J. Silver, eds. 1999. *Chaos and Governance in the Modern World System*. Minneapolis: University of Minnesota Press.

Arzt, Donna E. 2006. "Views on the Ground: The Local Perception of International Criminal Tribunals in the Former Yugoslavia and Sierra Leone." *Annals of the American Academy of Political and Social Science* 603:226–39.

Associated Press. 2012. "Ai Weiwei, Pussy Riot on Art World Power List." *Seattle Times*, October 18. http://seattletimes.com/html/entertainment/2019459345_apeubritainartpowerlist.html.

Baehr, Peter. 2002. "Identifying the Unprecedented: Hannah Arendt, Totalitarianism, and the Critique of Sociology." *American Sociological Review* 67 (7): 804–31.

Baiocchi, Gianpaolo. 2005. *Militants and Citizens: Local Democracy on a Global Stage in Porto Alegre*. Stanford, CA: Stanford University Press.

Baiocchi, Gianpaolo, and Ernesto Ganuza. 2012. "Politics without Banners. The Spanish Indignados' Experiment in Direct Democracy." In *Next Left: Building New Communities*, edited by Ernst Stetter, Karl Duffek, and Ania Skrzypek, 110–19. Brussels: FEPS.

———. Forthcoming. *Democracy in Motion: The Pitfalls of Participation in a Globalizing World*. Stanford, CA: Stanford University Press.

Baiocchi, Gianpaolo, Patrick Heller, and Marcelo K. Silva. 2008. "Making Space for Civil Society: Institutional Reforms and Local Democracy in Brazil." *Social Forces* 86 (3): 911–56.

Baiocchi, Gianpaolo, and Michael D. Kennedy. 2013. "Occupy Movements around the

World: How Is Brazil's Different?" *Huffington Post*, June 21. http://www.huffing-tonpost.com/gianpaolo-baiocchi/occupy-movements-around-t_b_3480620.html.

Baker, Stewart. 2012. "The SOPA War: Why the GOP Turned on Piracy." *Hollywood Reporter*, February 2. http://www.hollywoodreporter.com/news/sopa-hollywood-gop-piracy-286648.

Balaghi, Shiva. 2012. "Covering Iran's Ninjas." *Jadaliyya*, April 3. http://www.jadaliyya.com/pages/index/4923/covering-irans-ninjas.

———. 2011a. "Tragic Day for Norway; Shameful Day for Journalism." *Jadaliyya*, July 23. http://www.jadaliyya.com/pages/index/2202/tragic-day-for-norway;-shameful-day-for-journalism.

———. 2011b. "Why Tahrir Infuriates the Neo-Cons." *Jadaliyya*, February 15. http://www.jadaliyya.com/pages/index/647/why-tahrir-infuriates-the-neo-cons.

Balibar, Étienne. 2012. "What Democratic Europe? A Response to Jürgen Habermas." *Social Europe Journal*, January 10. http://www.social-europe.eu/2012/10/what-democratic-europe-a-response-to-jurgen-habermas/.

Ball, Patrick, Wendy Betts, Fritz Scheuren, Jana Dudukovich, and Jana Asher. 2002. "Killings and Refugee Flow in Kosovo March–June 1999: A Report to the International Criminal Tribunal for the Former Yugoslavia." American Association for the Advancement of Science, January 3. http://www.aaas.org/sites/default/files/migrate/uploads/ICTY2002.pdf.

Balmforth, Tom. 2013. "Out of Ukrainian Protests, a New Media Outlet Is Born." *RFE/RL*, December 13.

Bamyeh, Mohammed, ed. 2012. *Intellectuals and Civil Society in the Middle East.* London: I. B. Tauris.

Barker, Tyson. 2012. "Europe in Turmoil over Internet Anti-piracy Legislation." *The Atlantic*, February 27. http://www.theatlantic.com/international/archive/2012/02/europe-in-turmoil-over-internet-anti-piracy-legislation/253637/.

Barry, Andrew. 2013. *Material Politics: Disputes along the Pipeline.* London: Wiley Blackwell.

Baum, Deborah. 2012. "Building Brown, Building Futures." Brown University, February 15. http://news.brown.edu/features/2012/02/futures.

Bauman, Zygmunt. 1998. *Globalization: The Human Consequences.* New York: Columbia University Press.

———. 1987. *Legislators and Interpreters.* Cambridge, UK: Polity.

BBC News. 2006a. "Press Shivers from Gas Woes." January 3. http://news.bbc.co.uk/2/hi/europe/4578000.stm.

———. 2006b. "Putin Orders Oil Pipeline Shifted." April 26. http://news.bbc.co.uk/2/hi/europe/4945998.stm.

Beath, Andrew, Fontini Christia, Ruben Enikolopov, and Shahim Ahmad Kabuli. 2010. "Randomized Impact Evaluation of Phase-II of Afghanistan's National Solidarity Programme." http://www.nsp-ie.org/reports/BCEK-Interim_Estimates_of_Program_Impact_2010_07_25.pdf.

Beck, Ulrich. 2006. *The Cosmopolitan Vision.* London: Polity.

———. 2000. *What Is Globalization?* Translated by Patrick Camiller. Cambridge, UK: Polity, 2000.

Benda, Julien. 1927. *La trahison des clercs.* Paris: B. Grasset.

Berman, Paul. 2005. *Power and the Idealists, or the Passion of Joschka Fischer and Its Aftermath.* New York: Norton.

Bērziņš, Jānis. 2014. "Russia's New Generation of Warfare in Ukraine: Implications for Latvia's Defense Policy." National Defence Academy of Latvia Center for Security and Strategic Research. Policy Paper No. 2, April. http://www.naa.mil.lv/~/media/NAA/AZPC/Publikacijas/PP%2002-2014.ashx.

Beyer, Gerard J. 2010. *Recovering Solidarity: Lessons from Poland's Unfinished Revolution.* South Bend, IN: Notre Dame University Press.

Bhargava, Rajeev. 2002. "Ordinary Feelings, Extraordinary Events: Moral Complexity in 9/11." In *Understanding September 11*, edited by Craig Calhoun, Paul Price, and Ashley Timmer, 321–31. New York: New Press.

Biddle, Sheila. 2002. "Internationalization: Rhetoric or Reality?" American Council of Learned Societies Occasional Paper Number 56.

Blau, Peter, and Otis Dudley Duncan. 1967. *The American Occupational Structure.* New York: Academic Press.

Block, Fred, and Margaret Somers. 2005. "From Poverty to Perversity: Ideas, Markets, and Institutions over Two Centuries of Welfare Debate." *American Sociological Review* 70:260–87.

———. 2003. "In the Shadow of Speenhaland: Social Theory and the Old Poor Law." *Politics and Society* 31:283–323.

Blumgart, Jake. 2012. "The Next Left: An Interview with Bhaskar Sunkara." *Boston Review*, December 28. http://www.bostonreview.net/books-ideas/jake-blumgart-next-left-interview-bhaskar-sunkara.

Blyth, Mark. 2013. *Austerity: The History of a Dangerous Idea.* Oxford: Oxford University Press.

Bohdanova, Tetyana. 2013. "How Internet Tools Turned Ukraine's #Euromaidan into a Movement." *Global Voices*, December 9. http://globalvoicesonline.org/2013/12/09/how-internet-tools-turned-euromaidan-protests-into-a-movement/.

Bokor, Justin. 2012. *University of the Future: A Thousand Year Old Industry on the Cusp of Profound Change.* Ernst & Young. http://www.ey.com/Publication/vwLUAssets/University_of_the_future/$FILE/University_of_the_future_2012.pdf.

Bollinger, Lee C. 2012. "College Diversity at Risk." *Washington Post*, January 15. http://www.washingtonpost.com/opinions/college-diversity-at-risk/2012/01/13/gIQACxpn1P_story.html.

Bonilla-Silva, Eduardo. 1999. "The Essential Social Fact of Race." *American Sociological Review* 64 (6): 899–906.

Boog, Jason. 2011. "Occupy Wall Street Library Evicted." Galleycat, November 15. http://www.mediabistro.com/galleycat/occupy-wall-street-library-evicted_b42238.

Borgman, Christine L. 2007. *Scholarship in the Digital Age: Information, Infrastructure and the Internet.* Cambridge, MA: MIT Press.

Bose, Sugata. 2011. "Tagore in Today's World." *Asia Pacific Memo*, April 19. http://www.asiapacificmemo.ca/tagore-in-todays-world-harvard-professor-sugata-bose-video-interview.

Bourdieu, Pierre. 1988. *Homo Academicus*. Stanford, CA: Stanford University Press.

Bourdieu, Pierre, and Loïc Wacquant. 1992. *An Introduction to Reflexive Sociology*. Chicago: University of Chicago Press.

Bowen, John. 2004. "The Development of Southeast Asian Studies in the United States." In *The Politics of Knowledge: Area Studies and the Disciplines*, edited by David Szanton, 386–425. Berkeley: University of California Press.

Boyer, Dominic. 2005. *Spirit and System: Media, Intellectuals, and the Dialectic in Modern German Culture*. Chicago: University of Chicago Press.

BP. 2012. *Statistical Review of World Energy Report*, June. http://www.bp.com/content/dam/bp/pdf/Statistical-Review-2012/statistical_review_of_world_energy_2012.pdf

Bradatan, Costica, and Serguei Alex Oushakine. 2010. *In Marx's Shadow: Knowledge, Power and Intellectuals in Eastern Europe and Russia*. Plymouth, MA: Lexington Books.

"Brain Power." 2005. *The Age*, April 18. www.theage.com.au/news/Education-News/Brain power/2005/04/18/1113676693627.html.

Braun, Hannah. 2013. "The Articulation of Energy Affairs: An Analysis of the Production, Articulation, and Dissemination of the Knowledge of Energy Flows by the Oxford Institute for Energy Studies." Unpublished paper, Brown University, May.

Brecher, Jeremy, Tim Costello, and Brendan Smith. 2002. *Globalization from Below: The Power of Solidarity*. Cambridge, MA: South End Press.

Brinkerhoff, Jennifer M. 2009. *Digital Diasporas: Identity and Transnational Engagement*. Cambridge: Cambridge University Press.

Brophey, Paul C., and Rachel D. Godsil. 2009. "Anchor Institutions as Partners in Building Successful Communities and Local Economies." In *Retooling HJD for a Catalytic Federal Government: A Report to Secretary Shaun Donovan*, Penn Institute for Urban Research. http://community-wealth.org/content/chapter-8-anchor-institutions-partners-building-successful-communities-and-local-economies.

Brown, Keith S. 2006. "The New Ugly Americans? Making Sense of Democracy Promotion in the Former Yugoslavia." In *Transacting Transition: The Micropolitics of Democracy Assistance in the Former Yugoslavia*, edited by Keith Brown, 1–22. Bloomfield, CT: Kumarian Press.

Brown, Keith S., and Yannis Hamilikis, eds. 2003. *The Usable Past: Greek Metahistories*. Plymouth: Lexington Books.

Brown, Wendy. 2009. "Save the University: Wendy Brown, Part 6." September 25. http://www.youtube.com/watch?v=aR4xYBGdQgw.

Brundtland World Commission on Environment and Development. 1987. *Our Common Future*. New York: Oxford University Press.

Brysk, Alison. 2009. *Global Good Samaritans: Human Rights as Foreign Policy.* Oxford: Oxford University Press.

Burawoy, Michael. 2012a. "The Great American University." *Contemporary Sociology* 41 (2): 139–49.

———. 2012b. "The Public University—a Battleground for Real Utopias." Presentation at the annual meeting of the American Sociological Association. http://burawoy. berkeley.edu/Universities/The%20Public%20University%20as%20Real%20utopia.pdf

———. 2011. "The Last Positivist." *Contemporary Sociology* 40 (4): 388–404.

———. 2008. "A Public Sociology for California." *Critical Sociology* 34 (3): 339–48.

———. 2007a. "For Public Sociology." In *Public Sociology: Fifteen Eminent Sociologists Debate Politics and the Profession in the Twenty-First Century,* edited by Dan Clawson, Robert Zussman, Joya Misra, Naomi Gerstel, Randall Stokes, Douglas L. Anderston, and Michael Burawoy, 23–64. Berkeley: University of California Press.

———. 2007b. "Private Troubles and Public Issues." In *Collaborations for Social Justice,* edited by Andrew Barlow, 125–33. Lanham, MD: Rowman and Littlefield.

———. 2007c. "Public Sociology vs. the Market." *Socio-Economic Review* 5 (2): 356–67.

———. 2005a. "For Public Sociology." *American Sociological Review* 70 (1): 4–28.

———. 2005b. "Forging Public Sociologies on National, Regional, and Global Terrains." *E-Bulletin, The International Sociological Association* 2:42–52.

———. 2005c. "Public Sociology: Populist Fad or Path to Renewal?" *British Journal of Sociology* 56 (3): 417–32.

———. 2005d. "Rejoinder: Toward a Critical Public Sociology." *Critical Sociology* 31 (3): 379–90.

———. 2005e. "The Return of the Repressed: Recovering the Public Face of U.S. Sociology, 100 Years On." *Annals of the American Academy of Political and Social Science* 600:68–87.

———. 2004a. "The Critical Turn to Public Sociology." In *Enriching the Sociological Imagination: How Radical Sociology Changed the Discipline,* edited by Rhonda Levine, 309–22. New York: Brill.

———. 2004b. "Public Sociologies: A Symposium from Boston College." *Social Problems* 51 (1): 103–30.

———. 2004c. "Public Sociologies: Contradictions, Dilemmas and Possibilities." *Social Forces* 82 (4): 1603–18.

———. 2004d. "Public Sociology: South African Dilemmas in a Global Context." *Society in Transition* 35 (1): 11–26.

———. 2004e. "The World Needs Public Sociology." *Sosiologisk Tidsskrift* 12 (3): 255–72.

———. 2003. "Revisits: An Outline of a Theory of Reflexive Ethnography." *American Sociological Review* 68:645–79.

———. 1990. "Marxism as Science: Historical Challenges and Theoretical Growth." *American Sociological Review* 55:775–93.

———. 1989. "Two Methods in Search of History: Skocpol vs. Trotsky." *Theory and Society* 18:759–805.

Burawoy, Michael, Joseph A. Blum, Sheba George, Millie Thayer, Zsuzsa Gille, Teresa Gowan, Lynne Haney, Maren Klawiter, Steve H. Lopez, and Sean Riaian. 2000. *Global Ethnography: Forces, Connections and Imaginations in a Postmodern World.* Berkeley: University of California Press.

Burawoy, Michael, Alice Burton, Ann Arnett Ferguson, Kathryn J. Fox, Joshua Gamson, Leslie Hurst, Nadine G. Julius, Charles Kurzman, Leslie Salzinger, Josepha Schiffman, and Shiori Ui. 1991. *Ethnography Unbound: Power and Resistance in the Modern Metropolis.* Berkeley: University of California Press.

Burawoy, Michael, and János Lukács. 1992. *The Radiant Past: Ideology and Reality in Hungary's Road to Capitalism.* Chicago: University of Chicago Press.

Burris, Val. 2004. "The Academic Caste System: Prestige Hierarchies in PhD Exchange Networks." *American Sociological Review* 69 (2): 239–64.

Büyükokutan, Barış. 2011. "Toward a Theory of Cultural Appropriation: Buddhism, the Vietnam War, and the Field of U.S. Poetry." *American Sociological Review* 76 (4): 620–39.

Calhoun, Craig. 2013. *Cosmopolitanism and Belonging: American Power, European Integration, and Global Citizenship.* Unpublished manuscript.

———. 2012a. "Libyan Money, Academic Missions and Public Social Science." *Public Culture* 24 (1): 9–45.

———. 2012b. *The Roots of Radicalism: Tradition, the Public Sphere, and the Roots of Early 19th Century Radicalism.* Chicago: University of Chicago Press.

———. 2010a. "Introduction: On Merton's Legacy and Contemporary Sociology." In *Robert K. Merton: Sociology of Science and Sociology as Science*, edited by Craig Calhoun, 1–31. New York: Columbia University Press/SSRC Book.

———. 2010b. "Social Science Research and Military Agendas: Safe Distance or Bridging a Troubling Divide?" *Perspectives on Politics* 8 (4): 1099–1104.

———. 2007. *Nations Matter: Culture, History, and the Cosmopolitan Dream.* London: Routledge.

———. 2005. "The Promise of Public Sociology." *British Journal of Sociology* 56:355–63.

———. 2003a. "The Class Consciousness of Frequent Travelers: Toward a Critique of Actually Existing Cosmopolitanism." In *Debating Cosmopolitics*, edited by Daniele Archibugi, 86–116. London: Verso.

———. 2003b. "Information Technology and the International Public Sphere." In *Shaping the Network Society: The New Role of Civil Society in Cyberspace*, edited by Douglas Schuler and Peter Day, 229–51. Cambridge, MA: MIT Press.

———. 2001a. "The Critical Dimension in Sociological Theory." In *Handbook of Sociological Theory*, edited by J. H. Turner, 85–112. New York: Plenum.

———. 2001b. "Imagining Solidarity: Cosmopolitanism, Constitutional Patriotism, and the Public Sphere." *Public Culture* 14 (1): 147–71.

———. 1995. *Critical Social Theory: Culture, History and the Challenge of Difference.* Oxford : Blackwell.

———. 1994. *Neither Gods nor Emperors: Students and the Struggle for Democracy in China.* Berkeley: University of California Press.

——, ed. 1993. *Habermas and the Public Sphere*. Cambridge, MA: MIT Press.

——. 1989a. "Classical Social Theory and the French Revolution of 1848." *Sociological Theory* 7 (2): 210–25.

——. 1989b. "Tiananmen, Television and the Public Sphere: Internationalization of Culture and the Beijing Spring of 1989." *Public Culture* 2 (1): 54–70.

——. 1982. *The Question of Class Struggle: Social Foundations of Popular Radicalism during the Industrial Revolution*. Chicago: University of Chicago Press.

Calhoun, Craig, and J. McGowan. 1997. "Introduction: Hannah Arendt and the Meaning of Politics." In *Hannah Arendt and the Meaning of Politics*, edited by Craig Calhoun and J. McGowan, 1–24. Minneapolis: University of Minnesota Press.

Calhoun, Craig, Eduardo Mendieta, and Jonathan VanAntwerpen eds. 2013. *Habermas and Religion*. Cambridge, UK: Polity.

Calhoun, Craig, Paul Price, and Ashley Timmer, eds. 2002. *Understanding September 11*. New York: New Press.

Camic, Charles. 2010. "How Merton Sociologizes the History of Ideas." In *Robert K. Merton: Sociology of Science and Sociology as Science*, edited by Craig Calhoun, 273–96. New York: Columbia University Press/SSRC Book.

Camic, Charles, and Neil Gross. 2001. "The New Sociology of Ideas." In *The Blackwell Companion to Sociology*, edited by Judith R. Blau, 236–49. Oxford: Blackwell.

Camic, Charles, Neil Gross, and Michelle Lamont, eds. 2011. *Social Knowledge in the Making*. Chicago: University of Chicago Press.

Cantor, Nancy. 2011a. "Are College Rankings out of Step with America's Future?" *Huffington Post Commentary*, September 20. http://www.huffingtonpost.com/nancy-cantor/are-college-rankings-out-of-step_b_965864.html.

——. 2011b. "Is Syracuse University Sliding or Surging?" *Post Standard*, October 23. http://www.syracuse.com/news/index.ssf/2011/10/syracuse_university_nancy_cant.html.

——. 2007. "Higher Education on the World Stage of Democracy: Overcoming an 'Anemia of Deeds.'" University of Pennsylvania, Center for Community Partnerships, March 29. http://www.syr.edu/chancellor/speeches/upennConference.pdf.

Cardais, S. Adam. 2012. "Kosovo: Vetevendosje's 'Determination.'" *Transitions Online*, January 12. http://eastofcenter.tol.org/2012/01/kosovo-vetevendosjes-determination/.

Caron, James M. 2007. "Afghanistan Historiography and Pashtun Islam: Modernization Theory's Afterimage." *History Compass* 5 (2): 314–29.

Carothers, Thomas. 1999. *Aiding Democracy Abroad: The Learning Curve*. Washington, DC: Carnegie Endowment for International Peace.

Carr, Elizabeth. 2011. "Main Green Campout to Greet the Corporation." *Brown Daily Herald*, October 20. http://www.browndailyherald.com/2011/10/20/main-green-campout-to-greet-the-corporation/#.Tzvab13wOjE\.

Castells, Manuel. 2009. *Communication Power*. Oxford: Oxford University Press.

Chakrabarty, Dipesh. 2000. *Provincializing Europe: Postcolonial Thought and Historical Difference*. Princeton: Princeton University Press.

Chandler, David. 2010a. "The EU and Southeastern Europe: The Rise of Post-liberal Governance." *Third World Quarterly* 31 (1): 69–85.

———. 2010b. "Neither International nor Global: Rethinking the Problematic Subject of Security." *Journal of Critical Globalization Studies* 3:89–101.

Chari, Sharad, and Katherine Verdery. 2009. "Thinking between the Posts: Postcolonialism, Postsocialism and Ethnography after the Cold War." *Comparative Studies in Society and History* 51 (1): 6–34.

Charle, Christophe. 2004a. "The Intellectual Networks of Two Leading Universities: Paris and Berlin 1890–1930." In *Transnational Intellectual Networks: Forms of Academic Knowledge and the Search for Cultural Identities*, edited by Christophe Charle, Jürgen Schriewer, and Peter Wagner, 401–50. Frankfurt: Campus Verlag.

———. 2004b. "Introduction to Part II." In *Transnational Intellectual Networks: Forms of Academic Knowledge and the Search for Cultural Identities*, edited by Christophe Charle, Jürgen Schriewer, and Peter Wagner, 198–204. Frankfurt: Campus Verlag.

Charle, Christophe, Jürgen Schriewer, and Peter Wagner, eds. 2004. *Transnational Intellectual Networks: Forms of Academic Knowledge and the Search for Cultural Identities*. Frankfurt: Campus Verlag.

Chatterjee, Partha. 1993. *The Nation and Its Fragments*. Princeton: Princeton University Press.

———. 1986. *Nationalist Thought and the Colonial World*. London: Zed.

Chopan, Saghar, and Malaize Daud. 2009. "Political Leadership in Post-Taliban Afghanistan: The Critical Factor." In Middle East Institute, *Afghanistan 1979–2009: In the Grip of Conflict*, 97–101. http://www.e-ariana.com/ariana/eariana.nsf/allDo cs/2e94b90b9ffa8b80872576850076077d!OpenDocument&Click=.

Christensen, Clayton M., and Henry J. Eyring. 2011. *The Innovative University: Changing the DNA of Higher Education from the Inside Out*. San Francisco: Jossey-Bass.

Clark, Howard. 2000. *Civil Resistance in Kosovo*. London: Pluto Press.

Clawson Dan, ed. 1998. *Required Reading: Sociology's Most Influential Books*. Amherst: University of Massachusetts Press.

Cohen, David William. 2001. "International Expertise: A Position Paper." *Journal of the International Institute* 9 (1). http://quod.lib.umich.edu/j/jii/4750978.0009.106/- -international-expertise-a-position-paper?rgn=main;view=fulltext.

Cohen, David William, and Michael D. Kennedy. 2005. "Constituting Sacred Spaces, Producing Heretical Knowledge." In *Responsibility in Crisis: Knowledge Politics and Global Publics*, edited by David William Cohen and Michael D. Kennedy, 1–18. Ann Arbor: University of Michigan Scholarly Publishing Office.

Cohen, Kathryn. 2013. "Transformation from the Hollows: The Resource-Intervention Chain and Its Implications for Collective Action and Social Transformation." Academia.edu. http://www.academia.edu/3368849/Transformation_from_the_ Hollows_The_Resource-Intervention_Chain_and_its_Implications_for_Collective_Action_and_Social_Transformation.

Cole, Jonathan R. 2009. *The Great American University: Its Rise to Preeminence, Its Indispensable National Role, Why It Must Be Protected*. New York: Public Affairs.

Coleman, E. Gabriella 2013. *Coding Freedom: The Ethics and Aesthetics of Hacking.* Princeton: Princeton University Press.

Collier, Paul, V. L. Elliott, Havard Hegre, Anke Hoeffler, Marta Raynal-Querol, and Nicholas Sambanis. 2003. *Breaking the Conflict Trap: Civil War and Development Policy.* Washington, DC: World Bank and Oxford University Press.

Collins, Randall. 1998. *The Sociology of Philosophies: A Global Theory of Intellectual Change.* Cambridge, MA: Harvard University Press.

———. 1986. "Is 1980s Sociology in the Doldrums?" *American Journal of Sociology* 91:1336–55.

Comaroff Jean, and John L. Comaroff. 2011. *Theory from the South: Or, How Euro-America Is Evolving toward Africa.* Boulder, CO: Paradigm Publishers.

Connar, Walter, David E. Powell, and Anthony Jones, eds. 1991. *Soviet Social Problems.* Boulder, CO: Westview.

Connell, Raewynn. 2007. *Southern Theory: The Global Dynamics of Knowledge in Social Science.* London: Polity.

Cornwell, Grant H., and Eve W. Stoddard. 1999. *Globalizing Knowledge: Connecting International and Intercultural Studies.* Washington, DC: Association of American Colleges and Universities.

Coronil, Fernando, and Colloquium Speakers. 2001. "The Production of Knowledge and Indigenous Peoples." *Journal of the International Institute* 9 (1). http://quod.lib.umich.edu/cgi/t/text/text-idx?c=jii;cc=jii;q1=fernando%20coronil;rgn=main;view=text;idno=4750978.0009.104.

Coser, Lewis. 1986. Introduction to *The Social Role of the Man of Knowledge*, by Florian Znaniecki. New Brunswick, NJ: Transaction.

———. 1973. "The Intellectual as Celebrity." *Dissent* 20:46–56.

———. 1965. *Men of Ideas: A Sociologist's View.* New York: Free Press.

Court, Julius, and John Young. 2005. "Bridging Research and Policy in International Development: Context, Evidence and Links." In *Global Knowledge Networks and International Development*, edited by Diane Stone and Simon Maxwell, 18–36. London: Routledge.

Crews, Robert. 2006. *For Tsar and Prophet: Islam and Empire in Russia and Central Asia.* Cambridge, MA: Harvard University Press.

Cronon, Ciaran. 2011. "Cosmopolitan Democracy." In *Jürgen Habermas: Key Concepts*, edited by Barbara Fultner, 196–221. Durham, UK: Acumen Publishing, 2011.

Ćulibrk, Svetozar. 1971. "Cvijić's Sociological Research into Society in the Balkans." *British Journal of Sociology* 22 (4): 423–40.

Czerski, Piotr. 2012. "We the Web Kids." Pastebin, February 15. http://pastebin.com/0xXV8k7k.

Darden, Keith. 2014. *Resisting Occupation: Mass Schooling and the Creation of Durable National Loyalties.* Cambridge: Cambridge University Press.

Davenport, Lisa. 2009. *Jazz Diplomacy: Promoting America in the Cold War Era.* Jackson: University Press of Mississippi.

Dawes, Simon. 2011. "The 'Public University' as Response to Funding Cuts to

UK's Higher Education." *Truthout*, November 22. http://www.truth-out.org/public-university-response-funding-cuts-uks-higher-education/1321984014.

Dawson, Jane. 1996. *Eco-Nationalism: Anti-nuclear Activism and National Identity in Russia, Lithuania and Ukraine*. Durham, NC: Duke University Press.

De Graaff, Naná. 2012. "Oil Elite Networks in a Transforming Global Oil Market." *International Journal of Comparative Research* 53 (4): 275–97.

Dean, Meredith, Edna Gulley, and Linda McKinney. 2012. "Organizing Appalachian Women: Hope Lies in the Struggle." In *Transforming Places: Lessons from Appalachia*, edited by Stephen L. Fisher and Barbara Ellen Smith, 109–21. Urbana: University of Illinois Press.

Dewey, John. 1938. "Means and Ends." In *Their Morals and Ours*, by Leon Trotsky, John Dewey, and George Novack. Reprint, New York: Pathfinder Press.

Diebert, Ronald. 2012. "Big Data Meets Big Brother: The Political Economy of Cyber Security." Watson Institute for International Studies, Cyber Security Colloquium, October 10. http://watsoninstitute.org/events_detail.cfm?id=1904.

Diepenbrock, George. 2012. "KU, Military Connections Prove Mutually Beneficial." *LJWorld.com*, August 19. http://www2.ljworld.com/news/2012/aug/19/ku-military-connections-prove-mutually-beneficial/.

Dirks, Nicholas B. 2012. "Scholars and Spies: Worldly Knowledge and the Predicament of the University." University Lecture, Columbia University, February 20.

———. 2004. "South Asian Studies: Futures Past." In *The Politics of Knowledge: Area Studies and the Disciplines*, edited by David Szanton, 341–85. Berkeley: University of California Press.

Djagalov, Rossen. 2012. "Reflections on Occupy Harvard." Possible Futures, January 11. http://www.possible-futures.org/2012/01/11/reflections-on-occupy-harvard/.

Doig, Alan, and Martin Tisne. 2009. "A Candidate for Relegation? Corruption, Governance Approaches and the (Re)construction of Post War States." *Public Administration and Development* 29:374–86.

Dubet, François, and Michel Wieviorka. 1996. "Touraine and the Method of Sociological Intervention." In *Alain Touraine*, edited by Jon Clark and Marco Diani, 55–75. New York: Routledge.

Duncan, Otis Dudley. 1960. "From Social System to Ecosystem." *Sociological Inquiry* 31 (2): 140–49.

Duncan, Otis D., and L. F. Schore. 1961. "Cultural, Behavioral, and Ecological Perspectives in the Study of Social Organization." *American Journal of Sociology* 61:84–85.

Dutta, Debasish. 2001. "Teaching 'Global Product Realization' Globally." *Journal of the International Institute* 8 (3). http://quod.lib.umich.edu/j/jii/4750978.0008.302/--globalization-s-challenge-four-more-voices-join?rgn=main;view=fulltext.

Duus, Peter. 1998. *The Abacus and the Sword: The Japanese Penetration of Korea, 1895–1910*. Berkeley: University of California Press.

Eglitis, Daina Stukuls. 2002. *Imagining the Nation: History, Modernity and Revolution in Latvia*. State College: Pennsylvania State University Press.

Ehrlich, Vera St. 1976. "The Last Big Zadrugas: Albanian Extended Families in the Kosovo Region." In *The Zadruga: Essays by Philip E. Mosley and in His Honor*, edited by R. F. Byrnes, 244–51. Notre Dame, IN: Notre Dame Press.

Eidelson, Josh. 2011. "Fighting Privatization, Occupy Activists at CUNY and UC Kick into High Gear." *The Nation*, December 16. http://www.thenation.com/article/165195/ fighting-privatization-occupy-activists-cuny-and-uc-kick-high-gear#.

Elder, Miriam. 2012. "Pussy Riot Member Uses Freedom to Resume Protests against Vladimir Putin." *The Guardian*, October 12. http://www.guardian.co.uk/ music/2012/oct/12/pussy-riot-resume-protests-against-vladimir-putin.

Elliot, Gregory. 2009. *Family Matters: The Importance of Mattering to Families in Adolescence*. London: Wiley Blackwell.

Ellis-Kahana, Julia. 2012. "Transformative New Amazons or Destructive Neo-colonialists? An Exploration of Militant Nudity as a Method of Radical Activism for Women's Rights in Ukraine and Beyond." Unpublished paper, Brown University.

Engermann, David. 2010. *Know Your Enemy: The Rise and Fall of America's Soviet Experts*. New York: Oxford University Press.

Espeland, Wendy, and Michael Sauder. 2009a. "How Rankings Affect Diversity." *Southern California Review of Law and Social Justice* 18 (3): 587–608.

———. 2009b. "Rating the Rankings." *Contexts* 8:16–21.

EurActiv.com. 2013. "South Stream Bilateral Deals Breach EU Law, Commission Says." December 4. http://www.euractiv.com/energy/ commission-south-stream-agreemen-news-532120.

Eyal, Gil, and Larissa Bucholz. 2010. "From the Sociology of Intellectuals to the Sociology of Interventions." *Annual Review of Sociology* 36:117–37.

Eyres, Harry. 2012. "Pussy Riot, Punk and Holy Fools." *Financial Times*, October 12. http://www.ft.com/intl/cms/s/2/ef9b6884-06f7-11e2-92b5-00144feabdc0. html#axzz36yaK4Rm7.

Falk, Barbara J. 2003. *The Dilemmas of Dissidence in East-Central Europe*. Budapest: Central European University Press.

Filipowicz, Halina. 1996. "The Daughters of Emila Plater." In *Engendering Slavic Literatures*, edited by Pamela Chester and Sibelan Forrester, 34–58. Bloomington: Indiana University Press.

Fischer, Joschka. 2013. "Europe's Ukrainian Blunder." *Project Syndicate*, December 31. http://www.project-syndicate.org/commentary/joschka-fischer-places-the-blame-for-ukraine-s-turn-to-russia-squarely-on-europe.

Fisher, Stephen L., and Barbara Ellen Smith. 2012. "Placing Appalachia." In *Transforming Places: Lessons from Appalachia*, edited by Stephen L. Fisher and Barbara Ellen Smith, 1–18. Urbana: University of Illinois Press.

Fiss, Peer C., and Paul M. Hirsch. 2005. "The Discourse of Globalization: Framing and Sensemaking of an Emerging Concept." *American Sociological Review* 70:29–52.

Fleishman, Joel L. 2009. *The Foundation: How Private Wealth Is Changing the World: A Great American Secret*. New York: Public Affairs.

Fligstein, Neil, and Doug McAdam. 2012. *A Theory of Fields.* Oxford: Oxford University Press.

Foderaro, Lisa. 2011. "$60 Million Gift to Bolster Bard College's Global Work." *New York Times,* May 16. http://www.nytimes.com/2011/05/17/nyregion/bard-college-given-60-million-for-global-initiatives.html?_r=0.

Foucault, Michel. 1980. "Truth and Power." In *Power/Knowledge: Selected Interviews and Other Writings, 1972–77,* edited by Colin Gordon, 109–33. New York: Pantheon.

Fox, Benjamin. 2013. "In Search of Europe's Prophets." *European Observer,* April 19. http://euobserver.com/political/119856.

———. 2012. "Pussy Riot Lead Nominees for EU Freedom Prize." *EUobserver* September 26. http://euobserver.com/news/117668.

Frank, David John, and Jay Gabler. 2006. *Reconstructing the University: Worldwide Shifts in Academia in the 20th Century.* Stanford, CA: Stanford University Press.

Franklin, Cynthia G. 2009. *Academic Lives: Memoir, Cultural Theory, and the University Today.* Athens: University of Georgia Press.

Freedan, Michael. 2010. "On European and Other Intellectuals." In *European Stories: Intellectual Debates on Europe in National Contexts,* edited by Justine Lacroix and Kalpyso Nicolaidis, 77–86. Oxford: Oxford University Press.

Frickel, Scott, and Neil Gross. 2005. "A General Theory of Scientific/Intellectual Movements." *American Sociological Review* 70 (2): 204–32.

Friedman, Thomas L. 1999. *The Lexus and the Olive Tree.* New York: Anchor.

Friedman, Uri. 2013. "'Who, If Not Me?' Why One Ukrainian Activist Is Protesting." *The Atlantic,* December 5. http://m.theatlantic.com/international/archive/2013/12/who-if-not-me-why-one-ukrainian-activist-is-protesting/282077/%20%E2%80%A6.

Friedman, Victor. 2012. "Enhancing National Solidarity through the Deployment of Verbal Categories: How the Albanian Admirative Participates in the Construction of a Reliable Self and an Unreliable Other." *Pragmatics and Society* 3 (2): 189–225.

Front Line Defenders. 2013. "Kosovo: Human Rights Defender Ms. Nazlie Bala Attacked and Severely Beaten." http://www.frontlinedefenders.org/node/22176.

Funk, Nanette, and Magda Mueller, eds. 1993. *Gender Politics and Post-Communism: Reflections from Eastern Europe and the Former Soviet Union.* New York: Routledge.

Funk, Russell. 2013. "How Knowledge Categorization Systems and Evaluation Norms Enable and Constrain Network Change in Organizations." Unpublished paper, University of Michigan, October 10.

Gal, Susan, and Gail Kligman. 2000. *Politics of Gender after Socialism.* Princeton: Princeton University Press.

Galasinska, Aleksandra, and Dariusz Galasinski, eds. 2010. *The Post-Communist Condition: Public and Private Discourses of Transformation.* Amsterdam: Johns Benjamins.

Gellner, Ernest. 1990. "La trahison de la trahison des clercs." In *The Political Responsibility of Intellectuals,* edited by Ian Maclean, Alan Montefiore, and Peter Winch, 17–27. Cambridge: Cambridge University Press.

Gerber, Alexandra. 2011. "Being Polish / Becoming European: Gender and Knowledge in the Process of European Integration." PhD diss., University of Michigan.

Gessen, Masha. 2014. *Words Will Break Cement: The Passion of Pussy Riot*. New York: Riverhead Books.

Ghani, Ashraf. 2013. "Afghan National Identity at Risk." *Examiner.com*, January 4. http://www.examiner.com/article/ashraf-ghani-afghan-national-identity-at-risk?cid=rss.

———. 2011. "Sovereignty in Afghanistan." Lecture at Brown University, May 5. http://www.engagingafghanistan.org/videos-and-essays/democratic-possibilities.

Ghani, Ashraf, and Clare Lockhart. 2008. *Fixing Failed States*. Oxford: Oxford University Press.

Ghani, Mariam, and Ashraf Ghani. 2012. *Afghanistan: A Lexicon: 100 Notes—100 Thoughts*. Documenta 13, no. 029. Ostfildern, Germany: Hatje Cantz Verlag. http://www.amazon.com/Mariam-Ashraf-Ghani-Afghanistan-Documenta/dp/3775728783.

Gil, Federico G., Ricardo Lagos E., and Henry A. Landsberger, eds. 1979. *Chile at the Turning Point: Lessons of the Socialist Years, 1970–1973*. Philadelphia: Institute for the Study of Human Issues.

Gilman, Nils. 2003. *Mandarins of the Future: Modernization Theory in Cold War America*. Baltimore: Johns Hopkins University Press.

Ginsberg, Benjamin. 2011. *The Fall of the Faculty: The Rise of the All-Administrative University and Why It Matters*. Oxford: Oxford University Press.

Gitlin, Todd. 2012. *Occupy Nation: The Roots, the Spirit, and the Promise of Occupy Wall Street*. New York: IT Books.

Glaeser, Andreas. 2011. *Political Epistemics: The Secret Police, the Opposition, and the End of East German Socialism*. Chicago: University of Chicago Press.

Glenn, Alan. 2012. "Parting the Iron Curtain—with Music." *Michigan Today*, September 12. http://michigantoday.umich.edu/story.php?id=8462#.UFR3kRisM_V.

Global University Network for Innovation. 2014. *Higher Education in the World 5: Knowledge, Engagement and Higher Education: Contributing to Social Change*. London: Palgrave Macmillan. http://www.guninetwork.org/guni.report/heiw-5-2013.

Goffman, Erving. 1959. *The Presentation of Self in Everyday Life*. Garden City, NY: Anchor.

Goldthau, Andreas, and Jan Martin Witte, eds. 2010. *Global Energy Governance: The New Rules of the Game*. Washington, DC: Brookings Institute.

Gorz, Andre. 1967. *Strategy for Labor*. Boston: Beacon.

Goswami, Samir. 2012. "Will the Sanctions against Penn State Really 'Change a Culture'?" *Sociological Cinema*, July 24. http://www.thesociologicalcinema.com/4/post/2012/07/will-the-sanctions-against-penn-state-really-change-a-culture-only-if-we-also-stop-tolerating-a-culture-of-rape-on-college-campuses-as-well.html.

Gouldner, Alvin. 1979. *The Future of Intellectuals and the Rise of the New Class*. New York: Seabury.

Grady, Denise. 2012. "Ruling on Contraception Draws Battle Lines at Catholic

Colleges." *New York Times*, January 29. http://www.nytimes.com/2012/01/30/
health/policy/law-fuels-contraception-controversy-on-catholic-campuses.
html?pagewanted=all.

Graeber, David. 2013. *The Democracy Project: A History, a Crisis, a Movement*. New
York: Spiegel and Grau.

———. 2011. *Revolutions in Reverse: Essays on Politics, Violence, Art and Imagination*.
Brooklyn, NY: Autonomedia.

Gramsci, Antonio. 1971. *Selections from the Prison Notebooks*. Edited by Quintin Hoare
and Geoffrey Nowell Smith. New York: International Publishers.

Greenberg, Douglas. 2012. "Is There a Crisis in Public Higher Education?" Paper presented at "Knowledge: The Public University in the 21st Century," a conference at
Rutgers University Center for Cultural Analysis, February 24.

Greenberg, Michael. 2011. "In Zuccotti Park." *New York Review of Books* 17 (1): 2–14.
http://www.nybooks.com/articles/archives/2011/nov/10/zuccotti-park/.

Greenpeace International. 2006. "Baikal Victory: Putin Announces Oil Pipeline
Reroute." April 26. http://www.greenpeace.org/international/en/press/releases/
baikal-victory-putin-announce/.

Gregorian, Vartan. 1969. *The Emergence of Modern Afghanistan: Politics of Reform and
Modernization*. Stanford, CA: Stanford University Press.

Gudziak, Borys. 2014. "The Maidan, Christmas, the New Year and a New Ukraine."
KyivPost, January 6. http://www.kyivpost.com/opinion/op-ed/borys-gudziak-
the-maidan-christmas-the-new-year-and-a-new-ukraine-334710.html.

Guidry, John, Michael D. Kennedy, and Mayer Zald, eds. 2000. *Globalizations and
Social Movements: Culture, Power and the Transnational Public Sphere*. Ann Arbor:
University of Michigan Press.

Gumpert, Patricia J., ed. 2007. *Sociology of Higher Education: Contributions and Their
Contexts*. Baltimore: Johns Hopkins University Press.

Gusenbauer, Alfred. 2013. "For a New Social Deal. Believing in the Hopes That Social
Democracy Aspires to Be Entrusted With." In *Next Left: For a New Social Deal*,
edited by Ernst Stetter, Karl Duffek, and Ania Skrzypek, 11–21. Brussels: FEPS.

———. 2012. "Towards a New Narrative: Reconciling Progress and Emancipation."
In *Next Left: Building New Communities*, edited by Ernst Stetter, Karl Duffek,
and Ania Skrzypek, 21–27. Brussels: FEPS. http://www.feps-europe.eu/assets/
d30b8581-bf9d-43b3-9a9c-a086256f000c/next-left_vol_5.pdf.

———. 2011. "Making Progress a Meaningful Concept." *Queries* 7 (10): 11–15.

———. 2010a. "Reaching beyond Our Own Limitations." *Queries* 11:74–79.

———. 2010b. "The Social Democratic Mission: Lessons from History for the Next
Left." In *Europe's Left in Crisis: How the Next Left Can Respond*, edited by Sunder
Katwala and Ernst Stetter, 37–41. London: Fabian Society.

Gusenbauer, Alfred, and Ania Skrzypek. 2013. "The Next Social Contract: Progressive
Politics after an Era of Plenty." In *Progressive Politics after the Crash*, edited by Olaf
Cramme, Patrick Diamond and Michael McTernan, 233–43. London: I. B. Tauris.

Gustafson, Bret. 2012. "Fossil Knowledge Networks: Industry Strategy, Public Culture and the Challenge for Critical Research." In *Flammable Societies: Studies on the Socio-economics of Oil and Gas*, edited by John-Andrew McNeish and Owen Logan, 311–34. London: Pluto Press.

Gutmann, Amy, Charles Taylor, K. Anthony Appiah, Jürgen Habermas, Steven C. Rockefeller, Michael Walzer, and Susan Wolf. 1994. *Multiculturalism: Examining the Politics of Recognition*. Princeton: Princeton University Press.

Habermas Jürgen. 2012. *The Crisis of the European Union: A Response*. Cambridge, UK: Polity.

———. 2009. "An Avantgardistic Instinct for Relevances: Intellectuals and Their Public." Transformations of the Public Sphere. http://publicsphere.ssrc.org/habermas-intellectuals-and-their-public/.

———. 2006. *The Divided West*. London: Polity.

Haddad, Bassam. 2012. "Jadaliyya: A New Form of Producing and Presenting Knowledge in/of the Middle East (Interview with Bassam Haddad by Julia Elyachar)." *Jadaliyya*, February 8. http://www.jadaliyya.com/pages/index/4278/jadaliyya_a-new-form-of-producing-and-presenting-k.

Hagan, John, and Sanja Kutnjak Ivković. 2006. "War Crimes, Democracy, and the Rule of Law in Belgrade, the Former Yugoslavia, and Beyond." *Annals of the American Academy of Political and Social Science* 605:130–51. http://www.jstor.org/stable/25097802.

Halas, Elzbieta. 2006. "Classical Cultural Sociology: Florian Znaniecki's Impact in a New Light." *Journal of Classical Sociology* 6 (3): 257–82.

———. 2000a. *Florian Znaniecki's Sociological Theory and the Challenges of the 21st Century*. Frankfurt: Peter Lang.

———. 2000b. "The Humanistic Approach of Florian Znaniecki." In *Verstehen and Pragmatism: Essays in Interpretive Sociology*, edited by Horst J. Helle, 213–28. Frankfurt: Peter Lang.

Halimi, Zaniti. 2013. "Hindu Culture in the Kosovan Social Context." *Njohja* 2:83–90.

Hall, Robert B. 1949. *Area Studies: With Special Reference to Their Implications for Research in the Social Sciences*. Ann Arbor, MI: Edwards Brothers.

Hall, Stuart. 1996. "On Postmodernism and Articulation: An Interview with Stuart Hall." In *Stuart Hall: Critical Dialogues in Cultural Studies*, edited by David Morley and Kuan-Hsing Chen, 131–50. London: Routledge.

Halvorson, Dan. 2010. "Bring International Politics Back In: Re-conceptualizing State Failure for the Twenty-First Century." *Australian Journal of International Affairs* 64 (5): 583–600.

Hari, Johan. 2007. "Pseud's Corner." *New Statesman*, April 30. http://www.newstatesman.com/film/2007/04/slavoj-zizek-intellectual.

Harlow, Sioban. 2014. "Creating New Partnerships." *Journal of the International Institute* 8 (2). http://quod.lib.umich.edu/j/jii/4750978.0008.202/—globalization-s-challenge?rgn=main;view=fulltext.

———. 2004. "Science-Based Trade Disputes: A New Challenge in Harmonizing the Evidentiary Systems of Law and Science." *Risk Analysis* 24 (2): 443–47.

————. 2001. "Creating New Partnerships." *Journal of the International Institute* 8 (2). http://quod.lib.umich.edu/j/jii/4750978.0008.202/-- globalization-s-challenge?rgn=main;view=fulltext.

Hauser, Gerard A. 1999. *Vernacular Voices: The Rhetoric of Publics and Public Spheres.* Columbia: University of South Carolina Press.

Havel, Václav. 1999. "Kosovo and the End of the Nation State." Translated by Paul Wilson. *New York Review of Books* 46 (10): 4–6.

————. 1993. *Summer Meditations.* Translated by Paul Wilson. New York: Vintage.

————. 1990. "The Politics of Hope." In *Disturbing the Peace: A Conversation with Karel Hvizdala,* by Václav Havel, translated by Paul Wilson, 163–205. London: Faber and Faber.

Haysom, Keith. 2011. "Civil Society and Social Movements." In *Jürgen Habermas: Key Concepts,* edited by Barbara Fultner, 177–95. Durham, UK: Acumen Publishing.

Heath, Jennifer, and Ashraf Zahedi, eds. 2011. *Land of the Unconquerable: The Lives of Contemporary Afghan Women.* Berkeley: University of California Press.

Heath, Joseph. 2011. "System and Lifeworld." In *Jürgen Habermas: Key Concepts,* edited by Barbara Fultner, 74–90. Durham, UK: Acumen Publishing.

Heta, Albert, and Vala Osmani, eds. 2011. *Are You a Tourist or a Traveler? Discussions, Presentations and Papers from Politics of Contemporary Art.* Prishtina: Stacion Center for Contemporary Art.

Hoffman, Andrew J. 2011. "Talking Past Each Other? Cultural Framing of Skeptical and Convinced Logics in the Climate Change Debate." *Organization & Environment* 24 (1): 3–33.

Holohan, Ann. 2005. *Networks of Democracy: Lessons from Kosovo for Afghanistan, Iraq, and Beyond.* Stanford, CA: Stanford University Press.

Hoover, Eric. 2011. "Syracuse, Selectivity, and 'Old Measures.'" *Chronicle of Higher Education,* October 13. http://chronicle.com/blogs/headcount/ syracuse-selectivity-and-%E2%80%98old-measures%E2%80%99/28973.

Hopkins, Dwight. 2001. "The Religion of Globalization." In *Religions/Globalizations: Theories and Cases,* edited by Dwight N. Hopkins, Lois Ann Lorentzen, Eduardo Mendieta, and David Batstone, 7–32. Durham, NC: Duke University Press.

Hotson, Howard. 2011. "Don't Look to the Ivy League." *London Review of Books* 33 (10): 20–22. http://www.lrb.co.uk/v33/n10/howard-hotson/ dont-look-to-the-ivy-league#fn-ref-asterisk.

Hovorun, Cyril. 2013. "On Maidan." *The Raven,* December 13. http://sainteliaschurch. blogspot.it/2013/12/on-maidan-archimandrite-cyril-hovorun.html.

Howse, Christopher. 2010. "Cardinal Newman: The Victorian Celebrity Intellectual Who Brought Benedict to Britain." *The Telegraph,* September 11. http://www.tele- graph.co.uk/news/religion/7995294/Cardinal-Newman-The-Victorian-celebrity- intellectual-who-brought-Benedict-to-Britain.html.

Hudzik, John. 2011. *Comprehensive Internationalization: From Concept to Action.* Washington, DC: NAFSA.

Hughes, Everett C. 1961. "Ethnocentric Sociology." *Social Forces* 40 (1): 1–4.

Hurst, Cindy. 2010. "The Militarization of Gazprom." *Military Review* 5:59–67.

Hynes, James. 1997. *Publish and Perish: Three Tales of Tenure and Terror.* New York: Picador.

Hyseni, Agim. 2013. "Fehmi Agani (The Founder of Sociological Studies in Albanian Language)." *Njohja* 2:273–91.

Inkpen, Andrew, and Michael H. Moffett. 2011. *The Global Oil and Gas Industry: Management, Strategy and Finance.* Tulsa, OK: Penwell.

International Energy Agency (IEA). 2011. *World Energy Outlook 2011.* Paris: OECD/IEA.

IP Policy Committee Blog. 2012. "Lessons from the ACTA Battles and Opening Up New Fronts." *Transatlantic Consumer Dialogue,* July 4. http://tacd-ip.org/archives/704.

Ishchenko, Volodymyr. 2014. "Support Ukrainians but Do Not Legitimize the Far-Right and Discredited Politicians!" LeftEast, January 7. http://www.criticatac.ro/lefteast/author/volodymyr-ishchenko/.

Jacoby, Russell. 1987. *The Last Intellectuals: American Culture in the Age of Academe.* New York: Basic Books.

Janeway, William. 2012. *Doing Capitalism in the Innovation Economy: Markets, Speculation and the State.* Cambridge: Cambridge University Press.

Jaschik, Scott. 2013. "The Right to Remain Silent: Does Brown University Have a Problem with Free Speech?" *Inside Higher Ed,* October 23. http://www.slate.com/articles/life/inside_higher_ed/2013/11/brown_university_censorship_ray_kelly_speech_provokes_dissidence.html.

Judt, Tony. 2011. *Ill Fares the Land.* New York: Penguin.

———. 2009. *Reappraisals: Reflections on the Forgotten Twentieth Century.* New York: Penguin.

———. 1998. *The Burden of Responsibility: Blum, Camus, Aron and the French Twentieth Century.* Chicago: University of Chicago Press.

———. 1992. *Past Imperfect: French Intellectuals, 1944–1956.* Berkeley: University of California Press.

Kadushin, Charles. 2012. *Understanding Social Networks: Theories, Concepts, and Findings.* Oxford: Oxford University Press.

Kaldor, Mary, Sabine Selchow, Sean Deel, and Tamsin Murray-Leach. 2012. "The 'Bubbling Up' of Subterranean Politics in Europe." *LSE Research Online,* June. http://bit.ly/Tx6LTI.

Kalleberg, Ragnvald. 2010. "The Ethos of Science and the Ethos of Democracy." In *Robert K. Merton: Sociology of Science and Sociology as Science,* edited by Craig Calhoun, 182–213. New York: Columbia University Press/SSRC Books.

Kantor, Rosabeth Moss. 1977. *Men and Women of the Corporation.* New York: Basic Books.

Kantor, Tadeusz. 1993. *A Journey through Other Spaces: Essays and Manifestos, 1944–1990.* Edited by Michal Kobialka. Berkeley: University of California Press.

Kaplan, Robert D. 2012. "The Geopolitics of Shale." *STRATFOR,* December 19. http://www.stratfor.com/weekly/geopolitics-shale.

Karaganis, Joe, ed. 2011. *The Media Piracy Report*. Social Science Research Council Books. http://piracy.ssrc.org/the-report/.

Karatnycky, Adrian. 2005. "Ukraine's Orange Revolution." *Foreign Affairs*, March/April, 35–52.

Kaser, Karl. 1994. "The Balkan Joint Family: Redefining a Problem." *Social Science History* 18 (2): 243–69.

Katumaric, Vjeran. 2013. "National Independence, Democracy, and Development in the Balkan Ending of the Modern Myths." *Njohja* 2:91–108.

Keane, John. 2000. *Václav Havel: A Political Tragedy in Six Acts*. New York: Basic Books.

Keck, Margaret, and Kathryn Sikkink. 1998. *Activists beyond Borders: Advocacy Networks in International Politics*. Ithaca, NY: Cornell University Press.

Keller, Ann Campbell. 2009. *Science in Environmental Policy: The Politics of Objective Advice*. Cambridge, MA: MIT Press.

Kelmendi, Pellumb. 2012. "Civil Society and Contentious Politics in Post-conflict Kosovo." In *Civil Society in Kosovo since 1999*, edited by Mentor Agani, 33–57. Prishtina: Center for Political Courage.

Kennan, George F., ed. 1993. *The Other Balkan Wars: A 1913 Carnegie Endowment Inquiry in Retrospect with a New Introduction and Reflections on the Present Conflict*. Washington, DC: Carnegie Endowment Books.

Kennedy, Floyd D., Jr., and Michael D. Kennedy. 2014. "If the West Stands Up to Putin, Russian Economy Will Pay Heavy Cost." *Global Post*, March 5. http://www.globalpost.com/dispatches/globalpost-blogs/commentary/if-west-stands-putin-russian-economy-will-pay-heavy-cost.

Kennedy, Michael D. 2014a. "From Affirmative to Critical Solidarity." In *Framing a New Progressive Narrative*, edited by Ernst Stetter, Karl Duffek, and Ania Skrzypek, 30-47. Brussels: FEPS. http://www.feps-europe.eu/en/news/586_next-left-vol-viii.

———. 2014b. "Knowledge Networks and Former Students." Academia.edu, May 18. http://www.academia.edu/3532139/Knowledge_Networks_and_Former_Students.

———. 2014c. "Solidarity with Ukraine against Putin's Reality" *Public Seminar*, March 7. http://www.publicseminar.org/2014/03/solidarity-with-ukraine-against-putins-reality/#.Ux05G17TM7B.

———. 2013a. "Articulations of Transformation: Subjectivities and Structures in Crisis." *Njohja* (Prishtina) 2:109–34. http://www.academia.edu/3630827/_2013_Articulations_of_Transformation_Subjectivities_and_Structures_in_Crisis.

———. 2013b. "Engaged Ethnography under Communist Rule: Sociology, Solidarity and Poland." *Problems of Post-Communism* 60 (4): 28–34.

———. 2012a. "Burawoy and Public Sociology at Central European University: A Video with Summary." Academia.edu. https://www.academia.edu/3762795/_2012_Burawoy_and_Public_Sociology_at_Central_European_University_a_Video_with_Summary.

———. 2012b. "Cosmopolitanism and the Global Articulation of Consequential Solidarity." *Queries: The Next Mission of Cosmopolitan Social Democracy* 8:46–54.

———. 2012c. "Cultural Formations of the European Union: Integration, Enlargement, Nation and Crisis." In *European Identity and Culture: Narratives of Transnational Belonging*, edited by Rebecca Friedman and Markus Thiel, 17–50. Aldershot, UK: Ashgate.

———. 2012d. Foreword to *Next Left: Building New Communities*. Edited by Ernst Stetter, Karl Duffek, and Ania Skrzypek. Brussels: FEPS.

———. 2012e. "Keywords for Globalizing Knowledge across Contexts." In *Relevant/ Obsolete? Rethinking Area Studies in the U.S. Academy*, edited by Will Glover and Ken Kollman, 112–38. Ann Arbor: International Institute at the University of Michigan.

———. 2012f. "The Next Left and Its Social Movements." In *Next Left: Building New Communities*, edited by Ernst Stetter, Karl Duffek, and Ania Skrzypek, 98–109. Brussels: FEPS.

———. 2012g. "Poles Rallying for Our Digital Freedom." Editorial in *Providence Journal*, B6.

———. 2011a. "Afghanistan, Ashraf Ghani, and Democratic Possibilities." Engaging Afghanistan, May. http://www.engagingafghanistan.org/videos-and-essays/democratic-possibilities.

———. 2011b. "Arab Spring, Occupy Wall Street, and Historical Frames: 2011, 1989, 1968." *Jadaliyya*, October 11. http://www.jadaliyya.com/pages/index/2853/arab-spring-occupy-wall-street-and-historical-fram.

———. 2011c. "Cultural Formations of the Public University: Globalization, Diversity, and the State at the University of Michigan." In *Knowledge Matters: The Public Mission of the Research University*, edited by Diana Rhoten and Craig Calhoun, 457–99. New York: Columbia University Press.

———. 2011d. "Global Solidarity and the Occupy Movement." Possible Futures: A Project of the Social Science Research Council, December 5. http://www.possible-futures.org/2011/12/05/global-solidarity-occupy-movement/.

———. 2010a. "Area Studies and Academic Disciplines across Universities: A Relational Analysis with Organizational and Public Implications." In *International and Language Education for a Global Future: Fifty Years of Title VI and Fulbright-Hays*, edited by David Wiley and Robert Glew, 195–226. East Lansing: Michigan State University Press.

———. 2010b. "A Public Sociology of Emerging Democracies: Revolution, Gender Inequalities, and Energy Security." *Bulletin of University of Lviv: Sociological Series*, issue 3 [*Вісник Львівського університету. Серія соціологічна, Випуск 3*]. http://burawoy.berkeley.edu/PS/Applications/Kennedy.pdf.

———. 2010c. "Soviet Studies, National Security, and the Production of 'Useful' Knowledge: A Discussion of *Know Your Enemy and the Rise and Fall of Soviet Experts*." *Perspectives on Politics* 8:1163–66.

———. 2009. "On Public Sociology and Its Professional, Policy, and Critical Complements in America and the Postcommunist World." *Academic Studies from Lviv Sociological Forum "Traditions and Innovations in Sociology"* [Наукові студії львівського соціологічного форуму "Традиції та інновації в соціології"], 201–12.

——. 2008. "From Transition to Hegemony: Extending the Cultural Politics of Military Alliances and Energy Security." In *Transnational Actors in Central and East European Transitions*, edited by Mitchell Orenstein, Steven Bloom, and Nicole Lindstrom, 188–212. Pittsburgh: University of Pittsburgh Press.

——. 2006. "Calhoun's Critical Sociology of Cosmopolitanism, Solidarity, and Public Space." *Thesis Eleven* 84:73–89.

——. 2005. "The Ironies of Intellectuals on the Road to Class Power." *Theory and Society* 34:24–33.

——. 2004a. "Evolution and Event in History and Social Change: Gerhard Lenski's Critical Theory." *Sociological Theory* 22 (2): 315–27.

——. 2004b. "Poland in the American Sociological Imagination." *Polish Sociological Review* 4 (148): 361–83.

——. 2004c. "Transforming Globalization's University and the Challenge of Difference in an Age of Belligerence." In *Responsibility in Crisis: Knowledge Politics and Global Publics*, edited by David William Cohen and Michael D. Kennedy, 157–82. Ann Arbor: University of Michigan Scholarly Publishing Office.

——. 2003. "International Biographies: A. Nihat Gökyiğit." *Journal of the International Institute* 10 (3): 8–9.

——. 2002a. *Cultural Formations of Postcommunism: Emancipation, Transition, Nation and War.* Minneapolis: University of Minnesota Press.

——. 2002b. "Globalization Is US?" *Journal of the International Institute* 10 (1). http://quod.lib.umich.edu/j/jii/4750978.0010.101/—globalization-is-us?rgn=main;view=fulltext.

——. 2001a. "Engaging Globalization's Difference." *Journal of the International Institute* 8 (3): 10–11. http://quod.lib.umich.edu/j/jii/4750978.0008.306?rgn=main;view=fulltex.

——. 2001b. "Globalization's University Challenge." *Journal of the International Institute* 8 (2): 4–5. http://quod.lib.umich.edu/j/jii/4750978.0008.203/—globalization-s-university-challenge?rgn=main;view=fulltext.

——. 2001c. "Postcommunist Capitalism, Culture and History." *American Journal of Sociology* 106 (4): 1138–51.

——. 2000a. "Extending Contextual Expertise." *Journal of the International Institute* 7 (3): 12–13. http://quod.lib.umich.edu/j/jii/4750978.0007.307?rgn=main;view=fulltext.

——. 2000b. "The Global Politics of Intellectual and Institutional Responsibility." *Journal of the International Institute* 8 (1): 12–13.

——. 2000c. "On Collaboration and Diversity." *Journal of the International Institute* 7 (2): 14–15. http://quod.lib.umich.edu/j/jii/4750978.0007.208?rgn=main;view=fulltext.

——. 1999a. "The Liabilities of Liberalism and Nationalism after Communism: Polish Businessmen in the Articulation of the Nation." In *Intellectuals and the Articulation of the Nation*, edited by Ronald Grigor Suny and Michael D. Kennedy, 345–78. Ann Arbor: University of Michigan Press.

———. 1999b. "Poland's Critical Sociological Significance: A Comparative and Historical Approach to a Nation and Difference." In *Power and Social Structure: Essays in Honor of Włodzimierz Wesołowski*, edited by A. Jasinska-Kania, M. L. Kohn, and K. M. Słomczyński, 239–63. Warsaw: Wydawnictwa Uniwersytetu Warszawskiego.

———. 1994. "An Introduction to East European Ideology and Identity in Transformation." In *Envisioning Eastern Europe: Postcommunist Cultural Studies*, edited by Michael D. Kennedy, 1–45. Ann Arbor: University of Michigan Press.

———. 1992a. "The Alternative in Eastern Europe at Century's Start: Brzozowski and Machajski on Intellectuals and Socialism." *Theory and Society* 21 (4): 735–53.

———. 1992b. "Eastern Europe's Lessons for Critical Intellectuals." In *Intellectuals and Politics: Social Theory in a Changing World*, edited by Charles Lemert, 94–112. Beverly Hills: Sage Press.

———. 1991. *Professionals, Power and Solidarity in Poland: A Critical Sociology of Soviet-Type Society.* Cambridge: Cambridge University Press.

———. 1987. "Hermeneutics, Structuralism and the Sociology of Social Transformation in Soviet-Type Society." *Current Perspectives in Social Theory* 8:47–76.

Kennedy, Michael D., and Miguel Centeno. 2007. "Internationalism and Global Transformations in American Sociology." In *Sociology in America: A History*, edited by Craig Calhoun, 666–712. Chicago: University of Chicago Press / An American Sociological Association Centennial Publication.

Kennedy, Michael D., and Naomi Galtz. 1996. "From Marxism to Postcommunism: Socialist Desires and East European Rejections." *Annual Review of Sociology* 22:437–58.

Kennedy, Michael D., J. Timmons Roberts, Alissa Cordner, and Adam Kotin. 2012. "Environmental Knowledge Matters: Assessing Impacts of the Luce Foundation Initiative on Higher Education and Sustainability." Watson Institute for International Studies. www.luceenvironment.org.

Kennedy, Michael D., and Ronald Grigor Suny. 1999. "Introduction." In *Intellectuals and the Articulation of the Nation*, edited by Ronald Grigor Suny and Michael D. Kennedy, 1–51. Ann Arbor: University of Michigan Press.

Kennedy, Michael D., and Elaine Weiner. 2003. "The Articulation of International Expertise in the Professions." Paper presented at conference, "Global Challenges and US Higher Education," Duke University, January 23–25. http://ducis.jhfc. duke.edu/archives/globalchallenges/pdf/kennedy-paper.pdf.

Khalek, Rania, Richard Yeselson, J. A. Myerson, Katha Pollitt, and OpinionNation. 2013. "The Ray Kelly 'Shoutdown': Free-Speech Failure or Democracy in Action." *The Nation*, November 6. http://www.thenation.com/blog/177008/ray-kelly-shoutdown-free-speech-failure-or-democracy-action#.

Kharchenko, Sergii. 2013. "Ukraine: Euromaidan Kitchen Feeds Thousands Daily." DEMOTIX, December 5. http://www.demotix.com/news/3422105/ukraine-euromaidan-kitchen-feeds-thousands-daily/all-media.

Khazan, Olga. 2012. "Poland Has Fracking Tensions, Too." *Washington Post*,

October 30. http://www.washingtonpost.com/blogs/worldviews/wp/2012/10/30/poland-has-fracking-tensions-too/.

Kiley, Kevin. 2012. "A Fair Fare Affair." *Inside Higher Ed*, February 10. http://www.insidehighered.com/news/2012/02/10/brown-dispute-questions-whats-fair-payment-lieu-taxes.

King, Kenneth. 2005. "Knowledge-Based Aid: A New Way of Networking or a New North-South Divide?" In *Global Knowledge Networks and International Development*, edited by Diane Stone and Simon Maxwell, 72–88. London: Routledge.

King, Lawrence Peter, and Ivan Szelenyi. 2004. *Theories of the New Class: Intellectuals and Power*. Minneapolis: University of Minnesota Press.

King, Martin Luther, Jr. 1963. "Letter from a Birmingham Jail." Historical Text Archive, April 16. http://historicaltextarchive.com/sections.php?action=read&artid=40.

Kirschbaum, Erik, and Irina Ivanova. 2012. "Protests Erupt across Europe against Web Piracy Treaty." *Reuters*, February 11. http://www.reuters.com/article/2012/02/11/us-europe-protest-acta-idUSTRE81A0I120120211.

Kluz, Richard. 2012. "Anonymous Attacks Polish Government Sites." CNN iReport, January 21. http://ireport.cnn.com/docs/DOC-734863.

Knudsen, Rita Augestad. 2014. "Moments of Self-Determination: The Concept of 'Self-Determination' and the Idea of Freedom in 20th- and 21st-Century International Discourse." PhD diss., London School of Economics and Politics.

Kohl, Wilfrid L. 2010. "Consumer Country Energy Cooperation: The International Energy Agency and the Global Energy Order." In *Global Energy Governance: The New Rules of the Game*, edited by Andreas Goldthau and Jan Martin Witte, 195–220. Berlin: Global Policy Institute and Washington, DC: Brookings Institute.

Kohn, Melvin L. 1993. "Doing Social Research under Conditions of Radical Social Change: The Biography of an Ongoing Research Project." *Social Psychology Quarterly* 56 (1): 4–20.

———, ed. 1989. *Cross-National Research in Sociology*. Newbury Park, CA: Sage.

Kohn, Melvin L., and Kazimierz M. Słomczyński. 1990. *Social Structure and Self-Direction: A Comparative Analysis of the United States and Poland*. Oxford: Blackwell.

Kohn, Melvin L., Kazimierz M. Słomczyński, Krystyna Janicka, and Valeri Khmelko. 1997. "Social Structure and Personality under Conditions of Radical Social Change: A Comparative Analysis of Poland and Ukraine." *American Sociological Review* 62 (4): 614–39.

Konrad, Gyorgy, and Ivan Szelenyi. 1979. *Intellectuals on the Road to Class Power*. New York: Harcourt Brace Jovanovich.

Kostiuk, Olga, Lydia Liachkhova, Marina Lopato, and Tamara Rappe. 2003. "Applied Art." In *The Collections of the Romanovs: European Art from the State Hermitage Museum, St. Petersburg*, edited by James Christen Steward, with Sergey Androsov, 166–71. London: Merrell.

Krasniqi, Shemsi. 2010. "La mémoire face à l'oubli: 10ème anniversaire de l'expulsion Kosovo: 1999–2009." Unpublished paper, Prishtina, March.

Kroes, Nellie. 2012. "The European Public on the Net." Internet Freedom Republica conference, Berlin, May 4. http://europa.eu/rapid/press-release_SPEECH-12-326_en.htm?locale=en.

Kroll, Charlie. 2012. "A Strong Brown Boosts Providence." *Providence Journal*, April 12. http://digital.olivesoftware.com/OLIVE/ODE/PROJO/LandingPage/Landing-Page.aspx?href=VFBKLzIwMTIvMDQvMTI.&pageno=MTk.&entity=QXIwMTkwMA..&view=ZW50aXR5.

Krugman, Paul. 2012. "Unethical Commentary: Newsweek Edition." *New York Times*, August 19. http://krugman.blogs.nytimes.com/2012/08/19/unethical-commentary-newsweek-edition/.

Kubik. Jan. 2006. "Avant-Garde Theater contra State Socialism: What Was Global before the Era of Globalization (in Tadeusz Kantor's Theater)?" In *Stawanie sie Spoleczenstwa*, edited by Andrzej Flis, 267–91. Krakow: Universitas. (in Polish)

Kubik, Jan, and Amy Linch, eds. 2013. *Post-Communism from Within: Social Justice, Mobilization, and Hegemony.* New York: New York University Press/SSRC.

Kurti, Albin. 2011. "International Protectorate." November 8. https://www.youtube.com/watch?v=TYci38HqlDU.

Kurzman, Charles. 2008. *Democracy Denied, 1905–1915.* Cambridge, MA: Harvard University Press.

Kvit, Serhiy. 2014. "What the Ukrainian Protests Mean." *University World News*, January 8. http://www.universityworldnews.com/article.php?story=20140108164131129.

Lacroix, Justine, and Kalpyso Nicolaidis, eds. 2010. *European Stories: Intellectual Debates on Europe in National Contexts.* Oxford: Oxford University Press.

Lacroix, Serhiy. 2010. "Borderline Europe: French Visions of the European Union." In *European Stories: Intellectual Debates on Europe in National Contexts*, edited by Justine Lacroix and Kalpyso Nicolaidis, 105–21. Oxford: Oxford University Press.

Lagos, Ricardo. 2012a. "Social Democracy in the 21st Century: Some Experiences from Chile." In *Next Left: Building New Communities*, edited by Ernst Stetter, Karl Duffek, and Ania Skrzypek, 28–36. Brussels: FEPS.

———. 2012b. *The Southern Tiger: Chile's Fight for a Democratic and Prosperous Future.* New York: Palgrave Macmillan.

Laidi, Z., ed. 2008. *EU Foreign Policy in a Globalized World: Normative Power and Social Preference.* London: Routledge.

Landen, Simone. 2011. "Michigan Legislature Moves to Ban Domestic Partnership Benefits." *HuffPost Detroit*, December 8. http://www.huffingtonpost.com/2011/12/08/michigan-legislature-bans-domestic-partner-benefits_n_1135029.html.

Landerretche, Oscar. 2012. "New Collectivism, the Fourth Way." In *Next Left: Building New Communities*, edited by Ernst Stetter, Karl Duffek, and Ania Skrzypek, 68–87. Brussels: FEPS.

Larson, Magali Sarfatti. 1977. *The Rise of Professionalism.* Berkeley: University of California Press.

Lash, Scott, and Celia Lury. 2007. *Global Culture Industry.* London: Polity.

Latour, Bruno. 2005. *Reassembling the Social: An Introduction to Actor-Network Theory.* Oxford: Oxford University Press.

Leberecht, Tim. 2012. "Shaping the Values of Our Connected World." *World Economic Forum Blog*, November 9. forumblog.org/2012/11/shaping-the-values-of-our-connected-world.

LeCercle, J. J. 1990. "Textual Responsibility." In *The Political Responsibility of Intellectuals*, edited by Ian Maclean, Alan Montefiore, and Peter Winch, 101–21. Cambridge: Cambridge University Press.

Ledeneva. Alena. 2013. "A Critique of the Global Corruption Paradigm." In *Post-Communism from Within: Social Justice, Mobilization, and Hegemony*, edited by Jan Kubik and Amy Linch, 297–333. New York: New York University Press/SSRC.

Lee, Alfred McClung. 1986. *Sociology for Whom*. Syracuse, NY: Syracuse University Press.

Leites, Nathan. 1953. "Stalin as an Intellectual." *World Politics* 6 (1): 45–66.

Lenski, Gerhard. 1978. "Marxist Experiments in Destratification: An Appraisal." *Social Forces* 57:364–83.

———. 1966. *Power and Privilege: A Theory of Social Stratification*. New York: McGraw Hill.

Lenski, Gerhard, Patrick Nolan, and Jean Lenski. 1995. *Human Societies: An Introduction to Macrosociology*. 7th ed. New York: McGraw-Hill.

Leonard, Mark, and Nico Popescu. 2007. "A Power Audit of EU-Russia Relations." *European Council of Foreign Relations Policy Paper*, November.

Leporc, Alexey. 2003. "Nicholas I and the New Hermitage: The Ancien Regime Moving toward the Public Museum." In *The Collections of the Romanovs: European Art from the State Hermitage Museum, St. Petersburg*, edited by James Christen Steward, with Sergey Androsov, 28–35. London: Merrell.

Levi, Michael. 2012. "Five Myths about the Keystone XL Pipeline." *Washington Post*, January 18. Also available at Council on Foreign Relations, http://www.cfr.org/energyenvironment/five-myths-keystone-xl-pipeline/p27099.

Levy, David. 1990. "Politics, Technology and the Responsibility of Intellectuals." In *The Political Responsibility of Intellectuals*, edited by Ian Maclean, Alan Montefiore, and Peter Winch, 123–42. Cambridge: Cambridge University Press

Lewis, Tania. 2001. "From the Organic to the Celebrity Intellectual." *Minnesota Review* 52–54:215–24.

Lie, John. 2004. *Multiethnic Japan*. Cambridge, MA: Harvard University Press.

Lim, Linda. 2001. "Globalizing the Intellect." *Journal of the International Institute* 8(2) http://quod.lib.umich.edu/j/jii/4750978.0008.202/--globalization-s-challenge?rgn=main;view=fulltext.

Limani, Hana. 2013. "Articulating Africana Philosophy." *Njohja* 2:135–52.

Lipset, Seymour Martin. 1963. *Political Man: The Social Bases of Politics*. Garden City, NY: Doubleday.

Lo, Ming-cheng. 2002. *Doctors within Borders: Profession, Ethnicity and Modernity within Colonial Taiwan*. Berkeley: University of California Press.

Lock, Grahame. 1990. "The Intellectual and the Imitation of the Masses." In *The Political Responsibility of Intellectuals*, edited by Ian Maclean, Alan Montefiore, and Peter Winch, 142–60. Cambridge: Cambridge University Press.

"Looking Ahead at Brown." 2012. Editorial in *East Side Monthly*, March, 5.

Lowen, Rebecca S. 1997. *Creating the Cold War University: The Transformation of Stanford*. Berkeley: University of California Press.

Luci, Nita, and Linda Gusia. Forthcoming. "Our Men Will Not Have Amnesia: Civic Engagement, Emancipation and Gendered Public in Kosovo." In *Civic and Uncivic Values in Kosovo*, edited by Sabrina Ramet. Budapest: Central European University Press.

Luci, Nita, and Vjollca Krasniqi, eds. 2011. *Politics of Remembrance and Belonging: Life Histories of Albanian Women in Kosova*. Prishtina: Center for Research and Gender Policy.

Ludlow, Peter. 2013. "What Is a 'Hactivist'?" *New York Times Opinionator*, January 13. http://opinionator.blogs.nytimes.com/2013/01/13/what-is-a-hacktivist/.

Maclean, Ian, Alan Montefiore, and Peter Winch, eds. 1990. *The Political Responsibility of Intellectuals*. Cambridge: Cambridge University Press.

Majors, Dan. 2011. "24 Peacefully Protest against Mercer-Based Tear Gas Maker." *Pittsburgh Post-Gazette*, December 2.

Malcolm, Noel. 1999. *Kosovo: A Short History*. New York: Harper.

Maliqi, Shkëlzen. 2000. "Why Peaceful Resistance Movement in Kosova Failed." March 22. http://shkelzenmaliqi.wordpress.com/2000/03/22/why-peaceful-resistance-movement-in-kosova-failed/.

Mandelbaum, Michael. 2004. *The Ideas That Conquered the World*. New York: Public Affairs.

Marcus, George E. 2000. "Preface: A Reintroduction to the Series." In *Para-Sites: A Casebook against Cynical Reason*, edited by George E. Marcus, ix–xiv. Chicago: University of Chicago Press.

Marginson, Simon, and Imanol Ordorika. 2011. "El central volumen de la fuerza: Global Hegemony in Higher Education and Research." In *Knowledge Matters: The Public Mission of the Research University*, edited by Diana Rhoten and Craig Calhoun, 67–129. New York: Columbia University Press.

Marody, Mira. 1993. "Why I Am Not a Feminist: Some Remarks on the Problem of Gender Identity in the United States and Poland." *Social Research* 60 (4): 853–64.

Marx, Karl. 1845. *Theses on Feuerbach*. https://www.marxists.org/archive/marx/works/1845/theses/theses.htm.

Marx, Karl, and Friedrich Engels. [1848] 2012. *The Communist Manifesto*. Edited by Jeffrey Isaac. New Haven, CT: Yale University Press.

Maslen, Geoff. 2012. "Universities Face Uncertain Future without Radical Overhaul." *University World News*, no. 245, October 24. http://www.universityworldnews.com/article.php?story=20121024084857770.

Masuda, T., R. Gonzalez, L. Kwan, and R. E. Nisbett. 2008. "Culture and Esthetic Preference: Comparing the Attention to Context of East Asians and Americans." *Personality and Social Psychology Bulletin* 38:1260–75.

Matthau, David. 2011. "Sociologist Says Penn State Scandal Could Be the

Tipping Point." New Jersey 101.5, November 11. http://nj1015.com/sociologist-says-penn-state-scandal-could-be-the-tipping-point-video/.

Maxwell, Simon, and Diane Stone. 2005. "Global Knowledge Networks and International Development." In *Global Knowledge Networks and International Development*, edited by Diane Stone and Simon Maxwell, 1–17. London: Routledge.

McDonald, Brent. 2012. "Occupiers' 'Think Tank' Soldiers On, Nonconfrontationally." *New York Times*, February 1. http://cityroom.blogs.nytimes.com/2012/02/01/occupiers-think-tank-soldiers-on-nonconfrontationally/?ref=occupywallstreet&_r=0.

McDonald, Michael. 2012. "Harvard's Voluntary Tax Spurs Ailing Providence to Press Brown." *Providence Business News*, February 8. http://www.pbn.com/Harvards-Voluntary-Tax-Spurs-Ailing-Providence-to-Press-Brown,65222.

McQuarrie, Michael. 2011. "Who Is Responsible for Police Violence at UC Davis?" Possible Futures, a Project of the Social Science Research Council, November 28. http://www.possible-futures.org/2011/11/28/who-is-responsible-for-police-violence-at-uc-davis/.

Mearsheimer, John, and Stephen Walt. 2007. *The Israel Lobby and U.S. Foreign Policy*. New York: Farrar, Straus and Giroux.

Merkx, Gil. 2003. "Waves of Change: Internationalization in U.S. Higher Education." *International Educator* 12 (1): 6–12.

Merton, Robert K. 1973. *The Sociology of Science: Theoretical and Empirical Investigations*. Chicago: University of Chicago Press.

Mertus, Julie. 1999. *Kosovo: How Myths and Truths Started a War*. Berkeley: University of California Press.

Mews, Constant J., and John N. Crossley, eds. 2011. *Communities of Learning: Networks and the Shaping of Identity in Europe, 1100–1500*. Turnhout, Belgium: Brepols.

Meyer, John, Francisco O. Ramierz, David John Frank, and Evan Schofer. 2007. "Higher Education as an Institution." In *Sociology of Higher Education: Contributions and Their Contexts*, edited by Patricia J. Gumpert, 187–221. Baltimore: Johns Hopkins University Press.

Meyer, Michael. 2014. "Evgeny vs. the Internet." *Columbia Journalism Review*, January 2. http://www.cjr.org/cover_story/evgeny_vs_the_internet.php?page=all.

Mikdashi, Maya. 2011. "Waiting for Alia." *Jadaliyya*, November 20. http://www.jadaliyya.com/pages/index/3208/waiting-for-alia.

Min, Anselm. 2004. *The Solidarity of Others in a Divided World: A Postmodern Theology after Postmodernism*. New York: T & T Clark International.

Mishra, Pankaj. 2013. "Why Salman Rushdie Should Stick to Holding Obama to Account." *The Guardian*, January 4. http://www.guardian.co.uk/books/2013/jan/04/salman-rushdie-pankaj-mishra-yan.

———. 2012. *From the Ruins of Empire: The Intellectuals Who Remade Asia*. New York: Farrar, Straus and Giroux.

Mitchell, Timothy. 2011. *Carbon Democracy: Political Power in the Age of Oil*. London: Verso.

Molnar, Virag. 2005. "Cultural Politics and Modernist Architecture: The Tulip Debate in Postwar Hungary." *American Sociological Review* 70 (1): 111–35.

Monitor Group. 2007. "Project to Enhance the Profile of Libya and Muammar Qadhafi: Executive Summary of Phase I." http://www.motherjones.com/files/project_to_enhance_the_profile_of_libya_and_muammar_qadhafi.pdf.

Montefiore, Alan. 1990. "The Political Responsibility of Intellectuals." In *The Political Responsibility of Intellectuals*, edited by Ian Maclean, Alan Montefiore, and Peter Winch, 201–28. Cambridge: Cambridge University Press.

Moody, James. 2004. "The Structure of a Social Science Collaboration Network: Disciplinary Cohesion from 1963 to 1999." *American Sociological Review* 69 (2): 213–38.

Mooney, Tom, and Alisha A. Pina. 2012. "Mayor Says City near Bankruptcy." *Providence Journal*, February 3, 1, 2.

Moore, Barrington. 1966. *Social Origins of Dictatorship and Democracy*. Boston: Beacon Press.

Morgan, Mary. 1999. "99 Years Later, It's Still the Same Old Story." *Ann Arbor News*, M-Edition, September 2, 3.

Mosco, Vincent. 2000. "Webs of Myth and Power: Connectivity and the New Computer Technopolis." In *The World Wide Web and Contemporary Cultural Theory*, edited by Andrew Herman and Thomas Swiss, 37–60. New York: Routledge.

Moscow Times. 2012. "Putin Awards Foreign Executives." October 5. http://www.themoscowtimes.com/business/article/putin-awards-foreign-executives/469312.html.

Mueller, Milton L. 2010. *Networks and States: The Global Politics of Internet Governance*. Cambridge, MA: MIT Press.

Muller, Jan-Werner. 2010. "In the Shadows of Statism: Peculiarities of the German Debate in European Integration." In *European Stories: Intellectual Debates on Europe in National Contexts*, edited by Justine Lacroix and Kalpyso Nicolaidis, 87–104. Oxford: Oxford University Press.

Myers, Charles. 2002. "Teaching Rulers How to Govern: The World Bank and Its Governance Agenda." PhD diss., University of Michigan.

Nagl, John A., Andrew M. Exum, and Ahmed A. Humayun. 2009. "A Pathway to Success in Afghanistan: The National Solidarity Program." *Policy Brief for a New American Security*, March. http://www.cnas.org/files/documents/publications/CNAS%20Policy%20Brief%20-%20Supporting%20Afghanistans%20NSP%20March%202009.pdf.

Newfield, Christopher. 2013. "Seven Questions to the MOOCFest." Remaking the University, January 8. http://utotherescue.blogspot.com/2013/01/seven-questions-to-moocfest.html?m=1.

———. 2008. *Unmaking the Public University: The Forty-Year Assault on the Middle Class*. Cambridge, MA: Harvard University Press.

Nisbett, R. E. 2007a. "Cognition and Perception East and West." In *Psychological Science around the World*, edited by Q. Jing, 300–310. Beijing: International Psychology Press.

———. 2007b. Preface to Chinese edition of *The Geography of Thought*. Beijing: CITIC Publishing House / Informedia of China.

Northrop, Douglas. 2004. *Veiled Empire: Gender and Power in Stalinist Central Asia*. Stanford, CA: Stanford University Press.

Nowak, Andrzej. 2002. "Honing the Competitive Edge." *Journal of the International Institute* 8 (2). http://quod.lib.umich.edu/j/jii/4750978.0008.202/—globalization-s-challenge?rgn=main;view=fulltext.

Nowak, Leszek. 2012. "The Structure of Provincial Thought." In *Thinking about Provincialism in Thinking: 66 Poznan Studies in the Philosophy of the Social Sciences and Humanities*, edited by Krzysztof Brzechczyn and Katarzyna Paprzycka, 51–66. Amsterdam: Rodopi.

Office of the United Nations High Commissioner for Human Rights. 2014. "Report on the Human Rights Situation in Ukraine." May 15. http://www.ohchr.org/Documents/Countries/UA/HRMMUReport15May2014.pdf.

Olson, Kevin. 2011. "Deliberative Democracy." In *Jürgen Habermas: Key Concepts*, edited by Barbara Fultner, 140–55. Durham, UK: Acumen Publishing.

Onuch, Olga. 2014. "Social Networks and Social Media in Ukrainian 'Euromaidan' Protests." *Washington Post, Monkey Cage*, January 2. http://www.washingtonpost.com/blogs/monkey-cage/wp/2014/01/02/social-networks-and-social-media-in-ukrainian-euromaidan-protests-2/.

Oreskes, N. 2004. "Beyond the Ivory Tower. The Scientific Consensus on Climate Change." *Science* 306:1686.

Oreskes, N., and E. M. Conway. 2010. *Merchants of Doubt*. New York: Bloomsbury Press.

Orr, Matthew. 2013. "The Soul of the Square." *New York Times Video*, December 20. http://www.nytimes.com/video/world/europe/100000002614934/the-soul-of-the-square.html?smid=tw-share.

Ortner, Sherry. 2006. *Anthropology and Social Theory: Culture, Power and the Acting Subject*. Durham, NC: Duke University Press.

Osborn, Alan. 2013. "U-Multirank Is Launched, 500 Universities Expected to Sign Up." *University World News*, February 3. http://www.universityworldnews.com/article.php?story=20130201144343699.

Oshima, Kotoe. 2011. "Occupy Duke One of Few Collegiate Demonstrations." *The Chronicle*, November 2. http://www.dukechronicle.com/articles/2011/11/03/occupy-duke-one-few-collegiate-demonstrations.

Osman, Wazhmah. 2012. "Between a Rock and a Cave: The Uneven Development of the Afghan Public Sphere." In *Engaging Afghanistan*, edited by Shiva Balaghi and Michael D. Kennedy, September 11. http://www.engagingafghanistan.org/videos-and-essays/the-public-sphere.

———. 2011. "Thinking outside the Box: Television and the Afghan Culture Wars." PhD diss., New York University.

Osorio, Jonathan Kay Kamakawiwo'ole. 2002. *Dismembering Lahui: A History of the Hawaiian Nation to 1887*. Honolulu: University of Hawaii Press.

Padgett, John F., and Walter W. Powell. 2012. *The Emergence of Organizations and Markets*. Princeton: Princeton University Press.

Padilla, Arthur. 2005. *Portraits in Leadership: Six Extraordinary University Presidents*. Westport, CT: Praeger.

Page, Scott E. 2012. "Counterfactual Campus: Scott Page, 2112 and the Resilient Idea." WISC Institute for Discovery. http://vimeo.com/55045254.

Pagoulatos, George, and Xenophon A. Yataganas. 2010. "Europe Othered, Europe Enlisted, Europe Possessed: Greek Public Intellectuals and the European Union." In *European Stories: Intellectual Debates on Europe in National Contexts*, edited by Justine Lacroix and Kalpyso Nicolaidis, 183–202. Oxford: Oxford University Press.

Panofsky, Aaron L. 2010. "A Critical Reconsideration of the Ethos and Autonomy of Science." In *Robert K. Merton: Sociology of Science and Sociology as Science*, edited by Craig Calhoun, 140–63. New York: Columbia University Press/SSRC Books.

Pavgi, Kedar. 2011. "The FP Top 100 Global Thinkers." *Foreign Policy*, November 28. http://www.foreignpolicy.com/articles/2011/11/28/the_fp_top_100_global_thinkers#sthash.t8A4B9AN.dpbs.

Paxson, Christina, and Angel Tavares. 2012. "Swearer Center's 25 Years of Progress." *Providence Journal*, October 5.

Peacock, James. 2007. *Grounded Globalism: How the U.S. South Embraces the World*. Athens: University of Georgia Press.

Pendleton-Jullian, Ann. 2009. "Design Education and Innovation Ecotones." Scribd. http://www.scribd.com/doc/48937251/Design-Education-and-Innovation-Ecotones-Ann-jullian-Architect.

Pendleton-Jullian, Ann, and John Seely Brown. Forthcoming. *Design Unbound*.

Pigman, Geoffrey. 2007. *The World Economic Forum: A Multi-stakeholder Approach to Global Governance*. New York: Routledge.

Pina, Alisha A. 2012. "Brown University Agrees to Pay Providence $31.5 Million More over 11 Years." *Providence Journal*, May 1. http://news.providencejournal.com/breaking-news/2012/05/in-the-works-br.html. [no longer available, accessed May 2, 2012]

Piven, Frances Fox. 2008. "Can Power from Below Change the World?" *American Sociological Review* 73 (1): 1–14.

Pleyers, Geoffrey. 2010. *Alter-Globalization: Becoming Actors in the Global Age*. Cambridge, UK: Polity.

Polkinghorn, Brian. 2006. Review of *Networks of Democracy: Lessons from Kosovo for Afghanistan, Iraq, and Beyond*, by Anne Holohan. *American Journal of Sociology* 112 (1): 299–301.

Pozdorovkin, Maxim. 2013. "Pussy Riot: A Punk Prayer." *Global Comment*, June 25. http://globalcomment.com/pussy-riot-a-punk-prayer/.

Prahalad, C. K., and Kenneth Lieberthal. 2003. "The End of Corporate Imperialism." *Harvard Business Review* 81:109–17, 142.

Prakash, Gyan. 1990. "Writing Post-Orientalist Histories of the Third World: Perspectives from Indian Historiography." *Comparative Studies in Society and History* 32 (2): 383–408.

Prewitt, Kenneth, Thomas A. Schwandt, and Miron L. Straf, eds. 2012. *Using Science in Public Policy*. Washington DC: National Academies Press.

Prospect/Foreign Policy. 2005. "The Prospect/FP Top 100 Public Intellectuals: Who Are the World's Leading Public Intellectuals?" infoplease. http://www.infoplease. com/spot/topintellectuals.html#ixzz1vvNMNDpt.

Pula, Besnik. 2009. "The Permanent State of Exception: International Administration in Kosovo." In *Hegemonic Transformations, the State and Crisis in Neoliberalism*, edited by Yildiz Atasoy, 227–43. New York: Routledge.

———. 2004. "The Emergence of the Kosovar Parallel State, 1988–92." *Nationalities Papers* 32 (4): 797–826.

"The 'Punk Prayer' That Landed Pussy Riot in Court." 2012. *The Telegraph*, August 17. http://www.telegraph.co.uk/news/worldnews/europe/russia/9482190/The-punk-prayer-that-landed-Pussy-Riot-in-court.html.

Rachkevych, Mark. 2013. "How the Social Drivers of Euromaidan Differ from the Orange Revolution." *KyivPost*, December 6. http://www.kyivpost.com/content/ ukraine/how-the-social-drivers-of-the-orange-revolution-differ-from-euro-maidan-333171.html.

Rashid, Ahmed. 2008. *Descent into Chaos: The United States and the Failure of Nation Building in Pakistan, Afghanistan and Central Asia*. New York: Viking.

Rathbun, Brian. 2004. *Partisan Interventions: European Party Politics and Peace Enforcement in the Balkans*. Ithaca, NY: Cornell University Press.

Regulska, Joanna, and Magda Grabowska. 2013. "Social Justice, Hegemony and Women's Mobilizations." In *Post-Communism from Within: Social Justice, Mobilization, and Hegemony*, edited by Jan Kubik and Amy Linch, 139–90. New York: New York University Press/SSRC.

Reichman, Jerome. 2009. "Intellectual Property in the Twenty-First Century: Will the Developing Countries Lead or Follow?" *Houston Law Review* 46 (4): 1115–85. http://www.ncbi.nlm.nih.gov/pmc/articles/PMC3060777/.

Rensink, Emiline. 2013. "Anonymous Seattle Reaches Out to Public with 'Operation Rose Awareness.'" *Examiner.com*, January 27. http://www.examiner.com/article/ anonymous-seattle-reaches-out-to-public-with-operation-rose-awareness.

Rettman, Andrew. 2009. "Russia Invites Europe to Join New Energy Charter." *EUobserver*, April 21. http://euobserver.com/foreign/27970.

———. 2006. "Georgia Leader Wows MEPs with Anti-imperialism Speech." *EUobserver*, November 14. http://euobserver.com/foreign/22861.

Rhoades, Gary. 2007. "The Study of the Academic Profession." In *Sociology of Higher Education: Contributions and Their Contexts*, edited by Patricia J. Gumpert, 113–46. Baltimore: Johns Hopkins University Press.

Rhoads, Robert A., and Katalin Szelenyi. 2011. *Global Citizenship and the University: Advancing Social Life and Relations in an Interdependent World*. Stanford, CA: Stanford University Press.

Rhoten, Diana, and Craig Calhoun, eds. 2011. *Knowledge Matters: The Public Mission of the Research University*. New York: Columbia University Press.

Riabchuk, Mykola. 2013. "Ukraine: Across the Dividing Lines." *Al Jazeera*, December 16. http://m.aljazeera.com/story/2013121672720957494.

Rice, Andrew. 2012. "How Not to Fire a President: The Attack on Teresa Sullivan and the School That Rose to Her Defense." *New York Times Magazine*, September 16, 56–62, 65.

Roberts, Kenneth M. 2011. "Chile: The Left after Neoliberalism." In *The Resurgence of the Latin American Left*, edited by Steven Levitsky and Kenneth M. Roberts, 325–47. Baltimore: Johns Hopkins University Press.

Robertson, Roland. 1992. *Globalization: Social Theory and Global Culture*. London: Sage.

Robinson, Sophie. 2012. "Poems for Pussy Riot: Free Pussy." *English Pen*, September 26. http://www.englishpen.org/poems-for-pussy-riot-free-pussy-by-sophie-robinson/.

Rogers, Douglas. 2012. "The Materiality of the Corporation: Oil, Gas, and Corporate Social Technologies in the Remaking of a Russian Region." *American Ethnologist* 39 (2): 284–96.

Rohde, David. 2012. "The Jobs University: How to Turn Our Schools into Engines of Innovation." *Atlantic Monthly*, February 10. http://www.theatlantic.com/business/archive/2012/02/the-jobs-university-how-to-turn-our-schools-into-engines-of-innovation/252893/.

Roucek, Joseph S. 1936. "The Development of Sociology in Yugoslavia." *American Sociological Review* 1 (6): 981–88.

Rowsell, Ben. 2012. "Solving the Statebuilders' Dilemma." *Washington Quarterly* 35 (1): 97–114.

RT. 2012. "Nord Stream Launches Second Pipeline." October 8. http://rt.com/business/news/nord-stream-line-start-881/.

Rubbo, A. 2001. "Values and Architectural Education." *Architectural Theory Review* 6 (2): 65–80.

Runner, Philippa. 2009a. "Gas War Costing EU 'Hundreds of Millions a Day.'" *EUobserver*, January 14. http://euobserver.com/foreign/27410.

———. 2009b. "Russia and Ukraine Face EU Sanctions Threat." *EUobserver*, January 16. http://euobserver.com/foreign/27424.

Rutland, Peter. 2012. "What Links Pussy Riot with Dostoyevsky." *Moscow Times*, August 27. http://www.themoscowtimes.com/opinion/article/what-links-pussy-riot-with-dostoevsky/467138.html.

Ryan, James G., and James L. Garrett. 2005. "The Impact of Economic Policy Research: Lessons of Attribution and Evaluation from IFPRI." In *Global Knowledge Networks and International Development*, edited by Simon Maxwell and Diane Stone, 37–56. London: Routledge.

Sagrans, Erica, ed. 2011. *We Are Wisconsin: The Wisconsin Uprising in the Words of the Activists, Writers, and Everyday Wisconsinites Who Made It Happen*. Minneapolis, MN: Tasora.

Said, Atef. 2011. "Uprising in Egypt: America in the Egyptian Revolution." The Immanent Frame, April 11. http://blogs.ssrc.org/tif/2011/04/11/america-in-the-egyptian-revolution/.

Said, Edward. 2000. "The Treason of the Intellectuals." In *Masters of the Universe? NATO's Balkan Crusade*, edited by Tariq Ali, 341–44. London: Verso.

———. 1996. *Representations of the Intellectual.* New York: Vintage.

———. 1979. *Orientalism.* New York: Vintage.

Saito, Hiro. 2012. "The Fukushima Disaster and Japan's Occupy Movement." In Possible Futures: A Project of the Social Science Research Council, February 28. http://www.possible-futures.org/author/saito/.

Saito, Hiro, and Yoko Wang. 2014. "Competing Logics of Commemoration: Cosmopolitanism and Nationalism in East Asia's History Problem." *Sociological Perspectives* 57 (2): 167–85.

Sassen, Saskia. 2008. *Territory Authority Rights.* Princeton: Princeton University Press.

———. 2007. *A Sociology of Globalization.* New York: Norton.

Sauder, Michael, and Wendy Nelson Espeland. 2009. "The Discipline of Rankings: Tight Coupling and Organizational Change." *American Sociological Review* 74:63–82.

Schiffman, Richard. 2013. "'Frackademia': How Big Gas Bought Research on Hydraulic Fracturing." *The Guardian*, January 9. http://www.guardian.co.uk/commentisfree/2013/jan/09/fracking-big-gas-university-research.

Schor, Juliet. 2012. "Hours Reductions: Elements for a Red-Green Coalition." In *Next Left: Building New Communities*, edited by Ernst Stetter, Karl Duffek, and Ania Skrzypek, 165–76. Brussels: FEPS.

Schottler, Peter. 2004. "French and German Historians' Networks: The Case of the Early Annales." In *Transnational Intellectual Networks: Forms of Academic Knowledge and the Search for Cultural Identities*, edited by Christophe Charle, Jürgen Schriewer, and Peter Wagner, 115–33. Frankfurt: Campus Verlag.

Schriewer, Jürgen. 2004. "Multiple Internationalities: The Emergence of a World-Level Ideology and the Persistence of Idiosyncratic World-Views." In *Transnational Intellectual Networks: Forms of Academic Knowledge and the Search for Cultural Identities*, edited by Christophe Charle, Jürgen Schriewer, and Peter Wagner, 473–533. Frankfurt: Campus Verlag.

Schuessler, Jennifer. 2012. "Professor Who Learns from Peasants." *New York Times*, December 4.

Schulte, Barbara. 2004. "East Is East and West Is West? Chinese Academia Goes Global." In *Transnational Intellectual Networks: Forms of Academic Knowledge and the Search for Cultural Identities*, edited by Christophe Charle, Jürgen Schriewer, and Peter Wagner, 307–29. Frankfurt: Campus Verlag.

Schwab, Klaus. 2013. "Building Resilience to Global Risks." *World Economic Forum Blog*, January 8. http://forumblog.org/2013/01/building-resilience-to-global-risks/.

Schwandner-Sievers, Stephanie. 2013. "Democratisation through Defiance: The Albanian Civil Organization 'Self-Determination' and International Supervision in Kosovo." In *Civil Society and Transitions in the Western Balkans*, edited by Vesna Bojicic-Dzelilovic, James Ker-Lindsay, and Denisa Kostovicova, 95–116. Basingstoke, UK: Palgrave Macmillan.

Scott, James. 2012. *Two Cheers for Anarchism: Six Easy Pieces on Autonomy, Dignity, and Meaningful Work and Play*. Princeton: Princeton University Press.

Sekulic, Dusko, Garth Massey, and Randy Hodson. 1994. "Who Were the Yugoslavs? Failed Sources of a Common Identity in the Former Yugoslavia." *American Sociological Review* 59 (1): 83–97.

Selivanova, Yulia. 2010. "Managing the Patchwork of Agreements in Trade and Investment." In *Global Energy Governance: The New Rules of the Game*, edited by Andreas Goldthau and Jan Martin Witte, 49–72. Berlin: Global Policy Institute and Washington: Brookings Institution.

Senkevitch, Tatiana V. 2003. "Reflections on Projecting Petersburg." *Journal of the International Institute* 10, no. 3 (Spring/Summer): 4, 19.

Sewell, William H., Jr. 2005. *Logics of History: Social Theory and Social Transformation*. Chicago: University of Chicago Press.

Shaikh, Nermeen, and Amy Goodman. 2013. "Is Edward Snowden a Hero? A Debate with Journalist Chris Hedges and Law Scholar Geoffrey Stone." Debate on *Democracy Now*, June 12. http://www.democracynow.org/2013/6/12/is_edward_snowden_a_hero_a.

Shami, Seteney. 2011. "Announcing the Arab Council for the Social Sciences." *Jadaliyya*, October 29. http://www.jadaliyya.com/pages/index/3009/announcing-the-arab-council-for-the-social-science.

Shankar, Subramanian. 2001. *Textual Traffic: Colonialism, Modernity, and the Economy of the Text*. Albany: SUNY Press.

Shavarshidze, George. 2012. "Open Society Foundations: International Higher Education Support Programme Academic Fellowship Program." Open Society Foundation/Academic Fellowship Program Meeting, Budapest.

Sherman, Daniel. 2010. "Uncovering Sustainability in the Curriculum." In *Climate Neutral Campus Report*, edited by Melissa Daley, 70–73. San Francisco: Kyoto Publishing. www.climateneutralcampus.com.

———. 2008. "Sustainability: What's the Big Idea?" *Sustainability* 1 (3): 188–95.

Shevtsova, Lilia. 2014. "Blurred Lines between War and Peace." *American Interest*, July 11, 2014. http://www.the-american-interest.com/shevtsova/2014/07/11/blurred-lines-between-war-and-peace/.

Shils, Edward. 1972. *The Intellectuals and the Powers and Other Essays*. Chicago: University of Chicago Press.

Shils, Edward, S. Chandrasekhar, Roderick Childers, John Hope Franklin, Arthur Friedman, Jacob W. Getzels, Harry G. Johnson, Saunders Mac Lane, Edward Rosenheim, John Simpson, Lorna P. Straus, and H. G. Williams-Ashman. 1972. "A Report of the University of Chicago Committee on the Criteria of Academic Appointment." *University of Chicago Record* 4 (6) and 6 (1). http://provost.uchicago.edu/pdfs/shilsrpt.pdf.

Shwed, Uri, and Peter S. Bearman. 2010. "The Temporal Structure of Scientific Consensus Formation." *American Sociological Review* 75 (6): 817–40.

Sica, Alan. 2010. "Merton, Mannheim, and the Sociology of Knowledge." In *Robert*

K. Merton: Sociology of Science and Sociology as Science, edited by Craig Calhoun, 164–81. New York: Columbia University Press/SSRC Books.

Sierakowski, Sławomir. 2014. "Welcome Ukraine into the EU and Restore Faith in the Project." *The Guardian*, January 4. http://www.theguardian.com/commentisfree/2014/jan/04/welcome-ukraine-into-eu-project.

Sikkink, Kathryn. 2011. *The Justice Cascade: How Human Rights Prosecutions Are Changing World Politics.* New York: Norton.

Simonson, Peter. 2010. "Merton's Sociology of Rhetoric." In *Robert K. Merton: Sociology of Science and Sociology as Science*, edited by Craig Calhoun, 214–52. New York: Columbia University Press/SSRC Books.

Skocpol, Theda. 1979. *States and Social Revolutions: A Comparative Analysis of France, Russia and China.* Cambridge: Cambridge University Press.

Skocpol, Theda, and Margaret Somers. 1980. "Uses of Comparative Inquiry." *Comparative Studies in Society and History* 22 (2): 174–97.

Skrzypek, Ania. 2013. "The Next Social Contract: A New Vision for European Society." In *Next Left: For a New Social Deal*, edited by Ernst Stetter, Karl Duffek, and Ania Skrzypek, 24–59. Brussels: FEPS.

Slack, Jennifer Daryl. 1996. "The Theory and Method of Articulation in Cultural Studies." In *Stuart Hall: Critical Dialogues in Cultural Studies*, edited by David Morley and Kuan-Hsing Chen, 112–27. London: Routledge.

Sloterdijk, Peter. 2012. *The Art of Philosophy: Wisdom as Practice.* New York: Columbia University Press.

Smith, Mitch, and Kevin Abourezk. 2011. "Emails: Wisconsin and Michigan Opposed Nebraska's AAU Membership." *Lincoln Journal Star*, September 3. http://journalstar.com/news/local/education/emails-wisconsin-and-michigan-opposed-nebraska-s-aau-membership/article_19188dda-afe7-57c8-aa2c-c1939ec5acb4.html.

Snow, David A., R. Burke Rochford Jr., Steven K. Worden, and Robert D. Benford. 1986. "Frame Alignment Processes, Micromobilization, and Movement Participation." *American Sociological Review* 51:464–81.

Soens, Darren. 2012. "Firefighters Protest Tax Exempt Brown." *WPRI News*, February 9. http://www.wpri.com/dpp/news/local_news/providence/providence-firefighters-protest-tax-exempt-brown. [no longer available, accessed February 10, 2012]

Somers, Margaret. 1999. "The Privatization of Citizenship: How to Unthink a Knowledge Culture." In *Beyond the Cultural Turn: New Directions in the Study of Society and Culture*, edited by Victoria Bonnell and Lynn Hunt, 121–61. Berkeley: University of California Press.

———. 1995a. "The 'Misteries' of Property: Relationality, Families, and Community in Chartist Narratives of Political Rights." In *Early Modern Conceptions of Property*, edited by John Brewer and Susan Staves, 62–92. London: Routledge.

———. 1995b. "Narrating and Naturalizing Civil Society and Citizenship Theory: The Place of Political Culture and the Public Sphere." *Sociological Theory* 13:229–74.

———. 1995c. "What's Political or Cultural about the Political Culture Concept?

Toward an Historical Sociology of Concept Formation." *Sociological Theory* 13:113–44.

Soros, George. 2012. "Europe's Crisis of Values." *Project Syndicate*, December 31. http://www.project-syndicate.org/commentary/the-existential-crisis-of-the-european-union-by-george-soros.

———. 2008. *The Crash of 2008 and What It Means.* New York: Public Affairs.

Sowell, Thomas. 2009. *Intellectuals and Society.* New York: Basic Books.

Spolsky, Danylo. 2013. "One Minister's Dark Warning and the Ray of Hope." *KyivPost*, November 27. http://www.kyivpost.com/opinion/op-ed/one-ministers-dark-warning-and-the-ray-of-hope-332521.html.

St Felix, Doreen. 2013. "The Only Thing 'Uncivilised' about Ray Kelly's Talk at Brown Was Inviting Him." *The Guardian*, October 31. http://www.theguardian.com/commentisfree/2013/oct/31/brown-university-ray-kelly-protest-free-speech.

Stanfield, David, and Daniel Lincoln. 2012. "OECD, Boston College Explore Role of Research Universities." *University World News*, October 29.

Starr, S. Frederick. 2005. "The Baku-Tbilisi-Ceyhan Pipeline: School of Modernity." In *The Baku-Tbilisi-Ceyhan Pipeline: Oil Window to the West*, edited by S. Frederick Starr and Svante E. Cornell, Johns Hopkins University-SAIS. http://www.silkroadstudies.org/BTC_1.pdf.

Steinmetz, George. 2007. "American Sociology before and after World War II: The (Temporary) Settling of a Disciplinary Field." In *Sociology in America: A History*, edited by Craig Calhoun, 314–66. Chicago: University of Chicago Press/An American Sociological Association Centennial Publication.

Stern, Jonathan. 2012. Preface to *The Gas Relationship between the Baltic States and Russia: Politics and Commercial Realities*, by Agnia Grigas. Oxford Institute for Energy Studies NG 67. http://www.oxfordenergy.org/wpcms/wp-content/uploads/2012/10/NG_67.pdf.

———. 2006. "The Russian-Ukrainian Gas Crisis of January 2006." Oxford Institute for Energy Studies, January 16. http://www.oxfordenergy.org/2006/01/the-russian-ukrainian-gas-crisis-of-january-2006/.

Stetter, Ernst, Karl Duffek, and Ania Skrzypek, eds. 2013. *Next Left: For a New Social Deal.* Brussels: FEPS.

Steward, James Christen. 2003. "The Private Taste of the Romanovs in Eighteenth Century Russia." In *The Collections of the Romanovs: European Art from the State Hermitage Museum, St. Petersburg*, edited by James Christen Steward, with Sergey Androsov, 14–27. London: Merrell.

Stiglitz, Joseph E. 2011. "Of the 1%, by the 1%, for the 1%." *Vanity Fair*, May. http://www.vanityfair.com/society/features/2011/05/top-one-percent-201105.

Stillman, Amy. 2003. "Infinite Horizons: Engaging Global Diversity." *For a University of the World* (Webcast, March 27). *Journal of the International Institute* 10 (3): 2. http://quod.lib.umich.edu/cgi/t/text/text-idx?c=jii;view=text;rgn=main;idno=4750978.0010.302.

Stokes, Doug, and Sam Raphael. 2010. *Global Energy Security and American Hegemony.* Baltimore: Johns Hopkins University Press.

Stokes, Gale. 1997. "The Devil's Finger: The Disintegration of Yugoslavia." In *Three Eras of Political Change in Eastern Europe*, by Gale Stokes, 109–43. Oxford: Oxford University Press.

Stone, Diane. 2005. "Knowledge Networks and Global Policy." In *Global Knowledge Networks and International Development*, edited by Simon Maxwell and Diane Stone, 89–105. London: Routledge.

Strange, Rodney. 2008. *Newman 101: An Introduction to the Life and Philosophy of John Cardinal Newman.* Notre Dame, IN: Christian Classics.

Stripling, Jack. 2012. "UVa's Painful Public Lesson in Leadership." *Chronicle of Higher Education*, July 2. http://chronicle.com/article/ UVas-Painfully-Public-Lesson/132701/.

"Students Press Brown U to Pay More to Providence." 2012. *WPRO News Talk*, February 10. http://www.630wpro.com/Article.asp?id=2392398&spid=38785. [no longer available, accessed February 10, 2012]

Sudetic, Chuck. 2011. *The Philanthropy of George Soros: Building Open Societies* [with comments by George Soros and Aryeh Neier]. New York: Public Affairs/Perseus Group.

Suny, Ronald Grigor, Fatma Muge Gocek, and Norman M. Naimark, eds. 2011. *A Question of Genocide: Armenians and Turks at the End of the Ottoman Empire.* Oxford: Oxford University Press.

Suny, Ronald Grigor, and Michael D. Kennedy, eds. 1999a. *Intellectuals and the Articulation of the Nation.* Ann Arbor: University of Michigan Press.

———. 1999b. "Towards a Theory of National Intellectual Practice." In *Intellectuals and the Articulation of the Nation*, edited by Ronald Grigor Suny and Michael D. Kennedy, 383–417. Ann Arbor: University of Michigan Press.

Swartz, David. 1997. *Culture and Power.* Chicago: University of Chicago Press.

Szanton, David. 2004. "The Origin, Nature, and Challenges of Area Studies in the United States." In *The Politics of Knowledge: Area Studies and the Disciplines*, edited by David Szanton, 1–33. Berkeley: University of California Press.

Szelenyi, Ivan, and Katarzyna Wilk. 2013. "Poverty and Popular Mobilization in Post-Communist Capitalist Regimes." In *Post-Communism from Within: Social Justice, Mobilization, and Hegemony*, edited by Jan Kubik and Amy Linch, 229–64. New York: New York University Press/SSRC.

Sztompka, Piotr. 2011. "Another Sociological Utopia." *Contemporary Sociology* 40 (4): 388–404.

Tahiri, Lindita. 2013. "Internet Activism as Transformation of Political Discourse." *Njohja* 2:219–32.

Tamas, G. M. 1990. "The Political Irresponsibility of Intellectuals." In *The Political Responsibility of Intellectuals*, edited by Ian Maclean, Alan Montefiore, and Peter Winch, 247–56. Cambridge: Cambridge University Press.

Tansman, Allan. 2004. "Japanese Studies: The Intangible Act of Translation." In *The

Politics of Knowledge: Area Studies and the Disciplines, edited by David Szanton, 184–216. Berkeley: University of California Press.

Tarrow, Sidney, and Peter Hall. 1998. "Globalization and Area Studies: When Is Too Broad Too Narrow?" *Chronicle of Higher Education*, January 23. http://chronicle.com/article/GlobalizationArea/99332/.

Taum, Ramsay Remigius Mahealani. 2013. "Ancient Wisdom, Future Knowledge: Looking to the Past to Shape the Future." Presentation at Brown University, November 7.

Taylor, Charles. 2009. "Rethinking Secularism: The Philosopher Citizen." The Immanent Frame, October 19. http://blogs.ssrc.org/tif/2009/10/19/philosopher-citizen/.

———. 2007. *A Secular Age*. Cambridge, MA: Harvard University Press.

———. 1994. "The Politics of Recognition." In *Multiculturalism: Examining the Politics of Recognition*, edited by Amy Gutmann, Charles Taylor, K. Anthony Appiah, Jürgen Habermas, Steven C. Rockefeller, Michael Walzer, and Susan Wolf, 25–74. Princeton: Princeton University Press.

Thomas, Daniel C. 2001. *The Helsinki Effect: International Norms, Human Rights, and the Demise of Communism*. Princeton: Princeton University Press.

Thomas, Douglas, and John Seely Brown. 2011. *A New Culture of Learning: Cultivating the Imagination for a World in Constant Change*. Createspace Publisher, 2011.

Thomas, W. I., and Florian Znaniecki. 1958. *The Polish Peasant in Europe and America*. New York: Dover. Originally published 1918–20.

Thornton, Arland. 2004. *Reading History Sideways: The Fallacy and Enduring Impact of the Developmental Paradigm*. Chicago: University of Chicago Press.

Thorpe, Charles. 2006. *Oppenheimer: The Tragic Intellect*. Chicago: University of Chicago Press.

Thorpe, Holden, and Buck Goldstein. 2010. *Engines of Innovation: The Entrepreneurial University in the 21st Century*. Chapel Hill: University of North Carolina Press.

Till, Brian Michael. 2011. *Conversations with Power: What Great Presidents and Prime Ministers Can Teach Us about Leadership*. New York: Macmillan.

Tippee, Bob. 2012. "Defining Energy Security." *Oil and Gas Journal*, January 23. http://www.ogj.com/articles/print/vol-110/issue-1c/regular-features/journally-speaking/defining-energy-security.html.

Todorova, Maria. 1997. *Imagining the Balkans*. Oxford: Oxford University Press.

Tomasic, Dinko. 1941. "Sociology in Yugoslavia." *American Journal of Sociology* 47 (1): 53–69.

Tomusk, Voldemar, ed. 2007a. *Creating the European Area of Higher Education: Voices from the Periphery*. Dordrecht, Netherlands: Springer.

———. 2007b. "The End of Europe and the Last Intellectual: Fine-Tuning Knowledge Work in the Panopticon of Bologna." In *Creating the European Area of Higher Education: Voices from the Periphery*, edited by Voldemar Tomusk, 269–303. Dordrecht, Netherlands: Springer.

Torpey, John. 1995. *Intellectuals, Socialism, and Dissent: The East German Opposition and Its Legacy*. Minneapolis: University of Minnesota Press.

Touraine, Alaine. 2009. *Thinking Differently*. Cambridge, UK: Polity.

———. 2007. *A New Paradigm for Understanding Today's World*. Cambridge, UK: Polity.

Tucker, Aviezer 2012. "The New Power Map: World Politics after the Boom in Conventional Energy." *Foreign Affairs*, December 19. http://www.foreignaffairs.com/ articles/138597/aviezer-tucker/the-new-power-map?page=2.

Turner, Jonathan. 2002. *The Structure of Sociological Theory*. Belmont, CA: Wadsworth.

Tusk, Donald. 2012. "A Debate on Protection of Intellectual Property in the Internet." February 3. https://www.premier.gov.pl/en/news/news/a-debate-on-protection-of-intellectual-property-in-the-internet.html#content.

UIA/UNESCO. 1996. "Charter for Architectural Education." June. http://www. unesco.org/most/uiachart.htm.

U-M Faculty. 2001. "Globalization's Challenge." *Journal of the International Institute* 8 (2). http://quod.lib.umich.edu/j/jii/4750978.0008.202/ —globalization-s-challenge?rgn=main;view=fulltext.

Umland, Andreas. 2014. "Kyiv's Euromaidan Is a Liberationist and Not Extremist Mass Action of Civic Disobedience." *Open Letter to Journalists, Commentators and Analysts Writing on the Ukrainian Protest Movement Euromaidan*, Change. org, February 4. https://www.change.org/ru/%D0%BF%D0%B5%D1%82%D0 %B8%D1%86%D0%B8%D0%B8/to-journalists-commentators-and-analysts-writing-on-the-ukrainian-protest-movement-euromaidan-kyiv-s-euromaidan-is-a-liberationist-and-not-extremist-mass-action-of-civic-disobedience.

———. 2013. "How Spread of Banderite Slogans and Symbols Undermines Ukrainian Nation Building." *KyivPost*, December 28. http://www.kyivpost.com/opinion/ op-ed/how-spread-of-banderite-slogans-and-symbols-undermines-ukrainian-nation-building-334389.html.

Unger, Roberto Mangabeira. 2005. *The Left Alternative*. London: Verso.

Veblen, Thorstein. [1904] 2005. *The Higher Learning in America*. Reprint, New York: Cosimo Classics.

Verdery, Katherine. 1991. *National Ideology under Socialism: Identity and Cultural Politics under Ceausescu's Romania*. Berkeley: University of California Press.

Verger, Antoni. 2009. *WTO/GATS and the Global Politics of Higher Education*. London: Routledge.

Vitalis, Robert. 2010. "The Noble American Science of Imperial Relations and Its Laws of Race Development." *Comparative Studies in Society and History* 52 (4): 909–38.

———. 2002. "International Studies in America." *Items and Issues* 3 (3/4). http://www. ssrc.org/workspace/images/crm/new_publication_3/%7B219ac6a2-2060-de11-bd80-001cc477ec70%7D.pdf.

Voice of America (VoA). 2009. "Polish Defense Minister's Pipeline Remark Angers Germany." October 31. http://www.voanews.com/content/a-13–polish-defense-minister-pipeline-remark-angers-germany/327455.html.

Waggoner, Eric. 2014. "I'm from West Virginia and I've Got Something to Say about the Chemical Spill." *Huffington Post*, January 14. http://www.huffingtonpost.com/ eric-waggoner/west-virginia-chemical-spill_b_4598140.html.

Walaszek, Zdzislawa. 1977. "Recent Developments in Polish Sociology." *Annual Review of Sociology* 3:331–62. http://www.jstor.org/stable/2945940.

Wald, Alan. 1987. *The New York Intellectuals: The Rise and Decline of the Anti-Stalinist Left*. Chapel Hill: University of North Carolina Press.

Walder, Andrew G. 2004. "The Transformation of Contemporary China Studies, 1977–2002." In *The Politics of Knowledge: Area Studies and the Disciplines*, edited by David Szanton, 314–40. Berkeley: University of California Press.

Waldman, Katy, and Will Oremus. 2013. "An Idiot's Guide to the Reddit Thread, 'What's the Most Intellectual Joke You Know'"? *Slate*, June 28. http://mobile. slate.com/blogs/future_tense/2013/06/28/the_most_intellectual_joke_you_ know_an_idiot_s_guide_to_the_reddit_thread.html?fb_ref=sm_fb_share_ blogpost&original_referrer=https%3A%2F%2Fm.facebook.com.

Walker, Peter. 2012. "Tent City University: One of the Most Remarkable Aspects of Occupy London." *The Guardian*, January 19. http://www.guardian.co.uk/uk/2012/ jan/19/occupy-london-tent-city-university.

Wallerstein, Immanuel. 2012. "The World Left after 2011." January 1. http://www. iwallerstein.com/world-left-2011/.

———. 2002. "New Revolts against the System." *New Left Review* 18. http://newleftrev-iew.org/II/18/immanuel-wallerstein-new-revolts-against-the-system.

———. 1999. "The Heritage of Sociology, the Promise of Social Science." In *The End of the World As We Know It*, 220–52. Minneapolis: University of Minnesota Press.

———. 1996. *Open the Social Sciences*. Stanford, CA: Stanford University Press.

———. 1976. *The Modern World System*. Vol. 1. Waltham, MA: Academic Press.

Walsh, Katie. 2012. "Occupy Hits Pitt's Campus." *Te Duquesne Duke*, February 1. http://www.theduquesneduke.com/occupy-hits-pitt-s-campus-1.2761684#. UtFcmfbTM7B.

Waltz, Susan. 1999. "On the Universality of Human Rights." *Journal of the International Institute* 6 (3). http://quod.lib.umich.edu/j/jii/4750978.0006.302?rgn=main ;view=fulltext;q1=human+rights.

Wampler, Jan. 2001. *Open Notes for Harmony: Six Places*. Cambridge, MA: MIT, Department of Architecture.

Warczok, Tomasz, and Tomasz Zarycki. 2014. "Bourdieu Recontextualized: Redefi-nitions of Western Critical Thought in the Periphery." *Current Sociology* 62 (3): 331–51. http://csi.sagepub.com/content/62/3/334.abstract.

Warner, Michael. 2005. *Publics and Counterpublics*. New York: Zone Books.

Weber, Max. [1905] 1930. *The Protestant Ethic and the Spirit of Capitalism*. Translated by Talcott Parsons. New York: Scribner.

Weberman, David. 2013. "Philosophy as Self Transformation: From Socratic Wisdom to Foucauldian De-Naturalization." *Njohja* 2:233–47.

Wicke, Jennifer. 1994. "Celebrity Material: Materialist Feminism and the Culture of Celebrity." *South Atlantic Quarterly* 93 (4):751–78.

Williams, Alex. 2012. "Chris Hayes Has Arrived with 'Up.'" *New York Times*, June 22. http://www.nytimes.com/2012/06/24/fashion/chris-hayes-has-arrived-with-up. html?pagewanted=all&_r=0.

Williams, Jeffrey J. 2012. "Deconstructing Academe: The Birth of Critical University Studies." *Chronicle of Higher Education*, February 19. http://chronicle.com/article/ An-Emerging-Field-Deconstructs/130791/.

Williams, Raymond. 1977. *Marxism and Literature*. London: Verso.

Williams, Ross, Gaetan de Rassenfosse, Paul Jensen, and Simon Marginson. 2012. "U21 Rankings of National Higher Education Systems 2012." Universitas 21, May 10. http://www.universitas21.com/news/details/61/ u21-rankings-of-national-higher-education-systems-2012.

Wilson, Jeremy M. 2006. "Law and Order in an Emerging Democracy: Lessons from the Reconstruction of Kosovo's Police and Justice Systems." *Annals of the American Academy of Political and Social Science* 605:152–77.

Wilson, Robin. 2011. "As Chancellor Focuses on the 'Public Good,' Syracuse's Reputation Slides." *Chronicle of Higher Education*, October 2. http://chronicle.com/ article/Syracuses-Slide/129238/.

Wimmer, Andreas, and Brian Min. 2006. "From Empire to Nation-State: Explaining Wars in the Modern World, 1816–2001." *American Sociological Review* 71 (6): 867–97.

Winn, Peter. 2007. "Without Yesterday There Is No Tomorrow: Ricardo Lagos and Chile's Democratic Transition." *Footnotes*, February. http://www2.asanet.org/ footnotes/feb07/indexone.html.

Wittgenstein, Ludwig. 1953. *Philosophical Investigations*. New York: Macmillan.

Wolfe, Thomas C., and John Pickles. 2013. "Social Justice, Social Science, and the Complexities of Post-Socialism." In *Post-Communism from Within: Social Justice, Mobilization, and Hegemony*, edited by Jan Kubik and Amy Linch, 95–137. New York: New York University Press/SSRC.

World Economic Forum (WEF) on Europe and Central Asia. 2011. *Expanding the Frontiers of Innovation*. Forum held June 8–9, Vienna, Austria. http://www3.weforum.org/docs/EU11/WEF_EU11_Report.pdf.

Worsley, Peter. 1997. *Knowledges: Culture, Counterculture, Subculture*. New York: New Press.

Wynnyckyj, Mychailo. 2014. "Filtering through the Fog of War." Facebook posting, January 26. https://www.facebook.com/notes/mychailo-wynnyckyj/ filtering-through-the-fog-of-war/688664257851594.

——— . "We Are in Phase Four of the Euromaidan Revolution." Interview with Andrij Holovatyj, YouTube, January 16. http://www.youtube.com/ watch?v=pvBfFw9xKQQ.

Yemelianova, Galina M. 2002. *Russia and Islam: A Historical Survey*. Basingstoke, UK: Palgrave Macmillan.

Yglesias, Matthew. 2013. "Actually, Keynes Cared a Lot about the Long Run." *Slate*, May 6. http://www.slate.com/articles/business/moneybox/2013/05/

niall_ferguson_keynes_and_homosexuality_the_harvard_historian_s_ludi-
crous.html.

Zabala, Santiago. 2012. "Slavoj Zizek and the Role of the Philosopher."
Al Jazeera, December 25. http://www.aljazeera.com/indepth/opinion/
2012/12/20121224122215406939.html.

Zakharov, Yevhen, Serhiy Zhadan, Viktor Pushkar, Oleksander Severyn, et al. 2014.
"We Are Not Extremists!" January 25. http://ireport.cnn.com/docs/DOC-1078187.

Zarycki, Tomasz. 2014. *Ideologies of Eastness in Central and Eastern Europe*. London:
Routledge.

Žižek, Slavoj. 2012. *The Year of Dreaming Dangerously*. London: Verso.

———. 1999. "NATO, the Left Hand of God." June 29. http://www.lacan.com/zizek-
nato.htm.

Znaniecka, Eileen Markley. 1936. "Sociology in Poland." *American Sociological Review*
1 (2): 296–98.

Znaniecki, Florian. 1986. *The Social Role of the Man of Knowledge*. New Brunswick,
NJ: Transaction.

———. 1954. "Basic Problems of Contemporary Sociology." *American Sociological
Review* 19 (5): 519–24.

Zoellick, Robert. 2008. "The Key to Rebuilding Afghanistan." *Washington Post*,
August 22.

Zubrzycki, Genevieve. 2012. "Negotiating Pluralism in Québec: Identity, Religion
and Secularism in the Debate over 'Reasonable Accommodation.'" In *Religion at
the Edge: Toward a New Sociology of Religion*, edited by Courtney Bender, Wendy
Cadge, Peggy Levitt, and David Smilde, 215–37. New York: Oxford University
Press.

———. 2006. *The Crosses of Auschwitz*. Chicago: University of Chicago Press.

Zuckerman, Ethan. 2013. *Rewire: Digital Cosmopolitans in the Age of Connection*. New
York: Norton.

Zuckerman, Harriet. 2010. "On Sociological Semantics as an Evolving Research Program." In *Robert K. Merton: Sociology of Science and Sociology as Science*, edited by
Craig Calhoun, 253–72. New York: Columbia University Press/SSRC Books.

Zussman, Robert, and Joya Misra. 2007. "Introduction." In *Public Sociology: Fifteen
Eminent Sociologists Debate Politics and the Profession in the Twenty-First Century*,
edited by Dan Clawson, Robert Zussman, Joya Misra, Naomi Gerstel, Randall
Stokes, Douglas L. Anderston, and Michael Burawoy, 23–64. Berkeley: University
of California Press.

Zychowicz, Jessica. 2011. "Two Bad Words: Femen & Feminism in Independent
Ukraine." *Anthropology of East Europe Review* 29 (2): 215–27.

Index